M.A. ANSARI: GANDHI'S INFALLIBLE GUIDE

M.A. ANSARI

Gandhi's Infallible Guide

MUSHIRUL HASAN

MANOHAR
2010

First published 1987
Revised and enlarged edition 2010

ISBN 978-81-7304-850-0

Published by

Ajay Kumar Jain for
Manohar Publishers & Distributors
4753/23 Ansari Road, Daryaganj
New Delhi 110 002

Typeset at

Digigrafics
New Delhi 110 049

Printed at

Salasar Imaging Systems
Delhi 110 035

To the memory of
my brother

NAJMUL HASAN

Thandi thi jis ki chaon wo deewaar gir gai

ٹھنڈی تھی جس کی چھاؤں وہ دیوار گر گئی

Contents

Tables

Foreword

OVER THE YEARS, Mushir has earned for himself an enviable position among scholars through his writings on the role played by the Muslim community in the freedom struggle, and its relationship with the Indian National Congress, on the one hand, and with the Muslim League, which initiated the partition of the subcontinent in 1947, on the other. His scholarly writings are characterized by a liberal and secular vision, and behind his exploration lies a seminal question: Why did secular nationalism in India fail in creating a united nation, resting equally upon Hindu and Muslim participation, in 1947?

In the present volume, Mushir explores this theme through reflecting upon the political career of Mukhtar Ahmad Ansari, one of the most distinguished nationalist Muslims in the country. Ansari hailed from a section of the Muslim landed gentry in the United Provinces (as it was then known) which was turning increasingly to the liberal professions for sustenance, and which played a leading role in public life in the first half of the twentieth century. In portraying Ansari's stance on the great issues of the times, Mushir illumines the history of an entire class; though it would be wrong to assume that all its members possessed the professional eminence or the flawless integrity of Ansari. Be that as it may, this scholarly work looks upon the social underpinnings of political behaviour with sensitivity and skill, and in doing so, it throws a flood of illuminating light upon a seminal area of nationalist politics in the period under review.

Perhaps the first decade of the twentieth century was a crucial period for men like Ansari as they struggled to define afresh the position of their community within the framework of political society in India. This position, it needs to be stressed, was radically different from that of the Hindu community. So far as the latter was concerned, powerful elites drawn from the landed classes, or from the commerical and professional bourgeoisie, had already organized themselves under the aegis of the Congress against British imperialism. But the Muslim community found itself in a quandary and the nationalist stance was no easy stance for a Muslim leader. Like the Hindus, nationalism came to the Muslim elites through a heightened consciousness of their religious identity. For this very reason, it was difficult for the Muslim leaders, or for the rank and file of the community, to relate their identity to the resurgence of nationalism; more particularly, because the victory of nationalism could possibly result in a political society in which the numerical strength of a community played a crucial part in determining its access to power. In other words, the triumph of nationalism in India could pave the way for a democratic polity in which the Hindus, through sheer weight of numbers, could dominate those who subscribed to other religious world-views.

Ansari's entry into nationalist politics sensitively highlighted the dilemmas confronting Muslim leaders in the opening decades of the century. The strategy to which Syed Ahmad Khan and his followers had given currency earlier, namely, that it was inadvisable for the Muslims to associate themselves with the freedom struggle, had become somewhat discredited by this time. A new generation of Muslims—related as much to the land as to the liberal professions—were drawn increasingly to political action in the cause of nationalism. Behind this transformation lay a bitter realization of the humiliation which British imperialism had inflicted upon Islam within India as well as in the world community. The British assault upon the Turkish Empire in the nineteenth and twentieth centuries triggered off a powerful wave of anti-imperialism among young Muslims of Ansari's generation, and the growth of this sentiment lay behind the medical delegation which he led to Turkey with the objective of expressing the solidarity of the Indian Muslims with the international community of Islam. On his return from Turkey, Ansari suddenly found himself in a position of prominence within his community, and the pan-Islamic sentiment which he spearheaded and reinforced became the basis of a radical transformation of Muslim opinion within India. This was reflected in a change in the constitution of the Muslim League just as it was also reflected in the creation of a united front with the Hindus in the struggle against British imperialism.

The metamorphosis of anti-imperialism and pan-Islamic values into a national consciousness was a complex process bedevilled by serious inconsistencies and tensions. Mushir illumines this process with commendable skill through pursuing the career of Mukhtar Ahmad Ansari and other leaders like Maulanas Abul Kalam Azad and Abdul Bari, or the Brothers Shaukat and Mohamed Ali. Behind this transformation lay a crucial alliance between the Muslim professional classes and the landed gentry, on the one hand, and the clerical classes, led by the Deoband *ulama* and the religious leaders of Firangi Mahal, on the other. This alliance of nationalist Muslims and pan-Islamists in turn reached out to a wider leadership, prominent among them Mahatma Gandhi, in a bid to liberate India from British rule. Mushir portrays both the strengths and the weaknesses of such a nationalist consolidation which brought Hindus and Muslims together in a way they had never been united before. The popular character of non-cooperation during the years 1920-2 was largely the result of such a consummation. Yet from the very outset this alliance carried within itself the most serious contradictions. The sentiment of nationalism which non-cooperation conjured into existence among its supporters was a sentiment which drew heavily upon religion as a mediator between the citizen and the nation. Small wonder, then, that whatever be the short-term gains of such an alliance, in the long run it was designed to heighten the cohesiveness of religious communities at the cost of national solidarity. Indeed, the evidence which Mushir brings to light bears ample witness to the fragility of Hindu-Muslim unity which had been conjured into existence during the heyday of the non-cooperation movement. His perception of the reasons behind the breakdown of this, alliance, more particularly, of the tensions which developed between the two communities in the course of the anti-imperialist struggle, is equally significant. Perhaps there was a fatal flaw here upon which we shall dwell some more later.

Whatever be the reasons behind a growing religious cleavage in the 1920s, men like Ansari, who stood true to the cause of Hindu-Muslim unity, as they also stood true to the cause of nationalism, found themselves increasingly out of touch with the sentiments in the Muslim community. Indeed, the consequences of the political strategy adopted by Mahatma Gandhi during 1920-2 became manifest towards the end of the decade, when the nationalist leaders, young and old, radicals and conservatives, sought to bring different religious groups together in a movement which sought to achieve *purna swaraj*. The constitutional bargaining between Hindu and Muslim leaders, at this juncture, vividly reflects the extent to which communal and religious identities had hardened with the passage of time. Of course, the imperialist tactic of creating divisions among different classes and communities played a crucial role in all this; witness Birkenhead's taunt that the nationalist leaders were incapable of producing a constitution acceptable to everyone in the subcontinent. Nevertheless, it cannot be denied that the strategy of divide and rule was successful, to some extent, because of the religious cleavages within Indian society, which provided a backdrop to the confrontation between nationalism and imperialism. Ansari remained true to the vision of a united India, in which Hindus and Muslims would live as partners and equals, long after this ideal had been betrayed by men like the Ali Brothers, or Jinnah, who had entered politics as a staunch nationalist. Perhaps the stirring call which he gave for national unity, at the annual session of the Indian National Congress in 1927, over which he presided, provides a sensitive clue to the role which he sought to play at this juncture. Yet Ansari found himself utterly isolated at the fateful session of the Congress in Lahore, in December 1929, where a decision was taken to embark upon civil disobedience in order to achieve *purna swaraj*. As he pointed out to both the senior generation of leaders, represented by Mahatma Gandhi and Motilal Nehru, and the younger generation, represented by Jawaharlal Nehru and Subhas Chandra Bose, to embark upon a struggle against the British Government without ensuring unity between Hindus and Muslims was to take a step that could lead to the most fateful consequences. That Ansari's warning was prophetic is vindicated by subsequent events. Yet his tragedy lay in the lonesomeness of his position in 1930. As Mushir observes, even the staunch supporters of Ansari, like Mahatma Gandhi and Jawaharlal Nehru, turned a deaf ear to his warnings at this juncture. Yet there was a fearful price to pay for such indifference.

Although Ansari found himself isolated on the eve of the civil disobedience movement, this did not prevent him from attempting to put across the secular viewpoint to his co-religionists shortly afterwards. The All-India Nationalist Muslim Party, which he created in 1929 was his last and potentially most significant contribution to politics. Here was a heroic attempt to mobilize all Muslims, rich or poor, landlords or peasants, merchants or professionals, the *ulama* or the artisanate, on a common nationalist platform. Mushir pursues the fate of this gallant effort by Ansari in considerable detail. His assessment of the strengths and weaknesses of Ansari's leadership, who despite high-mindedness and sterling integrity was unable to reach out to the Muslim masses or provide them with a vision of the 'good society' with which they could identify, constitutes the finest section of this scholarly book and holds out a perceptive account of Muslim politics. It is difficult to fault Mushir's conclusion that Ansari fell between two stools; on the one hand, the indifference of the Muslim leaders and their followers to the nationalist position; and on the other, the pressures which even secular Hindu politicians experienced from their co-religionists. If Mushir's account of nationalist politics in the 1930s adds up to a depressing story, we have only to turn to communalism, as a divisive factor (and worse) within Indian politics, in our own times, to realize the validity of his perception.

What then (we may finally ask ourselves) was the solution to the communal problem in the 1930s? Or, for that matter, how can it be resolved in our own times? These are questions with which we may have to wrestle for quite some time in the future. Perhaps the solution to the communal problem lies in a total refusal to be drawn into any political dialogue along religious lines. This is not to deny the existence of a religious sensibility among different classes or communities; historically or contemporaneously. This is merely to argue that the only way of handling communalism is to banish it altogether from the domain of politics. The creation of a secular society is an ideal to which responsible Indians are as firmly committed today as they were during the course of the freedom struggle. Furthermore, it is obvious that secularism in India cannot replicate secularism in Western societies, where this term implies the displacement of the religious sensibility from the psyche of the citizen. Nevertheless, it is possible to work for a secular order in which religion is absent from the public domain, although it may exercise a powerful influence in the private domain. The creation of such a secular society calls for a vigorous effort by all concerned to devise a language of politics wherein religion occupies no place at all. No such solution to the communal problem was even attempted in the decades reviewed by Mushir in this scholarly work. Yet a refusal to be marginalized by the idiom of religious politics offers the only way out of a dilemma which has haunted India for a century and more. Indeed, this dilemma shall continue to bedevil politics in the subcontinent unless the people of India launch a bold assault upon the virus of communalism in the body politic.

Nehru Memorial Museum & Library RAVINDER KUMAR
New Delhi Director

Preface to the Second Edition

Reviewing *A Nationalist Conscience: M.A. Ansari, the Congress, and the Raj* in the Cambridge journal, *Modern Asian Studies*, the historian Francis Robinson bemoaned that many Indian Muslims may have lost interest in keeping the memories of Dr. Ansari and Maulana Abul Kalam Azad alive, and that Indian society as a whole no longer value, as before, and perhaps did not even know, the principles for which they stood.

First published in 1987, the book described Ansari's place in the history of the Indian national movement. As an ardent patriot he had many competitors, but among Muslims he had the field virtually to himself until his death in May 1936. Through the All-India Nationalist Muslim Party, in particular, he was instrumental in furthering secular and nationalist trends in politics. Even after its collapse, the central vitality, the genuineness and the persuasive sincerity of tone kept Ansari's message alive.

To most people, both in his lifetime and since his death, Ansari ranked as a nationalist, a great medical doctor, and an apostle of Hindu-Muslim unity. I hope this book will help explain the hold he secured upon his generation.

While revising and rewriting *A Nationalist Conscience*, I have resisted the temptation of incorporating some of my recent researches. However, I have included some rare photographs, introduced major editorial changes, and have appended the statement of Abdur Razzaq Ansari. It is drawn from the J.C. Curry Papers at the Centre for South Asian Studies, Cambridge. The extent of revision is indeed very substantial. Some gaps still exist; to complete the story I would recommend my own books, *From Pluralism to Separatism: Qasbas in Colonial Awadh* (2004) and *Moderate or Militant: Images of India's Muslims* (2008), for interpretation and additional information on Ansari's political profile. *Modernity to Nationalism: Halide Edip Encounters Gandhi's India* (2010) is, equally, a major source of information on Jamia Millia Islamia and its Chancellor, Ansari. The book covers a major part of his public life. So does *Partners in Freedom, Jamia Millia Islamia* (2007), an illustrated book co-authored by Rakhshanda Jalil.

Let me end with Francis Robinson's concluding remarks:

> . . . To a region increasingly beset by communalism the life of Ansari shows how during the freedom movement there were Muslims who worked for the highest secular ideals. To a region increasingly beset by religious intolerance the life of Azad reveals how the finest religious sensibility can fashion the most open and humane outlook in private and public life. These are lives which deserve to be known and studied outside the purely academic community. . . .

I owe the subtitle of this book to Mohandas Karamchand Gandhi. He was the one to describe Ansari as his 'Infallible Guide'.

This political biography will be followed by the publication of Ansari's speeches and correspondence.

I owe a great deal to Mohammed Javed Ansari for his secretarial assistance, and to Dr. Simi Malhotra for going through the final typescript with meticulous care. Ravinder Kumar is no more, but we cherish his memory.

October 2009 M.H.

Preface to the First Edition

This Book embodies elements of research and study done over more than a decade, beginning with my Ph.D. dissertation submitted at the University of Cambridge in 1977 and continuing until today. In my book *Nationalism and Communal Politics in India, 1916-1928*, I chose to take a closer look at some of the chief exponents of liberal and secular tendencies among Indian Muslims. The present work is part of the same endeavour—an exploration into the many facets of the nationalist struggle and an examination of the ideas and movements which concerned certain influential groups among Muslims. I have chosen Mukhtar Ahmad Ansari because he symbolized and represented a powerful nationalist strand during the epic struggles of the 1920s and the 1930s.

During the course of researching and writing this book I have incurred innumerable debts of gratitude. I am indebted, first and foremost, to the family and relatives of the man who forms the subject of this study: to Begum Zohra Ansari and Professor Azhar Ansari.

I have used a great number of libraries and archives in India, Pakistan and the United Kingdom. Without exception their librarians and archivists have been unfailingly helpful. Of the many people in Pakistan who have helped make my stay there a pleasure, I must mention at least two: Khalid Shamsul Hasan and Sharif al-Mujahid. The staff of the Nehru Memorial Museum & Library (NMML) in Delhi rendered all possible assistance to me. I am grateful, in particular, to Hari Dev Sharma, A.K. Awasthi, S.K. Bhatnagar, N.C. Mahajan, Umesh C. Mandal and Deepak Vashisht.

I owe a considerable debt to the Governing Council of the NMML which offered me a Professorial Fellowship for three years during which most of this book was written. My greatest debt is to Ravinder Kumar who read the whole text with care, offered suggestions for improvements, and agreed to write a thoughtful foreword to this book. His insights have done much to help my understanding of Indian nationalism and the communal question, though he cannot, of course, be held responsible for anything I have written here.

A special debt of gratitude is owed to a number of persons who read chapters in the state of their first creation. I am especially indebted to: S. Gopal, Azhar Ansari, Francis Robinson, V.C. Bhutani, Hari Dev Sharma, Muzaffar Alam and Shahid Amin. Zoya offered invaluable suggestions on style and content and provided much support to my modest scholarly endeavours. My father, Professor Mohibbul Hasan, has always been a source of inspiration to me. His thorough and insightful scholarship, combined with his professional integrity, has long set me a worthy standard.

Many other people have assisted by passing on references and other helpful information, provided hospitality during the course of my research, or taken time off their own work to seek out material for me. I would particularly like to thank the following: Khalid Shamsul Hasan, Arif Husain, Praveen Saberwal, Rewa Pathak and Abu Salman Shahjahanpuri.

A suitable title eluded everyone—except my friend Simon Commander, who came up with a balanced title/subtitle. I also enjoyed his hospitality during my stay in London.

The Indian Council of Historical Research offered me a modest study grant. Dr T.R. Sareen and S.M. Mishra were kind enough to have it sanctioned.

By an unwritten convention authors seldom venture to thank their publishers. I wish to depart from this custom by recording here my sincere appreciation of Ramesh C. Jain. His professional skill and integrity has won him many friends. I am privileged to be one of them.

I hope Barbara, Shaaz and Shehzad would derive some comfort from the fact that this book is dedicated to the loving memory of Sonny (Najmul Hasan) who is, alas, no more. His memory will always remain part of us. Faiz Ahmad Faiz summed up the feelings of a younger brother.

Mujh ko shikwa hai mere Bhai ki tum jaate hue
Le gaye saath meri umr-i guzashta ki kitab

Is men to meri bahut qeemti tasweeren theen
Is men bachpan tha mera aur mera ahd-i shabab
Is ke badle mujhe tum de gaye jaate jaate
Apne gham ka yeh damakta hua khoon-rang gulab
Aake le jaao tum apna yeh damakta hua phool
Mujh ko lauta do meri umr-i guzashta ki kitab

Jamia Millia Islamia M.H.
October 1986

Introduction

ON 14 MAY 1936, Asaf Ali, the Delhi lawyer, suggested to Mahatma Gandhi that an appropriate memorial be raised in memory of Mukhtar Ahmad Ansari and to associate his name with rural medical aid all over India in the form of 'Ansari Medical Corps' or 'Ansari Travelling Dispensary'.[1] But neither then nor later did such suggestions receive consideration.[2] Delhi's 'Ansari Road' is the only reminder of Ansari's long-standing association with the city as a physician-surgeon, political activist and educationist. His house—Dar-us-Salam—had been the venue of Congress meetings and the focal point of much political activity in the capital of British India.[3] But most people in the neighbourhood are unfamiliar with its significance and have not heard of its previous occupant.

Some time in 1934-5, Mohammad Mujeeb, then a teacher at the Jamia Millia Islamia, undertook to write Ansari's biography with the aid of a rich collection of papers which included letters, press clippings, pamphlets and books.[4] But the biography was never written.[5] The papers were promptly transferred to a basement in the Jamia Library, and were retrieved in the early 1960s. In the meantime, part of the collection, especially Ansari's correspondence from 1912 to 1925, was destroyed. Today, little is known of Ansari in the Jamia—an institution he nursed from the time of its inception in October 1920. A Health Centre housed in three small rooms was once Jamia's modest tribute to its founder and *Amir-i Jamia* (Chancellor). The M.A. Ansari Auditorium is a relatively recent addition.

Ironically, some historians in England, America and Australia have taken adequate notice of Ansari's commitment to inter-communal unity, his efforts in drawing Muslims into the freedom struggle, and his effective role as a mediator between his community and the Congress movement. However, historians in the subcontinent have ignored his active political life which spanned over two decades of a tumultuous phase in India's struggle for liberation from colonial domination.[6] It is easy to explain this omission in Pakistan, because Ansari's concerns were steeped in the essentially secular, democratic ethos of the nationalist struggle. As one wedded to the Congress ideals in the tradition of many of his predecessors and contemporaries, he would have poured scorn on the idea of Pakistan as unequivocally as he opposed the potentially divisive tendencies during his lifetime. The two-nation theory would have been as much an anathema to him as was the notion of granting separate electorates and communal representation to the Muslims. He was neither a theorist nor a creative thinker, but he certainly had a vision of a just society, a civilized and harmonious whole, a society in which there would be no friction on account of caste, regional, linguistic and religious diversities.[7] 'I consider the brotherhood of man as the only tie,' he declared, 'and partition based on race or religion are, to my mind, artificial and arbitrary.'

After Independence, there has been a stream of biographical literature on Gandhi and Jawaharlal Nehru who played so central a part in the shaping of modern India. Scholarly interest has also extended to such other leaders who possessed a distinct cultural, religious, or regional identity and have therefore inspired the particularist tendencies of certain castes, communities and regions. This is true of C.R. Das and Subhas Chandra Bose in Bengal, C. Rajagopalachari in Tamil Nadu, Madan Mohan Malaviya in UP and Lala Lajpat Rai in the Punjab—all identified with a particular region and placed in the category of 'heroes'. However, some other leaders bearing no specific affinity to a region or a religious group have not received much notice. Ansari is among them. Cut-off from his home state—UP—he lived in Delhi in a composite cultural environment and followed a political course which did not reflect the interests and aspirations of any particular region or community. In contrast with Ansari, Mohamed Ali, the popular hero of the Khilafat days, is appropriated by many Muslims in India and Pakistan today; they see in him a vocal champion of their communitarian concerns.

In popular perception, the Congress Muslims 'failed' to counter the two-nation theory, to present a viable enough alternative to the Muslim League, and to rally their community around the Congress banner. 'The collapse and elimination of the Nationalist Muslims as a group,' wrote Nehru, 'forms a pitiful story.'[8] Even if we accept this judgement, we are still called upon to analyse why they were marginalized and the *reasons* why they could not develop into an effective force in politics. Besides, 'success' stories alone do not form the core of a historian's concern. The emergence of Congress Muslim group and its subsequent 'decline' and 'disintegration' deserves critical appraisal in order to understand certain vital dimensions of the nationalist and communitarian processes.

The present work focuses on the career of one such person—Ansari—who put forward the point of view of the Congress Muslims with clarity, consistency and conviction. He succeeded—where others failed—in reconciling his community's concerns with the national interests and remained true to all that Indian nationalism stood for. Above all, his line of action inspired many of his comrades to stay clear of communal proclivities and leave behind a vibrant composite legacy. One of the purposes of this book is to uncover this essential but neglected legacy.

My aim is to reveal Ansari as what he undoubtedly was—an important figures in Indian politics—to delineate his principal political interests, to explore his ideological predilections and to draw a portrait that captures his flaws as well as his strong points, his failures as well as his successes. Wherever possible, I have tried to analyse his responses and attitudes in the larger historical context provided by colonial rule. I have alluded to the influences on the style and content of his politics, if not always given their full historical weight.

I have also attempted, with the aid of much fresh literature, to examine political developments from 1912 to 1936—the years covered in some detail in this study—to look afresh at the nature and character of the pan-Islamic movement and to review the existing notions on the 'communal question'. In so doing, I hope not only to throw light on certain important and unstudied dimensions, but also to suggest that the role of the Congress Muslims in general provides a useful entry for understanding certain facets of nationalism and communalism in India.

NOTES

1. Asaf Ali to Gandhi, 14 May 1936, F. No. G-21, 1936, All India Congress Committee Papers [AICC], Nehru Memorial Museum & Library [NMML].
2. 'I remember, of course, that nothing of the kind (Memorial Fund) has yet been done about Hakim Saheb, my father and Ansari. It is not for me to move in this matter and I suppose it is rather late now to take any step.' Jawaharlal Nehru to M.K. Gandhi, 9 February 1947, S. Gopal (ed.), *Selected Works of Jawaharlal Nehru* [*SWJN*], second series, vol. 3 (Delhi, 1985), pp. 496-7.
3. It was sold in 1946 by Shaukatullah Ansari and is now owned by a Jain trust. Zohra Ansari, Oral History Transcript, NMML.
4. Ansari transferred a large collection of his books, journals and magazines to the Jamia Millia Islamia. I have come across a list of 534 books which were donated by Begum Ansari in memory of her husband. But the Jamia Library has not preserved this collection.
5. Mujeeb noted in his preliminary draft of Ansari's unfinished biography that he was 'quite lost' because Ansari had little time to spare for interviews. He wrote a small section of chapter one—'The Lights and Shades'—but was unable to complete it. Draft, Mujeeb Collection, Dr. Zakir Husain Library, Jamia Millia Islamia [JMI].
6. The omission is surprising in the accounts of those writers who were associated with Ansari and followed his activities closely. See, for example, Mohammad Mujeeb, *The Indian Muslims* (London, 1967) which has no reference to Ansari; also, Abid Husain, *The Destiny of the Indian Muslims* (Delhi, 1970); Swaliha Abid Husain, *Jaane Walon ki yaad aati Rahi* (Delhi, 1974); K.G. Saiyidan, *Andhi me Chiragh* (Delhi, 1962); Imdad Sabri, *Dehli ki Yadgar Hastiyaan* (Delhi, 1972).
6. See, for instance, his presidential address at the All-Karnatak Hindi Prachar Sabha held at Mysore in 1929 and his address at the Bengal Nationalist Muslims Conference held at Faridpur in July 1931.
7. See, for instance, his presidential address at the All-Karnatak Hindi Prachar Sabha held at Mysore in 1929 and his address at the Bengal Nationalist Muslims Conference held at Faridpur in July 1931.
8. Jawaharlal Nehru, *An Autobiography: With Musings on Recent Events in India* (London, 1936), p. 139.

1

Ghazipur to Delhi

FOUNDED IN AD 1330, Ghazipur gained much importance in the sixteenth century as capital of a *sarkar* in the *suba* of Allahabad. In December 1763, the East India Company acquired control and appointed the collector of Banaras as its administrator. This arrangement continued until 1818, when Ghazipur was constituted as a district.

In the revolt of 1857 Ghazipur figured prominently. The bulk of the people, led by some zamindars who were aggrieved at their ejection by auction-purchasers, pillaged government offices and treasury. Reported an official: 'On all sides of the District, itself always most troublesome, were disturbances real or reported.'[1] In Zamaniah, one of the four *tahsils*, 'every building belonging to Government or Europeans was plundered and burnt'. H.R. Nevill's account reveals the distinct popular character of the revolt and, at the same time, the government's repressive measures to quell the disturbances.[2]

Muslims of Ghazipur[3] were in the forefront of the revolt, even though they formed just over 9 per cent of the population and were unevenly distributed in four *tahsils* (Table 1.1.)—Ghazipur; Zamaniah, which derives its name from Ali Quli Khan, Khan Zaman, who expelled the Afghans from Ghazipur in 1560 and was governor of Jaunpur in the reign of Akbar (1556-1605); Muhammadabad, an old Muslim settlement dating from the days of the Lodi Sultans (1451-1526); and Saidpur.[4] Most Muslims were Julahas or weavers, supporting themselves either in their own villages or in the mills of Calcutta, Kanpur and Bombay where they worked for short periods. The *District Gazetteer* described them as 'the most bigoted of all Mussalmans' and as 'a turbulent and lawless race',[5] an assessment obviously influenced by their participation in the 1857 revolt.

TABLE 1.1: POPULATION BY *TAHSIL* 1911

Tahsil	*Total*	*Hindus*	*Muslims*	*Others*
Ghazipur	246,861	226,539	20,052	260
Muhammadabad	197,428	177,474	19,716	238
Zamaniah	216,756	191,665	24,945	146
Saidpur	178,690	166,757	11,842	85

SOURCE: *Ghazipur: Supplementary Notes and Statistics to Vol. XXXIX of the District Gazetteer of the UP of Agra and Oudh* (Allahabad, 1915), Appendix I.

The Syeds were small in numbers and relatively uninfluential in the district. The Sheikhs, on the other hand, formed 15.8 per cent of the Muslim population. They claimed to be the descendants of the companions of the Prophet Muhammad (570-632), distinguishing themselves from one another by adding prefixes such as Ansari, Siddiqui and Qureshi. They were followed by the Pathans who traced their origin to the Afghan settlers of the days of Aurangzeb (1658-1707), when a powerful colony established itself in Mahaich and another occupied the *tahsil* of Zamaniah.[6] Most Pathans were traders or in service, though some had small landholdings as well.

Muslims in Ghazipur owned 148,610 acres, or 17 per cent of the land, a remarkably large proportion. The principal land owning families were the Syeds of Nonahara who traced their ancestry to Syed Masud Ghazi, the reputed founder of Ghazipur; the Siddiqui Sheikhs of Pahatia and the Usmani Sheikhs of Salempur, whose estate paid Rs. 3,868 as land revenue.

The Ansaris preferred not to use the prefix in order to distinguish themselves from the Julahas, who also claimed descent from the Ansars (aiders) of Medina. They had rendered assistance to Prophet Muhammad during his migration (*hijrat*) from Mecca. They traced their lineage from Abu Ayyub Ansari (d. 672), a close companion of the Prophet, his host at Medina, a warrior and a venturous conqueror who, when fighting across the Bosphorus at the age of ninety or more, was killed and buried in Constantinople. They were directly descended from the three sons of Khwaja Hamiduddin, who came from Arabia in the fourteenth century and settled in Shiraz from where his sons migrated to

Delhi. One of them was appointed *qazi* by Mohammad bin Tughlaq (1325-51). His nephew founded Yusufpur.[7]

The office of *qazi* continued to be held by members of the family even after the British introduced basic changes in the judicial structure which, as in the case of Bengal, displaced many Muslims from the judicial department and added to their impoverishment. Some members of the Ansari family were employed in government service. They were the one to purchase property in and around Ghazipur. Others either acquired land by purchasing the estates of the old families brought to ruin by the mismanagement or by the unsympathetic revenue administration, or retained their ancestral lands, as in the case of Bhitri which they had received from the Mughal emperor, Akbar. They held a fair amount of land in the neighbourhood, including Yusufpur itself, which was 327 acres in extent and was assessed at Rs. 712, the tenure being *bighadam*.

With Mukhtar Ahmad [hereafter referred to as Ansari], the youngest of the four sons of Haji Abdul Rahman, the Ansaris emerged from the position of an old Ghazipur family into national eminence. From the early 1920s, some of his close relatives—Aziz Ansari (1889-1985), Faridul Haq Ansari (1895-1966) and Shaukatullah Ansari (1908-72)—played an important part in political affairs. None succeeded in scaling the heights achieved by their mentor; yet, Aziz joined the Indian Medical Mission to Constantinople and went to jail during both the non-cooperation and civil disobedience agitations; Farid was member of the All-India Congress Committee (AICC) from 1927 to 1948, secretary of the Delhi Pradesh Congress Committee in 1929-30 and one of the founders of the Congress Socialist Party; Shaukatullah, Ansari's nephew and married to his adopted daughter, Zohra (b. 1913), floated the Azad Muslim Board and the All-India Muslim Majlis in support of the Congress. In 1940, he was elected general secretary of the All-India Azad Muslim Conference and, in 1944, he indicted the two-nation theory. Partition, according to him, 'would throw back India back to something like the state she was in after the Mughal Empire had collapsed and before the British Raj replaced it. For, once the frame of unity was broken, once the process of disruption had begun, it would not be likely to stop at the separation of Moslem State or States from Hindu India.'[8]

Born on 25 December 1880 in Yusufpur, Ansari had a quiet but deep pride in his ancestry. It pleased him to think that his roots lay deep in the soil of Arabia and that he belonged to a distinguished family with branches in different parts of the country. Mohammad Mujeeb (1902-85), records an interview in which he quotes Ansari as saying: 'My family originates from the Ansari. But then he stopped, then laughed. Why should one imagine that Ansaris are particularly few. There are as many as have been destined to be.'[9]

The Ansaris were not men of wealth or influence as their fortunes were substantially reduced in the second half of the nineteenth century. They held on to their small landholdings without making much out of them. Forced by circumstances they took to government service, a distasteful choice for those who were not yet reconciled to the reality of British rule. Ansari's father—Abdul Rahman—was an *amin* at Rasara in Ballia district. His fame rested on the loyal service he rendered to the British in the 1857 revolt for which he received a small estate near Yusufpur and granted exemption from the Arms Act. He prospered in a modest way.[10] Kadir Baksh, who amassed a fortune as a contractor to the commissariat department, was another well-known loyalist in Ghazipur. He received a land grant in Jamal-uddinpur in Jaunpur district.

Rahman (d. 1902), a devout Muslim who went on the arduous pilgrimage (*haj*) to Mecca, did not leave behind any great fortune for his sons to inherit, a fact which explains why they eventually moved out of Ghazipur after his death. But he had taken a close and guiding interest in his sons' education. Few middle class families, particularly in eastern UP, had paid as much attention to the education of their children as Rahman did.

Abdul Wahhab (d. 1946), the eldest son, specialized in the *yunani* system of medicine at the renowned Tibbia school in Delhi, run by Haziq-ul Mulk Hakim Abdul Majid Khan (d. 1901). He also went to the Dar al-ulum at Deoband, the famous religious seminary born in the throes of the 1857 revolt and was a *murid* of its founder, Rashid Ahmad Gangohi (1828-1905). In his days, his intellect was feared, his character praised, and his almost

M.A. Ansari

Family Re-Union: (1) Raza Nawaz Jung, (2) Ansari, (3) Hakim Abdul Wahab Nabina, (4) Hakim Abdur Razzaq, (5) Mohd. Umar Ansari, (6) Faridul Haq Ansari.

Ansari with member of his extended family. Hakim Nabina is sitting in the middle.
To his left is Abdur Razzaq Ansari.

legendary reputation as Hakim *Nabina* (for he was blind) spread to different parts of the country. He practiced in Hyderabad, Poona, Bombay and Delhi, where Khwaja Hasan Nizami (1878-1957) called him *Lukman-ul Mulk*.[11] Mujeeb, a visitor to his house on the western side of the historic Juma Masjid area, found 'an old, established system of preparing medicaments for the needs of the poor as well as the rich'.

Abdur Razzaq (1868-1930), also a renowned Hakim, did not attain the reputation of his elder brother. He spent many years in the Nizam's court at Hyderabad and was primarily responsible for drawing several members of his family to the Deccan. 'We soon began to practice apart,' stated Razzaq in his testimony (see Appendix 3), 'and lived in separate houses. We both had considerable success there and got large fees.' Although they were exiled for their part in the court intrigues, both the brothers, their family members continued to enjoy the patronage of several nobles who cherished their association with the two eminent hakims.

Wahhab and Razzaq were equal in their devotion to the *ulama* of Deoband. The former was a *murid* of Rashid Ahmad Gangohi; Razzaq of Mahmud Hasan (1851-1920), principal of the Dar al-ulum. Razzaq described his initiation:

> I had great respect for the Maulana and had determined to become his *murid*; so I went to Deoband and told him that both I and my mother wished to become his *murids*, but my mother was too old to travel. After some persuasion the Maulana agreed to break his usual rule and came to Delhi where my mother and I both became his *murids*. Dr. Ansari became his *murid* at the same time.

These connections proved advantageous when the Muslim divines were pressed into service to provide depth to the Khilafat agitation in India. Razzaq, influenced by Mahmud Hasan, was drawn into the 'Silk Letter Conspiracy'. Ansari, a *murid* of the renowned Deoband *alim* and of Hafiz Mohammad Ali of Gorakhpur, acted as an effective link between the *ulama* and the Western-educated Muslims and strengthened their alliance in 1919-22.[12] His wife, on the other hand, was a *murid* of Hafiz Ahmad Khan, *mohtasim* of Deoband, and corresponded with him to secure the release of Mahmud Hasan, interned in Malta for his part in the Silk Letter

Conspiracy.[13] When Ansari went to Edinburgh for higher studies, he took with him two firmly established family traditions: a vocational commitment to medicine and religious loyalty to the *ulama* of Deoband.

In spite of their brief forays into the political arena, Wahhab and Razzaq lived in a world divorced from politics. Both were deeply steeped in the Islamic heritage, frequenting *dargahs* of *pirs* and *madaris* of many a well-known *alim* to seek enlightenment, spiritual solace and guidance. Next to this, *hikmat* was their main concern; their astonishing success was matched only by the almost legendary popularity of Hakim Ajmal Khan (1863-1927), whose house and hospital were filled day by day with the sick and dying and who would minister to them, taking no fees from the poor.[14] Exceedingly generous, the two brothers earned vast sums of money and spent most of it on their family. Abdur Razzaq supported the education of Ansari and his cousin Mohammad Asghar in London, and later helped the former in setting up his practice in Delhi. 'I had to set him [Ansari] up in Delhi and sent him several thousand rupees for this, but he soon started well and I had no more need to send him money.' He was able to do so owing to the patronage of wealthy rajas and nawabs who almost of necessity maintained a retinue of hakims along with poets, writers and dancers. Such patronage brought immediate rewards. This is illustrated by the career of Ajmal Khan, who, according to one of his biographers, averaged a yearly income of Rs. 50,000.[15] It was considerably reduced in later years because some of his clients among the rajas and nawabs avoided him because of his activism.

The younger brothers—Mohammad Raza (d. 1935)[16] and Ansari—were cast in a different mould. This had much to do with their education in British schools and colleges, a fact which helped them to pursue careers different from their relations. While many of their background preferred the Aligarh College, Rahman, who felt that excellence came from the special nurturing of individual talent, sent his sons to the Muir Central College at Allahabad,[17] established in 1872 by the city's wealthy landowners, bankers and pleaders. Ansari studied English, Mathematics, Deductive Logic, Trigonometry and Geometrical and Conic Sections, Elementary Physics and Chemistry. The education he received proved to be valuable. In fact, this early association with

Allahabad's composite environment shaped his attitude towards other religions in particular and the communal problem in general. Wazir Hasan (1874-1947), who also attended the Muir Central College and became an important figure in both the Congress and the Muslim League organizations, observed that Western education promoted greater understanding and tolerance among the Hindus and Muslims, enabled them to recognize their common destiny above the 'existence of separate entities and the din of communal claims', and 'form conceptions of a broader obligation and wider responsibilities to their country as a whole'.[18] Henry Cotton, a civil servant sympathetic to India's nationalist aspirations, attributed unity of ideas to uniformity of training, and the ideal which was present in Sir Syed's mind when he founded Aligarh College. According to him, 'mutual trust, a desire for the achievement of common ends and objects, nationalism and self-government—these are the inspiration of the rising generation, not less of Mohammedans than of Hindus.'[19]

The Muir Central College was chosen in part because of its premier status in northern India and in part because Ansari's mother wanted him to remain close to the family in Ghazipur. For the same reason when Razzaq moved to Hyderabad in 1898 with his mother, Ansari accompanied them. There is little doubt that during his childhood and early youth he was the focus of a comfortable and loving family. In the future, the quiet solidity of the family home provided a necessary haven to which he could retreat from the rigours of an unexpectedly hectic political life.

Ansari passed his intermediate examination in 1896.[20] He then went up to Nizam College, founded by the Nizam. Soon after, he married Shamsunnisa (d. 1938), who turned out to be a pliant wife and a good housekeeper. Halide Edip (1884-1964), the Turkish author, remembered her as 'very pious, very charitable'.[21] What is perhaps not known is that the Begum did much public work. She was associated with the Anjuman-i Khuddam-i Kaaba, leading the appeal for moral and financial support along with the mother of the Ali Brothers and the wife of Mohamed Ali (1878-1931). Indeed, she headed the Delhi branch of the Women's Khilafat Committee,[22] and attended Congress sessions regularly; the only one she missed was the one at Belgaum (1925) owing to a motor accident. Confined to the domestic role expected of a woman of her time and station, Shamsunnisa found an outlet for her interests and energy in her husband's political career.

Ansari graduated in 1900. He did not do well in his examinations but impressed his teachers with his diligence and earnestness.[23] They recognized his potential and, in 1899, helped him to secure the state scholarship to study medicine in Great Britain. This was a dream come true. Looking ahead to a splendid future, men of Ansari's background yearned for an opportunity to obtain a degree from a British university, a valuable asset and a passport to joining the 'heaven born'.

Approaching twenty-one, Ansari sailed for London, being the first in his family to cross the seas. A cousin, Mohammad Asghar, a law student followed him in London, reporting himself to the educational adviser in London at 21 Cromwell Road and spending a couple of weeks in the accommodation provided for new arrivals, Ansari joined the Medical College in Edinburgh. By sheer talent and a capacity for prolonged and concentrated work, he secured the degree of Doctor of Medicine and Master of Surgery in 1908. Soon after, he served as resident medical officer in the Charing Cross Hospital in London, established in 1823 as the West London Infirmary, and was originally located in Villiers Street, near Charing Cross in the heart of the metropolis. Ansari was the first Indian to achieve such a distinction. This caused quite a furore in the local press. An evening newspaper published a leading story entitled 'Grave Injustice to British Doctors' with racist overtones. But the Governing Council of the Hospital stoutly defended Ansari's appointment. He already had the ambition to spark off enthusiasm among those he met. His selection, stated the Council, 'has been made purely on the basis of merit, and it will be disastrous for British hospitals if any other criterion was employed for appointment purposes'.[24]

This incident gained wide publicity. It was a matter of pride for many Indians that one of them had established his professional competence in the face of a racially arrogant section of the British press. Among Muslims, in particular, he became known as among the few who opted for the 'modern method' as opposed to the more commonly practiced *yunani tibb.* There are many others now who have done the same, but Ansari was the first to lead the way.

The youngman's stay in Britain from 1901 to 1910 is the least known period of his life. Not a single letter from these years survive, either written or received by Ansari, and it is only from isolated comments that one tentatively constructs, in a very limited way, the society in which he lived. We know, for instance, that he did indeed work hard, but also found time to be sociable,[25] to act in plays[26] and to make some lively and intelligent friends. He had many aristocratic attributes which infused his entire sensibility. In later years, they provided him with strength when standing out against orthodoxy. Although an entertaining and at times a fascinating companion with a great store of anecdotes and Urdu *ghazals* on which to draw, he was not by nature gregarious or sociable. Even in later years he did not easily admit those he met to his confidence or allow them to penetrate the warmth and humanity which lay behind his formidable defences. Serious intellectual doubts inhibited him from engaging wholeheartedly in any form of radical activism with revolutionary aims.

Most people found Ansari relaxed by temperament, cultivated and generous. According to Mujeeb's description in his unfinished biography, he was 'a distinctive figure of average height, broad pleasing looks, openness, of a voice somewhat musical, emotions gushing and effusive, but what struck people at once were his attractive eyes, his pompous moustache and profusive eye-brows'. He exuded the charm which swiftly won friends. Most of the friendships he formed in London lasted until his death; many were to play significant parts in his professional or political life. Jawaharlal Nehru (1889-1964) described meeting 'a smart and clever young man with a record of brilliant academic achievement behind him'.[27] Their meeting developed into a lifelong friendship. It was to him and his father that Ansari most readily confided his plans and his feelings, and it was to their home in Allahabad that he liked best to go for a vacation. It was a relationship so central to Ansari's life and which he took so much for granted, that he never felt the need to comment on it.

There was also Ajmal Khan, the scion of a family of physicians who had long served the Mughal court and, after their decline, the regional princes. The two first met in London only to find

In Edinburgh, 1901

As an actor in Othello staged in Edinburgh

Fellow-students in England:
Ansari, Inayat Ali Khan & Saeeduzzaffar Khan (standing)

Comrade-in-arms: Shaukatullah Ansari (right), Salimuzzaman (left). The other two are not identifiable. Sitting: Left to right—Ansari, Ajmal Khan and Qazi Abdul Ghaffar, his biographer.

Ansari with Hakim Ajmal Khan (in the middle) and others.

each other's company congenial. Their friendship ripened when they worked together in the Rowlatt satyagraha. There were few secrets between these two through the long unbroken years of friendship and few griefs in which they could not solace each other.

All who met Ajmal Khan succumbed to his irresistible spell. Tolerant, human and broad-minded, he counselled people who turned instinctively to him for guidance. A product of the finest composite cultural traditions and ideals, his belief in Hindu-Muslim unity was not a matter of policy but a part of his heritage; it was in his blood and the substance of his everyday life. He was loved and honoured, and most of all by those who themselves had high ideals of commitment and refinement.[28] C.F. Andrews (1871-1940) spoke of 'an ever deepening friendship' with Ajmal Khan and revered him for his integrity and dedication.[29] 'Quiet, humble, modest, with all the dignity of a man of character, learning and religious sincerity', wrote Andrews, 'Ajmal Khan was the one recognized head in Delhi who, all acknowledged as their moral leader, for his character and character alone.[30] Many years later Jawaharlal summed up his many qualities:

> As an ex-president of the Congress he was one of its elder statesmen; but he was something more also, and he occupied a unique place in the Congress leadership. Brought up as he was, entirely in the old conservative way, with no touch of modernism in it, and steeped in the culture of imperial Delhi of Moghal days, it was a delight to watch his fine courtesy and hear his unhurried voice and listen to his dry humour. He was, in his manners, a typical aristocrat of the old order, with princely look and princely ways, and even his face bore a marked resemblance to the miniatures of the Moghal sovereigns. Such a person would not ordinarily take to the rough-and-tumble of politics. . . . But even during the latter part of the War events, and the influence of his old friend and colleague, Dr. M.A. Ansari, were driving him to the Congress; and subsequent happenings—Martial Law in the Punjab and the Khilafat question—moved him deeply, and he turned with approval to the new Gandhian technique of non-cooperation. He brought a rare quality and precious gifts to the Congress—he became a link between the old order and the new, and gave the support of the former to the national movement. . . . He brought the Hindus and Muslims much nearer to each other, for both honoured him and were influenced by

his example. To Gandhiji he became a trusted friend, whose advice in regard to Hindu-Muslim matters was the final word for him. My father and Hakimji had naturally taken to each other.[31]

Such was the man Ansari met in London.

Another person of vigorous and independent mind in London was Mohammad Iqbal (1876-1938), already known through his poems *Nala-i Yatim* (Complaint of the Orphan) which he recited in 1899 at Lahore. In 1905, Iqbal left for Europe, studied at Trinity College, Cambridge, read German at Heidelberg, and submitted his doctorate dissertation at the University of Munich. Atiya Begum Fyzee, a cousin of Akbar Hydari (1869-1942), described the young brilliant student of those days; she met Iqbal first in London and later in Germany. She recorded the details of a party at her house on 23 June 1907. 'Dr. Ansari,' she noted, 'entertained us with songs, Lord Sinha's daughters . . . with music, and Iqbal with extempore compositions of clever and witty verses referring to almost every important guest present by making exaggerated remarks about their peculiarities, sending as all into roars of laughter.'[32] Atiya's sister-in-law, Rufiah Sultan Nazli Begum, also refers to a meeting with Ansari.[33]

Such social gatherings recreated the north Indian culture of the elite in an alien cultural milieu, but they were often attended by the former British civil servants and educationists who had served in India. Thus Ansari, Mohamed Ali and Fazl-i Husain (1877-1936) attended parties hosted by the families of Theodore Beck (1859-99), principal of the Aligarh College in Syed Ahmad Khan's (1817-98) lifetime and T.W. Arnold (b. 1864), who taught and wrote on Islam and the history of Muslims.[34] On 21 September 1898, Ansari found himself in the company of Mohamed Ali and Fazl-i Husain at 82 Brondesbury Villas in Kilburn, the home of Miss Beck. 'We passed an exceedingly pleasant evening,' recorded Fazl-i Husain, and 'talked literature, philosophy, politics, and what not.'[35]

Such meetings generated much lively discussions.[36] But there is no evidence to indicate Ansari's involvement in or his association with any student group, such as the Majlis in Cambridge, the Oxford Islamic Society, or, the Anjuman-i Islamia, later called the pan-Islamic society.[37] Some of his contemporaries—Abdul Majid Khwaja (1885-1962), Haroon Khan Sherwani (1891-1980) and Syed Mahmud (1889-1971)—read W.S. Blunt (1840-1922) and Professor E.G. Browne (1862-1920) of Cambridge and engaged with pan-Islamism and the nationalist movements in West Asia. Ansari did not make the acquaintance of either of them at this time; he devoted very little thought to politics, Indian or other.

Ansari returned to India in 1910 to be offered the principalship of the Lahore Medical College. But the terms of the scholarship on which he went to Edinburgh required that he serve the Hyderabad State for some years. He waited for a while to be placed in one of the medical institutions and toyed with the idea of moving to Calcutta. But the Raja of Mahmudabad (1879-1931) and Ali Imam (1869-1932), a lawyer and member of the governor-general's council at that time, saw a bright future for the young doctor in Delhi, the new capital of British India, and advised him accordingly. Besides being the imperial capital, Delhi was one of the main centres of the Urdu-speaking world, the home of Mir Taqi Mir (1733-1814) and Asadullah Khan Ghalib (1797-1869); in Ansari's own words, the 'cradle of Islamic civilization in India' and 'the city of Muslim memories'. 'Time has not yet effaced the landmarks of Islam in the history of this country,' he observed, 'nor has the dust of centuries buried the footprints of our ancestors.'[38] The decision to settle in Delhi was irrevocable. From this moment Ansari planned his life with a method rare among young men and adhered to his own rules with inflexible self-discipline. He had every reason to feel satisfied and some excuse for being self-satisfied. He had been successful and popular at the medical schools in London and faced the future with a confident belief in his ability to make the most of it.

Ansari's clinic was for several years housed in a portion of the Fatehpuri mosque in the old city, a mosque sold by the British to a Hindu banker after the 1857 revolt and returned to the Muslims by the viceroy, Lytton (1831-91). Here and later in Daryaganj he continued to practice as perhaps one of the few famous doctors of India. Among his patients were many leading Congressmen, princes, rajas and nawabs.[39] He gave certain hours to the poor daily, no matter what profit he could have made from those hours. The cases were almost all non-Muslim; the needing

Muslims were generally treated free directly or through relatives.[40]

Ansari's private house—*Behisht* (Paradise)—was by the old city walls, near the Mori Gate. It was in this house that Andrews and Mohamed Ali lectured on the sufferings of Indians in South Africa.[41] The distinguished English novelist E.M. Forster (1879-1970) and his companion Syed Ross Masud (1889-1937) stayed here during their visit in late October 1912. Forster described Ansari as 'a most charming Doctor' and was impressed with his hospitality.[42] 'I sit in the verandah of the house . . . with now a chicken running past and now a squirrel, and listen to the doves and green parrots making conversation in the garden. . . . Both garden and house are small, and it is a great kindness on Ansari's part to have put me up. Though a youngman, he has already a large practice. . . . He seems as competent as he is charming, and I think I would as soon rely on him as on certain paler skins at home. . . .'[43]

The *Behisht* was thronged by unexplained visitors—sitting cross-legged on the beds or on the luggage. There seemed to be no set meal times, but whenever Forster crossed the threshold, tea and poached eggs would appear and Ansari's wife, who observed *purdah*, would send cigarettes, betel nut and *itr* (scent).[44] 'I am in the middle of a very queer life,' he told a friend on 2 November 1912, 'whether typically Oriental I have no means of knowing, but it isn't English.'[45]

Forster described 'a very homely and pleasant' evening at a *nautch*, or party with dancing girls, arranged by Ansari. He admired the leading performer, a girl 'with a queer but very charming face and delightful manners' and was regaled by her dancing.[46] 'Emotion came to me through the harsh voice and music, so that I enjoyed myself', he wrote. 'When the singer sank down in our midst, with her scarlet and golden robes spread round us, and sang love songs, I realized what a *nautch* must be to Indians.'[47] The English novelist spent the evening in the company of, among others, Mohamed Ali, the volatile editor of the *Comrade* who even contemplated suicide as the message reached him that the Bulgarians were only 25 miles from Constantinople—'a name that had for five centuries been sacred to every Muslim as the centre of his highest hopes'.[48] Mohamed

Ali indiscreetly shared his experience at the *nautch* with a fellow-journalist, and not long afterwards, the *London Times* reported how a leading Muslim, on the eve of Turkey's defeat in the Balkan war, had spent his evening at an 'orgy'.[49]

In 1928, Ansari set up his clinic within the walled city in Daryaganj which remained a sparsely built-up area until 1908 when the stationed British troops were evacuated to the new cantonment on the Ridge. Gradually, however, some successful lawyers and doctors built some new houses. Ansari moved into one of them. Apart from sharing for some years with Dr. H.C. Sen the distinction of being the only Indian in Delhi to own motor cars,[50] he soon bought an elegant octagonal building, overlooking a square lawn, from Lala Sultan Singh for Rs. 50,000.[51] It was aptly called Dar-us-Salam, abode of peace. In the early 1930s, it became the venue of important meetings and conferences: a counterpart of Motilal Nehru's (1861-1931) Allahabad residence, Anand Bhawan. Halide Edip stayed in Dar-us-Salam for two months in 1935 and described it as 'an historical place where the ancient, the medieval, and the modern came together: the ideas and aspirations of divergent personalities meet, coalesce, and the personalities disperse to set in motion new trends elsewhere'. 'In the free India of the future,' she prophesized, 'that house will be one of the principal landmarks in its marking.'[52] The prophesy has not been fulfilled. Dar-us-Salam is, today, a visible symbol of neglect. The hustle and bustle of the 1920s and early 1930s is gone; instead, a group of half-naked *sadhus* congregate singing hymns.

Edip's account offers a glimpse of Ansari's family. In the left wing of the house lived Shamsunnisa who saw no men other than her relatives, except Gandhi. She spent her leisure reading the Quran, the *Gulistan* (Rose Garden: 1258) and *Bustaan* (Fruit Garden: 1257) of the Persian poet, Saadi (1184-1291) and Urdu short stories and poetry. Her attitude towards her servants reminded Edip of old Turkey. She would often hear young girls taking lessons from different teachers on the verandah behind the curtain. They were as free and as natural as the daughter of the house. There was no trace of class feeling.[53] Presumably, the lessons were in Quran and *Hadis.*

Zohra, lived in Dar-us-Salam. Her life, according to the Turkish author, 'seemed to be an Indian version of my life of thirty-five years ago in Turkey. She was too individualistic to fit into a fixed group whether inside or outside of Purdah.'[54] She described Zohra's interest in history and literature:

> She knew her country's history exceedingly well . . . she did not feel Muslims to be an alien race, a minority grafted on Indian soil, and doomed to remain as such. She was Indian to the core. Asoka was part of her past history just as much as humayun. . . . She both humanized and dramatized for me the great monumental edifices which would otherwise have been only heaps of stones more or less artistically arranged. She knew all the legends around the lives of those who had lived in those ruins.[55]

These impressions reveal Ansari's profound influence on the young Zohra, who continued the legacy of her father's catholic outlook. What is, however, not brought out is that children were a constant pleasure and interest to Ansari and that parenthood aroused the most delightful aspects of his character. He reserved his affection and care for Zohra, his letters to her sparkling with tenderness, humour and affection.[56] Zohra, on her part, proved to be a woman of strong character and intelligence who understood her father as no one else did; in return, Ansari confided everything to her, as he did to no one else, not even his wife. He found in Zohra the intellectual companionship and supportive admiration he needed.

NOTES

1. *Narrative of Events and the Restoration of Authority in the Division of Benares in 1857-1858,* UP State Archives (UPSA), Lucknow, Box No. 1.
2. H.R. Nevill, *Ghazipur: A Gazetteer,* vol. XXIX (Allahabad, 1909), pp. 171-4.
3. Passing through Ghazipur on 31 August 1824, Bishop Heber observed: 'The population is great, and the mosques, and Mussulmans in the shops and streets are so numerous, and there are so few pagodas of any importance visible, that I thought I had bidden adieu for the present to the followers of Brahma. Mr Melville, however assured me, to my surprise, that it was in the large towns only that the Mussulmans were numerous, and that, taking the whole province together, they were

barely an eleventh part of the population, among the remainder of whom Hindooism existed in all its strength and bigotry.' M.A. Laird (ed.), *Bishop Heber in Northern India Selection from Heber's Journal* (Cambridge, 1971), p. 126.

4. According to the 1911 Census, the Hindus were 90.7 per cent of the population and the Muslims 9.11 per cent. 'This is the smallest proportion of Musalmans on record, and is partly accounted for by their greater susceptibility to plague, partly perhaps by the fact that, the Ghazipur Muslims are mainly in poor circumstances. It has never been the experience of this district that Muslims increase more rapidly than Hindus.' *Ghazipur: Supplementary Notes and Statistics to Volume XXXIX of the District Gazetteer of the United Provinces of Agra and Oudh* (Allahabad, 1915), Appendix I.
5. *Ghazipur: A Gazetteer*, p. 90.
6. Ibid., p. 91.
7. Ibid., p. 99.
8. Shaukatullah Ansari, *Pakistan: The Problem of India* (Lahore, 1944), p. 103.
9. Draft note, Mujeeb Collection, JMI; M. Mujeeb, 'Dr Ansari: Chand Yaaden Baaten', *Aaj Kal* (Delhi), Ansari Number, January 1981, pp. 12-13.
10. Rahman was the son of Sheikh Mohammad Baksh who had two other sons—Mohammad Sadiq and Abdul Ghaffar. Sadiq (d. 1907/8) became an inspector of police in Punjab. One of his daughters was married to Ansari's brother Abdur Razzaq; the other to Maulvi Mohammad Talib of Ghazipur. Statement of Abdur Razzaq Ansari, J.C. Curry Papers, Centre of South Asian Studies, Cambridge. All subsequent references to Razzaq are drawn from the same statement.
11. Zia Ahmad Barni, *Azmat-i Rafta* (Karachi, 1961), p. 263.
12. Ansari kept the *Shaikh-ul Hind* informed of the government moves against him and his movement, and paid for his travel expenses to the Hijaz. Both he and his brother, Razzaq, provided funds to support his activities. H.A. Madani, *Naqsh-i Hayat: Khudnawisht Sawanah* (Karachi, 1979 edn.), p. 620.
13. 'Tehrik-i Azadi ka ek Khamosh Kaarkun: Abdul Ali Khan ke khudnawisht halaat-i zinaagi', *Jung* (Rawalpindi), 9 June 1964.
14. C.F. Andrews, *Zakaullah of Delhi* (Cambridge, n.d.), p. xxiii.
15. Rasheed Ahmad Khan, *Hayat-i Ajmal* (Delhi, 1931), p. 130.
16. On his death, Ansari wrote: 'My brother was a brother as well as a friend and his parting has been a great wrench. He was the most popular, the most respected and the most beloved state official in Hyderabad. His was a model life of service and dedication to the people in his charge. When he retired from service last year some ten or fifteen thousand people gathered to bid him farewell and the poor and

suffering people of Aurangabad raised a tearful wail when he left them. He was a truly pious and truly generous hearted man. He was equally respected by his colleagues and his superiors. In him, as I have said before, I lose a brother, a comrade and a true friend. I feel lonely and lost without him.' Ansari to S.A. Brelvi, 13 May 1935, Brelvi Papers, NMML.

17. For the early history of the college, see Irene A. Gilbert, 'Autonomy and Consensus under the Raj: Presidency (Calcutta); Muir (Allahabad); M.A.O. (Aligarh)', S.H. Rudolph and L.I. Rudolph (eds.), *Education and Politics in India: Studies in Organization, Society, and Policy* (Delhi, 1972), pp. 178-82.
18. *India*, 17 October 1913.
19. 'India: Old and New', *Asiatic Review*, July 1914.
20. *University of Allahabad Calendar 1896-97* (Allahabad, 1896), p. 547; *University of Madras: The Calendar for 1917* (Madras, 1917), vols. 1-2, p. 372.
21. Halide Edip, *Inside India* (London, 1936), p. 31; Zohra Ansari, 'Shamsunnisa awr Dr Ansari', *Aaj Kal*, January 1981, p. 14.
22. Gail Minault, *The Khilafat Movement: Religions Symbolism and Political Mobilization in India* (Delhi, 1982), pp. 36, 150.
23. Zohra Ansari, Oral History transcript.
24. Barni, *Azmat-i Rafta*, p. 106.
25. Zohra Ansari, Oral History transcript.
26. A photograph in this book shows Ansari playing the part of Othello in Edinburgh.
27. Nehru, *An Autobiography*, p. 17.
28. Mujeeb, *The Indian Muslims*, p. 536; for a more recent appreciation of Ajmal Khan's role, see Barbara D. Metcalf, 'Nationalist Muslims in British India: The Case of Hakim Ajmal Khan', *Modern Asian Studies*, 19, I, 1985, pp. 1-28.
29. C.F. Andrews, 'Hakim Ajmal Khan', in *Eminent Mussalmans* (Madras, 1926), p. 287.
30. *Modern Review*, 31, 6 June 1922, p. 686. Hardinge recalled that Ajmal Khan was much respected throughout India' and found him loyal in every way. He saw him at Delhi and often discussed Muslim affairs, especially in connection with the war. Hardinge to Chelmsford, 23 August 1916, MSS. EUR. E. 264 (15), Chelmsford Papers, IOL. Also, Ansari's account in Abdul Ghaffar, *Hayat-i Ajmal* (Delhi, 1950), pp. 110-11. The memoirs of Ansari, quoted at length by Ghaffar, are not traceable.
31. Nehru, *An Autobiography*, pp. 168-9.
32. Atiya Fyzee, *Iqbal* (Bombay, 1947).
33. Nazil Begum of Jangira, *Sair-i Europe* (Lahore, n.d.), p. 26.
34. Azim Husain, *Fazl-i Husain: A Political Biography* (Bombay, 1936),

p. 20; Afzal Iqbal, *Life and Times of Mohamed Ali* (Delhi, 1978), rpt., pp. 31-2.
35. MSS. EUR. E. 352 (2), Fazl-i Husain Papers, IOL.
36. Notice Fazl-i Husain's noting on 23 September 1898: 'In the evening we had a very hot discussion. Really we had not fixed upon the topic, the subject under discussion was quite vague and all the more vague because the branch of knowledge to which it belongs is far from precision. We were talking about Religion, Blind belief etc.' Ibid.
37. There was an Islamic Society in London, an Oxford University Indian Club and the Oxford Islamic Society. Haroon Khan Sherwani, then a student at Jesus College, Oxford, was president of the Oxford Islamic Society. Others associated with it were H. Fyzee, K. Tayebji, H.M. Shairani, father of the Urdu poet, Akhtar Shairani, Haroon Khan Sherwani Papers, NMML.
38. Speech at the All-India Muslim League Session, Delhi, 1918, Mushirul Hasan (ed.), *Muslims and the Cosngress: Select Correspondence of Dr M.A. Ansari, 1912-1935* (Delhi, 1979), p. 264.
39. He would charge Rs. 500 to 1,000 a day from the Nawab of Rampur and the Begum of Bhopal. His consultation fee in the early 1930s was Rs. 32. But he treated most Congress leaders free of charge. Motilal Nehru was his patient for long and Ansari was extremely solicitous of his health.
40. Zohra recalls some of Ansari's acts of generosity. See Oral History transcript.
41. Barni, *Azmat-i Rafta*, pp. 107-8. For Andrews on South Africa, Hugh Tinker, *The Ordeal of Love: C.F. Andrews and India* (Delhi, 1979), chapter five; Andrews to Tagore, 15 November 1913, *Andrews' Papers: Bunch of Letters to Rabindranath Tagore and M.K. Gandhi* (Deshbandhu Andrews Centenary Committee, n.d.).
42. To Mary Aylward, 30 October 1912, Mary Lago and P.N. Furbank (eds.), *Selected Letters of E.M. Forster, 1879-1920* (London, 1983), vol. I, p. 141.
43. To Laury Mary Forster, 31 October 1912, ibid., p. 144.
44. P.N. Furbank, *E.M. Forster: A Life: The Growth of the Novelist 1879-1914* (London, 1978), p. 228.
45. To Florence Barger, 2 November 1912, *Selected Letters*, p. 144.
46. To Alice Clara Forster, 6 November 1912, ibid., p. 149.
47. Quoted in Furbank, *E.M. Forster: A Life*, p. 229.
48. Mohamed Ali wrote: 'To return to that autumn night in 1912, I was saved a trial of my courage as well as cowardice by the unexpected appearance of a Muslim friend [Ross Masud] who had graduated from Oxford not long before and was on the occasion accompanied by an English fellow-graduate of that University [E.M. Forster] who was his guest and had expressed a desire to see an Indian *nautch*. Arrangements

had been made *sub rosa* and the place selected was the house of a barrister who was my next door neighbour. My friend insisted on my company and hard as I pleaded the excuse of a busy editor . . . my friend would not take any denial and almost bodily lifted me from the editorial sanctum and carried me by main force to the private *nautch* party next door.' Afzal Iqbal (ed.), *My Life a Fragment: An Autobiographical Sketch of Maulana Mohamed Ali* (Delhi, 1979 edn.), p. 38.

49. Furbank, *E.M. Forster: A Life,* p. 229; Mohamed Ali wrote: 'Thus it was that instead of being a horror of broken bones and bleeding body supposed to have accidentally alien down from a third storey, there I was "assisting" at the "orgy" that had been arranged by my young friend to gratify the curiosity of a brother Oxonian.' Ibid., pp. 38-9.
50. Narayani Gupta, *Delhi Between Two Empires, 1803-1931: Society, Government and Urban Growth* (Delhi, 1981), p. 58.
51. 'Tehrik-i Azadi ka ek Khamosh Karkun', op. cit.
52. Edip, *Inside India,* p. 27.
53. Ibid., p. 32.
54. Ibid., p. 33.
55. Ibid.
56. See, for example, Ansari to Shaukatullah Ansari, 21 May 1934, Hasan (ed.), *Muslims and the Congress,* p. 155.

A view of Dar-us-Salam.

Ansari's car

2

The Political Milieu, 1910-1917

> Delhi, in spite of her newly-conferred dignity, is still dominated by her past which broods over the lives and activities of the living as well as the smouldering remains of the dead. An ever present sense of her tragic history has created in her people a cynical disregard for her needs, the joys and sorrows of the present. She has rarely felt the new enthusiasms which render the lives of the modern cities so absorbing and fruitful and have made them the nerve-centres of the common life of the country. Her biggest sons would seem to an outside observer to be engaged in an incessant personal struggle to keep their heads above the water-line. Their horizon almost exactly resembles that of any out-of-the-way mofussil town whose entire consciousness is filled with the enormous figure of the District Magistrate.
>
> *Comrade*, 12 July 1913

THE INDIA TO which Ansari came in 1912, at the age of thirty-two, was a land of relative tranquility. The flames which had fired the Swadeshi movement in Bengal had been extinguished with the annulment of partition in 1911, and, for the time being, a major irritant in government's relationship with the Indian National Congress was removed. The 'moderates', epitomized by men like G.K. Gokhale (1866-1915), Pherozeshah Mehta (1848-1915) and Surendranath Banerjea (1848-1925), now came to dominate Congress affairs after having been eclipsed by the rapid rise of extremist nationalism in Maharashtra, Bengal and the Punjab. Their hopes of an ultimate victory were kept alive by the outcome of the Russo-Japanese war of 1904-5 and by another inspiring example, that of Mohandas Karamchand Gandhi (1869-1948), who led successful passive resistance struggles in South Africa between 1906 and 1914. The defeat of the Russian army and navy at the hands of a much smaller Asian country than India led the 'extremists' and their revolutionary allies to believe that if Japan could thwart an occidental giant like Russia, then India, a much larger country, could do the same to an insular power like Britain. This thinking encouraged the demand for swaraj in different parts of the country, including Delhi, the Imperial capital since 1 October 1912.

Delhi remained a political backwater until February 1917 when a branch of the Home Rule League was opened, a fact Ansari alluded to in his evidence before the Hunter Commission. This marked 'the entry of prominent local men', as Delhi's chief commissioner put it, 'into the all-India political arena',[1] and led to a sudden flurry of political activity: the Indraprastha Sewak Mandli was formed in May 1917 in response to Annie Besant's (1847-1933) advocacy of boy scouts' organization and a League Volunteer Corps—with Ansari, Ajmal Khan and Asaf Ali (1888-1953)[2] on the management committee—was raised in early 1918.[3] Contemporaries noticed the anti-government rumblings and suggested the not so unfamiliar remedy of educating the 'public mind on imperial lines'.[4]

Ansari, already known for his good work as leader of the Indian Medical Mission to Constantinople, was a key figure in Delhi's Home Rule movement. As its president he organized an intermittent but comprehensive scheme of propaganda, declared liberty of thought and speech to be every citizen's birth-right, and urged the people to condemn the arrest of Annie Besant. 'It is a matter which concerns not simply an individual community or province, but is an all-India question and touches the liberty and the rights of every Indian. Hence silence at a time like this is cowardly and disloyal to one's own people and to one's self.'[5]

Apart from local men like Asaf Ali, Shiv Narain Haksar, Abdur Rahman (b. 1888), R.S. Piyare Lal and Abdul Aziz (b. 1907), Ansari persuaded his younger friends to attend the League meetings in order to initiate them into the Home Rule crusade. Among those he influenced most was Khaliquzzaman (1889-1973), an Aligarh graduate, and Tassaduq Ahmad Khan Sherwani (1889-1935), a contemporary of Jawaharlal at Cambridge. Such men threatened to disturb Delhi's placid life and involve its citizens in an agitation of serious proportions.

In its historical sequence, the Home Rule agitation brought to the fore the organizing and leadership qualities of several fresh recruits to the nationalist movement. Among them were Mohammed Ali Jinnah (1876-1948), Jamnadas Dwarkadas, Shankarlal Banker (1889-95) and Umar Subhani (d. 1926) in Bombay; Jawaharlal, Harkaran Nath Misra (b. 1890), Khaliq-uzzaman, Khwaja and Sherwani in UP; Ansari, Ajmal Khan and Asaf Ali in Delhi. Jawaharlal recalled how 'the atmosphere became electric' with the younger men expecting 'big things to happen in the near future' and how Annie Besant's internment vitalized the Home Rule movement. The Leagues attracted the old 'Extremists' who had been kept out of the Congress since 1907, as well as large numbers of newcomers from the middle classes.[6] The *New Era* from Lucknow noticed how Annie Besant's incarceration 'unwittingly accomplished the purpose of an organized agitation and propaganda in a single day', and led to 'a fresh stirring in public life' and a 'stiffening of public resolve'.[7] Ansari, too, referred to its impact in Delhi, where

> the recent events have produced a great deal of feeling and people who were not Home Rule Leaguers have either joined the League or are thinking of joining it soon. Even some of the most conservative people have changed their views [and], have come to look upon the actions of some of the local Governments as highly unconstitutional and unwise.[8]

The Home Rule Leagues were dominated by Hindu theosophical ideas, and many of their patrons were connected with Hindu revivalist bodies. But, in general, they pursued a non-communal programme, a fact which encouraged educated Muslims to swell the ranks of Annie Besant's adherents. For instance, Abdul Majid Khwaja, a successful lawyer and Jawaharlal's contemporary at Cambridge, set up a Home Rule League branch in Aligarh with the backing of Haji Musa Khan, a leading *rais* of Datauli and one of the stalwarts at the Aligarh College. Some young lawyers and journalists did the same in Allahabad. Prominent among them were: Sheikh Zahur Ahmad, an Aligarh graduate; Manzar Ali Sokhta, whose father managed the Nehru household; Kamaluddin Jafri (d. 1933), a lawyer; Wahid Yar Khan, editor of *Nai Roshni*, a paper published from 1916 to 1918. In Agra, Syed Ali Nabi (d. 1927) led the Home Rule League. He was a member of the UP legislative council from 1909 to 1912 and chairman of the reception committee of the Muslim League in 1913. In Lucknow, its main adherents were Raja Ghulam Husain (1882-1917), editor of *Comrade* and *New Era*; Syed Jalib Dehlavi (d. 1930), editor of an Urdu daily, *Hamdam*; Hakim Abdul Wali (b. 1884), proprietor of the *Al-Bayan*, an Arabic-Urdu monthly of Lucknow, and owner of the famous Asi Press; Shuaib Qureshi, Khaliquzzaman and Abdur Rahman Siddiqi (1887-1953), Aligarh graduates and members of Ansari's medical mission to Turkey.

Some indication of their political preferences can be gauged from their support to Annie Besant's election as Congress president in 1917, as opposed to their patron, the Raja of Mahmudabad. The *New Era* insisted that the dictates of patriotism and national self-interest required that Mrs Besant be elected president of the national assembly. It appealed to the Raja to withdraw from the contest because, 'no other choice, whether of a Hindu or Muslim public man, would symbolize more effectively the faith and will of educated India or express the strength of the national resolve in a more decisive form'.[9] In a note submitted to the viceroy on 7 February 1917, James Meston (1865-1943), lieutenant-governor of UP, summed up the strength of nationalist feelings among such Muslims and lamented the declining influence of their detractors, especially those allied to the government. He observed with uncharacteristic frankness:

> In deciding either on the strategy of its *post-bellum* policy or to handle the Home Rule agitation, the Government of India will no doubt have regard to the strength of the Nationalist feeling in India at the present moment. It is unquestionably greater than it has ever been in our time. The Christmas meetings at Lucknow caught up and consolidated popular sentiment as few political events have done. Extremists and moderates have united after years of misunderstanding; and, greatest marvel of all, the Mohammedans also had come into the fold. A few Moderates may grumble here and there; and a few conservative Mohammedans may urge that the League does not represent their community. But they *do* nothing. They are voiceless in public; they do not hold meetings; they have completely lost command of the Press. For all practical purposes they have, for the time at least, disappeared as a separate party. *The resultant union of all voices has filled educated Indians with a pride and a feeling of nationality which is impossible to ignore* [italics mine].[10]

Political radicalism among Muslims was triggered by the annulment of Bengal's partition and the British machinations in Turkey. Paradoxical as it may seem, their 'extra-territorial patriotism' served to stimulate the development of their territorial patriotism also. The aggression of Western powers hastened their disillusionment with the policy of traditional reliance on the government, and the rejection of the Muslim university scheme and the Kanpur mosque incident made it clear that Muslim interests at home were of no greater consequence to their rulers than their sentiments with regard to their brethren abroad. The Balkan wars helped to unify Muslim sentiment, extend the pan-Islamic idea, and stimulated the 'hot-headed literati editors, schoolmasters and journalists' to conduct their anti-government agitation.[11] In these years, the rhetoric of Muslim political language moved from an emphasis on the preservation of elite interests to more emotive, populist, public symbols of Muslim corporate identity.[12]

It was left to Hardinge (1858-1944) to heal the wounds left by that deep gash in the body of India—the partition of Bengal. But his decision to revoke the partition embittered many Muslims and not just the Bengali Muslims. Moreover, the great Muslim university project, conceived by the successors of Syed Ahmad Khan, shuddered to a halt because the secretary of state for India and his council objected to both the term 'Muslim' in the nomenclature of the university and to the scheme to affiliate colleges outside the province. Lastly, the dictates of European diplomacy and the anti-Turkish strain of the British government constrained Hardinge. He tried to impress London with the strength of pan-Islamic feelings in India over the Italian attack upon Tripoli, but the India Office did not feel the feverishly rising pulse of pan-Islamism. Hardinge told the secretary of state that the Foreign Office did not sufficiently appreciate the difficulties which his government encountered over Turkey. Some years later, Montagu conceded that the Muslim 'resentment appears so remote from the minds of my colleagues'.[13]

The shift in government policy profoundly altered the tone and tenor of Muslim League politics. To begin with, an influential group of lawyers, journalists and a section of the *ulama* contested the methods of the first generation of Aligarh Muslim leaders, affirmed their commitment to agitational methods, and believed in working out the destiny of their compatriots in unison with the Congress. Instead of being haunted by the spectre of Hindu domination, they endorsed the Congress creed. The *New Era* wrote:

> A community of about 70 million . . . has to work out its political destiny in close and active cooperation with the rest of the Indian people. Any other alternative to a policy of trust resolutely striving for the complete unity of the Indian races is unthinkable. Any self-respecting Muslim who knows what political freedom means for the self-realization of individuals as well as communities can feel no enthusiasm for a political creed that does not aim at a free and united India.[14]

Shibli Nomani (1857-1914) was among the most influential exponents of the idea of cooperation with the Hindus in general and the Congress, in particular. In a series of essays published in 1912, he berated the Muslim League's political methods and the short-sightedness of its leaders. Whereas the Congress pursued a comprehensive and constructive economic and political programme, the League seemed solely interested in a larger share for Muslims in government services and in the extension of separate electorates to municipalities and district boards. In drawing yet another point of contrast, Shibli pointed out that the Congress leaders were not drawn from the titled and landed gentry, whereas the League was in their hands. Such people could not sacrifice their own material interests by taking a firm stand against the government. Above all, the eminent *alim* of Nadwa reminded readers of the bonds of unity which had prevailed between the two communities during medieval rule in India. This was an old story, 'but even today go to the villages and see for yourself the brotherly feelings that exist between Hindus and Muslims, and the two communities participate in each other's functions as if they were related to each other by family ties'.[15] Shibli was right. Khaliquzzaman recalled, from the vantage point of Pakistan, the dominance of the titled gentry, nawabs, landlords and *jee huzoors* and their self-seeking politics. The League activities were, consequently, confined to 'indoor political shows' and its annual sessions were held either in well-decorated *pandals* or in big halls where a few honourable members were allowed access by special cards.[16]

Changes in the League began to occur around 1911. The transfer of its office (January 1910) from Aligarh to Lucknow was a notable development. The League at Aligarh had been an adjunct of a college dominated by those who learnt their lesson of loyalty to government and opposition to Congress at the feet of Syed Ahmad Khan. But, with the initiative passing into the hands of the politically advanced Lucknow-based leaders, the newly-vitalized organization reflected, slowly but steadily, the radical temper of people like Shibli, Abul Kalam Azad (1888-1958), Mohamed Ali, Wazir Hasan, Zafar Ali Khan (1873-1956), Mazharul Haq (1866-1930) and their followers. Described as the 'younger men' and as the standard-bearers of 'new ideals', 'new forces' and *nai raushni*, these men secured their major victory in 1913. That is when the League's revised constitution incorporated a new clause proclaiming its aim to work with other groups for 'a system of self-government suitable to India'. But the old school of politicians could not swallow this bitter pill and launched a counter attack.[17] Mohammad Shafi (1869-1932) in Punjab, Nawab Ali Chaudhuri (d. 1921) in Bengal and Fateh Ali Khan Qizilbash (b. 1862) in UP denounced the self-government idea on the ground that it would irk Anglo-Muslim relations and irretrievably damage Muslim interests. An outraged Fateh Ali Khan exhorted members of the League: 'Its calamitous character is too obvious and before years add to its sanctity, Muslims must join in undoing the fair but deceptive foundations which they have dug.'[18]

Such warnings were ill-timed. The politics of Fateh Ali Khan and his counterparts in Bengal and Punjab was quite clearly divorced from reality and out of tune with the mainstream of political life. 'I am far from being out of sympathy with the young party,' wrote Meston, 'because I believe that it was an inevitable reaction against the dignified inefficiency of the old-fashioned Muslims.'[19] Meston should have added that proximity to the Raj contributed to their eventual ouster from the premier Muslim organization. The Aga Khan (1875-1958), who presided over the League's destiny from 1906 to 1913, suddenly bolted and resigned on 3 November 1913. Replying to Harcourt Butler (1869-1938), who constantly urged him to lead the Muslims, the Ismaili leader conceded that he was unable to do so, 'for my first advice will be loyalty of the kind that means trust and confidence and that trust and confidence the Muslims are not now giving to Government'.[20]

Heads rolled in the Aligarh College, once the most loyal of institutions. 'Things have been going very badly in Aligarh,' reported Meston, 'Aligarh is suffering from the ferment, like every other institution of its kind. The young party would be glad to see the European element entirely rejected and the whole place handed over to their own theories of education, which at present would be nothing short of a calamity. The older people are beginning to jib at the noisy domination of the younger clique, but have no constructive policy to set up against them.'[21] In August 1913, Ishaq Khan (1860-1918), honorary secretary, admitted that the moderate men had lost ground with the public and were afraid of being ridiculed. Hamid Ali Khan (1875-1930), the Nawab of Rampur, resigned from the visitorship of the college in disgust;[22] others found their position insecure because of Mohamed Ali, who, according to the panic-stricken viceroy, had turned the College into 'a hot-bed of sedition'. Forster, who visited Aligarh in October 1912, sensed the drift of things. 'Life at Aligarh shows many seams', he noted in his diary on 25 October 1912:

> The English staff complained that they were not trusted to give the help they had hoped to give, but would be turned adrift as soon as the Mohammedans cd. stand without them: they could make some way with the students—not much, owing to the influence of *The Comrade*, a forward Islamic paper 'which told lies';—and none at all with the government body. The Mahammedans had an air of desperation, which may be habitual, but was impressive; why should Sir Edward Grey have been the *first* to recognize Italian rule in Tripoli (By the Peace of Ouchy in 15 October 1912, Turkery recognized the Italian occupation of Tripoli, its erstwhile province), they asked, and pertinently.[23]

Changes in Aligarh and other places in northern India had no real impact on Delhi, a city where Muslims had no organized political life of their own. The Muslim League had a branch with a limited membership of 1,316; the rest were educational and religious bodies, such as the Ahl-i Hadis Conference, founded in

1912, the Anjuman-i Ahmadi, formed in 1880, and the Anjuman-i Hidayatul Islam, established in 1906 to propagate Islamic education in the countryside through the setting up of *madaris*. Their activities were centred round the Juma Masjid, the Fatehpuri mosque and the famous *madaris* which had retained their hold despite the presence of high-profiled and renowned seminaries like the Dar al-ulum at Deoband and the Nadvat al-ulama in Lucknow. But there was little talk of politics in Delhi generally and among Muslims particularly. Many eschewed politics, because they could recount the trauma of 1857 when their co-religionists paid a heavy price for taking part in the revolt. But the Turko-Italian war transformed the political scene. It generated religious fervour by a sudden burst of political activity, gave rise to a steady rise in the publication and circulation of newspapers and led to the mushroom growth of organizations which were formed to befriend the beleagured Turkey. A weekly report of the Director of Intelligence observed:

> ... the war is now the one topic of conversation among Muhammadans, who are daily growing more and more excited over the wrongs suffered by Turkey. Passengers in the Durbar Railway trains also are seen eagerly reaching and discussing the latest newspaper war supplements, and even Khansamahs and other Muhammadan servants employed in various camps are said to be taking an extraordinary interest in the War news. The sober treatment of the subject that first characterized the utterances of leading Muslim journals is fast disappearing, and is giving way to denunciation of European Christian Powers in general and of Italy in particular.[24]

The diffuse sentiment against the tyranny of the Christian countries found focus and leadership in the activities of Mohamed Ali. It was officially recorded that pan-Islamism had little footing in India till 1912 when he removed the *Comrade* to Delhi.[25] Soon after, it had the company of the *Hamdard* in Urdu. These journalistic ventures received unprecedented popularity. Mohamed Ali's energy, skill and buoyancy would have probably ensured this anyway; but the fact that they caught the tide of public opinion at the turn and expressed pungently and clearly what scores of Muslims were vaguely thinking, proved to be an added asset. In more specific terms, the *Comrade* and the

Hamdard offered a platform for voicing the uneasiness and dissatisfaction of important Muslim groups, moulded their attitudes towards government and, above all, focused on the news from the Balkan front which unfolded the story of Turkey's military reverses and, at the same time, raised the spectre of European forces advancing into the heartlands of the Islamic world.

Mohamed Ali's influence was unrivalled in his days. Most Muslims followed his every move avidly and with overwhelming approval. He acted as guide and counsellor of many, including Ansari who rarely acted against his advice. It is easy to understand why this was so. Since the foundation of the Muslim League in December 1906, Mohamed Ali was the very model of a leader on the move—bold, outspoken to the point of brashness and confident as reformer and social radical, as crusader for the Turkish cause and as champion of Muslim political interests.[26] And one other thing: he did not shun the limelight. Always an activist, always restless, always eager and always imbued with a profound sense of playing the leading part in a great drama, he took centre stage so quickly and so dramatically that his detractors often suspected him of being in the middle of one conspiracy and on the fringe of another. But there was nothing of the conspiratorial or the surreptitious about his interests or actions. However, cynical and ill-informed government officials—his *bete noire* for long—attributed motives of money and publicity to denigrate him and pooh-poohed the causes he so vociferously championed.

Mohamed Ali's personality was as many-faceted as his political accomplishments. A highly emotional man, he was easily touched to tears and profoundly stirred by glamorous and ardent actions. He combined insatiable curiosity with a reluctance to dwell on anything that did not serve his political concerns; reticence with sociability, elaborate courtesy with moody neglect; a yearning for attention with a demand for privacy. He had a flair for the unorthodox, a freedom of thought and behaviour and a personal dynamism, but his great asset was that he possessed to the full the resources of traditional oratory and journalism. Few among his contemporaries could match his combination of qualities: his range of articulate emotions, his capacity for analytical argument, his pathos, fantasy and wit and his power to marshal all these, through a command over the resources of the language, towards ends clearly discerned and passionately desired. He also had considerable poetic talent, which combined with his fervour and the desperate situation in which Turkey found herself after the war, to create in him a feeling of impending martyrdom. In a scarcely veiled reference to the government's repressive policies, he wrote from Chhindwara: 'Such sufferings and privations as ours have only too often been the lot of mankind, in all ages and climes, and even today so many of our own countrymen and co-religionists have had to bear far worse things than have yet fallen to our share.'[27]

Mohamed Ali, at this period, was primarily a mass-appeal man. Party ties meant little to him; he preferred the role of a lone wolf outside the pack, neither subordinating himself to a group nor subordinating a group to himself except by the force of tongue. He did not allow others to equivocate: they were either for him or against him. For all his self-confidence, he was highly sensitive to criticism, quick to resent opposition and to take it as a personal attack. He therefore made no effort to conceal his scorn for those who disagreed with him and cared little whom he offended by plain speaking. This was true of dissenting comrades; if, however, they reverted to his orthodoxy he welcomed them back. He often disregarded Gandhi's admonishment and considered violence a legitimate, indeed a preferred method, and advocated it coldly. The end hallowed all means. Money and other forms of aid could not be tainted by their source, the cause purified them.

The extent of Mohamed Ali's influence is evident from the fact that two of his favourite projects—the medical mission and the Anjuman-i Khuddam-i Kaaba—struck the most respondent chord in the hearts of the Delhi Muslims. Traders, merchants and weavers generously funded the mission. The Anjuman, on the other hand, increased its membership from 900 to 2,000 in June 1914 owing to the active and enthusiastic backing of the hide and shoe merchants, the butchers, the artisans of the city and the students of the *madaris*, including those from the Nazarat al-Maarif al-Quraniya, an institution founded in 1913 by Maulana Ubaidullah Sindhi (1872-1944) of Deoband to extend the teaching of the Quran and Islamic theology to members of the 'new Muslim party'.

The troubles, observed H.C. Beadon, deputy commissioner of Delhi, began in 1912-13 when Mohamed Ali started his two newspapers and launched the Anjuman-i Khuddam-i Kaaba. He made much of the close Turkish connection and seized the opportunity of the Balkan wars to excite Muslim feelings.[28] All this made it inevitable that the Khilafat question, when it became a political issue in 1919, had its supporters in Delhi already organized. Ansari, fresh from his professional success in England, entered into Delhi's political scene unobtrusively.

NOTES

1. *The Disorders Inquiry Committee* [hereafter *DIC*], vol. I, *Delhi* (Calcutta, 1920), p. 123. For political developments, Gupta, *Delhi Between Two Empires*, pp. 196-200; Donald W. Ferrel, 'The Rowlatt Satyagraha in Delhi', Ravinder Kumar (ed.), *Essays on Gandhian Politics: The Rowlatt Satyagraha of 1919* (London, 1971), pp. 192-8.
2. Asaf Ali was in England from 1911 to 1914 and returned to India as a barrister in December 1914. His first public appearance in political affairs was as member of the Home Rule League which he joined in March 1917. Later, he took a prominent part in the Rowlatt satyagraha and the Khilafat and non-cooperation movements. He led a strike in the Government Press, Delhi, and gave up his practice in August 1920. He opposed council elections, 'practiced general intimidation through his volunteers at polling stations, and organized a partial social boycott of candidates'. In November 1921 he led volunteers to picket shops of cloth dealers and was soon put in jail. Home Poll. F. No. 366, 1930, NAI. Some of these details are missing in Sudhir Pant, *Asaf Ali: Patriot and Humanist* (Delhi, 1984).
3. The first recorded volunteer organization in Delhi was the Muslim League Volunteer Corps, founded in November 1918. By the end of 1920, there were five more: the Askar-i Islamia (literally the Army of Islam), the Khilafat Volunteer Corps, the Khuddam-i Watan (Servants of the Nation), the Khilafat Workers Association, established in March 1919, and the Muslim Razakar Volunteer Corps. The chief commissioner of Delhi reported that these bodies were in practice indistinguishable, for 'they execute the decision of the local Khilafat Committee and act in perfect cooperation'. They were subsequently declared 'unlawful' for being a 'serious menace to the social life and public liberties of peaceful and

law-abiding citizens'. Home Poll. F. No. 35, 1920; Home Poll. Deposit, February 1921, F. No. 77, 1921, NAI. A general extension of the volunteer movement in UP also took place. When a rough statement of its strength was prepared in November 1921, there were Khilafat volunteers in some 35 out of 41 districts from which reports had been received. They were drawn from Azamgarh (1,423), Saharanpur (926), Gorakhpur (405), Moradabad (400) and Aligarh (387). Muzaffarnagar returned 258 volunteers, Meerut 250, Budaun 200 and Gorakhpur 189. Numbers in Bulandshahr, Mainpuri, Etah, Ballia, Unnao and Gonda also ran into three figures. GAD, F. No. 604, 1920, UPSA.

4. 'History of the Non-Cooperation and Khilafat Movements in Delhi' in Mushirul Hasan and Margrit Pernau (eds.), *Regionalizing Pan-Islamism: Documents on the Khilafat Movement* (Delhi, 2005).
5. *New Era* (Lucknow), 30 June 1917.
6. Nehru, *An Autobiography*, pp. 31-2.
7. *New Era*, 23 June 1917.
8. Ibid., 30 June 1917.
9. Ibid., 11 August 1917.
10. Note for the viceroy by Meston, 7 February 1917, MSS. EUR. F. 36 (6), Meston Papers, IOL. The League, according to the lieutenant-governor, had collapsed and was merely doing the bidding of the Congress. 'I am not sure that this state or affairs can last; but we have to accept the fact, for the time being, that on paper the Mahomedans have now come into the Nationalist camp.' Meston to Chelmsford, 11 January 1917, MSS. EUR. E. 264 (18), Chelmsford Papers, IOL.
11. To Secretary, Home Department, 11 October 1913, Hardinge Papers (86), Cambridge University Library, Cambridge. 'Note on Serious Disturbances and Political Troubles in India from 1907 to 1917', Home Poll Deposit, February 1918, 31, NAI.
12. Metcalf, 'Nationalist Muslims in British India', op. cit., p. 19.
13. Montagu to Chelmsford, 31 March 1919, Chelmsford Papers (5).
14. *New Era*, 26 May 1917.
15. *Maqalat-i Shibli* (Azamgarh, 1938), vol. 6, pp. 161-90; also summary in K.B. Sayeed, *Pakistan: The Formative Phase, 1857-1948* (Karachi, 1968 edn.), pp. 36-7.
16. Choudhry Khaliquzzaman, *Pathway to Pakistan* (Lahore, 1961), pp. 137-8.
17. I have discussed the background to these developments in *Nationalism and Communal Politics in India, 1885-1930* (Delhi, 1990); Francis Robinson, *Separatism Among Indian Muslims: The Politics of the United Provinces' Muslims 1860-1923* (Cambridge, 1974).
18. To members of the All-India and Provincial Muslim League, 7 July 1913, enclosure in Fateh Ali Khan to Meston, 24 August 1913, Meston Papers (6).

19. To Chelmsford, 11 January 1917, ibid., (1). Earlier assessments of Hardinge and Butler also deserve mention. According to the viceroy, the Muslim League was 'like a sheep without a shepherd' and its leadership 'want to do something, but they do not know what to do or how to do it.... The Aga Khan is finished as a leader, and we must hope for and look forward to some moderate men to come to the front and assume the leadership.' Butler's estimate of the leaders was: 'Aga Khan is clever but a weather cock. Mahmudabad is weak as water, so is Rampur, and unreliable to boot. The Nawab of Dacca hates Aligarh and all its works as much as he hates Aga Khan. The Secretary of the Muslim League, Wazir Hasan, is a born intriguer and a mischievous fellow. He is a Shia and plays on Mahmudabad's religious weakness and at present has great influence with him.' Hardinge to Sydenham, 27 March 1913, Hardinge Papers (85); Butler to Allan, 6 April 1913, Butler to Lovat Fraser, 8 April 1913, Butler Papers, MSS. EUR. E. 116 (71), IOL.
20. To Harcourt Butler, 3 March 1913, Butler Papers (71). For the resignation letters of Ameer Ali and the Aga Khan, see Mushirul Hasan (ed.), *Mohamed Ali in Indian Politics: Select Writings* (Delhi, 1982), vol. I, pp. 188-94. His attitude towards the Aligarh Muslim University question and the annulment of Bengal's partition was linked with his attempts to have his status defined by the British government. Complaining that he often faced embarrassing and painful situations, as in Zanzibar where he received no formal recognition owing to the 'ambiguity' of his position, the Aga Khan urged the viceroy to recommend four more guns as an entirely personal distinction, in addition to the 11 which would mark his status, 'for I am regarded by the Indian public as more respected a person than many different gun chiefs'. The Aga Khan to Hardinge, 11 December 1915, IVPS/10/58, IOL.
21. Meston to Ramsay MacDonald, 11 September 1913, Meston Papers (3). Also, W.S. Marris informed the lieutenant-governor: 'I do not want to trouble you with Aligarh affairs: but things are going decidedly bad at the College ... I don't think the sleeping dogs can be let lie much longer.' To Meston, 11 December 1913, Meston Papers (6). Compare his earlier assessment of the Aligarh situation, quoted in Gilbert, 'Autonomy and Consensus', op. cit., pp. 198-203.
22. To Meston, 21 August 1913, and resignation of the Nawab of Rampur in enclosure, Ishaq Khan to Meston, 20 November 1913, Meston Papers (6). Also, the comment of the Governor of Bombay that the 'moderate men are nowhere' and ignorant and self-seeking youngermen—some of them products of Aligarh—were giving dangerous counsels'. Sydenham to Hardinge, 18 March 1913, Hardinge Papers (85).
23. Furbank, *E.M. Forster: A Life,* p. 227.
24. Home Poll. B, January 1912, 121-3, NAI.

25. Note by S.H. Fremantle, December 1917, Meston Papers (15).
26. I have examined his ideology and politics in *Mohamed Ali: Ideology and Politics* (Delhi, 1981).
27. To James DuBoulay, 18 February 1919, Hasan (ed.), *Mohamed Ali in Indian Politics*, vol. 2, p. 193. His political rhetoric is the subject of a study by Greogory C. Kozlowski, 'The Power of Language and the Language of Power: A Study on Mawlana Mohammad Ali's Political Rhetoric', *South Asia*, vol. 5, 1, June 1982.
28. *DIC*, p. 134. Also, Aparna Basu, 'Mohamed Ali in Delhi: The Comrade Phase, 1912-1915', Mushirul Hasan (ed.), *Communal and Pan-Islamic Trends in Colonial India* (Delhi, 1985 edn.); Ferrel, op. cit.

The All-India Medical Mission in Constantinople.

The Mission's hospital at Chanak Kila.

With Abdur Rahman, friend and colleague.

With the members of the Medical Mission: C. Khaliquzzaman (right), Aziz Ansari (left)
Sitting: Left to right—Abdur Rahman Sindhi, M.A. Ansari and Shuaib Qureshi.

3

Pan-Islamism at Home and Abroad

> How long this provoking hurricane of injustice and trouble?
> This delight at wailing and crying—how long?
> How long will ye take vengeance for the victor of Ayyub?
> You will show us the sight of the crusaders—how long?
>
> SHIBLI NOMANI

> Dr Ansari was the head of the Mission and, to me, the most representative Indian Muslim. Externally he has not changed much. The same small moustache, the brooding mouth . . . black and energetic eyebrows stretched over his deep-set eyes. They were purposeful eyes, very kind in spite of the unwavering determination in their depths. His clothes had that masculine elegance which one associated with London. He talked very little, but always to the point and said next to nothing about India. Barring a distinct individuality he was not different from our own eminent physicians.
>
> EDIP, *Inside India*, p. 17

UNDER THE INFLUENCE of Mohamed Ali, for whom he retained a deep and lasting veneration, Ansari embraced politics less for ambition than from a sense of duty. He strove for power not for the sake of material rewards or personal prestige, but because he knew that he possessed talents and wanted to use them to do some good—by which he meant promoting the interests of the country and the *qaum*. But, then, he had his own way to make in the world. Unlike many of his friends, he had no family wealth or connections to hoist him into a readymade political niche.

Events in the Balkans, which turned out to be a prelude to the final dismantling of the Ottoman empire, influenced Ansari most. As news of the Italian invasion of Tripoli trickled through the columns of the *Comrade*, he discerned clear signs of a conspiracy to destroy and annex the few remaining Muslim states. He was disturbed by Britain's role, for it became evident that much water had flown since that country fought side by side with Turkey against Russia half a century ago. The view gained credence, not unjustifiably, that Britain had acquiesced in the Italian assault upon Tripoli. This triggered off a reaction of serious proportions and virtually guaranteed new spates of headlines in the newly emboldened Urdu press. 'There is a great agitation,' reported the viceroy, 'in Muslim circles over the war in the Balkans, and a general feeling that the Christians are combining to thrust the Muslims out of Europe.' The government, which had hitherto regarded the events in the Balkans with cool disdain, was forced to say that it could no longer cover up British culpability.

Indian Muslims conceived a number of projects to voice their concern. The Anjuman-i Khuddam-i Kaaba was one; the medical mission to Turkey was another. Ansari's active association with the mission was a turning point in his public life and his political ideas were affected strongly by his experience in 1912 and 1913. Of all his life, these were the most formative years. News of the medical mission appeared in the *Comrade* on 19 October 1912: 'Those who know Dr Ansari's greatest ability as physician and surgeon will hail the idea of a relief mission under his direction with delight.' Ansari's own views appeared in the *Comrade* of 26 October. The Turk, he wrote,

> has been fighting ever since he established his empire on the shores of the Bosphorus and has so far survived the deadliest of struggles. Yet never before in the annals of the Ottoman empire had he to face a situation so critical in nature, so difficult to handle and so dangerous in consequences as he has now before him. It is perfectly obvious that the very existence of the Turkish nation depends upon the issue of this war. Firstly, the medical service in the Turkish army has been very recently organized and as such will be unable to cope with the requirements of such a deadly war. Secondly, Turkey's foes are already receiving, on a very large scale, medical . . . help from all parts of Europe; and the poor Turk is left entirely to his own limited resources. What we can do to lighten his burden is to provide an efficient field-hospital where a fair number of the sick and wounded can be accommodated.

Ansari's appeal for public subscription met with an immediate and overwhelming response; by the end of November 1912, the total contribution for the Turkish Relief Fund reached Rs 1,18,762.[1] Delhi's Red Crescent Society and other Muslims raised Rs 32,000. Contributions also came from the ladies of Hyderabad, from the *dargah* at Ajmer, and from the *sajjadanashin* of Fatehgarh and Sassaram.[2] Remarkably, the mission received government support as well. Ansari noted, just before it set out: 'So far the Government of India have not in any way shown any dislike for our human(e) Mission, nor should I think they are likely to do so. My own impression has been that they have been very fair to us and have given every legitimate help and support.'[3]

'It is gratifying to notice,' Ansari announced, 'that the men who have joined the Mission are from the cultured middle and higher class families, representing the flower of Muhammadan youth, who are fully alive to the responsibilities and nature of the work with which they are entrusted.'[4] Five doctors,[5] seven dressers,[6] and ten male nurses and ambulance bearers made up the mission.[7] The Old Boys' of the Aligarh College were well represented, no less than eight of the twenty-one proceeding from India had studied for some time at and, in some cases, graduated from Aligarh. Among them were Abdur Rahman Siddiqi, Shuaib Qureshi and Khaliquzzaman, all bound to Ansari by deep personal loyalty and affection. Khaliquzzaman, who met Ansari on 13 November 1912 at Aligarh, recorded his meeting:

> News was received which spread like wildfire in the College of an attack of the Balkan powers on Turkey. We had already decided to give up meat diet during the Tripoli war agitation and now we took steps to collect funds between ourselves and sent the savings to the Red Crescent Society in Turkey. . . . One day while I was playing tennis in front of my room . . . I was introduced as the football captain of my College eleven to Dr Ansari. I expressed my joy and admiration for him for having undertaken the responsibility of leading the Medical Mission. He told me that he had come to Aligarh to find some youngmen to go with him to help him in the discharge of his duties. I said, 'I am not a doctor'. He replied, 'You can do managerial work as well as some nursing', after which he left me seriously cogitating over the matter. By the evening I had made up my mind to join the Mission.[8]

The idea of a medical mission carried to Turkey a message of deep sympathy and goodwill from India; Viqar-ul-Mulk (1841-

1917), secretary of the Aligarh College, said so in his letter of 29 June 1913.[9] In Delhi alone, 15,000 Muslims accompanied the mission all the way from Juma Masjid to the railway station to bid them farewell.[10] Mohamed Ali was jubilant: 'In joy and in grief the heart of Islam beats in unison, but this is the first time in the history of Indian Mussalmans that their sympathy had taken shape as a humane and beneficent measure to relieve the sufferings of their brethren abroad who lie torn and bleeding. The moral value of this fact can hardly be overestimated.'[11] Ansari might have recognized the throng on the railway platform. The viceroy had sent a representative; Ajmal Khan stood on the platform with his beard and animated gestures, leaning on his walking stick with its silver band and braced for a parting of poignant significance. Several Muslim divines were associated with this departure of the mission and their blessings bestowed upon it. Shibli Nomani touched Ansari's feet at the Lucknow railway station in a touching demonstration of his affection for the leader of the medical mission.[12] Mohamed Ali was there of course, because he had much to do both with the choice of Ansari as leader of the mission and with the setting of this scene. Ansari seemed a trifle overawed. His short speech was diffident. Habitually modest, he took care to emphasize that the send-off was not a tribute to himself but to the people who helped organize the mission.

The mission sailed from Bombay on 15 December 1912, reaching Constantinople on 1 January. The story of its work and experience was told with a minute exactitude in Ansari's letters, the longest and most descriptive he ever wrote. They present his experiences, embellished as a theatrical panorama, with himself a figure in centrestage. They reveal the unflagging interest in Turkey which never left him and further indicate that his experiences set him on the path of strong opposition to British imperial rule which characterized so much of his life.

When Ansari reached Turkey, the long night of Hamidian despotism was over and the dawn of freedom had come in July 1908 when the constitution had once again been proclaimed and elections ordered. The Young Turk Revolution, led by the Committee of Union and Progress, achieved many of its objectives and its three important leaders—Enver Bey (1881-1922), Talat

Bey (1872-1926) and Kemal Bey (1840-88)—remained in effective control. But it was not all smooth sailing, as Ansari's despatches revealed. Dissenters both within and outside the Party merged to form the Liberal Union (*Hurriyat wa Itilaf*) on 21 November 1911. But the political crisis was deepened by the 'big stick election' in April 1912, the subsequent repressive policies of the Unionists against their opponents, reports of setbacks at the war front against Italy and internal revolts in many of the provinces, notably in Salonika. In the midst of such troubles, a group of 'Saviour Officers', formed in May-June 1912, went into action and forced Said Pasha (1863-1921) and his Cabinet to resign. But the new Cabinet, headed by Ghazi Ahmed Mukhtar Pasha (1839-1918), was short-lived. Taking advantage of their preoccupation with the Italian war and the attack of the Balkan allies in October 1912, the Unionists launched their surprise assault on the Sublime Porte on 23 January 1913. Led by Enver Bey, a small party of officers forced their way into the Cabinet room, shooting the Minister of War and forcing the aged Kamil Pasha to write out his resignation. From then until 1919 Turkey was governed by a virtual military dictatorship, dominated by Enver, Talat and Kemal Pashas. Their rule ended only with Turkey's defeat in 1918, when the Committee of Union and Progress disbanded itself, its leaders fled abroad and the liberal spokesmen emerged from exile, concealment or insignificance to preside over the dissolution of the Ottoman empire.[13]

Ansari was fascinated by the activities of the Young Turks, baffled by the machinations of European powers and aghast at the 'inhuman deeds done by the Balkan armies during the occupation of Salonika and Kavalla'. He was therefore determined 'to do all that lay in our power to lessen the sufferings, to sympathize with and soothe the bleeding hearts of our fellow-Muslims in Turkey'.[14] The mission set up hospitals, build bridges and pitched tents in the teeth of a most bitterly cold wind and the mud almost knee-deep.[15] They were at times frustrated as well. 'I cannot tell you what difficulties are placed in our way here in arranging a small matter,' complained Ansari. 'Our things have all arrived last week, and in any other country but Turkey everything would have been arranged in a day or two.'[16] He went on to utter a cry of absolute despair: 'My men and myself have been driven to eating nothing but cheese and bread for three days, owing to the box containing our provisions having been stolen by some-one.'[17] Yet, 'we have all been working terribly hard,' he reported on 22 February 1913. 'I may tell you that our field-hospital, if not the best, is second to none in Turkey. Not only are our wards, dispensary, operating theatre and general provision most excellent, but every member of the Mission has got the zeal and energy of ten persons and a most excellent *espirit de corps* exists among them, of which I naturally feel very proud.'

Entranced by Turkey, the last vestige of Islamic activity, Ansari was impressed with its military prowess both in the past and in his own times. He was carried away by the ruins of the fortress in Vienna, which was captured by the Turks under Suleiman (1496-1566). With his imagination fired by brilliant scenes of the past, almost as if he had lived it, he recalled the glories of the Turkish empire extended over three continents: from Baghdad to Budapest and from Cairo to the boundaries of Morocco. 'It had been a remarkable career of achievements', he wrote in 1925, many years after Turkish military prestige had declined and the myth of the invincibility of Turkish troops shattered. Ansari continued: 'Probably in no other dynasty in the world's history has there ever been a succession of such brilliant rulers. . . . The Turk may well take immense pride in his glorious military heritage.'[18]

Ansari identified Turkish military prowess with the Young Turks, who had salvaged the country's waning prestige. This is borne out by his description of the *coup d'etat* engineered by Enver Bey on 23 January 1913. Commenting on the coup and on Enver Bey's success, Ansari opined: 'It is obvious that the Young Turks have saved the prestige of Turkey and mean to die honourably, if death *must* come. It is impossible even for an adversary to abstain from admiring their pluck, although it still remains to be seen whether this pluck is going to save Turkey.'[19] He admired Enver Bey, 'a youngman of about 35, exceedingly handsome, with most expressive eyes full of determination [and] with a demeanour of a very strong man, chastened with hardships and sufferings'.[20] Enver Bey 'believed in working loyally for his God and country' and was sure that Turkey would rise soon to 'its full glory and power'. Recently, he informed Mohamed Ali, 'he has had a narrow escape from death by drowning; but he is destined to perform greater work for his nation and God saved him'.[21] Ansari also got together with Halide Edip, one of the leading lights of the Party of Union and Progress, a silent, though very effective power working behind the scenes';[22] Khalil Beg 'a gallant soldier' who performed invaluable service against the Bulgarian regiment with his band of volunteers from Crete, Arabia and Anatolia; Talat Bey, with whom Ansari discussed the proposal for the sale of Turkish bonds in India; and Sheikh Abdul Aziz Chawish, 'a very impressive man who chooses every word before uttering it'.[23]

Besides medical relief, Ansari promoted schemes to render moral and material support to and reaffirm his countrymen's solidarity with the Turks; in fact, he indicated in some of his speeches that he thought less of the medical work he had done than of the political results between Turkey and the Indian Muslims and that in doing so he was no ideologue but a patient, open-minded and resourceful pragmatist. The sale of Turkish bonds, originating in a discussion with Talat Bey, was one of his favourite schemes. So great was his enthusiasm that he planned an extensive tour to popularize it in India. 'I would deal in my lectures,' he wrote to Mohamed Ali, 'with Turkey, its people, its institutions, its government, the war and its results . . . , the future of Turkey and the way in which the Mussalmans of India can best help the Turks and themselves . . . I wish to start in Bombay, go to Hyderabad, Bhopal, Lucknow, Rampur, Aligarh and Delhi. And then later on I will go to Lahore, Meerut, Allahabad, Banaras, Bankipur and Calcutta.'[24] He also planned setting up a Muslim Bank, a Cooperative Society and a university at Medina. Urging Mohamed Ali to discuss the much-canvassed university scheme with Shibli and Iqbal, Ansari wrote: 'We have sent you a cable and hope you will not spare any pains in preparing the constitution and curriculum for the University of Medina on the lines of the Aligarh University.'[25] Then, there was the colonization scheme for refugees in Anatolia 'to sow the seeds of greater things'. 'We have had several meetings of the Colonization Society,' Ansari reported to Mohamed Ali on 27 May 1913, and a definite plan of work has been decided. Tomorrow a committee consisting of five persons [Ansari, Zafar Ali Khan, Agah Bey (representing Ottoman Red Crescent, Saleh Bey, an agricultural expert and Ahmed Foad] is going to Anatolia to see the tracts of the land the government is willing to place at the disposal of the Society. . . . The Committee has been given every facility by the government to inspect these tracts. The members are going first to Angora to see 65,000 acres of land in Qara Ilias, then to Konia and Oulihishla by train and from there by carriages to Adana, where 45,000 acres of land near Jabali—Barakat are available. The exact location of the two villages would be decided after the completion of the tour.[26]

Many of these projects were ignored in Turkey and forgotten in India, but not the sincere and devoted work of the mission. The scenes of leave-taking at Hindia and Sanjak Tepi where the two hospitals were established, were 'most touching and will remain in our memory'.[27] Ansari would have felt the same way when he and his men reached Bombay on the first part of their journey on 4 July 1913. Arriving at the Ballard Pier, leaning on the arm of Mohamed Ali and looking pale and worn out but in good spirits, the mission was greeted by Fazulbhoy Currimbhoy (b. 1872) and Umar Subhani and by cheering crowds bearing banners with hospitable inscriptions and carrying garlands and flowers.[28] A similar welcome awaited them in Delhi on the evening of 10 July. The *Comrade* reported:

Long before the time of arrival large crowds of people had begun to assemble on the platform and along the approaches to the railway station. . . . As the train moved slowly in, the air was rent with glad shouts of welcome. Thousands on the platform pressed forward to catch a glimpse of the man and his lieutenants, who had rendered good services to Islam, to kiss their hands and offer them flowers and garlands. . . .

As the party entered the vast courtyard of the mosque [Juma Masjid] it was greeted by thousands of Muslims of Delhi. . . . They were all inspired by a single sentiment and filled with a single aim—to do honour to the men who had made sacrifices in the cause of Islam. . . . After the Maghrib prayers the procession was formed again and it started along a different route for the Fatehpuri Mosque. . . . The entire Muslim Delhi seemed to have turned out for the occasion, [and] nothing but surging masses of humanity were visible in unbroken waves as far as the eye could reach in either direction. . . . Every now and then loud and irresistible voices called Dr Ansari to stand up and show himself and he could not but obey the call. And one can never forget the emotion of the moment as the hero of the occasion raised himself bashfully from his seat and in his characteristically modest way acknowledged the vociferous greetings of thousands of his admiring brethren—the lusty cheers of the youth, the applause of the grown-up men and the blessings of the aged. It was amidst such thrilling scenes that the long route was slowly traversed and the procession reached its destination. . . . Such remarkable tributes of love and admiration are ample rewards for men who serve a noble cause and prove themselves of some use to their fellow-beings.[29]

Soon after his return from Turkey, Ansari got embroiled in the Kanpur mosque episode—an episode sparked off by the sacrilege committed by the municipality in demolishing a portion of the Machli Bazar mosque as part of the city improvement scheme. But his part in the agitation, whipped up by the irrepressible Mohamed Ali, did not extend beyond accompanying Ajmal Khan on his weekly visits to Kanpur to treat the wounded in the police firing of 3 August.[30] His role in the Muslim university movement was also limited. Though a member of the Foundation Committee and of several deputations, his own links with the college were tenuous. Not being an 'Old Boy' he could hardly share the enthusiasm of the Ali Brothers, Abdur Rahman Siddiqi, Shuaib Qureshi and Khaliquzzaman. He supported the university cause owing to his loyalty to Mohamed Ali combined with the need to remain in the mainstream of Muslim political life.[31] At the same time, his political interests were widening and he was not only learning rapidly but growing in stature all the time. To compare Ansari of 1912-13, at the time of the medical mission, with Ansari at the time of the Muslim League session in 1918, is to see at once the distance he had travelled and the confidence he had gained. The same determination and ability were there, but tempered by a maturing of powers, a deepening of character and experience.

Ansari's heart was in several pan-Islamic schemes. Notable amongst them were the Anjuman-i Khuddam-i Kaaba and the Nazarat al-Maarif al-Quraniya, set up in the Fatehpuri mosque not far from Ansari's consulting chambers. He was one of the patrons of this Quranic school, having helped to raise financial support from the Nawab of Rampur, the Begum of Bhopal and a number of wealthy Muslim traders from Bombay and Karachi. 'My cousin', Khaliquzzaman wrote in *Pathway to Pakistan*,

> Istafa Karim, who, after graduating from Aligarh had joined the Arabic institution *Nazaratul Ma'arif* started by Maulana Ubaidullah Sindhi at Delhi, asked me to meet the Maulana in the Fatehpuri Mosque. I found the Maulana as full of anti-British sentiments as myself. In his talk he argued and tried to convince me that the time for Jihad had arrived. . . . He was a pupil of Maulana Mahmud Hasan of Deoband, who was in close touch with Dr Ansari, the Ali Brothers and Hakim Ajmal Khan. Money was collected in different centres to feed the revolutionary activities but the principal centre was at Delhi where Hakim Ajmal Khan and Dr Ansari with their great influence on the Nawab of Rampur, Begum of Bhopal and the titled gentry, big and small, all over India, were exerting every nerve not to allow the movement to suffer from lack of funds. . . .[32]

Ansari also helped to bring about close relations between the *ulama* and the Western-educated Muslims. He was in an ideal position to do so because of his family connections with Deoband. He introduced Ubaidullah Sindhi to Mohamed Ali and Azad.[33] He came into contact with Abdul Bari (1878-1926), the distinguished *alim* of Firangi Mahal, Lucknow, when the Maulana and his *madrasa* students travelled in UP collecting money for Turkish relief and for the Red Crescent Medical Mission. Mahmud Hasan, Ansari and Ajmal Khan mooted the scheme to set up the Nazarat al-Maarif; it was designed to provide the necessary thrust to the converging courses in politics of the modern and the traditionally educated. Likewise, the Jalsa-i Dastarbandi, convened in 1910 and attended by a delegation from Aligarh led by Aftab Ahmad Khan (1867-1930), the Jamiyat al-Ansar, founded by Ubaidullah Sindhi and the Anjuman-i Khuddam-i Kaaba, established in May 1912, sought to bridge the gulf which separated the modern and the traditionally-educated Muslims. Such initiatives were inspired by the mutual recognition that a unified effort alone could build a powerful movement in defence of Muslim interests in India and abroad. Consequently, the 'orthodox' and the 'anglicised' saw that after all they were not so unlike each other as they had imagined. 'Once more,' declared Mohamed Ali, 'Muslim society in India presented a level of uniformity and the bitterest opponents of a generation ago stood shoulder to shoulder. . . . If even a decade previously anyone had ventured to foretell such a result, he would have been laughed at for such a fantastic prophesy.'[34]

The Muslim League session of December 1918 provided the most striking evidence of the growing fraternization between the 'orthodox' and the 'anglicised' Muslims. A large number of *ulama*, who were drawn from different regions and theological schools, gathered in Delhi on the occasion. They had not done so before. Equally, they asserted, for the first time in recent history, their right to be consulted on both the political and the religious issues. They not only appeared at all subsequent League and Khilafat conferences, but also influenced major policy decisions. They realized that they must now be active in addressing themselves to the current anxieties—political, social and religious—of Indian Muslims, or else see true Islam as they understood it and their own claims to guide the community go by default.

The presence of the *ulama* was largely due to Ansari's effort. He invited them in order to add weight to the Khilafat protest, assured them a prominent place on the platform and sang paeans of praise in their honour. As the star performer as chairman of the reception committee, he delivered a powerful speech, later proscribed by the Punjab government. His address, according to a government report,

> resembled the sermon of a fanatic more than the address of a politician and amounts to a condemnation to death of the King of the Hejaz and an exhortation to Jehad if Mesopotamia, Arabia and Palestine are not handed back to Turkey. It accuses Great Britain of breaking her promise to respect the sanctity of the holy places and demands the independence of the Muslims of North Africa and Central Asia. Dr Ansari's demands were supported throughout by quotations from the Quran and the Hadis, and the speech . . . had an extraordinary effect on the audience. The Muslim League of that period regularly took its cue from the Congress and the methods employed to stampede opinion into the ultra extremist camp met with as great success as in the Congress pandal. As

they dispersed, members were heard cursing the destroyers of Islam and strong anti-British feeling was evident.[35]

Interspersed with extensive quotations from the Quran and the *Hadis*, Ansari tried to reassure the *ulama* and allay their fears about the League's *la-dini* (religion-less) character. Setting out his ideas with an eloquence and personal feeling that were rare to his time, he echoed the pan-Islamic concerns and the religious demands of the *ulama*. His manner was direct, his language simple. What he said could scarcely ever be misrepresented; where he stood none could mistake. With his frank, serious look, he attracted attention in any crowd by the firmness of his views and the force of his personality.

Ansari had reached the moment when honours began to fall on him like the leaves of autumn—public receptions, the acclaim of his community and the second class of the Usmaniah Order, conferred by the Sultan of Turkey in recognition of his services.[36] The Anjuman-i Islamia of Bombay gave him a welcome. Here he spoke of the success of the medical mission, a 'wonderful conception' on the part of Indian Muslims.[37] The Begum of Bhopal feted him and showered words of praise for his devotion.[38] He was specially invited to the Friday congregation at the Delhi Juma Masjid on 11 July 1913, where he described the struggle of the Turks against the Christian powers, 'who are bent upon wiping Islam from the face of the earth'.[39] For obvious reasons, he tried to smother their deficiencies under a flood of eloquence about their patriotic cause. A day later, he lectured amidst a rousing reception at the Aligarh College, where he had raised Rs 45,000 for the medical mission on his last visit. Here he boasted that the most important result of his trip was the fusion of a union between Turkey and India.[40] On 29-30 November, he spoke on the colonization scheme in Amritsar and gave an illustrated account of his work at the two hospitals, one near Chetalja at Hindia and the other at Chanak Kila, near Dardanelles.[41]

Mohamed Ali 'privately' suggested to Meston to honour Ansari by making him the viceroy's surgeon and to grant him and other members of the mission the Kaiser-i Hind medal.[42] Shibli Nomani sang paeans of praise and expressed the gratitude of the Muslims in a poem which came to be recited in the towns of northern India.[43] This must have surely gladdened Ansari. To him the trip to Turkey was a novel experience and, coming on top of the impressions left by his journey around the world, it had a powerful effect in crystallizing his ideas. His journey in 1913 provided the experience he needed to fire his imagination and opened a new world to him. He returned intellectually stimulated, full of ideas and with the energy to put them across.

When the intelligence department secured some letters implicating Ansari in a pan-Islamic conspiracy, Meston declared that he was not the stuff of which conspirators were made.[44] His professional character 'stands high, unlike that of some of the other men who have recently been interned. Quite moderate men think well of him and regard him as a capable professional man, distinguished by his friendships abroad and reasonably interested in Muhammadan politics generally, without committing himself in any way, so far as they know, to extreme views.'[45] Opposing the move to arrest Ansari, the lieutenant-governor concluded:

> In Moslem circles he commands considerable respect and moderate men regard him much more highly than, for example, Muhammad Ali or those who have been more recently interned. His work in the Mission during the last Turkish War is a matter of pride to them, as well as the professional position which he occupies in India; a firebrand is not what he is generally regarded as being.[46]

NOTES

1. *Comrade*, 16 November 1912; Ghaffar, *Hayat-i Ajmal*, p. 122.
2. *Comrade*, 9 November 1912.
3. To Mohamed Ali, 29 November 1912, Hasan (ed.), *Muslims and the Congress*, p. 1. It is rather surprising that contemporary accounts of Turkey make no mention of Ansari's medical mission. Mary Poynter, for instance, merely refers to other missions: the British Red Crescent Hospital, to the work of Lady Lowther, the wife of the British Ambassador and to the hospital of Major Doughty-Wylie. See Mary A. Poynter, *When Turkey was Turkey: In and Around Constantinople* (London, 1921).
4. *Comrade*, 30 November 1912.
5. M.A. Ansari, Ali Azhar H. Fyzee (Bombay), Mohammad Naim Ansari

(Jaunpur), Mahmudullah (Calcutta) and Shamsul-Bary (Gaya)—all professional doctors.

6. Ghulam Ahmad Khan (Lahore), M. Nurul Hasan (Meerut), Mohammad Chiraghuddin (Delhi), Syed Tawangar Husain (Karnal), Itamid Rasul (Chapra), Abdul Waheed Khan (Mirzapur), and Husain Raza Beg.
7. Abdur Rahman Siddiqi, Shuaib Qureshi, Aziz Ansari, Khaliquzzaman, Abdur Rahman, Qazi Bashiruddin Ahmad, Manzoor Ali—all educated in or connected with the Aligarh College. Besides, there were Yusuf Ansari (Gangoh: district Saharanpur), Ismail Husain Shirazi (Sirajganj: Bengal) and Tafazzul Husain.
8. Khaliquzzaman, *Pathway to Pakistan*, p. 21.
9. R.A. Jafri, *Karawan-i Gumgushta* (Karachi, 1971), pp. 333-4.
10. *Comrade,* 9 August 1912.
11. Ibid., 14 December 1912; Ghaffar, *Hayat-i Ajmal*, pp. 122-3.
12. Sulaiman Nadvi, *Hayat-i Shibli*, p. 595; Jafri, *Karawan-i Gumgushta*, pp. 315-16.
13. This paragraph is based on Bernard Lewis, *The Emergence of Modern Turkey* (London, 1961), p. 222.
14. *Comrade*, 25 January 1913.
15. Ibid., 22 February 1913.
16. Ibid., 15 February 1913.
17. Ibid., 22 February 1913.
18. Ansari to Mohamed Ali, 25 July 1925; *Comrade*, 18 September 1925.
19. *Comrade*, 22 February 1913.
20. Ibid., 15 February 1913.
21. Ibid.
22. Ibid., 8 February 1913. 'The picture of Halide Hanoum,' wrote one of her admirers, 'confronts us on all sides throughout Anatolia. Among the heroes of the revolution, the Turks reverence her as their Joan of Arc. No history of the Nationalist movement can ever be attempted or thought of without a full record of her courageous loyalty and untiring patriotism.' Grace Ellison, *An Englishwoman in Angora* (London, 1923), p. 214.
23. *Comrade,* 8 February 1913.
24. Ibid., 17 May and 7 June 1913.
25. Ibid., 31 May 1913.
26. Ansari to Mohamed Ali, 27 May 1913, Ansari Collection, NMML. Also, see report submitted by B. Lindsay and Abdur Rauf on the internment of the Ali Brothers. Hasan (ed.), *Mohamed Ali in Indian Politics*, vol. 2, pp. 145, 159-61. The scheme of colonization was supported by the *Comrade* in a series or articles contributed by Abdur Rahman Siddiqi. See Bamford, *Histories,* p. 113. Urdu extract of Ansari's letters are quoted in Jafri, *Karawan-i Gumgushta*, pp. 326-8.

27. Ansari to Mohamed Ali, 27 May 1913, Ansari Collection, NMML; *Comrade*, 31 June 1913.
28. *Comrade*, 5 July 1913; Jafri, *Karawan-i Gumgushta*, p. 337.
29. Ibid., 12 July 1913.
30. Ghaffar, *Hayat-i Ajmal*, pp. 136-7.
31. In 1917 Ansari took the lead in founding the 'Central Bureau for the release of Muslim Internees' and was the chief campaigner, besides Gandhi, for the release of the Ali Brothers from internment. The Raja of Mahmudabad was the president of the Bureau. Ansari and Syed Abdul Rahman of Delhi its secretaries, and Ajmal Khan the treasurer. *New Era*, 24 November 1917. In September 1917 Ansari reaffirmed his loyalty to Mohamed Ali by canvassing for his election to the presidentship of the Muslim League. 'It is imperative,' he wrote to Abdul Majid Khwaja, 'to hold public meetings where popular voice should with all force and unanimity declare him to be the only person fit for this honour.' He and Mazharul Haq wrote a joint letter to the members of the Muslim League in a similar vein. They referred to his 'noble services rendered at the most psychological moment in the history of the community to which he belongs' and which 'mark him out as one of the most potent factors in the formation of the Indian nation'. Ansari to Khwaja, 3 September 1917; Circular letter, 3 September 1917, Abdul Majid Khwaja Papers.
32. Khaliquzzaman, *Pathway to Pakistan*, pp. 31-2; Minault,. *The Khilafat Movement*, p. 30; Ghaffar, *Hayat-i Ajmal*, pp. 129-30.
33. Ubaidullah Sindhi, *Khutbat-i Sindhi*, p. 28, quoted in Minault, *The Khilafat Movement*, p. 30.
34. Afzal Iqbal (ed.), *My Life: A Fragment*, p. 44.
35. *History* (Delhi), p. 3. Hasrat Mohani made an interesting reference to Ansari's address in one of his poems. The message was not lost on his readers. He wrote:

    Khutba-i League hai kafara gunah-gaari ka
    ab hamen shikwa nahin Doctor Ansari ka
    kaash samjhen ise asbab-i hukumat ki nahin
    dakhl is pairu-e sidq men ghadari ka
    khud hi insaf se kahye ki utha rakhha hai
    aap ne koi daqeeqa bhi dil-azaari ka
    Hasrat is khutbe se nalaan hon na kiyon ahl-i fareb
    raaz makhfi na raha un ki gunah-gaari ka

    The address at the League is an atonement for [its past] sins: now we have no complaint against Dr Ansari.
    Would the government realize that there is nothing treacherous in following the path of righteousness.
    Judge for yourself, have you left any stone unturned to bring distress to ourhearts?

O Hasrat! how should the deceivers not be annoyed at this 'address'?
The secret of their sins is no longer hidden.

Khalid Hasan Qadiri, *Hasrat Mohani* (Delhi, 1985), pp. 204-5.

36. Ansari to Secretary, Government of India, Foreign and Political Department, 28 February 1914, Home Poll. Deposit, July 1914, 17, NAI.
37. *Comrade*, 5 July 1913.
38. Ibid.
39. Bamford, *Histories*, p. 113.
40. Ibid.
41. *Comrade*, 20 December 1913.
42. Mohamed Ali to Meston, 30 June 1913, Hardinge Papers (85).
43. *Ada karte hai hum shukr janab-i hazrat-i baari*
ke khairiyat se aye membaran-i wafd-i Ansari
yehi tha dard-i Islami yehi thi rasm-i gham khwaari
hazaaron kos jaa kar bhaiyon ki tum ne khidmat ki
tumhara naaz uthayen ahl-i millat jis qadar kam hai
ke tum ne ghaziyaan-i deen ki, ki hai naaz bardaari

We thank the Almighty for the safe return of the members of the Ansari mission.
You've served your brethren thousands of miles away. This was consistent with the spirit of Islamic compassion and the tradition of sharing mutual grief and sorrow.
Your deeds surely deserve glorification, for you have heightened the morale of the conquerors in the way of the Faith.

44. 'On the other hand', he continued, 'the more respectable Mahomedans have considerable regard for him; they are rather proud of the part that he took in organizing and taking out a medical mission to Turkey during the last Balkan War. Since his return his prestige has been considerable; he has a large medical practice of a thoroughly reputable character; and I believe he has taken to the ordinary duties of intelligent citizenship in Delhi'. Meston to Chelmsford, 7 September 1916, Chelmsford Papers (17).
45. Meston to Charles Cleveland, 6 September 1916, Meston Papers (4).
46. Note on Ansari's arrest, 6 September 1916, Meston Papers (1). The viceroy agreed and the proposal to arrest Ansari was dropped. Chelmsford to Meston, 16/17 September 1916, Chelmsford Papers (17).

4

Among the Satyagrahis

> Until the transfer of the capital from Calcutta, Delhi was practically free from agitation. But the seditionist has already invaded its precincts and achieved considerable success in converting the minds of the inhabitants of Delhi, who loved peace and pleasure even to a fault. . . . I have no hesitation in saying that no other city in India can claim the unenviable notoriety that Delhi enjoys for simmering popular discontent and even active contempt for British institutions and the British point of view. The result is that *within a few years of the change of capital the people of Delhi have become adept in organizing demonstrations and using strong language from the pulpit and in the press* [emphasis added]. Once Delhi decided to assume an hostile attitude, the suggestion was taken up by other towns connected with Delhi by railway and postal communications.
>
> Home Department, F. No. 36, 1920
> Delhi Archives

THE COUNTRYWIDE agitation against the Rowlatt Bills, enacted by the government and foisted on the country with scant regard for public opinion, offered Ansari an opportunity to plunge into national politics. By 1919, this shy and youthful doctor with limited experience of public life moved to the epicentre of the Rowlatt satyagraha.

Though Mohamed Ali inspired Ansari's political exertions in his early years, he was captivated by the charisma, prestige and personal authority of Gandhi. He admired him from afar and was won to him by personal contact in the course of the agitation for Mohamed Ali's release from internment. He was so moved by his initiatives that, at the 1918 Muslim League session, he extolled Gandhi as the 'acknowledged intrepid leader of India who is never afraid to speak out the truth and who has, by his noble actions, endeared himself as much to the Mussalmans as to the

Hindus'.[1] The extent to which his appeal had aroused sentiments against the Rowlatt Bills, impressed itself forcibly upon Ansari and he plunged into the Rowlatt satyagraha as the Mahatma's chief lieutenant in Delhi.

The Rowlatt Bills, rushed through the imperial legislative council in the teeth of opposition from all Indian members, evoked widespread indignation in India. Gandhi, the hero of Champaran, Kaira and Ahmedabad, voiced the country's rage and revulsion. From his sick bed, he condemned the 'devilish legislation'—not just 'a stray example of lapse of righteousness and justice'—but 'evidence of a determined policy of repression'. When his repeated appeals to the viceroy to withhold his assent from the 'black bills' went unheeded, he decided on satyagraha, a weapon he had effectively put to use in South Africa. The man who had made common cause with the British in the war and conducted a personal recruitment campaign now advocated satyagraha as 'a process of self-purification' in the 'sacred fight' against the Raj. 'I think the growing generation will not be satisfied with petitions etc.,' he wrote to Dinshaw E. Wacha (1844-1936) on 25 February 1919, 'we must give them something effective. Satyagraha is the only way, it seems to me, to stop terrorism'. In major cities and provincial towns alike people went up against the new legislative provisions. The young Jawaharlal was 'afire with enthusiasm' because Gandhi offered at last 'a way out of the tangle, a method of action which was straight and open and possibly effective'.[2]

Various historical accounts have described the upswell of sentiment in favour of the Gandhian movement, delineated the process which enabled divergent groups, often with dissimilar and contradictory interests, to coalesce in a most vigorous assault on government authority, and revealed how the social and economic dislocation caused by the First World War and the Muslim frustration over the indeterminate future of the Khilafat sparked off a serious confrontation with the Raj.[3] In such circumstances, the Rowlatt Act provided the catalyst and Gandhi the spark for ventilating the anger and resentment of aggrieved classes and communities. The Mahatma's ingenuity lay in canalizing their grievances, both latent and active in form, into a massive protest movement.[4]

The quickening pulse of political life, following Gandhi's intervention, had an appreciable impact on Delhi society. Those who earlier noted the apparent quiescence of political life, noticed the people's broadened political outlook. The capital was now the centre from which disturbances in the Punjab and in parts of UP were promoted. 'Delhi is radiating sedition [and] is the principal source of inspiration for local agitations in the districts around,' exclaimed an official.[5] Delhi's agitators stirred up trouble in the Meerut division, going in motors as far as Garhmukteshwar, and devoting special attention to Hapur. Delhi's traders refused to restock the shops of their clients in Moradabad and Bareilly districts on the ground that they had not followed up their movement.[7] J.P. Thompson, chief secretary to Punjab government, disclosed on 28 April 1919 that in distant Multan people were watching Delhi—which is important not only as the historic *and present* capital, but as the centre of the present disturbances.[8]

The 'fissiparous' tendencies were attributed to the spirited local organizations like the Indraprastha Sewak Mandli, Boy Scouts, the Home Rule League, the Muslim Volunteers and the Delhi Volunteer Corps; to the virulent campaign of newspapers—the *Qaum*, the *Inqilab*, the *Congress* and the *Vijaya*; and to the role of Swami Shraddhanand (1856-1926), who 'played a prominent part in stirring up trouble over the Rowlatt Bills and in fomenting unrest'.[9] Beadon, Delhi's deputy commissioner, noted the transition from a mofussil town to a centre of political turbulence. 'It will I imagine be readily recognized,' he put down on 20 May 1919,

> that before the Delhi Durbar Delhi was a simple mofussil town, with little knowledge on politics, with no political agitations beyond a few anarchists . . . [and] with no indigenous press. . . . Since Delhi became the capital all this had changed, for the place has been flooded with agitators and politicians from all parts of India and has been the scene of countless political demonstrations and meetings.[10]

Beadon's exposition fell short of pointing out that the war-time clampdown and the stagnation of political advance had accentuated 'fissiparous' trends, given rise to disaffection, perked up nationalist sensitivities, and enabled Gandhi's campaign against the Rowlatt Bills to gain a firm foothold in Delhi and elsewhere.

Ansari was Delhi's most prominent satyagrahi, the first president of the Satyagraha Sabha, formed on 24 February 1919 and also the first to take the satyagraha vow when Gandhi visited the city on 7 March.[11] His house was the venue of many important meetings and his voice was heard from many platforms, as, on 24 March, when he declared that satyagraha was adopted by the Prophet Muhammad himself. He urged all Muslims to take the vow.[12] He influenced Ajmal Khan, Hasrat Mohani, Asaf Ali, Abdur Rahman, Arif Husain Hasvi (1888-1936) and Shuaib Qureshi to join the Rowlatt satyagraha and to align themselves with the Mahatma. In general, his yeoman service during the months of February to April proved crucial in ensuring popular enthusiasm for the Gandhian movement in Delhi. That is why some officials, as mentioned earlier, considered putting him in jail; others preferred deportation. But the idea was eventually dropped on the grounds that either of these stringent measures would help foster Hindu-Muslim unity and affect government's credibility.[13]

Some clues to Ansari's role and political disposition are offered in his evidence before the Hunter Commission. From his written statement, submitted on 3 November 1919, we can guage his commitment to satyagraha and to the element which Gandhi stressed most strongly, non-violence. We are told:

> India's share in the war had largely contributed to the entertainment of high aspirations by Indians, which, however, turned out to be extravagant in view of the later development of government's policy. The introduction of the Rowlatt legislation led to unprecedented agitation throughout India. But government enacted the objectionable measure in the teeth of universal opposition, causing profound disappointment and resentment. This naturally led to the adoption of passive resistance in the form of *satyagraha*, i.e., insistence on truth and negation of all violence.
>
> At such a time Mahatma Gandhi had a message of hope to the people of India, satyagraha or passive resistance against the Rowlatt Bills was inaugurated at a meeting held at the Ashram of Mahatma Gandhi at Ahmedabad on Friday, the 24th February 1919. He advocated the only remaining and the most effective constitutional method of agitation against the unjust measures, by practising satyagraha or civil resistance.

The Mahatma had given to the matter his serious consideration and it was with the sense of full responsibility that he started the satyagraha campaign. His own words show the amount of concern and care with which he took this step. . . .

It has been alleged in certain quarters that satyagraha was the cause of all disorders during March and April last. This is an absolutely baseless assertion, as can be proved by facts. The principles advocated by satyagraha, as described above, had been strictly observed by all satyagrahis. Not a single satyagrahi has been convicted of any violence. On the contrary, satyagraha sabha and satyagrahis have always scrupulously observed non-violence and have helped the authorities in restoring order. In Delhi, Ahmedabad, Bombay, concrete instances can be shown to prove this assertion.[14]

There was nothing new, ominous or threatening in the hartals, which, in connection with the satyagraha observance, were enjoined as a sign of general protest on the passing of the Rowlatt Act. Ansari pointed out that:

Hartal or the suspension of all business is not a new thing in this country. From olden times it has been practised at various special occasions to express the general sorrow or trouble. In Delhi as in many other towns all business was suspended and shops were closed on receiving the news of the death of Queen Victoria and King Edward the VII, in recent years. . . . There is nothing, therefore, new or ominous and threatening in *hartal*, as has been stated recently by some persons, in England, as showing the disposition of the people to disorder.[15]

And finally, he spelt out Gandhi's success in terms of the amorphous but widespread discontent against the government. The burden of his argument, quite convincingly proved by recent historical researches, was that the tinder of unrest had been drying for months and Gandhi's satyagraha was merely the spark which started the conflagration. According to him, it appealed to the masses because India was essentially a religious country and in the mind of the masses any religious creed could easily gain legitimacy and a stronghold. 'Satyagraha as such is a creed and I think the masses follow it most extraordinarily implicitly.'

Fearful of violence, Ansari's task was to ward off a possible direct confrontation with the local authorities. But his labours proved fruitless when, during his absence from Delhi from

26 March to 2 April, violent and bloody clashes occurred on 30 March. This spelt danger to the passive resistance movement. So, on his return he tried, along with Shraddhanand and Ajmal Khan, to prevent another round of hartal which was planned on 6 April as a day of 'humiliation and prayers'. On the strength of Gandhi's statement of 3 April that violence was inconsistent with satyagraha, he persuaded the Satyagraha Sabha to give up hartal.[16] He recounted:

> It became clear in the morning that *hartal* had taken place and an informal consultation of the leading citizens of Delhi took place in my consulting rooms at Fatehpuri to devise means to divert the people from collecting in the Chandni Chowk and the central places of the town. Some two hundred volunteers were sent out to help the preservation of order in the town. A large crowd of people were taken to Fatehpuri mosque to attend the *Fateha* of those who had died of wounds. Permission was obtained from the deputy commissioner to hold a public meeting soon after the *Fateha* was over in Edward Park in order to divert the crowd from the Chandni Chowk and with the same purpose another mass meeting was held at Daryaganj, right away in the outskirts of the town. The day passed off quietly and on the next day, the 7th April and the following days, 8th and 9th, business was resumed all over the town and everything was normal.[17]

The police firing on 30 March had, however, inflamed passions to such an extent that support for a radical course of action gained momentum; the flames of revolt rose high and every funeral of the victims of police firing occasioned more deaths.[18] At the same time, Ansari's mediatory role, as indeed that of Ajmal Khan, ensured the peaceful observance on 10 April when the news of Gandhi's arrest spread like wild fire and led to a complete hartal in Delhi. It continued until 19 April and led to fierce clashes between the police and the satyagrahis, and to the mob assuming control of the agitation. While Ansari and Ajmal Khan could not control the multitude, they managed to persuade local authorities, with whom they were *en rapport*, to exercise restraint in dealing with the outburst.[19] This minimized the loss of lives and diffused the growing tension.

Ansari's mediatory role did not go down well with the pan-Islamists among the *ulama*, who were keen to intensify the agitation even at the risk of violence. Their spokesman was the firebrand Sahban-ul Hind Maulvi Ahmad Said (1888-1959) of Madrasa-i Aminia, who led the local pressure to extremism. In early 1919, he upbraided Muslims who were not prepared to die for the Khilafat and who, by doing good to the Europeans, did harm to their country. He was backed by Qazi Abbas Husain, editor of the *Qaum*, and Arif Husain Hasvi, editor of the *Congress*. These papers, along with the *Inqilab*, commended Asaf Ali's suggestion to call the place round the Clock Tower as *Khuni Chauraha* (bloody intersection) to perpetuate the memory of the Delhi martyrs, just as the *Khuni Darwaza* reminded the people of the 1857 revolt.[20] 'These two rags,' an angry official had written, 'are mushroom growths and yet a month old and I doubt whether the sediment of political excitement left by the Congress and Muslim League meetings will furnish sufficient soil to nourish them through six months of existence.'[21] He was wrong. These newspapers had a growing readership which began to respond, albeit slowly, to the anti-government rumblings in Delhi.

Ansari responded to their militancy with commendable firmness. He worked quietly, often unobtrusively, to pacify his militant colleagues and warned them of the hazards of violence. When his endeavours came to naught, he resigned from the Satyagraha Sabha. Writing to Mohamed Ali, who was still interned in Chhindwara (Central Province), Ansari questioned the purposefulness and efficacy of the satyagraha movement. The letter, intercepted by Chhindwara's deputy commissioner, reveals Ansari's ability to take an independent position on political issues and pursue it even if it alienated close comrades. He wrote:

> You must have learnt of my differences of opinion from Shaukat Bhai. Then I was against Hijrat (migration) only, but I was entirely in favour of Satyagraha. In Delhi, I have had ample experience of Satyagraha. Though on the 30th March I was not in Delhi, but from the 1st of April, to its end whole day and night I spent all my time in observing the movement of satyagraha with its result and in allaying the excitement and uneasiness that was then common in the public mind and eventually I came to the conclusion that it was possible to carry on the satyagraha on the principles on which its originator M. Gandhi wishes it to be carried on in the present circumstances. There are many causes for its

failure and some of those causes are such that we have, if not absolutely none, very little control over them.

In these circumstances I consider the satyagraha movement to be practically impossible and wholly unprofitable and severed my connection with the Satyagraha Sabha. This is my opinion about Indians generally except some selected people I consider Mussalmans generally absolutely unfit to act on the principles of satyagraha. In my humble opinion satyagraha is an impracticable movement, of course, under the direct supervision of M. Gandhi this movement may perhaps succeed to a certain extent.[22]

Ansari's letter to the organizers of a meeting, held in Delhi on 13 May to express loyalty to the government in view of the threatened Afghan invasion[23] and his joining a gathering to thank the authorities for their handling of the situation in April, caused quite a flutter.[24] Much was also made out of his resignation from the Satyagraha Sabha. According to one source, he quit because 'his views regarding the practicability of the passive resistance movement had changed when he saw excesses to which it led to'. It was rumoured that he had suggested that the signatories to the vow in Delhi be given an opportunity of saying whether, in the light of the incidents since 7 March, they still wished to be considered satyagrahis. 'Presumably, reckoning on a general recantation,' concluded an intelligence report, 'the Committee decided instead to abolish the Sabha and proceeded to burn the list of adherents and the papers on which they had signed the vow.'[25]

It is easy to discern a slight vacillation in Ansari's disposition, but it did not mean a shift in his commitment to satyagraha. There was also no wavering in his devotion to Gandhi; he continued to believe that the movement could still succeed under his 'direct supervision'. Genuinely captivated by his personality, his idealism, his concern for the poor and the downtrodden, the Mahatma became his unquestioned leader; he idolized him, followed him and assisted him in future political crusades. He enjoyed both his friendship and confidence which, at that time, was the biggest political asset he could have. Others also fell in behind his programme in 1919 without having either worked with him or, in some cases, even having met him. He endeared himself to

Ansari's younger colleagues—Shuaib Qureshi and Abdur Rahman Siddiqi—owing to the asceticism of his style of life and his moves towards communal unity on the basis of championing specifically Muslim grievances, such as the future of the Khilafat and the Holy Places of Islam.[26] They looked up to Gandhi for counsel and leadership on these overtly religious issues.

Gandhi was initially unsure of his own strategy, though his early contacts with the Muslims had enabled him to comprehend the import of religious institutions and symbols in Indian Islam. He could therefore appreciate and partake in Muslim anxiety over the Khilafat question. No Hindu Congressman before him had made such an endeavour—which may, perhaps, explain why no other Hindu before Gandhi was so well thought of and earned so much popularity among Muslims. The early Congress leaders were insensitive to Muslim religious susceptibilities and interposed Hindu symbols and rituals in their political campaigns. Gandhi avoided doing so. With his sharp political acumen, he played up the Khilafat cause so as to transmute the Muslim into the nationalist cause.

Gandhi had worked with Muslims in South Africa and, after his return to India, forged friendly links with some influential Muslims. He met the Ali Brothers in Aligarh and Delhi in 1915, and early in 1916. His circle of Muslim friends widened after meeting Ansari and Abdul Bari.[27] With his vigour, charm and obvious organizational flair, Ansari seemed a suitable ally. The Mahatma tried in vain to see the Ali Brothers in the Chhindwara prison, but he did not give up his resolve to secure their release. He told delegates at the 1917 Muslim League session that Hindus were with them to a man in their just struggle for the Ali Brothers' release, pleaded with the viceroy to release them, arguing that they were loyal to the Raj and that their internment irritated both Hindus and Muslims. He sought definite assurance for Turkey's future before endorsing the loyalty resolution of the Delhi War Conference. When the viceroy ignored his pleadings, the Mahatma announced his decision to engage the government in a duel.[28] The fight for Mohamed Ali's release, though a 'crushing burden', had to be borne.[29] He went on to assure Bi Amma—Mataji—that he would leave no stone unturned to secure their honourable release.[30] Elsewhere, he argued that his own political advancement lay through an alliance with Mohamed Ali and other Muslims.

Gandhi wanted to secure Mohamed Ali's collaboration in advancing Hindu-Muslim unity, having made it an essential part of his mission to India. *'My interest in your release'*, he told him, *'is quite selfish. We have a common goal and I want to utilize your services to the uttermost in order to reach that goal. In the proper solution of Mohammedan question lies the realization of Swaraj'* [emphasis added].[31] Convinced that self-government could only be achieved if Hindus and Muslims worked hand in glove, he tried to secure 'permanent unity' between them.[32] The Khilafat issue gave him a unique opportunity of doing so—a chance that would not arise in a hundred years.[33] His inner voice told him that the two would stand shoulder to shoulder one day because there was no other course open to them but to be brothers.[34] The Khilafat agitation was 'the great churning process of the ocean that India is. Why should we worry as to what will come out (poison or nectar) from the movement? Is it not enough if we are certain that that activity is pure and righteous.'

Gandhi assumed that Mohamed Ali, as a representative of Muslim opinion, was an ideal instrument for creating Hindu-Muslim comradeship with the aim of obtaining swaraj. Because to him swaraj meant not just political Home Rule but a state of communal harmony, the Rampur-born and Oxford-educated Mohamed Ali was valuable to both as an issue on which to cement an inter-communal combination and also because he symbolized the mingling of Hindu and Muslim culture in UP.[35] Mohamed Ali reciprocated. Full of admiration, he subscribed to the non-violent programme against the Rowlatt Act which, in his words, were 'enacted in the most tyrannical manner', ending 'the reign of law' and substituting 'a reign of terror in its place'.[36] While in Chhindwara, he corresponded with Gandhi regularly on various theological questions, and appreciated his efforts to secure his release.[37] At the end of 1919, he said:

> Long before we were free we had made up our minds to bring about a complete entente between Hindus and Muslims . . . and the best man among the Hindus to deal with was Mahatma Gandhi, a peace-loving and non-violent patriot who was intensely religious without the fury of

a theologian and whose honesty all could rely upon. He found us to be equally religious and equally without the fury of the theologian, and as Muslims we could not pledge ourselves to remain non-violent in all circumstances, he found that we too regarded force at present to be futile, and above all he could trust our word as much as we trusted him. Even if we ourselves wished to use force immediately, which we did not and could not, we would have lost his support and thus have lost the chance of bringing about the Hindu-Muslim entente and of bringing the government to its senses.[38]

Such a subservient posture was no doubt distasteful to some *ulama*, particularly to Syed Ahmed Raza Khan (1856-1921) of Bareilly. But people like him wielded limited influence during the popular pan-Islamic upsurge. Most *ulama* favoured accommodation with Congress and making common cause with the Hindus because of their support for the Khilafat cause. For this reason alone they cast in their lot with Gandhi and hitched their fortunes to the Congress star. For example, Abdul Bari, the spiritual preceptor of Ansari and the *pir* of the Ali-Brothers, became an important adherent to the Gandhian movement. He met the Mahatma at the Lucknow Congress in December 1916. They saw each other again in February/March 1918 at Ansari's home in Delhi and then in March 1919. After the second meeting, Abdul Bari followed Gandhi's lead. His motive was simple: the Mahatma was the only guarantor of Congress support to the Khilafat demands. 'I have accepted his [Gandhi's] support in getting our aims fulfilled,' he wrote in November 1920, 'and for that purpose I think it is necessary to follow his advice. . . . *I know that the strength of Islam lies in association with him*' [emphasis added].[39] In deference to his wishes (though Gandhi did not make the abandonment of cow-slaughter a condition of his support), Abdul Bari decided to eschew the sacrifice of cows and appealed to his co-religionists to do the same. Such a gesture of goodwill towards the Mahatma was important for sustaining the Hindu-Muslim rapprochement.

Khwaja Hasan Nizami, the scholar attached to the shrine of Nizamuddin Auliya, also favoured such a move. The Prophet Muhammad, he stated, slaughtered a cow only once in his lifetime, that the Quran did not enjoin upon the faithful to slaughter cows specially and the same religious, cultural and economic compulsions which prompted Hindus to save the cow applied to the Muslims as well.[40] He was also converted to satyagraha and non-violence. 'I have decided to adhere to the principles (*tariqa*) laid down by Mahatma Gandhi.'[41]

Muslim artisans, merchants, mill-workers and weavers rallied round Gandhi and took part in the hartal on 6 April. His success in securing their adherence was due to the consummate skill with which he capitalized on the indignation against the government's policy towards Turkey as well as the fear that the Rowlatt Bills were intended to enable officials to coerce the Muslims and 'prevent them from giving trouble so as to facilitate the dismemberment of Turkey'. Secondly, the economic distress fanned the steadily growing resentment against British domination. During World War I, a sharp increase took place in the prices of basic commodities such as rice, wheat, salt and cooking oil. In UP, food grain production fell sharply because of lack of rain and large areas were hit by famine or scarcity. The province, like other regions, was afflicted by the great influenza which caused the death of at least five to six million people. Gandhi used these discontents to organize a spectacular movement of popular protest.

An important outcome of the political excitement in the years 1918-19 was the uprecedented Hindu-Muslim comradeship. 'Though the Rowlatt Act sits like a dread nightmare on our breasts,' wrote the editor of *Amrita Bazar Patrika,* 'it has united both Hindus and Mussalmans in a way which has never been witnessed.'[42] There were reports of satyagraha in Muzaffarnagar, and of meetings on Hindu-Muslim relations. The Muslims went so far as to allow *chandan* to be put on their forehead and promised to abstain from killing any cows at the next Id.[43] The commissioner of Banaras division took note of the Maulvis of Jaunpur forfeiting their right to sacrifice cows at the next Id.[44] At Delhi, Shraddhanand addressed the Friday congregation at the Juma Masjid. Elsewhere, sadhus spoke from pulpits and Muslim divines addressed mixed audiences in Hindu temples.

The message was not lost on Ansari. The experience of the Rowlatt satyagraha convinced him that there were many issues which concerned Hindus and Muslims equally; consequently, there were objective reasons for them to coalesce in advancing the country's interests generally. Unity between them was not only desirable but necessary for the nationalist movement. With this conviction, he decided to devote himself whole-heartedly to cementing their bonds of friendship. Up to 1919, he had given convincing proof of his ability as a man of action, as advocate, negotiator and organizer. In the following years, he revealed other and rarer gifts as a leader and policy-maker which hitherto had not been brought fully into play.

NOTES

1. Hasan (ed.), *Muslims and the Congress*, p. 274.
2. Nehru, *An Autobiography*, p. 41.
3. See contributions in Kumar (ed.), *Essays on Gandhian Politics*.
4. Ravinder Kumar, *Essays in the Social History of Modern India* (Delhi, 1983), pp. 21-3; Ferrel, 'The Rowlatt Satyagraha in Delhi', op. cit.; Gupta, *Delhi Between Two Empires*, pp. 204-5.
5. Home Poll, A, May 1919, 19-20, NAI.
6. C.L. Alexander to W. Raw, 17 April 1919, General Administration Department [GAD], F. No. 262, 1919, Box 131, UPSA.
7. Ibid.
8. Ibid.; Home Dept. to the Chief Commissioner, Delhi, 20 April 1919, *DIC*, p. 209.
9. Home Poll. B, January 1910, 160-3, NAI; *History* (Delhi), op. cit.
10. Home Poll. B, May 1919, 119-20, NAI.
11. Ibid., 268-73, ibid.
12. Ibid., 141-7, ibid.
13. Ibid., 119-20, ibid.
14. *DIC*, pp. 201–2.
15. Ibid., p. 202.
16. Ibid., p. 102.
17. Ibid., p. 202.
18. Ferrel, op. cit.
19. *DIC*, pp. 202–3.
20. Ibid., pp. 145-6.
21. FR, second half of February 1919, Home Poll. Deposit, March 1919, 17, NAI. In Delhi the main newspapers with a pan-Islamic outlook were: *Congress, Fateh, Fatehmand, Khilafat, Hurriyat* and *Sabah*. Their combined circulation was just over 6,000, but they fared better than the literary and commercial journals which, according to a government report, 'last a few months, perish and are replaced . . .'. *Annual Report of the Newspapers Published in the Delhi Province*, 1920. Home Poll. F.

No. 4, 1921, NAI; *Annual Report of the Newspapers Published in the Delhi Province, 1921*, Home Poll. B, F. No. 12, 1922, NAI.

22. Home Poll. A, September 1919, 406-28, NAI; Hasan (ed.), *Mohamed Ali in Indian Politics*, vol. I, pp. 253-4.
23. Ansari wrote: 'At a time when there is danger of foreign invasion on our motherland, it is the imperative duty of all true and patriotic Indians whether Hindus or Muslims to sink all their differences with the Government and give it their whole-hearted support. Even if we put aside all the higher patriotic and ethical considerations, our self interest demands that we should make common cause with our rulers at this juncture. For, we must bear in mind that "Home Rule", "Responsible Government" and all our highly cherished ideals of constitutional rights and personal liberties could be gained only when there is perfect tranquility inside the country and no apprehension of an attack from outside.' Home Poll. A, May 1919, 119-20, NAI.
24. Mushirul Hasan and Margrit Pernau (eds.), *Regionalising Pan-Islamism*, p. 5. Home Poll. A, September 1919, 406-28, NAI; Bamford, *Histories*, p. 142.
25. FR, first half of May 1919, Home Poll. Deposit, July 1919, 49, NAI.
26. Hasan, *Nationalism and Communal Politics in India*, pp. 114-15.
27. Speech on Khilafat, Bombay, 9 May 1919. *The Collected Works of Mahatma Gandhi* [*CWG*], vol. 15, p. 295.
28. Gandhi to Maffey, 12 July 1918, Chelmsford Papers (21).
29. 11 April 1918, Mahadev Desai (ed.), *Day-to-Day with Gandhi* (Varanasi, 1968), vol. I, p. 93.
30. 6 August 1918, ibid., p 211; also, To Shuaib Qureshi, 24 September 1918, pp. 256-7.
31. Gandhi to Mohamed Ali, 18 November 1918, Hasan (ed.), *Mohamed Ali in Indian Politics*, vol. 2, p. 117.
32. *CWG*, vol. 15, p. 296.
33. Ibid.
34. *Day-to-Day with Gandhi*, vol. 1, p. 56.
35. J.M. Brown, *Gandhi's Rise to Power: Indian Politics 1915-1922* (Cambridge, 1972), p. 152.
36. Mohamed Ali to Chelmsford, 24 April 1919, Hasan (ed.), *Mohamed Ali in Indian Politics*, vol. 2, pp. 232-3.
37. For example, Mohamed Ali to Gandhi. 20 February 1919, ibid., pp. 239-41.
38. Quoted in Brown, op. cit., p. 331.
39. Home Poll. Deposit, 1921, 4, NAI; WRDCI, March 1919, Home Poll. B, April 1919, 148-52, NAI.
40. Hasan Nizami, *Tark-i Gayekushi* (Delhi, 1920), pp. 6-7, 16. Abdul Bari thanked Gandhi for the success of the Day of Prayer and conveyed

Maulana Sulaiman of Phulwari's message that the Hindus of the city, acting on Gandhi's instructions, 'have made us so much obliged that we ourselves have determined not to sacrifice cow in future'. Abdul Bari to Gandhi, n.d., Abdul Bari Papers, Firangi Mahal, Lucknow.

41. Hasan Nizami, *Government awr Khilafat* (Gurdaspur, 1922 edn.). The pamphlet was first published in 1920.
42. M.L. Ghose to Mohamed Ali, 14 April 1919, Hasan (ed.), *Mohamed Ali in Indian Politics*, vol. 2, p. 220.
43. P.W. Marsh to W. Raw, 27 April 1919, GAD, F. No. 262, 1919, UPSA.
44. Commissioner of Banaras Division to A.C. Chatterji, chief secretary to UP government, 29 April 1919, ibid.

5

The Khilafat Experience: Theory and Practice

> It is difficult for anyone not an Indian Moslem to realize what pan-Islamism means to the Indian Moslems. . . . It is a sentiment of which the prayers for Turkish success in the Tripolitan and Balkan wars, the Relief Fund, the Medical Mission and even Khilafat movement were weak but faltering expressions. It is not a sentiment inspired by interest, policy or worldly wisdom: it has no practical end in view [M.A. Ansari].
>
> Introduction to Halide Edip, *Conflict of East and West in Turkey* (Delhi, n.d), pp. iv-v

> *Husain ibn-i Ali Aao Khilafat chheeni jaati hai*
> *Madad kije khudara ab dam-i mushkil kushai hai*
>
> [Mohammad Haider of Pilibhit]
> Proscribed Publications (43), IOL

THE INDIAN MUSLIMS, who share certain religious beliefs and practices with their brethren elsewhere, have been conscious of their fraternal links with them. Some have been following their histories, deriving comfort in their accomplishments, and lamenting their steady decline. By the nineteenth and twentieth centuries, in particular, when Islam seemed to fall on evil days because of the European imperial penetration into the heartlands of the Muslim world, the heritage of the past stood forth as a symbol of community pride and distinction; in fact, everywhere Muslims were told to look to their own glorious Islamic past as the source for their inspiration, identity and unity. This was expressed in the adventurist and revivalist movements of Mohammad ibn Abdul Wahhab (1703-92) in Arabia, Syed Ahmad Barelvi (1786-1831) in India, Mohammad Ali ibn al-Sanusi (1787-1859) in Nigeria and Mohammad Ahmad (1848-85), the Mahdi of the Sudan. All of them re-emphasized that their socio-moral revival required political action, an activism epitomized by *jehad,* the exertion to realize God's will through moral self-discipline and, when necessary, military combat or warfare. At another level, they defended Islam from the polemical and hostile attacks of nineteenth-century Western orientalists and against the intellectual and moral imperialism of the West. They laid stress on the original message of Islam which had provided the ideal pattern for traditional Muslim society and remained eternally valid, and on the fact that Muslims were fully equipped to respond to the political, cultural and scientific challenge of the West. Thus Syed Ahmad Khan, a major catalyst for reform and change in India, and his contemporary, Mohammad Abduh (1845-1905) in Egypt, tried to show the compatibility of Islam with modern ideas and institutions.

Such currents, which gripped the Muslim countries from North Africa to South-East Asia, were reflected in Altaf Husain Hali's (1837-1914) lamenting the 'ebb' of Islam in the famous *Musaddas,* in Shibli Nomani's pan-Islamic anguish in the topical poem on the 'Trouble in the Balkans', and in Mohammad Iqbal's nostalgic ode to once Arab Sicily. Shibli and Ameer Ali (1849-1928), too, espoused Turkey's cause in the first quarter of the twentieth century, singling out the European powers as enemies of Islam. Elsewhere, similar reactions were triggered against the French occupation of Tunisia in 1871, the British possession of Egypt in 1882, the Russian conquest of Merv in 1884, the Italian seizure of Tripoli in 1911 and the Balkan war of 1912-13. Muslim responses to the Western aggression ranged from rejection to adaptation, from withdrawal to acculturation and reform. Most notably, however, the examples of German and Italian unifications suggested the potency of movements for unity of divided territories behind a single government.[1] This idea formed the basis of the pan-Islamic euphoria in the last quarter of the nineteenth century.

For most, the overriding consideration was the status of Turkey's Sultan as the custodian and defender of the Holy Places in the area known as *Jazirat al-Arab.* With the sanctuaries and symbols of Islam exposed to danger,[2] they demanded the *Jazirat al-Arab* to remain under Muslim sovereignty (according to the injunctions of the Prophet) with the Khalifa as its warden. With this as the rallying point, money and ornaments poured into the Khilafat fund, thousands flocked to the protest meetings and some even left the fields and factories to migrate to the Dar al-Islam in response to a call for *hijrat*. Students joined the swelling ranks of non-cooperators, while many of their elders gave up their lucrative jobs and high-sounding titles. Never before did so many Muslims unite on a common platform to fight a common cause.

In explaining this outburst, one must take into account the strength of the unifying powers of religious symbols in Indian Islam. Some of these symbols—mosque, *haj*, sufi shrine—fostered a sense of belonging to a common fraternity of Islam and thus made it easier for the pan-Islamic notion to permeate Muslim consciousness. Equally, one will do well to reckon with the theme of 'Muslim unity', echoed by the *ulama* of Firangi Mahal, Deoband and the Nadvat al-ulama, and how this concept eventually merged into the stream of pan-Islamic consciousness.

Among Sunni Muslims, who formed the overwhelming majority of the Muslim population, Turkey's Sultan was the *Amir al-Muminin* (Commander of the Faithful) and the protector of the Holy Places. The Khilafat was the viceroyalty of the Prophet of Islam, ordained by Divine Law for the perpetuation of Islam and the continued observance of its *sharia* (Islamic law) and the Khalifa (derived from the word 'Khalafa'—to leave behind) was both a spiritual and temporal head. Allegiance to him was obligatory which explains why some Sultans of Delhi bore the names of Khalifa on their coins and often received investitures as legal sanction for their rule. The name of the Abbasid Khalifa, Al-Mustasim, continued on the coins for about 40 years after the sack of Baghdad at the hands of the Mongols. It was probably an expression of the sentiment: 'The Khalifa is dead, long live the Khalifa.' The Mughal Emperors as well as some independent Muslim rulers in the eighteenth century often turned towards the Ottoman Khalifa as a source of strength. In 1785, Tipu Sultan sent an embassy to the Ottoman Sultan and his emissaries secured for him letters of investiture which allowed him to assume the title of an independent ruler.[3]

Interest in Turkey's welfare continued: each time it was involved in hostilities—the Russo-Turkish war of 1877-8 or the Greco-Turkish war of 1897—Indian Muslims took up the cudgels for Turkey, reaffirmed their attachment to its Sultan and prayed for his well-being. 'If the Muhammadans of the world were compared to the human body,' wrote the *Akhbar-i Am*, 'the Sultan would be the heart and brain.'[4] Anthony Macdonnell (1844-1919), lieutenant-governor of UP, quoted to the viceroy, Elgin (1849-1919), a leaflet describing the Ottoman Sultan as *Amir al-Muminin* and *Padshah-i Mussalmanan* and noted the sympathy with Turkey partly due to incitement from outside India and partly spontaneous—a feeling which, according to him, was fostered by Muslim schools and was more widespread than before. He was told by Agra's commissioner that many more people had taken to wearing the Turkish *fez*, and that was perhaps the straw indicating how the wind was beginning to blow.[5]

The 'incitement from outside', came from two distinct sources. In the first place, the British government exploited pro-Turkish sensibilities in order to secure Indian Muslim loyalty, as in 1857, and to protect their imperial interests from Russian encroachments by bolstering 'the sick man of Europe', as they did from the Crimean war of 1853-6 onwards. Then, the Sultan of Turkey, Abdul Hamid II (1842-1918), sent his agents to India, as other lands, to rally Muslim support and enthusiasm for his feeble regime threatened by external aggression and internal strife, caused by nationalist movements sprung up among his Christian Balkan subjects (Armenian, Greek, Romanian, Bulgarian) in south-east Europe.

Syed Ahmad Khan disputed Abdul Hamid's pretensions. The pan-Islamic surge threatened to wreck his effort to prop up the Anglo-Muslim alliance in India; so he spoke against the Turcophilia among his co-religionists, arguing that they were legally bound to obey the writ not of an external Muslim Khalifa but of the British Indian government. But such exhortations fell on inattentive ears as the fellow-feeling for Turkey extended to far-flung parts of northern India. Nawab Mohsin-ul-Mulk (1837-1907), one of Syed Ahmad Khan's successors at the Aligarh College, learnt his lesson the hard way. When he opposed the holding of pan-Islamic meetings on the campus, some of his colleagues described him as a 'downright sycophant'.[6]

The most bitter criticism of Syed Ahmad Khan's views came from an unexpected quarter—from that celebrated roving reformer, teacher and political agitator, Jamaluddin al-Asadabadi 'al-Afghani' (1839-97).[7] He regarded the Aligarh reformer's religious views and his educational programme as ancillaries to his political servitude and chided him for relying on the British instead of joining hands with the Indian nationalists. Afghani considered Syed Ahmad Khan as his main adversary in India, opposed to pan-Islamism, isolating the Indian Muslims from the rest of Dar al-Islam, especially from the Turks, and hostile to the conception of a universal Muslim Khilafat. According to him, the reassertion of Muslim identity and solidarity were prerequisites for the restoration of political and cultural independence, and unity and solidarity were essential at both levels.[8]

Afghani spent the greater part of his life travelling from one country to the other (Afghanistan, India, Iran, Egypt and the Ottoman Empire) as the chief exponent of pan-Islamism. His life, one of endless wanderings, touched and deeply affected Muslims in the last quarter of the nineteenth century; his pan-Islamic vision inspired various activist groups in different lands and lives on patiently, if amorphously, in the aspirations of many Muslims.[9] Curiously enough, his political programme of combined radicalism, modernism, nationalism and pan-Islamism became a serious political agenda of a vibrant and spirited opposition in the Khilafat agitation in India, years after his death.[10]

Among those who came under Afghani's spell was Shibli Nomani who visited Istanbul in 1893, received a medal from Abdul Hamid and parleyed with Afghani's co-worker and disciple, Mohammad Abduh.[11] His pan-Islamic ideas were echoed in Hali's *Musaddas* while his strong advocacy of the coexistence of diverse religious faiths was in accord with Mohamed Ali's idea, expressed in his Congress presidential address in 1923, of the 'Federation of Faiths'. Ansari developed his view of a natural solidarity beyond the nation: that which binds together all the peoples of the East threatened by the West.[12] At the All-India Khilafat Conference held on 27 December 1922, he underlined the need for an Asiatic Federation to promote solidarity among the peoples and countries of Asia with a view to rescuing them from the political and economic bondage of the West.[13] Afghani had put forward this idea first, though it became known to his contemporaries two decades earlier.

Afghani also influenced Iqbal and Azad. The former became interested most of all in his endeavour to find in Islam a means of unification for resisting the domination of the West. He also shared his desire to express unity on the religious basis of Muslims as a supra class and a supra-national entity. On the eve of and during World War I, Iqbal tied his hopes for liberation from colonial dependency to pan-Islamic solidarity. This was reflected in his poem *Shama Awr Shair* (The Candle and the Poet), written in 1912.[14] In his reply to the *Shikwa* (Complaint of God), he struck the same note:

> The trouble that is raging in the Balkans
> Is a message of awakening to the forgetful
> Thou may'st think it the means of vexing thy heart
> But in reality it is a test of thy self-sacrifice and self-reliance.

As for Azad, Afghani's influence can be seen from the time of his stay in Constantinople and Cairo when he developed close relations with the *Al-Manar* (The Lighthouse) group of Syrian and Egyptian scholars. He developed the nationalist and anti-imperialist thrust of Afghani's ideas in the *Al-Hilal*, inspired by the *Al-Urwa al-wuthqa* (The Indissoluble Link), an anti-imperialist journal published in collaboration with Abduh. He, too, bitterly attacked Syed Ahmad Khan's attitude to the Turkish Khilafat and urged on the authority of the Quran that *jehad* was imperative against those who had occupied even a part of the Dar al-Islam. Political fidelity was due to the Ottoman Khalifa; it was binding on the faithful to obey him and to comply with his wishes.[15]

Azad stood strongly for inter-communal union, citing the Prophet Muhammad's covenant with some Jews as a valid historical precedent for an integrated alliance with the Hindus. According to him, it was obligatory to unite with one category of non-Muslims, the Hindus, against another category of non-Muslims. Mohammad Idris Qandhari, an *alim* of Deoband, justified the alliance with the Hindus on the ground that they were *Ahl-i Sulah* as opposed to *Ahl-i Harb* (enemies of Islam).

In a similar vein, Ansari, in December 1920, quoted the *Sura-i Mumtahanah* (60: 8-9) to argue that Indian Muslims should behave 'righteously, affectionately and in a friendly manner towards all those non-Muslims who are neither at war with Muslims nor are they assailants intending to invade or occupy their territories'.[16]

This emphasis on a peaceful *modus vivendi* with the followers of another faith underlined the importance of forging links with men of different faiths; in fact, Afghani called upon India's Muslims to make common cause with the Hindus on national interests,[17] advocated inter-communal oneness, and defied any breach in the anti-British front. In his articles published in the Hyderabad journal, *Muallim-i Shafiq,* he evoked not only the universal Islamic but also national aspirations with special emphasis on the affinity of Hindu-Muslim interests. And just as he helped awaken Egyptian nationalism by alluding to the ancient glories of the past, so in India, even when talking to a primarily Muslim audience, he harped on the glory of the Indian Hindu past.[18] His appeal was no different from his earlier exhortation to Egyptian Muslims to seek inspiration from pre-Islamic Egyptian greatness. In both cases he appealed to an effective basis for solidarity against the foreigner.[19]

Afghani's attempt to reconcile pan-Islamism with nationalism carried conviction. Various theories were therefore worked out to remove the widespread conception that the essence of pan-Islamism implied a break with territorial nationalism. The Muslim ideologues, in particular, insisted that its sum and substance was to remove foreign domination; so their activities were inextricably bound with the concept of an emerging Indian nation. They pointed out that, in spite of their pan-Islamic ambition, or fantasy as some preferred to call it, they always had their own *Indian* community most clearly in mind and were sensitive to its trials and tribulations. The emblem used on the Khilafat delegation stationery—made up of twin circles of equal size and overlapping, with the word 'Khilafat' on one and the word 'India' on the other—symbolized their patriotism and illustrated the link between their vision of a free India and the liberation of the Muslim countries from the yoke of colonial rule. Ansari, for instance, established the connection between British colonial policies and the larger interests of the West in perpetuating 'the bondage and slavery of Asiatic people'. To him it was not only a question of India's honour and freedom, but of a great struggle for emancipating all the enslaved people from the thraldom of the West.[20]

The relationship between the Indians and the Turks was in the nature of a compact, because both Turkey and India were subjected to colonial rule. For this reason, Azad observed that the agitation in India had at first been directed towards the salvation of the Khalifa and the Ottoman empire, but the problem of the Khalifa was part of the larger issue of British imperialism. Khilafat workers must win India's freedom by means of non-cooperation; only then would they be able to save the Khalifa.[21] Mohamed Ali offered the same advice: Muslims must fight for swaraj with their non-Muslim brethren, for only in this way they would achieve the Khilafat aim.[22] He made the most passionate and detailed attempt to demonstrate that pan-Islamism and nationalism were compatible, arguing that Western aggression hastened Muslim disillusionment with their traditional reliance on the British government and thereby contributed greatly to Indian unity.[23] He further stated that the Muslims have had a pre-eminent sense of community in their *Weltanschauung* and especially so in India, where their adherence to Islam made them unique and gave them their 'communal consciousness'. 'I have a culture, a polity, an outlook on life—a complete synthesis which is Islam,' he said at the Round Table Conference in 1930. He did not, however, believe that being a Muslim he was any less an Indian. His religious beliefs, as indeed his commitment to nationalism, did not appear to him to be incompatible.[24] He could—and must—be true to both Islam and India. He took pains to explain that 'where India is concerned, where India's freedom is concerned, where the welfare of India is concerned, I am an Indian first, an Indian second and nothing but an Indian'.[25] Many others shared this conviction. As a result, they were able to easily swing back and forth between pan-Islamic and local nationalist appeals, depending upon which was a more appropriate anti-imperialist weapon in a specific regional situation.

The Khilafat movement has often been denounced as unrealistic on the grounds that its emphasis on extra-Indian loyalties stood in the way of genuine unity. It has also been pointed out that the alliance of the Congress Muslims with the nationalist forces was of an ephemeral and opportunistic nature. The roots of this assumption lay in the unexpressed postulate that Muslims were unpatriotic because they were moved only by loyalty to the invisible theocracy of which God was the ruler and that they had developed a nationalism of their own which was Islamic in tone and content. 'Under the circumstances,' observed the Congress and Hindu Mahasabha leader B.S. Moonje, 'how can peace and amity now grow between the Hindus and the Muslims unless either the Hindus surrender and become a consenting party to the Islamic Mission or if they are equally determined to preserve their essentially scientific identity separate from the one-sided Nationalism of the Muslims'.[26] The reality is that the Khilafat movement had merged into a general political struggle far outstripping its original limitations. Indeed, the Khilafat committees in some areas were often indistinguishable from local Congress bodies, volunteer groups, Kisan Sabhas and Home Rule Leagues. 'There is nothing to choose locally,' commented an official, 'between a gathering under the auspices of the Kisan Sabha or of the Khilafat Committee. Both movements appear to have been completely captured by the non-cooperation party.'[27] This was not just a joyful demonstration of the newly-found sense of solidarity, but an awareness of the 'extraordinary stiffening-up' of a demoralized, backward and broken-up people taking part in disciplined, joint action on a countrywide scale.[28]

In several areas of UP, the Khilafat Committees and the Kisan Sabhas acted in unison in attacking their common identifiable enemy—the landlord. Herein lay the danger in official assessment, a fact referred to when the secretary of the Rae Bareli Khilafat Committee spoke at a Kisan Sabha meeting on 6 February. 'What might have been in its way a harmful and beneficent movement,' he declared, 'is in danger of being rapidly perverted into a vehicle for virulent abuse of and violent agitation against the Government.'[29] Evidence of the potentially dangerous alliance came from other areas as well. The Khilafat activists organized a Kisan Sabha rally at Fyzabad, held on 20-21 December 1920.[30] Local Khilafat leaders—Lai Mohammad and Maulvi Riasat Husain—addressed a similar gathering at village Salethu in

Maharajganj on 2 February 1921; Amid Syed, a local agitator, organized a protest meeting at village Balla in the same police station area a week earlier.

Such meetings established a definite link between the demands of the Kisans and the Khilafatists, on the one hand, and the attainment of 'swaraj', on the other; in fact, words like 'Khilafat', 'Kisan ekta', 'swaraj', 'Gandhi' conjured up in the minds of the people a picture of bringing about a better world under the direction of better leaders.[31] Thus Maulvi Salamatullah, associated with Maulana Abdul Bari, declared that the peasant interests would be protected only after the Khalifa's dignity and prestige was restored. Kamaluddin Jafri, the Allahabad-based lawyer, linked the redressal of their grievances with the attainment of swaraj under the Congress directives. Hafiz Alam and Mohammad Nabi of Tanda, important Khilafatists in eastern UP, endorsed this view.[32]

The collaboration between the Khilafatists and groups of peasants and workers was equally pronounced in Bengal and Punjab. In Bengal, it was facilitated by the failure of harvests between 1918 and 1922, the rise in prices, the fall in the prices of jute and the influenza and cholera epidemics. In Punjab, the North-Western Railway strike, which was initially called at the end of April 1920 for improving the workers' material conditions, coalesced with the Khilafat agitation as the strikers began to perceive it as a protest against a 'tyrannical and exploitative' government.[33]

It is also worth noting that the Congress-Khilafat-League meetings began to be held in the same city and around the same time; often, the Khilafat Committee and the Muslim League took their political cue from the Congress and endorsed its decisions. The 1918 League session, for instance, did so and, as in the Congress, so in the League, wrote an intelligence officer, 'the moderates have lost all control'. The same spirit prevailed a year later, though the speeches 'were more violent in their language and defiant in their general attitude than the extremist Hindus at the meetings of the Congress'. Anti-British spirit, he emphasized, 'reigned supreme'.[34] In July 1920, the League insisted that the Congress met first so that it could recommend the course of action for the Muslims.[35]

Such demonstrations of political unity were matched by spontaneous expressions of communal harmony. In Delhi and Punjab, in particular, the Prem Sabhas and Anjuman-i Islam worked strenuously to ensure the peaceful observance of religious festivals.[36] Zafar Ali Khan captured the spirit of the time in the verse:

Aaee hain Aasman se chal kar woh quwaten
Jo Muslim-o-Hunood ko sheer-o-shakar karen.

Heavenly forces have helped to forge the bonds of friendship between the Hindus and the Muslims.

So did Agha Hashr:

Ho gaeen bikhri huee eenten baham tameer ki
Mil gaee har ek kari tooti huee zanjeer ki
But-shikan wahdast-parast ek jism ek jaan ho gaye
Ghul hua duniya me phir kafir Mussalman ho gaye.

The disjointed pieces have been put in order again
The links of the broken chain have been discerned
The idol-worshippers and the iconoclast have joined hands
There is a dinning clamour that the *kafirs* have again
embraced Islam.

Short-lived as this unity was, such sentiments indicated the strength and fervour of the nationalistic spirit of which it was the outward expression. 'The scenes that were enacted before my eyes,' wrote the Secretary of the Bengal Khilafat Committee, 'made me feel that the artificial barriers that had long been preventing the two major communities of the country to come together, had been miraculously swept away by the onrush of the all-embracing non-cooperation movement.'[37]

ANSARI AND THE KHILAFAT PROTEST

Ansari was the first to voice the growing disquiet over the future of Turkey and the Holy Places from an organized political platform—the All-India Muslim League session in December 1918. First, he concentrated on the dismemberment of Muslim states because of the 'avarice and greed of the Chancelleries of Europe', and warned that his community was concerned over the fate of 40 million Muslims in the world. He stressed that the integrity and independence of the present Muslim states be maintained, and besides redressing the wrongs done to the Arabs of North Africa and the Tartars and Turks of Central Asia, they should be given a free chance to choose their own government. Next, he turned to the relationship between the government and the Muslims, describing it as 'one varying from bias against them to that of antipathy, suspicion, mistrust and even dislike', and went on to express the sense of having been tricked, which Muslims felt from the time of the annulment of Bengal's partition. Now, he pointed out, the secretary of state and the viceroy were against separate electorates and communal representation, 'the life and soul of all our activities of the present day'.[38] He referred to the interference with religious liberty, guaranteed under the proclamation of 1858, 'the fundamental basis of [Muslim] allegiance to the Crown', the internment of Mahmud Hasan, Azad and the Ali Brothers and the strangulation of the *Comrade*, the *Hamdard*, the *Al-Hilal* and the *Zamindar*. Ansari had come to believe, slowly, but with growing conviction, that those who clung to the doctrine of *force majeure* advocated an imperial philosophy whose vigour was already spent and which was no longer a solution for the problems of the day. 'Had it not been that our rulers were engaged in a struggle of life and death,' he observed, 'the Mussalmans would have taken such constitutional measures as would have compelled action.'

Ansari reiterated his faith in the Lucknow Pact, hammered out in December 1916, and in the making of which he played a major part.[39] On Hindu-Muslim *entente*, he contended:

> The Mussalmans have fought the battle of India shoulder to shoulder with their Hindu brethren, their political programme has come in line with that of the Hindus, the Hindu-Muslim rapprochement entered into at Lucknow has, year after year, gained strength and vitality and I believe that as time goes on we shall understand each other better and any causes of friction that remain shall cease to exist. It is my firm conviction that a true Mussalman is always a good Nationalist.

He concluded on the note that India's exclusion from the application of Woodrow Wilson's (1856-1924) fourteen points was inexcusable in the light of its contributions and sacrifices during the War. It seemed to him a ridiculous paradox that India alone should escape from a movement of political thought that affected every other part of the British empire. Making a strong plea for self-determination, he set forth:

> Out of the welter and blood of the Armageddon have emerged certain definite principles on which will be based the foundations of a new and better world. . . . They have been repeated, explained and amplified time after time, until no doubt has been left in the minds of men that their application will be universal and not confined to the geographical limits of a country or continent nor will they be circumscribed by the prejudices of race, colour or creed. To my mind there is but one single doctrine in which is focussed the entire thought of the whole human race. This doctrine, Gentlemen, is the doctrine of self-determination.[40]

Muslims in northern India heeded Ansari's address; it summed up their own fears and frustrations arising out of British policies both in India and in Turkey. In fact, Ansari's effort to stir them out of their torpor was rewarded by a slow but steady surge of resentment against the government. 'There is no doubt', reported an intelligence officer, 'that the masses were grieved to hear of the Sultan's defeat. . . . Now Dr Ansari's address with its quotations from the Quran and the support of the ulamas [*sic*] been widely read and by now every Mussalman knows that the Holy Places are going out of the hands of the Mussalmans sovereign and that the English are responsible.'[41]

Fresh from his success at Delhi, Ansari devoted the next three years spreading the Khilafat message. In January 1919, he helped to distribute an *istifta* (questionnaire) issued by Abdul Bari in order to obtain an authoritative pronouncement from the leading *ulama.* He led the Khilafat delegation to the viceroy on 19 January 1920, and joined the second deputation to London in February 1921. He submitted a report of its activities and suggested that the Central Khilafat Committee depute knowledgeable people to Europe to remain in touch with the situation there as well as with 'Near Eastern affairs'. In early 1922, he joined hands with Ajmal Khan, Seth Chotani (1873-1932), Syed Mahmud (1889-1971) and A.H.S. Khatri in setting out the Khilafat claims. They laid out a scheme of political activity for their Muslim brethren with emphasis on attainment of swaraj under Gandhi's leadership. Ansari co-authored, with Ajmal Khan, a manifesto, issued in March 1922, demanding the restoration of the Turkish portion of the Ottoman empire to Turkey with full sovereign rights, the liberation of the Arabic-speaking areas—Palestine, Syria, Mesopotamia and Hejaz—from non-Muslim control and the maintenance of the Sultan's authority over the Holy Places.

The manifesto explicitly linked the Khilafat demands with the overall national struggle against British *imperium*. 'The world of Islam,' its authors stated:

> has grown wise in adversity. We are no longer easily duped by specious pretences. Turkey and the Khalifa of Islam have too often been betrayed by European Powers for us to trust in their good faith today. Only by genuine actions can Europe again win the friendship of the Islamic world. The settlement with Turkey must include the release of the *Jazirat-ul-Arab* from all suggestion of control by a non-Muslim Power and the Khalifa's authority over the administrations of the Holy Places must be recognized. It must include the complete independence of the Khalifa in his own capital. It must include the granting to the Muslims of Syria, of Palestine, of Iraq and of Egypt the common right of determination. No other statement will bring peace. These are the only terms on which Islam can with self-respect admit the Powers to friendship. If these terms are refused today they will be offered tomorrow, since Truth must prevail and the Federation of the Islamic peoples of the world grows stronger every day. Let the recent speech of His Majesty the Amir of Afghanistan warn the Powers of Europe that in sympathy Islam is one and undivided as it is in the Faith. Muslims demand only freedom for Islam—freedom to develop the civilization and the culture we know to be true and beautiful. This freedom is our God-given right and we can be content with nothing less. Islamic civilization cannot develop and thrive if it is in bondage, even if the bonds are called Mandates. . . .
>
> *Our Hindu brothers are with us in our struggle. Their numbers give us confidence in our strength and they are our brothers in all truth for the Holy Quran teaches that the friends of the Faith are our brothers* [emphasis added]. In all mankind it is only enemies of the Faith who are not brothers to true Muslims. Our Hindu brothers are doubly so for they love our country as we do, the country is their's as well as our's to love. *And they suffer with us and for us in the common cause Indians have made to win freedom by non-violent Non-cooperation. Together we will win Swaraj—a Swaraj that will enable us to secure justice for Islam*

[emphasis added]. Our enemies seek daily to divide us but let us not fear their intrigues. We have given final proof of our brotherhood in that the Muslims have loyally accepted the dictatorship of that great saint and thinker—Mahatma Gandhi—in our struggle for freedom. Henceforth Hindu-Muslim unity will prevail. We Muslims are called the Army of the Faithful the world over. At this crisis in the history of Islam let us merit the description. Let us remain faithful in thought, word and deed, faithful to our cause, to our country, to the leader we have chosen—Mahatma Gandhi. Though the powers of Europe may seek to deceive us again in the matter of the Khilafat claims, let us have no doubt but that truth will prevail. Making our voice heard and our demands known, let us work loyally for freedom and Swaraj through non-violent non-cooperation. Let us above all remain the Army of the Faithful. India's Muslims have achieved and suffered a great deal for the Faith. Perhaps they believe their suffering has been in vain. But the truth is that through suffering they have grown stronger far more than formerly. And much more remains to be done—much more must be suffered—before we win complete victory—complete freedom for Islam and India. The immediate work before us is that we must—

(1) Collect fifty lakhs for the Angora Fund.
(2) Be prepared to fill the gaols of British India when our Dictator Mahatma Gandhi bids us.
(3) Preserve non-violence at all costs because success depends on this.
(4) Preserve inviolate the sacred spirit of Hindu-Muslim unity.
(5) And last but not least follow Mahatma Gandhi unflinchingly.[42]

Ansari presided over district, provincial and all-India gatherings enlisting popular support for the Khilafat and the Congress movements. He took the lead in convening the All-India Muslim Conference at Lucknow on 21 September, and when the conference observed 17 October as 'Khilafat Day'—a day of mourning and protest—he ensured its success in Delhi. He headed the Anti-Peace Celebration Committee, financed the Khilafat volunteer corps in the capital, and reinvigorated the local Khilafat committee. This committee had come into existence on 5 November 1919 at Ajmal Khan's residence, some months after the founding of the Central Khilafat Committee. It included journalists, *ulama*, lawyers and a few petty traders who had earlier patronized the Anjuman-i Khuddam-i Kaaba. Maulvis

Kifayatullah, Ahmad Said and Nur Muhammad had played an active part in the Rowlatt satyagraha. Abbas Husain, Arif Husain Hasvi, Qazi Abdul Ghaffar and Tajuddin—all journalists—were also catapulted to the fore during the Rowlatt satyagraha.

This unique combination of the Western and the traditionally-educated turned the once benign imperial capital into a stormy centre of activism. The first fortnight of December 1919, reported the government, 'has only been remarkable in Delhi on account of the Khilafat agitation and the anti-peace celebration campaigns'.[43] In November 1919, the Delhi Khilafat Committee convened and hosted an All-India Khilafat Conference—attended by, among others, Gandhi and Shraddhanand. Its decisions—to boycott the peace celebrations planned by government for 13 December and to withhold cooperation with the government unless the Khilafat issue was settled in accordance with Muslim wishes—radicalized the Khilafat movement in Delhi. The other resolution proposing the boycott of British goods did not find favour with Gandhi. So the only resolutions passed thanked him and other Hindus for their support and proposed a boycott of peace celebrations. The extent of Gandhi's influence was also apparent at the Muslim League session in Amritsar in December 1919. In deference to his wishes and as a reciprocal gesture, the League substituted the slaughter of other animals in place of cows on the occasion of Baqr Id. It is noteworthy that Ansari introduced this resolution.

From January to March 1920 the Khilafat protest in Delhi reached a new level of intensity owing to the release of Mohamed Ali and Shaukat Ali as a result of the amnesty which accompanied the royal proclamation of the Montagu-Chelmsford reforms. The Ali Brothers made their first triumphal entry into Delhi on 9 January. In Ansari's open motor car, they were driven through the main streets of the old city decorated with garlands, crescent-emblazoned flags and archways at the various intersections. Khilafat volunteers, stated a government report, 'turned out for their first mass operations on the occasion of the triumphal arrival in Delhi of the Ali Brothers. . . . They took complete charge of the Chandni Chowk and endeavoured violently but unsuccessfully to control the assembled crowds.'[44] Mohamed Ali returned to the city on 16 January and asked Muslims to sacrifice their 'health, wealth and life in the name of God'; Azad said on the same occasion that the proposed Khilafat deputation to the viceroy had no request to make, but would simply inform him of the Islamic obligations.

Ansari was wholly behind the drive to implement non-cooperation. On 10 September he spoke at the Gora Bazar in Ghazipur on non-cooperation.[45] Towards the end of 1920, he presided over the 13th Muslim League session and dwelt at length on *tark-i mawalat*, or the abandonment of friendship with those who were at war with Islam and Muslim countries. He said that a government could only survive with the people's active cooperation or passive acquiescence and the only way of reforming it was to cease cooperation. The principle of *tark-i mawalat*, he emphasized, was a clear and definite injunction of the *sharia* which Muslims had consigned to oblivion. But Gandhi's 'far-sighted mind' saw in this religious principle an effective method of wide application, well-suited to the country's political requirements and in conformity with satyagraha. Ansari reminded his audience that non-cooperation was not only a political and moral necessity but a religious obligation; hence they had a greater responsibility in carrying it out.

Ansari accompanied Jawaharlal to Banaras and helped organize a non-cooperation committee at the university. He did the same in Allahabad, Aligarh and Agra. At the League session, he referred to the 'marvellous patience and fortitude' of the Aligarh students, students who left their College to join the National Muslim University, familiarly known as the Jamia Millia Islamia. Soon, Jamia became Ansari's lifelong passion and he devoted himself to its development.

NON-COOPERATION AT ALIGARH AND THE FOUNDATION OF JAMIA MILLIA ISLAMIA

Addressing a students' gathering at Ahmedabad on 28 September 1920, Gandhi had said:

> If [however] all government schools are left empty I promise that you will see the face of India changed within a month. Nothing else will have the same impact on the public and our rulers as that produced by every student leaving his or her school or college forthwith in a day.[46]

This call to national service and self-sacrifice elicited a ready response among diverse types of students; in fact, statistics for the boycott of schools and colleges were far more impressive than for boycott of courts or resignation from government service. The Congress Civil Disobedience Enquiry Committee noted that the ranks of Congress workers was swelled by 'the more ardent young men whose patriotism and enthusiasm have greatly advanced the cause of the country'.[47] This was true of, among other places, the M.A.O. College at Aligarh where non-cooperation was a spectacular success.

The college of Syed Ahmad Khan's days was ardently pro-British and steered clear of political entanglements. It was hard to be otherwise. Its founder considered education as the sole means for regenerating his community and regarded Anglo-Muslim rapprochement as a necessary condition for its upliftment. The *raison d'être* of his college was to make Muslims 'worthy and useful subjects of the Crown', to groom students to go on to British universities, and to train them for government employment so that they could join the 'heaven born'. Such expectations were fulfilled during Syed Ahmad Khan's lifetime. Students cultivated English habits and tastes, expressed loyalty to the Crown by decorating their rooms with portraits of Queen Victoria and the Prince of Wales, and heeded repeated admonitions to eschew politics. Consequently, Syed Ahmad's crusade against the Congress struck a favourable chord in Aligarh.

In the early years of the twentieth century, however, this academic centre suddenly exploded into political activity confronting the British with a serious movement of dissidence. The agitation against the Nagri resolution of 18 April 1900, followed by the students' strike of February 1907, represented a trend to steer the educated Muslims on a course different from that plotted by Syed Ahmad Khan. Contemporaries pointed out how, just a few years before they appeared, there was not the slightest sign of their imminence in Aligarh. This earlier quiescence, attributed to Syed Ahmad Khan's influence and to the pre-dominance of landed interests in the board of trustees, was gradually replaced by a radicalized posture. The Aligarh students threw to the winds all the caution they had learnt at the feet of the grand old man.

Inspired by the emotionally charged poems of Shibli Nomani and Hasrat Mohani and by the exalted prose of Mohamed Ali's *Comrade*, Azad's *Al-Hilal*, and Zafar Ali Khan's *Zamindar*, political rumpus gathered momentum during the course of World War I. Students raised funds for Turkey and prayed for the success of its armies in the Balkan wars. Four Aligarh graduates were part of Ansari's medical mission and at least one Aligarh Old Boy—Mahendra Pratap—was involved in the 'Silk Letter Conspirarcy' and at the head of the 'Provisional Government' in Kabul. This was not all. The themes of capitalist exploitation, of class conflict, of revolt against imperialism, and of socialism figured in the prose of Sajjad Hyder Yaldaram (1880-1943), Vilayat Ali 'Bambooq' (1885-1918), Abdul Ghaffar, and Abdur Rahman Bijnori (d. 1918), and in the inspiring *ghazals* of Hasrat Mohani and other younger poets at Aligarh. Syed Mohammad Tonki, a leading non-cooperator who later turned to 'Islamic socialism' under the influence of Hasrat Mohani, recalled receiving M.N. Roy's (1887-1954) writings, 'which discussed the Russian revolution, the reality of the socialist system, and the weakening of big empires as a result of capitalist and imperialist exploitation'. He and Kunwar Mohammad Ashraf (1903-62), who rose to political eminence in the 1930s, often discussed 'what a socialist system might achieve in India'.[48] The Progressive Writers' Association, formed in the early 1930s, followed many of the literary and political trends set by writers who were either in or closely connected with Aligarh. Some of its leading lights gave Urdu literature a vital stimulus, a new vigour, and a liberating consciousness.

Amidst this flurry of activity, the non-cooperation programme in September 1920 offered to these radical elements a rallying point.[49] Gandhi fired the first shot. He reached Aligarh on 11 October with Ansari, Azad, Ajmal Khan and the Ali Brothers to address a students' meeting. He spoke haltingly in Hindustani, trying to find the right words but his accent seemed droll to his 'pseudo-sophisticated' audience whose political and economic background and affiliations did not predispose them to accept his radically new doctrine of non-cooperation.[50] He then appealed to the trustees to decline any further government grant, disaffiliate the institution, and reject the charter of the Muslim University.

He urged the Aligarh boys to wash 'their hands clean of an institution acknowledging the aegis of Government that has forfeited all title to the allegiance of Islam and India and to bring into being a larger, nobler and purer Aligarh that would carry out the most wishes of its great founder'.[51]

The trustees were not impressed. They unanimously decided to run their institution on 'old established lines' and 'to make the Mussalmans of India worthy and useful subjects of the British Crown'. Mohamed Ali, the doyen of agitational politics, was able to activate only ten members; the remaining 48 at the meeting rallied round the loyalist principal, Ziauddin Ahmad (1878-1947), a Cambridge Wrangler who expended his talents in administration and petty politicking.

Unruffled by this rebuff, Ansari, Azad Subhani (1873-1926), Azad and the Ali Brothers reappeared in Aligarh on 23 October with a small group of students led by Zakir Husain (1897-1969), a student-lecturer in economics, and Ashraf, who had already left college and joined the non-cooperators. On this occasion, K.G. Saiyidain (1904-71) responded, together with Zakir Husain, to Gandhi's call 'The tumultuous scene at the Students' Union Hall,' recalled one of their contemporaries, 'dwells vividly in one's memory and the din of acclaim that greeted Dr Saiyidain's gesture rings in one's ears to this day'.[52] Mohammad Abid Husain, a graduate student, 'Respectfully I beg to inform you,' wrote to the principal,

> that I have got my doubts removed within the last four or five days, and I am now strong supporter of non-cooperation. The application which I sent to you a few days ago informing you of my intention to appear at the Allahabad University examination for B.A. degree should be considered as withdrawn. I can and will read in your college only in the case it is nationalized [*sic*], otherwise I am ready to face the doom awaiting my non-cooperating brothers. I consider it my duty to intimate you of these views, so that I may not be considered a double game [*sic*] player.[53]

Nurul Hasan of Azamgarh was so enthralled by the speeches of Azad and Azad Subhani that he joined the growing number of non-cooperators.[54] Amidst fiery and passionate speeches, resolutions, promises and assurances, many more students—estimates

Zohra Ansari, Ansari, Halide Edip and Sarojini Naidu.

The architects of Jamia Millia Islamia in Vienna (1925). In front (left to right): Abid Husain, Ansari, Ajmal Khan and Mohammad Mujeeb; (2nd row, left to right): K.A. Hamied, Barkat Ali and Vali Mohammad

range from 200 to 700—enrolled themselves with the Jamia Millia Islamia. Mohamed Ali thus scored a major victory; the college authorities were humbled. The pan-Islamic fervour, combined with the nationalist tide, swept the campus and Syed Ahmad Khan's vision of sustaining the Anglo-Muslim combination through the M.A.O. College was all but shattered.

Carried on the crest of the nationalist tide, the Jamia came into being at Aligarh in those days of 'unlimited dreams, fervent determination and enthusiastic nationalism'.[55] At the opening ceremony (29 October 1920), Mahmud Hasan [his address was read in his absence], explained that Jamia's *raison d'être* was to keep Muslim education free from external control so that 'we may be perfectly immune from pernicious alien influences in our ideas and beliefs, our morals and actions, our character and conduct'. Consequently, besides independence of government aid and control, Jamia evolved a philosophy of education which was consonance with national characteristics, with the Islamic spirit,[56] and with the idea of communal peace and religious understanding.[57] Halide Edip observed in 1935 that Jamia's general aim was to create a harmonious nationhood and that in its goal, if not always in its procedure, it was nearer to the Gandhian movement than any other Muslim institution she had come across.[58] Ansari presided over its destiny until his death in 1936.

Jamia's noticeable contribution was to familiarize the youth with their own cultural heritage without rejecting what was true and useful in the culture of others. In this way the founders hoped to create both a good Muslim in the traditional sense and a good citizen of an independent India. Recalled Mohammad Mujeeb, one of Jamia's prized acquisitions in 1926:

> We agreed that Muslim or non-Muslim, our student should learn to represent the values of his religion, of his moral and cultural tradition, that he should make himself a useful citizen by being cultured, modest, thoughtful and competent. The forms in which these qualities were to express themselves were those of the Indo-Muslim culture of the 19th and 20th century. This was the common culture of the region.[59]

Gandhi, one of Jamia's chief benefactors, went a step further. He hoped that it would interpret Muslim culture in a manner consonant with truth and the requirements of a people, diverse in culture, striving to achieve political unity, and that it would produce men of refinement and character living according to the highest moral standards and serving the people with devotion and sincerity.[60] He also expected the Jamia to be a Muslim stronghold of the national movement. Others nurtured the same expectation. The *Nation* of Lahore opined on 11 February 1925: 'Al-Azhar in Egypt was the birth place of Egyptian nationalism and is today the sternest opponent of all that Lord Allenby stands for and we trust and believe that the National Muslim University at Aligarh . . . will prove to be the Al-Azhar of India.'

On 2 November 1927, Gandhi visited the new campus at Okhla for the first time after it had moved from Karol Bagh. The Ali Brothers, Hakim Ajmal Khan, Ansari, Jamnalal Bajaj and Mahadev Desai accompanied him. Boys sat on either side of the passage leading up to the dais, spinning the *takli.* He looked closely at everything and seemed pleased. He narrated the story of his friend from his Satyagraha (literally, 'soul force') days in South Africa, Ahmad Mahomed Kachhalia, whom he regarded as a true patriot. He then went on to speak of the memorable day, 11 October 1920, when he had urged Mohamed Ali and his friends to start Jamia:

> Even after seven years, I don't feel the least sorry for that nor do I think that I committed a blunder in that. I believe that those who gave up their studies at the Government institutions did a great service to the country. I am sure that when the history of that period in India will be written the historian will no doubt have to write that those who boycotted Government institutions did great good to themselves and to their country . . . I am glad to find here some of the traces of those proud days, and I am very happy that you are trying your utmost to keep the flag flying. Your number is small, but the world never overflowed with good and true men. I ask you not to worry yourselves about the smallness of the number, but to remember that however few you may be the freedom of the country depends on you . . . I do not mind the unsatisfactory state of your finances. In fact I am glad that we should be living from hand to mouth, so that we may all the better cherish our Maker and fear Him.

Again, on a subsequent visit in 1930, he said, 'when I come to the Jamia, I feel I have come home.' He continued to participate in its activities. In 1935 he presided over Edip's lecture. In her words,

> Mahatma Gandhi sat on a cushion, surrounded with charcoal braziers, for the night was cold. Eyes from the packed crowd in the hall and eyes from the packed crowd on the spacious platform were riveted on him. The atmosphere vibrated with a mixture of profound affection and mystic fervour. And the fragile figure was more like Buddha than ever. Though I was delivering a speech on a historic phase of a distant country, I was conscious of a distinct line of thought which had nothing to do with what I was saying. I was thinking about the quality of Mahatma Gandhi's greatness.

'In many matters,' wrote Mujeeb in *Education and Traditional Values*, 'I did not understand him and in many I disagreed with him, but the fact that he had succeeded in identifying himself with India and Indians through his faith in non-violence was a tremendous force compelling me to discover for myself some means of identification.' In 1931, Maulvi Saad Ansari and Devadas Gandhi, Mahatma Gandhi's son, became satyagrahis, while students like Krishna Nair and Husain Hassan courted imprisonment. So did Shafiqur Rahman Kidwai (1901–53), who wore *khaddar* and the Gandhi cap. He had already been jailed during the Non-cooperation movement in 1920; in fact, C. Rajagopalachari had written: 'Of Shafiqur Rahman [Kidwai] of Aligarh, what shall I say,' he noted in his diary. 'I count it as a privilege to know such a man—I have not known a better young man or a more self-restrained, a more truly God-fearing, finer or noble soul.'

Jamia students and teachers spread Gandhi's gospel during the non-cooperation days and popularized the constructive programme in the Bardoli resolution. According to the *Swarajya* of Madras, Jamia trained more than 200 people to keep alive the torch of national idealism.[61] Even afterwards, Jamia stood by the Congress. And when Delhi was torn by communal strife in 1947-8, it remained one of the few islands of peace. In November 1946, the vice-chancellor, Zakir Husain, spoke of the fire of mutual hatred which was ablaze in the country and pleaded with them to put their heads together and extinguish the fire. 'This is not the time,' he said, 'to investigate and determine as to who lighted the fire, how it was lighted. The fire is blazing; it has to be put out.'[62]

Jamia's nationalist stance was, not surprisingly, distasteful to many, including a group of Muslims who called themselves *Khadim-i Millat* (servants of the community). In a lengthy memorandum they indicted their *bete noire*, Ansari and Zakir Husain, for turning Jamia into a Hindu stronghold, pointed out that the syllabi as well as magazines, such as *Payam-i Taleem*, stressed patriotism to the exclusion of Islamic worship (*ibadat*), and concluded that its orientation was prejudicial to Islam and its followers in India.[63] Zakir Husain and his colleagues brushed aside such criticism, which the Muslim League voiced particularly after the Wardha scheme of education was put into practice in the Jamia school.

Dependent on public subscriptions, Jamia managed its affairs in the initial spate of enthusiasm. But its existence was in jeopardy soon thereafter. Many students, drawn in the expectation of a political revolution or bright career prospects, drifted elsewhere; some staff members also deserted, thinking that they had performed their proper share of national service. 'With the receding tide,' observed the *Comrade* of 7 August 1925, 'the little bark was grounded into the shifting sands of ephemeral politics. Tossed now here, now there, it knew not where it was drifting. The helmsman stood aghast not knowing whether it was wise to flee from his post or to stick on where he was and painfully watch the slow but seemingly sure wreck of his little ship.' Mohamed Ali, the editor, had been Jamia's first principal. With his eyes fixed on Aligarh, he believed that the institution had outlived its usefulness.[64] He became increasingly averse to Jamia's nationalist orientation as he gradually developed narrow communitarian concerns.

Acute paucity of funds threatened the Jamia's existence. Though initially propped up by public contributions and by a monthly grant from the Central Khilafat Committee, these sources gradually dried up and the Jamia was hard pressed to pay salaries to its teachers and provide the minimum of facilities to the 225 students in 1923. Yet their enthusiasm was not dampened. Determined to make the Jamia an example and an inspiration in educational renaissance, the teachers, mostly dedicated to the cause of education, were out to convince themselves as well as others that they were part of a free national establishment and the symbol of a novel experiment in education.[65]

Some time during 1925, Ansari and Ajmal Khan, while in Europe, prevailed on three students in Germany—Zakir Husain, Abid Husain (1896-1978) and Mujeeb—to join Jamia. 'We asked several questions,' recalled Abdul Hamied (1898-1972), a nephew of A.M. Khwaja, 'about the Jamia and we pledged our loyalty to these great leaders and thanked them to have kept Jamia alive.'[66] In January 1926, they left the shores of Europe to join an institution with an uncertain future. Zakir Husain, a Pathan from Qaimganj, had taught Economics at Aligarh before joining the Berlin University where he wrote a thesis on the agrarian policies of the British in India; Abid Husain studied at the same University and researched on the educational philosophy of Herbert Spencer (1820-1903); in Jamia, he taught, administered and wrote on India's composite cultural traditions;[67] Mujeeb, cousin of Khaliquzzaman and son of a successful Lucknow barrister, Mohammad Naseem, studied History at Oxford and printing in Germany (1922-4). Halide Edip met him and Zakir Husain at Munich in 1923. 'With this austere young man [Zakir Husain], so obviously mature,' she reminiscenced, 'was another young student, Mujeeb by name. He was utterly different from Zakir Husain, with a delicate physique, refined features, thoughtful, tortured eyes. A temperament of artistic nature was written all over him. But outwardly he had the same quiet way, the same determined look as his companion. These were the first young Indians to make me wonder whether the talkative, versatile Indian students I had hitherto met, with their emphatic and passionate reactions, were really typical: certainly they were as different from these taciturn young men as Nordics and Latins.'[68]

Back home, a group of selfless teachers, Shafiqur Rahman Kidwai, A.G. Kellat (1871-1951), Aslam Jairajpuri (1882-1955), Hafiz Fayyaz Ahmad (1897-1964), Saeed Ansari (1904-84) and Irshadul Haq (1901-74) included, pledged to serve the Jamia for at least twenty years on a monthly salary of not more than Rs 150. They worked amidst and through poverty. Without the shelter of houses, they pegged away in tents and under the open sky. Yet, they cheerfully faced the hard trials 'in an atmosphere of freedom, enthusiasm and an indestructible optimism'. Zakir Husain remembered those years of deprivation as 'days of joy'. 'There was a longing to build', he said, 'and nothing to build with. There were no resources, only the will to achieve. In the eyes of every child who came to us we saw the image of freedom. Every child seemed to give us all that we had been deprived of by political enslavement.'[69] Some financial assistance came from outside, but it was not enough. In January 1928, Gandhi gave assurances of putting Jamia on a sound financial basis,[70] and launched a fund drive in memory of Ajmal Khan.[71] For the purpose, he urged G.D. Birla's (1894-1984) for a 'gift' of Rs 75,000.[72]

In its years of grinding poverty, Ansari turned out to be Jamia's saviour. Succeeding Ajmal Khan as *Amir-i Jamia* (Chancellor), he led a delegation to raise funds in March 1923, proposed diverting part of the Khilafat funds to the Jamia,[73] and pleaded for rescuing the institution from a serious financial crisis at the Gaya Khilafat Conference the same year. The Aga Khan, a patron of the Aligarh College, offered a modest annual grant of Rs 1,200; Jamnalal Bajaj (1889-1942) donated Rs 10,000; Birla grudgingly gave Rs 50,000.[74] The nawabs and taluqdars of U.P., who were otherwise the main benefactors of Muslim educational centres, avoided helping a Congress-backed institution. Other affluent groups, on the other hand, considered the Jamia an improvized rival to the more established university at Aligarh. They pinned their hopes on the 'Muslim Oxford' where a degree could still be a passport to government service.

Ignored by the Muslims and only marginally backed by the Congress, the Jamia faced the prospect of closure in the early 1930s. Yet Ansari did not despair. He was a doer. Instead of worrying he worked. Nothing was more characteristic of him than his tenacity, the refusal to let go of a problem until he could hit on a way of solving it. With a begging bowl he went around the country collecting funds and explaining his mission. He possessed prodigious energy and spent it prodigally as if he knew he would not be there long. In May 1933, he wrote to Abdul Majid Khwaja, Principal of the Jamia, in a state of anguish:

You are fully aware of the tremendous difficulties and the untold hardships which the Jamia has gone through since 1930 after my going to jail. The Hyderabad grant which was just about to be started was stopped and the grant from Bhopal was also stopped. . . . You can imagine in the absence of even the meagre allowances given to the teachers of Jamia how poor and destitute and half-starved they must be. It is really pitiable to see their plight and yet like brave fellows, they are going on. Now, however, there is a chance of re-starting both the Hyderabad and Bhopal grants if only we would put in all our best efforts.[75]

Ansari's efforts bore fruit; generous donations poured in from Bhopal, Hyderabad, Rampur and Madras. This enabled him to strengthen Jamia's educational programmes, organize lectures of leading educationists and invite representatives from Turkey to promote cultural friendship and understanding between different peoples and to keep Indians actively interested in great movements of the outside world. Though he did not pretend to be an intellectual, he respected men of intellect, whatever their backgrounds and knew how to make the best use of their brains. Thus Rauf Bey, the Turkish soldier and statesman, Dr Behdgt Wahby, the scientist, and Halide Edip, the educationist, novelist and historian of the national revival in Turkey, lectured at the Jamia. Edip, whom Ansari met at Constantinople in 1913, impressed most. Her eight lectures, delivered in January-February 1935, had a marked impact on her audience. Ansari extolled her virtues as a novelist, a social philosopher and an educationist.

She has worn military uniforms and served at the headquarters of the nationalist army, with the din and the smoke of a grim battle around her. She has also been a rebel against customs and traditions that fettered life . . . she has loved and served her people, but with a large heartedness that could look beyond them to the greater human family; she has thrown herself heart and soul into the struggle of her nation for life and liberty, but never ceased to be aware of the worldwide moral and cultural conflicts of which it formed a part. She speaks, therefore, with greater authority than any person living on the fundamental problems on whose solution will depend the future of the East.[76]

Ansari's abiding interest in the Jamia was, in the main, due to its secular and composite ideology. He was keen to keep it going as a vibrant symbol of the Khilafat and non-cooperation days.

To him, the college was much more than an experiment in basic education; it represented the national urge to participate in the larger educational and political processes and contribute to the intellectual awakening of the less privileged sections of society. He wanted the Jamia to be a model Muslim educational centre and a hub of nationalist activities to serve his ideal of promoting Hindu-Muslim integration.

Ansari's initiatives were not wasted. Much of his work has endured. The Jamia remains true to at least some of the goals set by its benefactors. Led by Zakir Husain and ably aided by his two comrades—Mujeeb and Abid Husain—it has chartered a course which was consistent with Ansari's vision. In the 1930s and the 1940s, they accepted Gandhi's guidance in working for an institution entirely free of British control and accepted him as their leader and guide in politics without being lured by office, power and authority. And when Delhi was tormented by bloody communal riots during Partition, the Jamia teachers and students organized relief for the victims and helped heal the communal wounds.[77] Ansari had done the same during his eventful public life; his successors at Jamia followed the example set by their chief benefactor.

THE KHILAFATISTS IN DISARRAY

The Khilafatists in India gave the impression of being cohesive, inspired by a common cause and motivated by mutually shared ideals. The deliberations of the Khilafat Conferences, however, reveal their personal feuds and ideological wranglings. The *ulama*, for instance, were at odds with each other exposing the fissures in their apparently solid phalanx of orthodoxy. Though leading *ulama* of Firangi Mahal and Deoband buried their differences temporarily to keep up the semblance of unity, their zealous followers conducted their bitter doctrinal debates unabashedly. Likewise, their alliance with the modern-educated allies was ruptured on the method and strategy of conducting the Khilafat movement. Most *ulama* criticized the subservient posture of Ansari and the Ali Brothers towards Gandhi and the Congress. Many Western-educated Muslims were, on the other

With overseas guests.

Ansari and Rauf Bey, president of the Angora National Assembly, with a Jamia student

Ansari with Rauf Bey

With the Egyptian guests

hand, not just uneasy with the Muslim divines but were wary of their growing political ascendancy.

The first potential threat to the alliance surfaced early in 1921 when differences cropped up over the future course of the non-cooperation movement. Was it to be conducted on the familiar lines of non-violence, as advocated by Gandhi? Or, was the use of force a viable method for pressurizing the government? Earlier, all had agreed to follow Gandhi's ideal of satyagraha. But, in the summer of 1921, some people began to question the efficacy of his methods. Some *ulama* expressed dissatisfaction with the limited vigour with which he had prosecuted the Khilafat agitation and wanted its scope to be defined and extended according to the *sharia*. At the Central Khilafat Committee and the Jamiyat al-ulama meetings on 21-22 December 1921, considerable friction occurred before Ansari, Azad and Ajmal Khan persuaded the *ulama* to accept that the time was not yet ripe for civil disobedience. They were mollified for the time being. But the showdown came at the end of the year when Hasrat Mohani put up a plucky fight for the 'complete independence' resolution. Gandhi threw his weight against this move, arguing that it could not be incorporated in the Congress creed without Hindu-Muslim unity. The Congress backed Gandhi, as did the Muslim League Subjects Committee. Hasrat's resolution was rejected by thirty-six votes to twenty-three.[78]

Ansari softened the acerbities that embittered politics and made for divisions and strife in the Congress-Khilafatist axis. But when matters came to a head, he came on the side of Gandhi and the Congress. He realized that, if Muslim religious enthusiasm went out of hand, the ensuing violence would have communal repercussions. Their carefully structured alliance would crumble for good and with it Muslim hopes of saving the Khilafat and the Holy Places. Thus when Mohamed Ali raised the spectre of an Afghan invasion in early 1921, Ansari quickly dispelled the fears of some Hindu activists. Again, when Abdul Bari delivered an intemperate speech on 3 March 1922, Ansari checked his frenzy which threatened to destroy his aim of building bridges between pan-Islamism and nationalism, a lesson he had learnt from Jamaluddin Afghani and his disciples in India. The causes of

Islam and India, according to him, had to go hand-in-hand and Muslims had therefore to continue to work for freedom, which was essential if they were to secure justice for Islam. The goal of redressing the Khilafat grievance was by no means enough; Ansari's sights, as always, were centred on India.[79]

On the complex and divisive issue of council entry, Ansari refused to join the Congress-Swaraj-Khilafat party under the leadership of C.R. Das (1870-1925) and Motilal Nehru. His reasons, as indeed those of Rajagopalachari (1879-1972) and K.R. Iyengar (1859-1923), were set out in the Report of the Congress Civil Disobedience Enquiry Committee (1922). All three argued that council entry violated the principle of non-cooperation, that the people opposed any change in the Congress programme, that entry into councils would be futile, and that the avowed purpose of obstructing all measures, whether good or bad, was 'obnoxious' to the principle and the spirit of Gandhi's movement.[80] Thus, in November 1922 Ansari challenged Motilal Nehru's motion in favour of council entry and secured an adjournment of the discussion until the Gaya Congress in December. Working hand-in-hand with Gandhi, he continued to favour the no-change party and worked to prevent party divisions from becoming deeper. This had been the refrain of his speech at the special Congress session on 15 September 1923. While reaffirming his opposition to council entry, he pleaded for unity in the Congress camp. 'It is a truism,' he said, 'but would bear repetition that no work, which requires our united energies and single-minded efforts, is possible unless we first remove other pre-occupying differences among ourselves.'[81]

NOTES

1. Nikkie R. Keddie, *Sayyid Jamal ad-Din 'al Afghani': A Political Biography* (Los Angeles, 1972), p. 130.
2. It was exemplified, for instance, in the following poem:

Ae barq aaj shola-fishan kyon nahin hai tu
Ae raad aaj garm fughan kyon nahin hai tu
Ae abr aaj girya kunan kyon nahin hai tu
Darya-i qahr aaj rawan kyon nahin hai tu
Islam aaj kufr ke narghe men aa gaya
Badal siyah rang ka Kaaba pe chha gaya

O the thunderbolt why doesn't you scatter flames?
O the lightening why thou wailest not?
O the clouds why weepest not thou?
Why is it that the river of curse is a frozen puddle and flows not?
Islam has been swamped and overwhelmed by the unbelief
And the Kaaba has been engulfed by darkness.

Proscribed Publications (8), IOL. Also, see 142, 152, 153.

3. R.P. Tripathi, *Some Aspects of Muslim Administration in India* (Allahabad, 1936), p. 37; Mohibbul Hasan (ed.), *Waqa-i Manazil-i Rum: Diary of a Journey to Constantinople* (Delhi, 1968).
4. *Akhbar-i Am*, 14 March 1895, Punjab Native Newspaper Reports.
5. Quoted in Peter Hardy, *The Muslims of British India* (Cambridge, 1972), p. 177. W.S. Blunt (1840-1922) was told on the eve of his visit to India that he should not say anything against the Sultan of Turkey because his name was now venerated in India as it has not formerly been. W.S. Blunt, *India Under Ripon: A Private Diary* (London, 1909), p. 13. Halil Halid was told by an Englishman who had followed the Prince of Wales during his tour around the colonies that the further one went from Turkey the greater was the influence of the Sultan among Muslims. Halil Halid, *The Diary of a Turk* (London, 1903) and *The Crescent Versus the Cross* (London, 1907).
6. *Jasus* (Agra), 14 July 1906; *Al-Aziz* (Agra), 28 July 1906, United Provinces Newspaper Reports.
7. Afghani was in India from 1857 to 1865. He came again in 1879 to spend three years in Bombay, Hyderabad, Bhopal and Calcutta. The purpose of his visit was to meet with all the *navvabs* and princes and *ulama* and grandees of that land and to explain to them one by one the results that are manifested from unity and solidarity in the whole world and the injuries that have appeared from division and disunity; and to caress their ears with the mystery of the *hadith*, the faithful are brothers; and to express inspiring and prudent words and to attract the friendship and cooperation of the learned and the eloquent; and to breathe into them the new spirit of love of nationality and to rend the curtain of their neglect to explain to them the place of the luminous Sultanate in the world of Islam; and to reveal and make manifest to this group the fact that the perpetuation of religion depends on the perpetuation of this government. And in all the mosques of the famous cities I shall light a flame in their inner hearth by means of appealing sermons and *hadiths* of the Best of the Prophets, and I shall together burn out their patience and long-suffering.

   Keddie, *Sayyid Jamal ad-Din 'al-Afghani'*, pp. 134-5.
8. Aziz Ahmad, *Studies in Islamic Culture in the Indian Environment* (London, 1964), pp. 55-6; Keddie, op. cit., p. 167.

9. Fazlur Rahman, *Islam* (London, 1966), p. 227; Anwar Moazzam, *Jamal al-Din al-Afghani: A Muslim Intellectual* (Delhi, 1983), p. xiii. His main contribution, according to Moazzam, was in providing a 'broad intellectual framework' for redefining the relationship between Islam and the changing world.
10. Keddie, *Sayyid Jamal ad-Din 'al-Afghani'*, p. 26. Elie Kedourie has argued that Afghani's reputation was to a large extent posthumous and was the work of disciples, or else of academic writers and publicists, 'eager to discover trends and precursors' to magnify the importance of their subjects. Elie Kedourie, *Afghani and Abduh: An Essay on Religious Unbelief and Political Activism in Modern Islam* (London, 1966), p. 3. This is not right, for there is adequate evidence to indicate his charisma on his contemporaries and greater evidence of his impact on subsequent political and intellectual movements in Muslim countries. Aziz Ahmad and Keddie also write of Afghani's limited hold. According to them, the people he met exercised no political or religious influence among Muslims, and his articles, published in an obscure journal of Hyderabad, did not cause any stir at the time. But their own evidence does not warrant this conclusion; in fact, the works of Blunt point to Afghani's influence. Kedourie's cynical view of Afghani becoming a 'British agent' is typical of his attempt to denigrate him and to underplay the role of ideology in politics.
11. Shibli Nomani, *Safarnamah-i Misr-o-Shaam* (Agra, 1894), pp. 129-32. Aziz Ahmad, *Islamic Modernism in India and Pakistan 1857-1964* (London, 1967), p. 129.
12. Albert Hourani, *Arabic Thought in the Liberal Age 1798-1939* (Oxford, 1970), pp. 118-19.
13. H.N. Mitra (ed.), *The Indian Annual Register (IAR)*, January-July 1923, vol. I, p. 921.
14. L.R. Gordon-Polonskya, 'Ideology of Muslim Nationalism', Hafeez Malik (ed.), *Iqbal: Poet Philosopher of Pakistan* (New York, 1971), pp. 115-16. For Afghani's influence, see Mohammad Iqbal, *The Reconstruction of Religious Thought in Islam*, p. 92, quoted in Ahmad, *Islamic Modernism*, pp. 129, 136.
15. Ahmad, *Studies in Islamic Culture*, p. 67 and his *Islamic Modernism*, pp. 129, 136. For Afghani's influence on Qazi Abdul Ghaffar, one of Azad's devoted followers, see Abdul Ghaffar, *Jamaluddin Afghani*, in Urdu (Delhi, 1941). Afghani's stay in India is referred to on pp. 12-13, 16-17, 35-7. Also, Annemarie Schimmel, *Gabriel's Wing: A Study into the Religious Ideas of Sir Muhammad Iqbal* (London, 1963), p. 21.
16. *Al-Ahkamul Quraniya mavalat-al Burtaniya* (Delhi, n.d.), p. 15; Pirzada (ed.), *Foundations of Pakistan*, vol. I, p. 547.
17. Hourani, *Arabic Thought in the Liberal Age*, p. 118.
18. Keddie, *Sayyid Jamal al-Din 'al-Afghani'*, pp. 155, 159-60.

19. Ibid., p. 160; N.R. Keddie, *Islamic Response to Imperialism: Political and Religious Writings of Sayyid Jamal al-Din 'Al-Afghani'* (California, 1968), p. 59.
20. Pirzada (ed.), *Foundations of Pakistan*, vol. 1, pp. 545-6.
21. W.I. Watson, Muhammad Ali and the Khilafat Movement' (unpublished M.A. thesis, 1955, McGill University), p. 64.
22. Muhammad Ali, *His Life, Service and Trial* (Madras, n.d.), p. 151.
23. *IQR*, July-December 1923, p. 30.
24. Mushirul Hasan, *Mohamed Ali: Ideology and Politics* (Delhi, 1982), p. 115.
25. Ibid.
26. 7 August 1926, Moonje Dossier, Pad No. 35, National Library, Calcutta.
27. S.R. Mayers to A.G. Shirreff, deputy commissioner, 25 February 1921, GAD, F. No. 50, 1921, Box No. 135, UPSA. All subsequent references, unless otherwise stated, are drawn from the same file.
28. Nehru, *An Autobiography*, p. 76.
29. Note on Rae Bareli disturbances, op. cit.
30. M.H. Siddiqi, *Agrarian Unrest in North India: The United Provinces 1918-22* (Delhi, 1978), p. 149; Kapil Kumar, *Peasants in Revolt: Tenants, Landlords, Congress and the Raj in Oudh* (Delhi, 1984), pp. 146, 165.
31. This idea was beautifully summed up in the verses of Mohammad Haider, a school teacher in Pilibhit. He wrote:

    Jama do qaum ka sikka baja do deen ka danka
    Mohamed, Shaukat-o Gandhi ke pairokaar ho jao
    Swadeshi se karo raghbat bidesi se karo nafrat
    Ki jis se muflisee ho door aur zardaar ho jao

    Let the respect for the nation be restored
    And the trumpet of the faith heralded
    Follow Mohamed (Ali), Shaukat and Gandhi
    Adopt all that is Swadeshi and shun that which is from outside
    So that you may remove poverty and achieve self-reliance.

    Proscribed Publications (43). Also, see the collection of poems in *Bulbulan-i Hurriyat* in Proscribed Publication (47). The collection was published by the Khilafat Committee in Jaunpur.
32. Police Dept., F. No. 51-N, 1921, UPSA: Note by Lakhte Husain and Jagannath, 28 January 1921, op. cit.
33. Khizar Humayun Ansari, 'The Emergence of Muslim Socialists and their Ideas in India Between 1917 and 1947' (Ph.D. thesis, University of London, 1985), pp. 83-5.
34. Home Poll. B, January 1919, 160-3, NAI; WRDCI (January 1920), Home Poll. Deposit, February 1920, 52, NAI.
35. Zahur Ahmad to G.N. Misra, 26 July 1920, F. No. 18, 1920, AICC Papers (Suppl.), NMML. In distant Malabar every mosque became a centre of

Congress Khilafat activity. Taluq and district level leaders toured the Muslim centres with Muslim colleagues, organization and Khilafat volunteers. E.M.S. Namboodripad, *How I Became a Communist* (Trivandrum, 1976), p. 35.

36. *Tribune*, 13 October 1919; *Fateh* (Delhi), 1 July 1920; Shraddhanand, *Inside Congress* (Bombay, 1946), pp. 68-70.
37. Abul Hayat, *Mussalmans of Bengal* (Calcutta, 1966), p. 37.
38. In the *Report on Indian Constitutional Reforms* (1918), communal representation was condemned on the ground that it perpetuated class distinctions, stereotyped existing relations, and constituted a serious hindrance to the development of the self-governing principle. Speech by Ansari at the All-India Muslim League, December 1918, Home Poll. A, March 1919, 251-9, NAI.
39. The pact was concluded between the representatives of the Congress and the Muslim League. The Congress agreed to separate electorates, to the principle of Muslim representation in the legislative councils and to weightage of seats to Muslims in excess of their proportion of the population in areas where they were in a minority.
40. Quoted in Ferrel, op. cit., p. 201.
41. Ibid.
42. Bamford, *Histories*, pp. 186-7, 194-5.
43. Home Poll. D, January 1920, 44, NAI.
44. *History of the Non-Cooperation and Khilafat Movements in Delhi*, p. 10; Minault, *The Khilafat Movement*, p. 85.
45. Ansari's speech 'clearly has attempted to bring into hatred or contempt or attempted to excite disaffection towards the Govt. . . . His purpose admittedly is to paralyse the Govt. And he says that no Govt. can carry on its operations when the inhabitants decide to give it no assistance and he preaches that no assistance should be given.' The official proposed Ansari's prosecution. Note on 2 October 1920, Home Police, F. No. 16/7, Box No. 58, UPSA.
46. *CWMG*, vol. 18, pp. 297, 280.
47. *IQR*, 1922-23, vol. 1, p. 84.
48. Syed Mohammad Tonki, in Horst Kruger (ed.), *Kunwar Mohammad Ashraf: An Indian Scholar and Revolutionary 1903-1962* (Berlin, 1966), p. 344.
49. K.M. Ashraf on Himself, in ibid., p. 391.
50. This is based on K.G. Saiyidain's memory of Gandhi's visit. He came into personal contact with the Mahatma in 1937 at the First National Education Conference in Sevagram. See *Gandhian Ideas on Education: Their Relevance to our Times* (New Delhi, n.d.), pp. 6-7.
51. *CWMG*, vol. 18, p. 369.
52. S. Bashiruddin, 'Dr K.G. Saiyidain: An Appraisal of Personality and Ideals' and K.A. Abbas, 'Thanks, Bhaijan!', in S. Abid Husain and Abdur

Rashid (eds), *Commemoration Volume* (Delhi, n.d.), pp. 45, 65. Referring to the speech made by Saiyidain on the occasion, his brother Khwaja Ahmad Abbas recalled: 'The impact of that speech must have left a deep impression on my subconscious because since then, even as a boy, I could not be swayed by the passion-filled arguments of the communalists. If the secular and humanistic concept of life has remained an integral part of my own personal credo, I owe it first of all to that speech.' Also, K.A. Abbas, *I am not an Island: An Experiment in Autobiography* (Delhi, 1977), pp. 50-1.

53. M.A. Husain to Ziauddin, 24 October 1920, Sir Syed Academy, Aligarh Muslim University, Aligarh. For details, see Mushirul Hasan, 'Nationalist and Separatist Trends in Aligarh, 1915-1947', *The Social and Economic History Review,* January-March 1985.
54. Nurul Hasan to Ziauddin Ahmad, n.d., ibid.
55. W.C. Smith, *Modern Islam in India* (Lahore, 1943), p. 150. Jamia's history is traced by one of its teachers, Abdul Ghaffar Mudholi, *Jamia ki Kahani,* in two volumes (Delhi, 1965).
56. *Jamia Millia Prospectus 1924-25* (Aligarh, n.d.), pp. 1-2.
57. Zakir Husain, quoted in Abid Raza Bedar, *Mata-i Faqir* (Delhi, 1969); Sheila McDonough, 'The Spirit of the Jamia Millia Islamia as exemplified in the writings of S. Abid Husain, R.D. Baird (ed.), *Religion in Modern India* (Delhi, 1981); Freeland Abbot, *Islam and Pakistan* (New York, 1968), pp. 135-6, 145.
58. Edip, *Inside India,* p. 95.
59. *The Jamia College: Its history and Significance* (Delhi, n.d.), p. 7.
60. Ibid., pp. 1-2. As its first *Amir-i Jamia,* Ajmal Khan wanted the students to know each other's culture: 'the firm foundation of a united Indian nationhood depends on this mutual understanding'. Cited in Metcalf, op. cit., p. 25.
61. 23 January, quoted in *Prospectus 1924-25,* p. 55.
62. M. Mujeeb, 'Dr Zakir Husain and the Jamia Millia Islamia', V.S. Mathur (ed.), *Zakir Husain: Educationist and Teacher* (Delhi, 1969), p. 45.
63. *Millat-i Islamia awr Jamia Millia Islamia, Delhi* (Calcutta, 1941), Quaid-e-Azam Academy, Karachi.
64. Mohamed Ali said in September 1923: 'I never concerned of the Jamia's growth and permanence at all. The Jamia's existence today is rather like that of the refugees and the Prophet's helpers at Medina who were lying in wait for the conquest of Mecca. Our real objective is Aligarh which some day we shall conquer.' Quoted in A.G. Noorani, *President Zakir Husain: A Quest for Excellence* (Bombay, 1967), p. 25. On this point, see Mujeeb, Oral History transcript (407), p. 35, NMML.
65. M. Mujeeb, *Dr Zakir Husain: A Biography* (Delhi, 1972), p. 40. Details of initial financial support and later difficulties are discussed in *Jamia Millia Islamia: Some Appreciations* (Aligarh, 1923), p. 1; Mujeeb, 'Dr

Zakir Husain and the Jamia Millia', Mathur (ed.), op. cit., p. 38; FR, first half of February 1923, Home Poll. F. No. 25. 1923, NAI.

66. K.A. Hamied, *An Autobiography: A Life to Remember* (Bombay, 1972), pp. 45-6. Mujeeb. Oral History transcript, pp. 30-1.
67. His scholarly pursuits were impressive. He translated a large number of German, English and French works into Urdu. These included Gandhi's *An Experiment with Truth*, Nehru's *Autobiography, Glimpses of World History* and *Discovery of India*, Immanuel Kant's *Critique for Pure Reason,* Bernard Shaw's *St. Joan,* Edward Spangler's *Psychology of Youth*, and Goethe's *Faust*. For an appreciation of his role in Jamia and the list of his publications, see *Abid Husain Felicitation Volume* (Delhi, 1974); pp. 11-12; McDonough, op. cit.
68. Edip, *Inside India*, p. 97. Gandhi described Mujeeb as 'one of the purest minded young men whom I have the pleasure of knowing'. To Mohammad Naseem, November 1929, *CWMG*, vol. XLII, p. 117.
69. *Jamia Silver Jubilee,* op. cit., pp. 2-3; also, Saiyidain's convocation address at Jamia, 10 November 1965, quoted in Malik Ram, Abid Raza Bedar (eds), *Afkar-i Saiyiadain* (Delhi, 1978), pp. 12-15. In 1923 a number of distinguished scholars served on the teaching faculty. Khwaja Abdul Hai gave lessons in *tafsir*, Aslam Jairajpuri taught *seerat* and Islamic history, Abdul Majid Khwaja taught law, Zakir Husain lectured on economics, while Jwala Prasad Singhal, S.M. Tonki and Moazzam Ali taught Hindu ethics, Urdu and History/Political Science, respectively. The Syndicate of Jamia comprised, among others, Ajmal Khan, Ansari, the Ali Brothers, Khwaja, Sherwani—also the Secretary (*Nazim*), Moazzam, H.M. Hayat who was also the Registrar (*Musajjil*), Nawab Ismail Khan, Syed Mahmud, Hasrat Mohani, Azad Subhani, Syed Sulaiman Nadwi, Abdul Majid of Budaun and Amir Mustafa Khan. See Mudholi, *Jamia ki Kahani*, appendix, and K.G. Saiyidain, Oral History transcript (3), NMML.
70. Message to Jamia Millia Islamia, 9 January 1928; telegram to M.M. Malaviya, 9 January 1928, *CWMG*, vol. 35, p. 449.
71. In his appeal, Gandhi wrote:

    In my humble opinion, it is the duty of Hindus and Mussalmans who believe in unity to perpetuate Hakim Saheb's memory in the tangible form proposed. It is their duty to ensure the stability of the Jamia, for it was a creation of the times when it was thought that the two communities were united for ever. And if the non-cooperating national colleges do not stand for, work for and finally ensure unity, nothing else can or will. I hope, therefore, that all the lovers of unity will liberally subscribe to the Fund. There are today two hundred students studying in the central institution and seventy-four in the city branch. There are moreover two night-schools which draw nearly two hundred students. The Jamia has a staff of twenty-three workers. The highest salary being paid is Rs 265, the lowest being Rs 35. The idea constantly before the Principal is to have volunteers who would draw just enough for their wants. The salaries amount in all to Rs 2,300 per month, the house rent is Rs 425 per month. The total monthly expenditure is Rs 4,800. The regular income, including boarding fees Rs 1,300, is Rs 2,700. There is thus a deficit of Rs 2,100. This was somehow met whilst Hakim Saheb was alive. Before the teachers create for themselves a name and a prestige enough to command help, the deficit must be met by the public. And the memorial cannot be considered lasting till the Jamia has a building of its own. The subscribers will, therefore, in deciding the amount of donation bear in mind what is required.

Young India, 19 January 1928, ibid., p. 4.

72. Gandhi to Birla, 7 February 1928, G.D. Birla, *Bapu: A Unique Association* (Bombay, 1977), vol. 1, pp. 85-6; also Gandhi to Birla, 21 February 1925, G.D. Birla, *In the Shadow of the Mahatma: A Personal Memoir* (Calcutta, 1953), pp. 8-9.
73. Appeal (with Shafee Daoodi), August 1928, Habibur Rahman Ludhianvi Papers, NMML.
74. Birla was pestered by Gandhi to give away the money. His own impression of Jamia was less favourable. He felt that it was 'more a communal institution than a national one. . . . Everywhere you smell nothing but Muslim culture.' But he allowed Gandhi to 'pay any sum which he decides as a suitable amount from all points of view'. Birla to Mahadev Desai, 17 March 1928, *Bapu*, vol. 1, p. 90.
75. Ansari to Khwaja, 2 May 1933, Hasan (ed.), *Muslims and the Congress*, p. 138.
76. Edip, *Conflict of East and West in Turkey*, p. iii.
77. Begum Anis Kidwai, *Azadi Ki Chaon Me* (Delhi, 1980), pp. 44, 47, 53-5, 61. This is an excellent account of the communal holocaust in the aftermath of the Partition of India.
78. The preceding paragraphs in the conclusion are based on my *Nationalism and Communal Politics in India*. The process is also discussed in Minault, *The Khilafat Movement*, pp. 186-8, Robinson, *Separatism*, chapter nine.
79. Minault, op.cit., p. 180.
80. Ravinder Kumar and D.N. Panigrahi (eds.), *Selected Works of Motilal Nehru* (Delhi, 1984), vol. 3, pp. 56-8, 61-2.
81. F. No. 9, 1923, AICC Papers.

6

The Heading Touch

> Hindu-Muslim unity. We have talked of it for years. The unity, so rich in aspiration, is still poor in practical life. . . . It must be confessed Hindu-Muslim unity is not strong enough, not deep enough, yet.
>
> *New Times* (Bombay), 14 April 1923

> It has to be mournfully confessed that at no time in our national history the sapling of Hindu-Muslim unity wore a more sickly or anaemic look than it does now.
>
> *Young India*, 10 May 1923, p. 159

THE YEAR 1921 was one of feverish political activity. The non-cooperation campaign generated unprecedented enthusiasm. In the joyful din of bold and determined opposition to government, the forces of unity and cohesion acquired strength, a fact which enabled the non-cooperators to achieve greater support for their campaign. But the suspension of civil disobedience in February 1922, followed by widespread Hindu-Muslim rioting, destroyed the edifice of unity. The over-inflated bubble of popular expectation burst and the disappointment was as overwhelming as the previous optimism had been exaggerated. 'Complete Hindu-Muslim unity which ought to have been a settled fact today,' lamented Ansari in September 1923, 'is conspicuous by its absence. Years of hard work in various fields have failed not only to make unity a permanent and solid factor of civic life but even to check the present recrudescence of communal discord, the neglected disease which now threatens the very existence of Indian nationalism.'[1]

While visiting Punjab in March 1923, Das, Motilal, Sarojini Naidu (1879-1949), Azad and Ajmal Khan found the situation virtually beyond hope. They noticed that each community had practically arrayed itself in an armed camp against the other.[2] Trouble had blown up at Multan during Muharram in April 1923 as a sequel to a violent outburst a year earlier.[3] Panipat and Amritsar were ablaze from April to July. 'It was a cruel irony of fate,' wrote the *Servant of India*, 'that the fourth anniversary of the Jallianwala Bagh, where four years ago common aspirations and common sufferings brought the Hindus and Mussulmans closer together than ever before, Amritsar should have witnessed a serious Hindu-Muslim riot and that British soldiers should have been called in to protect members of each community against the hooligans of the other.'[4] Scenes of bloodshed and strife afflicted Delhi on 11-12 July 1924. On 9-10 September, a major outbreak at Kohat in the North-West Frontier Province[5] led Gandhi to undertake a 21-day fast on 18 September 1924. The Congress drew up plans to renew the Hindu-Muslim *entente* and adopted pious resolutions on communal harmony. The meeting at Delhi in September 1923 was hosted by Ansari and chaired by Azad. The outcome was the formation of a committee, with Ansari and Lajpat Rai (1865-1928) as its members. These two individuals, representing two very different ideological strands, and united only by common loyalty to the Congress, set out to draft a 'National Pact'.

Some of the features of the pact were attainment of complete swaraj, establishment of a federal and democratic government and full religious liberty—of belief, worship, propaganda, association and education. Provision was made for joint electorates with reservation of seats for the minorities in proportion to their population in the constituencies. On cow-slaughter, the playing of music before mosques and the route of religious processions, Muslims were urged to give up cow-slaughter except on Baqr Id, music in front of places of public worship was forbidden, and the local conciliatory boards were asked to determine the route and time of religious processions.[6]

In marked contrast to these provisions—many of which formed part of the 1916 Congress-Muslim League scheme—Das, with a generosity that seemed extravagant, made large promises to the Muslims in Bengal.[7] While Ansari and Lajpat Rai proposed communal representation in the legislatures alone, Das extended it to local bodies and appointments to government posts. Das' terms relating to cow-slaughter and music before mosques also favoured the Muslims.

The Das pact, concluded with the obvious intention of buying Muslim support at the ballot box and in the Bengal legislative council, impinged on the interests of the Hindu landed, commercial and professional classes who faced the cheerless prospect of losing their advantages to a relatively new class of Muslim professional men and up-country merchants.[8] Its author's eloquent pleading that he did not concede to Muslims 'more than they were entitled to get in fairness and justice', failed to convince most educated Bengali Hindus. Das warded off the attacks against him by prevailing upon the Bengal Provincial Conference to ratify that pact in May 1924. But the Swaraj party repudiated it soon after his death a year later. It did so in deference to the Hindu supporters who had consistently opposed any concessions to Muslim pressures, especially over tenancy legislation, the opening of Islamia colleges and schools, and the appointment of Muslims in the Calcutta corporation.[9] It did not need any great degree of perception to understand that, if the Swarajists were to maintain their ascendancy in Bengal politics, they would have to stop pandering to the Muslims. Any attempt to enforce the Bengal pact was bound to drive the new mass Hindu electorate into communal organizations.

In actual fact, the Ansari-Lajpat draft was eclipsed by the bitter and acrimonious debate generated by the Bengal pact. 'Public view' was so 'befogged' that it failed to evoke a balanced appraisal.[10] In general, provincial and local Congress Committees were averse to it,[11] taking strong exception to the clauses on cow-slaughter and communal representation.[12] Muslim organizations, such as the Khilafat Committees at Gujranwala and Sialkot in Punjab and Noakhali and Calcutta in Bengal, regarded such provisions as an infringement of their political, religious and economic interests.[13] The Punjab Muslim League produced its own pact,[14] while the All-India Muslim League, the Khilafat Conference and the Jamiyat al-ulama preferred the Bengal pact.[15] 'The Mussalmans,' observed Ansari and Lajpat Rai in their report to the AICC, 'have been quite needlessly alarmed by some of its provisions and have allowed their judgement to be influenced by passing events.'[16] What they did not point out was that the Muslims were not prepared to accept anything short of what was conceded to them in the Act of 1919. Besides, given the history of Congress' political understanding with the Muslim League on the basis of separate electorates, weightage and communal representation, they were willing to accept a political settlement only within a self-perpetuating communal framework. In effect, therefore, the Ansari-Lajpat pact could neither satisfy their political aspirations nor contain the vociferous Hindu opponents of communal representation.

The Congress, wallowing in its seemingly eternal dissensions, made familiar noises as the violent conflagration reached serious proportions in Punjab, UP and Bengal. But apart from Gandhi whose personal anguish was reflected in his decision to go on a 21-day fast, most leaders were indifferent to resolving the communal problem. New political conclaves, such as the 'Unity Conference' at Delhi and the 'All-Parties Conference', were the outcome. Ansari, Ajmal Khan and Mohamed Ali convened the 'Unity Conference' in Delhi on 26 September 1924, but after all the ballyhoo things ran their course much as they did before. Some pious resolutions were passed, but the basic malady, as Jawaharlal retrospectively observed, could not be cured by conferences. A solution could not be reached by a majority of votes but by virtual unanimity and there were always 'extremists' whose idea of a solution was a complete submission of all others to their views.[17] The smiles and handclasp of Delhi faded ingloriously into oblivion.

In November of the same year Gandhi discussed the Hindu-Muslim problem despite the hemming and hawing of the hard-liners. This led to a conference at Delhi on 23 January 1925. He proposed a sub-committee to move on beyond the propagandistic mudslinging and the barren exercises of the past few years. But Madan Mohan Malaviya (1861-1946), Lajpat Rai and Shraddhanand refused to oblige. They knew that any compromise would endanger their political survival. And when the committee was eventually formed at the instance of Jawaharlal and Annie Besant, mutual bickerings marred its deliberations. Each side naturally made the best of its case and each, when forced to retreat, spoke of taking up fresh positions. Trouble started when Lajpat Rai took the line that the sub-committee's decisions would remain tentative without the Hindu Mahasabha's acquiescence. Here, it might have been thought, was the end of the matter. But

Lajpat Rai and his associates referred to a 'Muslim conspiracy' for bringing about an invasion of India. Ansari, who played a leading part in the conference, felt disconcerted. His own feeling was one of utter disgust so much so that he felt like retiring from public life altogether.[18] On 28 January, Motilal announced that, 'we were not able to reach final conclusions'.

When the committee reassembled in February-March, it accomplished nothing. The All-Parties Conference, wrote a distraught Jawaharlal in February, 'have not been a success so far. The discussions were painful to listen to. I am afraid the time has not yet come for an agreement which satisfies all parties.'[19] Only fourteen of the fifty-three members attended the final session on 1 March. They included Gandhi, the Nehrus, the Ali Brothers, Jinnah, Shraddhanand, Mohammad Yaqub (1879-1942) of Moradabad, and N.C. Kelkar (1872-1947). If Ansari had been more experienced and less enthusiastic, he might have realized that there was very little that he or, for that matter, Gandhi and Motilal could do to rescue the conference from being wrecked. Neither side felt there was much chance of an agreement but each thought, for different reasons, that they ought to go through the motions of trying.

The events of the next few weeks, and the statements and communiqués which ensued, must be considered with the scepticism needed to understand the story of inter-community feuds. The failure of the January conference, together with the growing incidents of riots, led Gandhi to declare that he saw no daylight out of the impenetrable darkness.[20] Later, he admitted his own imperfection as an instrument for bringing about communal peace,[21] and in despair said: 'I have learnt more and more to resign myself utterly to His grace.' Such a frank admission by the country's most consistent proponent of Hindu-Muslim amity augured ill for national unity and integration.

'The idea of a National Pact,' wrote the *Young India* of 3 January 1924, 'is sound and from a purely political point of view necessary.' 'Precedents in pact making,' it continued, 'for the protection of sectional interests may be lacking, but that fact need not bother us.' The communal issue was thus much too frequently considered from the standpoint of the early attainment of swaraj rather than that of nation-building and there was a far greater desire to work for a patch-up unity than to work towards a long-term and enduring solution. The flurry of stop-gap measures were hardly bolstered by carefully calibrated long-term policies. Centrality was, instead, accorded to 'Unity' and 'All-Parties' gatherings and much effort went in the drawing up of manifestos, declarations and resolutions, directed less to the reconciliation of rival policies than to the maintenance of an outward unity on some working formula of compromise. Devoid of any ideological content and lacking in the appreciation of the complex nature of the communal phenomena, such endeavours came to naught. The want of clear ideals and objectives in the freedom struggle undoubtedly helped the spread of communalism.[22]

On the basis of his presence in and association with the 'Unity' and 'All-Parties' gatherings, it is possible to argue that Ansari shared his perspective on the communal question with Gandhi and the Nehrus. He, too, saw its resolution in terms of political accommodation with the Muslim representatives in the Muslim League as well as in the regional formations.

CHAAK KAR DI TURK-I NAADAN NE KHILAFAT KI QABA [IQBAL]

Events in Turkey, meanwhile, went their own way. In August and September of 1922, Mustafa Kemal (1880-1938) routed the Greeks, completed the reconquest of Anatolia, and wrested a new treaty from the European powers to establish complete and undivided Turkish sovereignty in almost all the territory included in the present-day Turkish Republic. Indian Muslims were jubilant. 'Muslims throughout the country,' noted the viceroy, 'have been profoundly stirred and much pleased by the news of the Kemalist victories.'[23] Buoyed up by optimistic misinformation about the situation in Turkey, they failed to see the implications of the Grand National Assembly's momentous decision, adopted on 1 November 1922, to separate the offices of Sultan and Khalifa, divesting the latter of his temporal powers and making him into a symbolic 'pontiff' without even the aura of nominal suzerainty. The general disposition was to believe in Mustafa Kemal as a proud saviour of his country and champion of Islam.[24] A manifesto issued by Ansari and Ajmal Khan stated that the selection of a new Khalifa by the Assembly was a return to the great tradition of elected Khalifas, which would strengthen and not weaken his hand. As president of the Khilafat Conference held in December 1922, Ansari argued that the Turks had not really separated the Khalifa's spiritual and temporal powers, but had only made the Sultan a constitutional monarch. The Khilafat Conference expressed pleasure at the restoration of the earlier practice of electing the Khalifa. Mustafa Kemal was given the title of *Saif al-Islam* (The Sword of Islam), a term used in the past for conquering sultans.[25]

In the meantime, Ameer Ali (1849-1928), a Shia with close links with the government and the Aga Khan, leader of the Ismaili community, wrote to Turkey's prime minister, Ismet Pasha, suggesting that any diminution in the Khalifa's prestige or his elimination would mean the disintegration of Islam and its practical disappearance as a moral force in the world. They emphasized the 'imminent necessity for maintaining the religious and moral solidarity of Islam by placing the Khalifa-Imamate on a basis which would command the confidence and esteem of the Moslem nations and thus impart to the Turkish state unique strength and dignity'.[26] This letter alarmed the Turkish government;[27] it was actually insinuated at Angora—though not officially—that Ameer Ali and the Aga Khan had acted at the behest of the British government.[28] The fateful letter, according to some historians, influenced and possibly precipitated the decision to do away with the Khilafat.[29] The fact is that Mustafa Kemal realized that, as long as the Khalifa maintained his position, it would be difficult to establish a modern national state and a Turkish nation. The Khalifa, still supported by loyal followers, was ready to take part with any strong power to turn against his own people and render the idea of a modern republic meaningless.[30] His presence, besides impeding the foreign and internal political union of Turkey, was a source of 'strife and duplicity'.[31] 'There had been cruel and corrupt Sultans in Turkey,' wrote Halide Edip, 'there had been imbeciles and drunkards in its history, but never before had a son of Osman fallen so low as to maneuver [*sic*] for the subjugation of Turkey so that he might live comfortably'.[32]

After a preliminary preparation, the Khilafat was abolished on

3 March 1924. This was followed by the closure of the ministry of *shariat* and of the religious courts and by the unification of the judicial system. Traditional institutions which had governed society and government for centuries, were liquidated and the way was opened to a new mode of life.[33]

The Indian Muslims had another surprise in store. Two days after the trauma of seeing the Khilafat disappear, the pretentious Hashemite ruler of the Hijaz, King (formerly Sharif) Husain proclaimed himself Khalifa. With the exception of Abdul Bari, leading Khilafatists in general rejected the claim of an imperial stooge and a traitor to the Turks and therefore to pan-Islamic solidarity. Then, in late 1924, Abdul Aziz b. Saud, the Wahhabi chieftain of Nejd, attacked the Hijaz, captured Mecca and Medina, and destroyed a number of tombs and shrines in the holy cities. This caused a split in the Khilafat party with Abdul Bari and other leading *ulama* supporting the Hashemite claim and denouncing the Wahhabi ruler for his 'profanity', his religious insensitivity, and his territorial aggrandizement. Mohamed Ali, on the other hand, regarded him as a helpful co-adjutor in realizing his own ultimate goal—resuscitation of the Khilafat. The two most important factions, headed by Abdul Bari and his *murid*, Mohamed Ali, reached a parting of ways. This symbolized the disintegration of the alliance between the religious and the political wings of the Khilafat party.

With Turkey rejecting pan-Islamism and Muslims in other countries establishing national states independent of external ties of domination, Mustafa Kemal emerged as the symbol of Turkish nationalism, Zaghlul Pasha as the spearhead of the emerging national consciousness of Egypt, and the King of Hijaz as the rallying centre of so many Arab aspirations. But the Khilafat leadership in India remained ignorant of the potent force of Arab nationalism and the widespread enthusiasm and idealism which expressed itself in movements to eliminate completely Anglo-French domination. The 'Muslim World', which was a relatively closely woven whole during the pre-war days, was no longer the same. Territorial nationalism, race movements, and socialist ferments worked as solvents in the blood of pan-Islamic unity. Yet, the Khilafat leaders clung to the symbol of Islamic solidarity—the Khalifa—knowing full well that he was thoroughly discredited in the eyes of most Turks. This was because he had used his religious powers to stamp out the nationalist movement and thus sanctioned indirectly the foreign occupation of Turkey in violation of his basic religious obligation to defend the community against outside invaders. In addition, the Indian leadership failed to realize that the Khilafat was too remote and exalted an institution to mean much to, say, an average Anatolian peasant. That is why the Turks allowed an age-old institution to disappear with utter calm and indifference.[34] 'The absence of any reaction among the people is noteworthy', observed Halide Edip,

> for it proved beyond doubt that the Caliphate no longer commanded the allegiance of the Turkish people. . . . As a force of inter-Islamic unity within the Turkish Empire the Caliphate had proved itself ineffective. Abdul Hamid's policy of using it as a political bogey to frighten the West produced disastrous results. The "Jihad" proclamation during the Great War was a farce. Further Vahideddine's [*sic*] troops, fighting under the name of the Caliphate army against the people who are defending their honour and their existence smothered whatever respect and love for the institution still remained in the minds of the people.[35]

Even so, the Khilafat agitation showed no signs of having run its course. Its protagonists continued to believe that the institution they were trying to defend was 'with all its weaknesses, anti-Islamic trends and digression into pure imperialism . . . had served as a symbol of Muslim political unity and a powerful inspiration for the Muslim mind in India to retain its international character'.[36] There was a feeling of despondent bewilderment mingled with indignation towards the National Assembly whose drastic action weakened and isolated the one state on whose revival high hopes were set. Some mournfully recorded that an institution hallowed with traditions of thirteen centuries passed away, 'as if in a twinkling of an eye', and the 'edifice which looked as firm as a rock and promised to last as long as the world would last, was swept away by the flood of phenomena'.[37]

In marked contrast with the boisterous elation of the closing months of 1922, when, on the morrow of the Kemalist military successes, no voice was raised, whatever misgivings were secretly felt, to challenge the abolition of the Sultanate and its inevitable sequel—the expulsion of the Khalifa from Turkey—the reforms the Angora Assembly were now regarded as a calculated system of 'moral disintegration'. Mustafa Kemal, a name to conjure with twelve months ago, was in 1924 an 'Unbeliever' and a 'Salonica Renegade'. 'Is it not our bitter experience,' asked the indignant editor of the widely-circulated *Tarjuman* of Calcutta, 'that when the Turks required our moral and financial support, they exploited our feelings of fraternity, but as soon as they were able to stand on their own legs, they abolished the Khilafat without consulting us?'[38] Shaukat Ali was bluntly told by Ismet Pasha that his government's action was a purely domestic concern of the Turkish people, for whom the Khilafat had been an embarrassment and trouble in both internal affairs and foreign relations.[39]

Mustafa Kemal's decision to burst the Khilafat bubble impacted on the existing political alliances. The rapprochement between various Muslim groups, in particular, ended in the absence of a sound basis for permanent adjustments of diversified and, in some cases, conflicting interests.[40] Once the euphoria had worn thin, the dissensions in the leadership, which were so far kept under control, surfaced. Clearly, Islam had served as a focal point of unity in the face of a commonly perceived danger, but soon enough, material and political interests gained primacy over other considerations. For their part, the main thrust of Muslim organizations was to promote them even if it meant inter-community antagonisms.

The collapse of the movement profoundly affected the Muslim divines. Rebuffed and ignored by their comrades on the issue of council entry and continuing civil disobedience, they now found themselves isolated, confused and even inactive. Having once mobilized new groups, roused their religious fervour and articulated their grievances, they were now like a contrary jack-in-box refusing to retire, to seek new outlets for their energy and to build something out of their political experience. Some doggedly kept the Khilafat movement gasping, some capitulated to the communalist camp, but most, including the *ulama* of Deoband, entered the arena of religious controversies and organized the *tabligh* and *tanzim* societies as a counterpart to *shuddhi* and *sangathan*. They had a facility for kicking in doors that others could not open and a lack of wisdom that some felt helped reduce their credibility. The Jamiyat al-ulama split into factions with Nisar Ahmad of Kanpur and Abdul Majid of Budaun founding a parallel organization in Kanpur. Abdul Bari spoke the language of a zealot, urging Muslims to sacrifice cows without regard for Hindu religious susceptibilities. Addressing the All-India Sunni Conference (*Ahl-i Sunnat wal Jamaat*) in Moradabad on 17-19 March 1925, Syed Jamaat Ali Shah rejected un-Islamic practices which were subservient to Prophet Muhammad, and maintained adherence to the fundamentals of Islam.[41]

The Khilafat agitation provided the *ulama* with distinct enemy and goals; when the enemy and goals proved elusive other whipping boys and solutions had to be found. Much of their concerns, geared to religious goals, remained, because they seemed to be the hope of their followers. In consequence, some reverted to their former religious preoccupations. The Jamiyat al-ulama, despite its nationalist sympathies, moved along a course parallel to that of the Congress Muslim leadership: its chief project was to secure safeguards against interference with the *sharia* and guarantees for its propagation and implementation. In 1940, however, a section became the nucleus of various nationalist organizations. The Congress, which was otherwise vociferous about the secularization of politics, exploited this reserve of influence to counteract the Muslim League.[42]

Meanwhile, another group parted company with the Congress to organize the socialist and communist movements, especially in Bengal. Others, however, became enmeshed in sectarian causes in order to defend their faith. In Punjab, Saifuddin Kitchlew launched the Jamiyat-i Tanzim which, in accordance with its constitution of August 1925, consolidated various aspects of Muslim religious, cultural and educational life,[43] while the Anjuman-i Khuddam-i Al-Sufia, founded by the followers of Ahmad Reza Khan, countered the activities of the *shuddhi* and Arya Samaj bodies by establishing *madaris* and mosques. Of the 40 *madaris*, two each were established in Kashmir, Jammu, and Baroda and the remaining 24 in Agra, Mathura, Delhi, Etah, Bulandshahr, Gurgaon, Aligarh, Farrukhabad and other parts of northern India.[44] In Delhi and parts of UP, Syed Abdul Hai started the Jamiyat-i Tabligh al-Islam. From 1923 to 1928, this organization, formed as a counterpart to the *shuddhi* sabhas, progressed. Over 370 workers toured widely, converted 15,000 to Islam, and 're-admitted' 10,000 to the Islamic fold.[45]

The Congress politicians, including the 'Nationalist Muslims', gradually deserted Mohamed Ali; yet he clung to the much-maligned Khilafat committees. His defence of Ibn Saud, who had demolished numerous sepulchres held sacred by Muslims, alienated him from his spiritual mentor, Abdul Bari, and other friends. But he did not learn from his own experiences. During his visit to the Arab lands in June 1926, he discovered the squalor of Mecca and Medina, the barrenness of the surrounding land, the degeneracy of the social conditions, and the mismanagement of the *haj* traffic. Yet, he insisted on the Khilafat committees bringing about a truly Islamic rule in the Holy Land. He wanted India's Muslims to form a party around the nucleus of the Khilafat group, persuade others to their way of thinking, and thus achieve a united Muslim voice. He wanted them to contribute money, time, technical assistance and moral support to the Hijaz, devote themselves wholeheartedly to the reformation of the centre of Islam, and thus earn the good requital in both worlds. He was confident that it was possible to resist Ibn Saud's arrogation of control of the Holy Land and help re-establish a genuine Islamic rule.

Mohamed Ali paid scant regard to his own comrades who had followed his lead in the past but were no longer prepared to do so. His protégés in UP—Khaliquzzaman and Shuaib Qureshi—opposed his plan of sending three deputations to the Middle East. In neighbouring Delhi, Ansari resigned from the Khilafat committees in July 1926. In Punjab, the Muslim Swarajists took less interest in the Khilafat affairs; the main opposition to the Ali Brothers came from Saifuddin Kitchlew.

In sum, Mohamed Ali failed to recognize that 'Muslim identity' in a plural society had to be defined in response to the specific historical and contemporary experiences of the Muslim communities in the subcontinent. This fact had been underlined in Syed Ahmad Khan's rejection of pan-Islamism towards the end of the nineteenth century. But Mohamed Ali, who was swayed by his own religious/Islamic rhetoric, refused to accept that

Muslims themselves had played the final part in destroying what he was almost single-handedly fighting to maintain.

Mohamed Ali, a well-intentioned bull, charged round the China-shop, breaking up a good deal of worthless bits and pieces. The resurgence of communal violence and the squabbles over separate *versus* joint electorates and reservation of seats in legislative bodies and public services offered him an opportunity to indict the Congress. According to him, Gandhi, in particular, and the Congress, in general, were soft on people like Malaviya and Lajpat Rai. 'It is my sad conviction,' wrote the Maulana in the *Comrade* of 17 July 1925,

> that not one of these pseudo-Nationalists would have talked so glibly of Nationalism, majority rule and mixed electorates, if his own community had not been in the safe position of an overwhelming majority. It is they who are the real culprits as narrow communalists, but since the position of the community is safe enough they mouth all the fine phrases of nationalism and parade themselves as nationalists. The cow question provides the best topic for the exposure of their pseudo-nationalism, for in the name of nationalism they make demands on their fellow-countrymen that none has ever heard of them in any country or nation in the world.

In the circumstances, the Khilafat committees alone could advance 'Muslim interests' in India and abroad. Buoyed up by ill-founded expectations of what could be achieved, Mohamed Ali assured his readers that they were keen to bring about a truly Islamic rule in the Holy Land and outlined what the Indian Muslims should do; first of all, they should attempt to persuade other Islamic peoples to their way of thinking, and contribute money, time, technical assistance, moral support to the Hijaz. Above all, they should devote themselves whole-heartedly to the reformation of the centres of Islam and thus earn the good requital in both worlds.[46]

If Mohamed Ali's motives were less complicated than is sometimes believed and his technique more counter-productive, his influence on his followers was more complete than popular legend usually asserts. Some of his comrades viewed his indictment of the Congress with scepticism and ignored his plea for retaining the Khilafat committees, which had ceased to have a mass appeal and backing and were confined to those who were struggling to retain the name of the organization rather than to achieve its purpose.[47] According to Mushir Hosain Kidwai (1878-1937), one of the founders of the Anjuman-i Khuddam-i Kaaba and vice-president of the Oudh Provincial Khilafat Committee, the Khilafat question was 'no longer one which should cause anxiety to Indian Muslims'.[48] Equally important was Iqbal's reaction. Having regarded the Khilafat movement, which gave so much fervour to his community, as a means for strengthening the cause of Islam, it unfolded later on aspects in which 'no sincere Muslim could join for a single minute'. Instead of denouncing Mustafa Kemal and his policies, he commended Turkey for shaking off the fetters of medieval mentality and finding a way of life of her own.[49]

In marked contrast to Mohamed Ali, Ansari joined hands with the nationalist forces in breaking the communal impasse. Influenced by Congress' historic role in the nationalist struggle and the commitment of its leaders to communal amity he saw the fortunes of the religious minorities inextricably linked with it. On the other hand, he spoke against the Khilafat committees and their newly found allies in the Muslim League for orchestrating sectional interests and adopting a political strategy which suited the interests of the government and its collaborators in the landed, business and service classes. He found himself increasingly at variance with their purpose and methods. He stuck to his guns and was finally driven to take the painful but irrevocable decision of resigning from the Central Khilafat Committee. 'On my return from England in June', he wrote to Shaukat Ali on 16 July 1926:

> I found that communal passions had run amuck. . . . I therefore felt impelled to . . . fight the demon of communalism which was devastating the country and was breaking asunder strong ties formed between the Hindus and Muslims after centuries of intimate associations and common sufferings and sacrifice. As an Indian owing allegiance first to the motherland, I feel I must sever my connections with all communal or sectional political organizations.[50]

Ansari and the Ali Brothers were old comrades, but circumstances had now driven them into opposing camps and into conflict.

Ansari visited Turkey in the summer of 1925. His reactions

were refreshingly different from many of his Khilafat colleagues. This is reflected in his regular reports of the country's material progress accomplished by the Kemalist Republic.[51] Turkey in 1925 was markedly different from what Ansari saw on his last visit in 1912. The country was then in the throes of a crisis, internally divided and externally besieged by enemy powers. But it was now engaged in the stupendous task of reconstruction and on its way to achieving rapid progress. Ansari was impressed by the people he met. Then, he added a sweetener for the Angora people. They were not quite as difficult or dreadful; in fact, they were quite the reverse. He found them willing to discuss every aspect of a question, anxious to clear misunderstanding, keen on placing their point of view, appreciating to the full the opposite viewpoint and amenable to reasonable suggestions.[52] He rebutted the charge of widespread irreligiousness and impiety:

> I have not seen a more baseless and hollow charge. . . . There are a number of free-thinkers, agnostics or atheists, as there are in all Eastern countries. . . . But is this, phenomenon new, or peculiar to Turkey? I have talked to people of different strata of society; I have visited mosques and public places of worship at all odd hours and I am convinced that in spite of the high priests of free-thinking modernism and laocity [*sic*], the Turk is today as good a Muslim as he was ever before and more true to his faith than the Indian, the Syrian, the Palestinian or the Egyptian.[53]

Ansari's studied and balanced response is also reflected in his introduction to Halide Edip's *Conflict of East and West in Turkey*. He appraised the pan-Islamic sentiment in India, explained why his community placed on the Turks the burden of defending the honour of Islam, and lamented that they did not appreciate their 'quaint romanticism' and 'chivalry' or endure their 'oppressive affection'. If the Turks had known what pan-Islamism meant to the Indian Muslims and why the 'pan-Islamist sentiment' was their 'most sacred and exalted passion', they would have understood their frustration over the collapse of the Khilafat. Ansari observed that

> time has no doubt healed their wounds and they do not now reflect on the matter in the light of sentiment alone. But their world is still bleak

and desolate and the wrecks of their dreams lie around them. The pan-Islamism that was once an ideal is now a vague grievance; what was once a hope and an inspiration is now a sorrow. God is still in heaven, but the world has apparently lost its balance. For the hero of the Islamic community has now become the Prodigal Son.[54]

Ansari conceded that the Khilafat involved the Turks in pretensions which gave them a certain prestige but which also exposed them to the jealous wrath of their enemies and the shiftiness of selfish friends. The Indian Muslims did not appreciate this, because they tended to identify belief, manners and customs with the prescriptions of faith. Religion and social life were no doubt inseparable and a society that altogether overlooked the religious element was sure to drift from one vicious whirlpool to another. But India's Muslims were, according to Ansari, unable to distinguish between conservatism and stagnation; so they were ignorant of the good done by Mustafa Kemal. In a tone uncharacteristic of a professional surgeon and with a clarity and frankness rare among many of his colleagues, Ansari not only justified Turkish reforms but also made out a case for liberally interpreting religious decrees. He wrote:

Religion is the permanent basis of life, but the true religious spirit does not seek to shackle life in order to preserve a theoretical consistency between fact and belief. It endeavours rather to discover fresh sources of inspiration, which are really nothing more than fresh points of contact between the personality of the founder of a religion and of the follower across the gulf of time and altered social conditions. *Rigid conformity to the latter . . . may be as injurious to society as frivolous disregard for truth. There can thus be need for reform even when the law is all written down* [emphasis added].

The essence of Ansari's belief was that religion and politics no longer formed an indissoluble unity: they were separate realms concerned with different issues and functions, decided and performed by different experts.

JOURNEY TO CONSTANTINOPLE

Ansari sailed from the Bombay harbour on 10 April 1925 in the company of his ailing friend, Ajmal Khan. Both were to receive medical treatment in Paris and London. This voyage was different from his previous two. Ansari first went to England as a student; later, he travelled to Constantinople as a relatively unknown doctor. Now, his reputation both as a professional surgeon and a public figure were firmly established. He could have well anticipated the welcome that awaited him.

Ansari's first port of halt was Port Said, where he and Ajmal Khan were enchanted by the reception extended by some distinguished Egyptians. He wrote: 'The crowding of the main deck by long-robed officials, the warmth of their welcome, the flow of eloquent and sonorous Arabic in high-pitched voices, accompanied by even more eloquent gestures, though it warmed our hearts greatly, caused a little flutter in official dovecotes.'[55] The reference was to the viceroy of India, Reading (1860-1935), who was on his way to London.

Paris was the next stop. Judging from their letters home, both Ansari and Ajmal Khan were ecstatic to be in the French capital and to see much that was new, such as the mosque and the Muslim Institute, situated on the same side of the river Seine as the University of Sorbonne and the Quartier Latin.[56] They were also introduced to the *savants* of the Sorbonne and the University of Paris, received as officials of Jamia at a gathering of the *Rapprochement Universitaire*, and feted and lionized by the Carnegie Foundation, a melange of poets, artists, writers and rich young hangers-on. They lectured at the Societe de Sociologie de Paris and the Ligue du Droit de l'Homme et du Citoyen on the non-cooperation movement, conducted discussions with prominent Indians which convinced them that India's salvation lay in Gandhi's non-violent non-cooperation programme,[57] and kept up with the rapid, esoteric chatter that swirled around them. They were even quicker at becoming adept at the nightly partying. Ansari, in particular, looked every inch the polished performer.

After a month long stay in Paris, the doctor and the hakim spent six weeks in Lausanne where, 'at last we have got that complete rest and peace which has done us a world of good'. The trip was all sweetness and light. Vienna was their next halt. Here they saw the Medical Exhibition and purchased pathology specimens, charts and maps for Delhi's Ayurvedic and Yunani Tibbia College. They also went sight-seeing, though Ansari was depressed that the 'magnificent capital of the old dual monarchy looked like a ghost of its former self. The chateaux, palaces, monuments, public buildings, squares and boulevards in Vienna stood neglected, reminding one of their past splendour.[58]

Ansari made a round of the hospitals and clinics to acquaint himself with the regenerative methods of treatment, watch with care the technique of different workers, and discuss their results with them. He visited Paris, Lucerne and Vienna specially and saw the work of Eugene Steinach, Robert Lichtenstern, a urologist, and S. Voronoff. He gained much in practical and clinical knowledge which was reflected in his paper presented at the Delhi Medical Association in October 1925.

Ansari parted company with Ajmal Khan in Vienna. While the hakim left for Marseilles, Ansari boarded the Orient Express on its journey to Turkey. He reached Constantinople on 19 July 1925. But it was a city with a difference. On 13 October 1923, the National Assembly had voted that Angora (old Ancyra), founded by the Phrygian king Midas in the seventh century BC and once a great centre from which caravan roads led off into Persia, Syria and Armenia, be the seat of government. The decision to move the capital from Constantinople (Istanbul) into central Anatolia was because Anatolia was now located in Turkey, unencumbered by European, Arab or African provinces. The shift also symbolized a clean break with the Ottoman past.[59] Ansari noticed the change. He reported that Constantinople did not show the same 'bustle and activity' as in the days of the Ottoman empire. He found large buildings, military barracks, depots and arsenals empty and bare. Caught up in post-war lethargy and weariness, the people were hungry, taxes were heavy and food scarce. Ansari wrote of 'a vast number of poor, ill-clad, starving humanity begging in the streets'.[60] He referred to the uphill task of making a 'civilized' nation out of nothing, though he was acutely aware of the futility and superficiality of certain reforms, such as the 'Hat Law', being part of the much-advertised modernism. Meeting old friends and comrades convinced him that, despite external threats and internal feuds, Turkey surged ahead on the road to progress.[61]

According to Ansari's assessment, the Turks endorsed the national ideals and aspirations of the Indians and believed that the greatest service they could render to world peace was to attain freedom speedily. Their message to the pan-Islamists in India was equally significant. In the first place, they made plain that Turkey was beset with great external and internal difficulties and could not therefore participate in 'any movement involving fresh responsibilities'. Secondly, they 'should not even think of electing a Khalifa' and '*on no account lend themselves to perpetuate autocracy of an individual or a dynasty in any guise or shape*' [emphasis added]. Finally, Ansari stated that the Turkish officials maintained that it was better to have no Khalifa rather than to have one who would be 'ineffective' and even 'injurious'.[62] They could not have disavowed their remaining links with the pan-Islamists in India in a more forthright and categorical manner. Ansari's impressions, published in the *Comrade* of 18 September, sealed their fate. In fact, when Ansari returned to India at the end of 1925 he found the Khilafatists deep in the hot cauldron of party quarrels because their movement had lost its *raison d'être*. The Khilafat party was split into factions and the factions into fractions.

NOTES

1. F. No. 9, 1923, AICC Papers.
2. Quoted in Page,. *Prelude to Partition*, p. 85.
3. Commenting on the Multan riots in 1922, C. Rajagopalachari wrote: 'These terrible events remind us of how much ignorance, false religion and brute passion yet remains to be purged and how much watchful care on the part of leaders is necessary'. *Young India*, 21 September 1922, p. 381.
4. 19 April 1923. Selection from Newspapers in Bombay, 1923, p. 389.
5. For details and analysis of communal riots between 1922 and 1928, see *Report on the Working of the System of Government, U.P. of Agra and Oudh 1921-28* (Allahabad, 1928); *Indian Statutory Commission*, vol. 1, p. 27.
6. F. No. 25, 1924. AICC Papers.
7. Hasan, *Nationalism and Communal Politics*, p. 212.
8. I have examined the implications of the Das Pact in ibid., pp. 213-16; for Hindu opposition, see press clippings in Home Poll. K.W. II to 66, 1924, NAI.

9. K. Mcpherson, *The Muslim Microcosm: Calcutta 1918-35* (Heidelberg, 1974), pp. 84-6.
10. F. No. 25, 1924, AICC Papers. Ansari stated that there was much misunderstanding about the two pacts. If the principle of the National Pact was applied to any of the Muslim-majority provinces, the implications would be the same as in the Das Pact. He said: 'I do not see what the trouble is and where lies the unfitness of the Bengal Provincial Congress Committee Pact. If you are not prepared to concede the just rights of whatever community they may be . . . I assure you that you can never come to any agreement, there can never be peace, there can never be unity and I am afraid there will never be swaraj'. *Report of the Thirty-eighth Indian National Congress held at Coconada, 28-31 December 1923 and 1st January 1924* (Coconada, 1924), pp. 112-14.
11. For example, the Bihar and Maharashtra Provincial Congress Committees.
12. Shraddhanand to Ansari, 13 December 1923, F. No. 10, 1924, AICC Papers; Resolution of the Hindu Dharma Sangha of Calcutta in enclosure to Ansari, 27 February 1924, F. No. 25, 1924, AICC Papers.
13. F. No. 10, 1924, AICC Papers; Home Poll. K.W. II to 66, 1924, NAI.
14. *Tribune,* 27 January 1924, Home Poll. K.W. II to 66, 1924, NAI.
15. Ibid., 8 January 1924; *IQR,* July-December 1923, p. 193 for Jamiyat al-ulama; and p. 188 for Khilafat Conference.
16. F. No. 25, 1924, AICC Papers.
17. Nehru, *An Autobiography,* pp. 139-40. For proceedings of the Conference, see *IQR,* July-December 1925, pp. 149-60.
18. F. No. 13, 1925, AICC Papers.
19. Nehru to Syed Mahmud, 3 February 1925, in V.N. Datta and B.E. Cleghorn (eds.), *A Nationalist Muslim and Indian Politics* (Delhi, 1974), p. 32.
20. Cited in Mohibbul Hasan, 'Mahatma Gandhi and the Indian Muslims', in S.C. Biswas (ed.), *Gandhi Theory and Practice: Social Impact and Contemporary Relevance* (Simla, 1969), p. 143.
21. I can understand all about the Hindu-Muslim question, but have been reduced to a state of helplessness.' Gandhi to G.D. Birla, 23 May 1926, G.D. Birla, *In the Shadow of the Mahatma: A Personal Memoir* (Calcutta, 1953), p. 16.
22. Nehru, *An Autobiography,* p. 137.
23. Home Poll. 197-1, 1923, NAI; Mohammad Sadiq, *The Turkish Revolution and the Indian Freedom Movement* (Delhi, 1983), pp. 10-19.
24. *Pioneer,* 4 January 1924, quoted in Foreign and Poll. Dept., 228 (3)-X, 1923, pp. 64-5. Also, see statements issued by prominent Khilafatists in Home Poll. 721-II, 1922, NAI.
25. Home Poll. 60, 1923, NAI; Minault, *Khilafat Movement,* p. 202.

26. 24 November 1923, Foreign and Poll. Dept., 228(3)-X, 1923, NAI.
27. Ismet Pasha is reported to have said that these two Shia leaders had no right to make 'suggestions' and 'observations' in the name of Sunnis. Also, that they did not have 'the right knowledge and experience' to express views on the 'fundamental law of Turkey from a religious point of view'. *Pioneer,* 31 December 1923, quoted in ibid.
28. The Aga Khan denied the charge in a letter to *The Times*. The essential unity of Islam, he stated 'is of far greater importance than any sectarian differences. For this reason I have advocated the establishment of a strong Khilafat above parties and politics.' *Pioneer*, 19 December 1923, quoted in ibid.; Minault, *Khilafat Movement*, p. 203.
29. Ahmad, *Islamic Modernisn*, p. 138; Minault, op. cit., p. 203.
30. P.M. Holt, A.K.S. Lambton and Lewis (eds.), *The Cambridge History of Islam: The Central Islamic Lands* (Cambridge, 1970), vol. I, part IV, p. 533; Lewis, *Emergence of Modern Turkey*, p. 258.
31. The High Commissioner of Constantinople to the Foreign Office, 6 February 1924, Foreign and Poll. Dept., 34-X, 1924, p. 3.
32. Halide Edip, *The Turkish Ordeal* (London, 1928), p. 12.
33. Soon after the abolition of the Khilafat, a movement arose among the *ulama* of Al-Azhar of reviving the Khilafat in Cairo and vesting that office in the person of the King of Egypt. The *Lujnatual-Khilafat-ul-Azhar* was formed to convene an Islamic world congress in March 1925. And when little enthusiasm was shown by Muslim countries, the proposed congress was postponed to May 1926 on the plea of unsettled conditions obtaining in Egypt and the necessity of carrying out preliminary propaganda. *Cambridge History of Islam*, pp. 533-4.
34. It is one of the ironies of history that although the Turks scarcely lifted a finger to preserve the Khilafat, many of them fought doggedly against the new law, introduced by the Kemalist Republic, compelling all male citizens to wear hats instead of the *fez*. G.L. Lewis, *Turkey* (London, 1955), p. 92.
35. Edip, *Conflict of East and West in Turkey*, p. 118; Edip, *Turkish Ordeal*, p. 104.
36. Khaliquzzaman, *Pathway to Pakistan*, p 74.
37. Mohammad Barkatullah, *The Khilafat* (London, 1924), p. 1.
38. *Tarjuman* (Calcutta) 16 February 1926, Native Newspaper Reports (Bengal), 27 February 1926, p. 109.
39. Foreign and Poll. Dept., 34-X, 1924, p. 21.
40. Khaliquzzaman aptly summed up the widespread confusion in Muslim circles. 'As a result of this catastrophe,' he wrote:

    For practically one decade they [Muslims] suffered from deep inertia and pessimism and were incapable of any organised mass action either for the freedom of India or for the protection of their own Muslim interests in the country. Khilafat Committee continued for a few years more but it ceased to have a mass appeal or backing.... As time went on their energy also began to be misdirected and found its escape in fighting for offices in the organisation or for the formation of new parties with new names but no programmes. The Khilafatists who were once known as Khilafat-Congressmen became Congress-Khilafatists and some, after some time, purely Congressmen. Others remained nothing but Khilafatists with no work. The history of the next sixteen years of Muslim India is a mass of confusion and a chapter of political benightedness.

Khaliquzzaman, *Pathway to Pakistan*, p. 74.

41. *Fil Badih Khutba-i Sadarat* (Lahore, n.d.), pp. 43-66.
42. For a brief outline of the role of the *ulama,* see Mushirul Hasan, 'Religion and Politics: The Ulama and the Khilafat Movement', *Economic and Political Weekly*, 15 May 1981.
43. *Jamiyat-i Markaziya Tanzim ka Mujawaza Dastur-ul Amal* (Amritsar, 1925), p. 7. Among the members of the All-India Tanzim Committee were: Maulvi Rahim Baksh (Karachi), Malik Barkat Ali (Lahore), Abdul Talib of Delhi, Mohammad Shafi, Zafar Ali Khan and Raja Ghazanfar Ali Khan of Lahore, Nawab Mohammad Ismail Khan of Meerut, Maulana Mazharuddin, editor of the Delhi weekly *Al-Aman* and Zahur Ahmad of Lucknow.
44. *Fil Badih*, op. cit., pp. 15-16.
45. Syed Ghulam Bhik Nairang, *Jamiyat-i Markaziya Tablighal Islam Ambala shehar ki Satarsala khidmat ka khulasa* (Ambala, 1940), pp. 4-5.
46. Watson, op. cit., pp. 88-9.
47. Khaliquzzaman, *Pathway to Pakistan*, p. 74.
48. *Kaiser-i Hind*, 1 July 1923, Native Newspapers Report, Bombay, 1923, p. 626.
49. Cited in Annemarie Schimmel, *Gabriel's Wing: A Study into the Religious Ideas of Sir Muhammad Iqbal* (Leiden, 1963), pp. 47-8.
50. Ansari to Shaukat Ali, 16 July 1926, Hasan (ed.), *Muslims and the Congress*, p. 19.
51. These were published in the *Comrade.*
52. *Comrade*, 18 September 1925.
53. Ibid.
54. Introduction, *Conflict of East and West in Turkey*, pp. v-vi. All subsequent references are drawn from the introduction.
55. *Comrade*, 10 July 1925; Ghaffar, *Hayat-i Ajmal*, p. 336.
56. Ibid., 17 July 1925.
57. Ibid., 30 June, 24 July 1925.
58. Ibid., 18 September 1925.
59. Lewis, *Turkey*, p. 76; Poynter, *When Turkey was Turkey*, p. 138. For an account of the state of affairs in Angora by an English writer—the first

to visit the city after the Kemalist revolution—see Grace Ellison, *An Englishwoman in Angora*, pp. 135-6. See Edip, *Turkish Ordeal*, p. 49, for an extract from Mustafa Kemal's letter in which he advocated the necessity of transferring the seat of Parliament to Anatolia.

60. *Comrade*, 18 September 1925.
61. Ansari's account is similar to that of the British writer Ellison, who appreciated Mustafa Kemal's contribution in the building up of a strong and united Turkey. See Grace Ellison, *Turkey To-day* (London, 1928).
62. *Comrade*, 18 September 1925.

ANNEXURE I

The Draft Indian National Pact

WHEREAS INDIA being a dependency of the British Government has been deprived of all the rights and privileges of a free country and Indians are denied even full citizenship rights in several parts of the British Empire and the present foreign government does not use and in the nature of things cannot be expected to use all its resources to uphold the dignity and protect the elementary rights of Indians; whereas it is essential for the free and full moral and material development of her citizens and the enforcement of due respect for their human rights and their liberties in all parts of the globe that Indians should before all else possess in India the rights and privileges that the free nations of the world enjoy in their respective countries; whereas it is necessary that all the peoples of India, of whatever religion, race or colour should unite together and apply all their resources, moral, mental and material, for the attainment of Swaraj and the only obstacle is the want of cooperation among the different communities due to misunderstanding and mutual suspicion about each other's aims and intentions and whereas a joint declaration by all communities of the goal which they seek to attain and the rights which they wish to secure for the people, which a Swaraj Government will be pledged to guarantee and safeguard, will be beneficial to the creating of that confidence and toleration, which are absolutely essential for a common endeavour.

It is hereby resolved that all the communities and committees represented by the signatories to this document shall enter into an agreement in terms of the following resolutions which shall be known as the Indian National Pact:

In pursuance thereof it is hereby resolved:

1. It shall be the firm and unalterable object of the communities represented by the signatories to this pact to secure complete Swaraj for India, that is to say, the Swaraj which will secure and guarantee to Indians the same status, rights and privileges in India as every free and independent nation enjoys in its country.
2. The form of Government under Swaraj shall be democratic and of the federal type; but the exact nature of this Government shall be fixed and determined hereafter by a National Convention consisting of representatives of all communities and all shades of political opinion.

3. Hindustani shall be the national language of India. It shall be permissible to write it in either script Urdu or Devanagari.
4. Full religious liberty, i.e., liberty of belief, worship, propaganda, association and education, is hereby guaranteed to all the communities forming the Indian Nation and shall form a constitutional right which it shall never be lawful for any government to annul, modify, suspend or otherwise the aforementioned liberties shall, however, be exercised subject to such disciplinary rules and regulations as may be found necessary to preserve peace and order and to eliminate force or compulsion by any one party in derogation of the rights of others.
5. To prevent any particular religious denomination being given undue preference over any other, no government funds or funds collected by local bodies from public revenue and public taxes including cesses shall be devoted to the promotion and furtherance of any denominational institutions or purposes.
6. When once the Swaraj has been achieved it shall be the sacred duty of every Indian, be he Hindu, Mussalman, Sikh, Parsi, Christian or of any other denomination to defend it against all attack—external or internal.
7. In view of the present state of feeling prevailing in the different communities and in view of the insufficient development of political sense and responsibility in them, it is necessary for some time to afford adequate protection to the interests of minorities. It is therefore hereby agreed that the various communities shall have separate representation in the Legislatures, both State and Federal.

   (NOTE: Dr Ansari wishes to extend this principle to municipalities and local boards. Lala Lajpat Rai does not agree to this. As an alternative Lalaji proposes that a time limit may be fixed during which communal representation will be enforced and at the expiry of which it will be abolished altogether.)

   Such representation shall throughout the country be in proportion to the numerical strength of each community in the constituencies (Lala Lajpat Rai wants that special provision shall be made for the small minority such as Christians and Parsis, etc. Dr Ansari suggests that large minorities such as Sikhs and Christians may be given special representation in the Federal Legislatures but only very small minorities such as Parsis should be given special representation both in the Federal and State Legislatures). But the electorate in all cases will be joint.

   There shall be no communal or colour or caste distinction in public services and in the educational institutions.
8. In order to achieve national unity and out of regard for the religious feelings of their Hindu compatriots the Mussalmans of India do hereby by a solemn self-denying ordinance bind themselves to give up cow-

slaughter except in connection with Id-i-Azha when it will be done, in such a manner as will not injure the feelings of Hindus.

9. In order to secure and preserve a calm atmosphere for public worship it is hereby declared that no music shall be allowed in front of places of public worship at such time as may be fixed by local mixed conciliatory boards.
10. Religious processions of different denominations when falling on one and the same date shall follow such different routes or be fixed for such different times as may be determined by local mixed conciliatory boards.
11. In order to prevent friction and settle all questions giving rise to differences and conflicts between different religious communities, e.g., on the occasion of Dussehra, Muharram, Rath Yatra procession, Sikh Divans, etc., etc., provincial and local joint boards will be appointed to act as conciliatory and arbitration boards.
12. While cherishing feelings of the most friendly nature towards all the nations of the world at large it is further resolved that the people of India should participate in the formation of a Federation of Eastern countries to be established for purposes of mutual help in trade and commerce and the emancipation of the East from economic exploitation and domination by Europe and with a view to encourage and support Oriental culture and generally to maintain good and friendly relations between the various nationalities all over the East.

(Dr Ansari wishes to incorporate in the National Pact provision 2 to clause 4 of the Lucknow Pact also which runs as follows: 'Further that no bill, nor any clause thereof, nor a resolution affecting any community, which question is to be determined by the members of that community in the Legislature concerned, shall be proceeded with, if three-fourths of the members of that community in the particular Legislature, Federal or State, oppose the bill or any clause thereof or resolution.' But as there is no time to get Lala Lajpat Rai's opinion it is submitted with his recommendation only.)

LAJPAT RAI
M.A. ANSARI

Report of the Committee

Preamble & Clauses I & II. The preamble and the first 2 clauses of the draft pact appear to have evoked no criticism or only of an insignificant nature except in one or two prominent cases, where doubts are expressed as regards the form of government adumbrated in our draft, otherwise they have been generally accepted.

Clause III. The third clause relating to a common national language has called forth varying opinions; Mussalmans, in general, favouring 'Urdu' against 'Hindustani', while some political and denominational opinions are in substantial agreement that Hindustani (in both Urdu and Devanagari script) should be the *lingua franca* of India, but each province should retain and use its own vernacular.

Clause IV. Clause IV has again called forth differing opinions. But some Hindus would discourage 'Propaganda and proselytization'. Others regard this clause as one of the most salutary provisions and one, at least, calls it a constitutional right, which must be made inviolable by any government. There is an overwhelming consensus of opinion in favour of its retention and such amendments as are proposed are verbal and insignificant.

Clause V. This too is upheld by a considerable majority. But some gentlemen would see this provision restricted to future arrangements only and two or three others would relax it in favour of some denominational institutions which may be engaged in social work also. . . .

Clause VI. This is almost unanimously agreed to by all.

Clause VII. Clause VII has evoked the largest quantity of comment and criticism. While opinions are more or less equally divided as regards Dr Ansari and Lala Lajpat Rai's notes to this clause, there seems to be a fair consensus on the point of 'separate representation' for the present, i.e., with a time limit. But Mussalman opinion does not favour joint electorates though enlightened Muslim opinion is almost unanimously for common electorates in regard to municipalities and local boards as a necessary step towards the extension of the principle in regard to Federal and State legislatures, when the time may be ripe for such a change and when minorities themselves may ask for it. Nearly all Hindu opinion is for a time limit for 'separate representation'. As regards the question of public services, again, Hindu and Mussalman opinion is sharply divided. The former condemn (though not unanimously) proportionate distribution of posts according to numerical strength and the latter unanimously insist on it, only some individual Mussalmans accept departments where expert knowledge is essential. By far the most controversial part of the whole draft is Article 7, which has been made the subject of keen and earnest comment by individuals, associations and the press alike.

Clause VIII. Clause VIII again has evoked earnest comment. Some Hindus have urged its abrogation as redundant, and some others including some prominent public men, have insisted on the omission of Id-i-Azha also as an exception. Similarly a majority of Mussalmans have emphatically condemned it as subversive of 'freedom of action', while a few have endorsed it subject to the condition that the Hindus should leave the matter entirely to the good sense of the Muhammadans—an opinion shared by the Bihar

Provincial Congress Committee. One or two Mussalmans hope that it will not be regarded a 'bargain' but a voluntary concession to Hindu susceptibilities.

Clause IX. With reference to the playing of bands before places of public worship also, there is some difference of opinion. Some prominent Hindus would stop 'music', 'uproar of processions' before all places of public worship at all times of day and one or two would restrict the operation of this clause to only 'Moslem places of worship' and yet there are others who think that genuine worship ought not to be disturbed by any noises. But the balance of opinion, we think, is in favour of the provision.

Clauses X & XI. Clauses X and XI are almost unanimously agreed upon by all parties.

Clause XII. Clause XII has aroused quite unnecessary suspicion and opposition in many persons. Some of them (both Hindus and Mussalmans) regard it wholly premature. They do not feel sure that the time has yet arrived for us to think of an Asiatic Federation. One critic condemns the ideas as 'Western' and advises the country to rise above any cramped ideas of Asiatic Federations and expects a development, by India, of the idea of international brotherhood. But the sting of the suspicion we fear seems to lie (at least in the objections of some of the critics) in the erroneous notion that the said federation is meant to provide an opportunity for a certain important minority in India to enter into relations with Afghanistan and Turkey! One critic goes to the extent of saying that none but China and India are the victims of Europe's policy of 'economic exploitation of the East' and, therefore, no league with other Asiatic countries is necessary. And yet there are others who think that the object of the federation would be 'the emancipation' of Asia from the economic exploitation of Europe, America or Japan.

The sum and substance of the entire criticism of this clause seems to be that its scope and real object have been wholly missed or imperfectly realized by those who have viewed it with distrust and therefore pronounced it premature.

Last Note. Dr Ansari's last note has been almost generally endorsed by all.

In our opinion, however, our draft-pact has quite unjustifiably suffered by contrast with other documents on the same subject, which came into existence since its publication. It has not been made the subject of calm and considered judgement by either Hindus or the Mussalmans—although the Christians, the Sikhs and the Parsis seem to have treated it seriously. The attention of the former has been very largely and we feel unduly absorbed by other documents referred to above and they have not accorded to our draft, the thought and consideration which it deserved at their hands; and, again, the Mussalmans have been quite needlessly alarmed by some of its provisions and have allowed their judgements to be influenced by passing events.

Of the omissions pointed out we have noted three.

(1) It is said that we should have treated the interests of 'labour', the Sikh and the Parsi communities specifically in separate clauses. But that is taking us too far. In so far as the adjustment of the 'causes of conflict' are concerned, we have, we think, comprehensively dealt with them in this pact—including the principles of special representation. But we do not think that we were required to go further than the settlement of the elementary principles. The deduction of details concerning the allotment of representation (which would include the interests of 'Labour' no less than 'Capital', 'Landholders' and 'Tenants') is left to the *National Convention*, which is to draft the constitution of our Federal or State Legislatures.
(2) It is urged that the actual Pact to be subscribed by the representatives of various communities should be written in *Hindustani*. The suggestion is premature, but, we regard it with the *same* respect which it deserves.
(3) Supplementary clauses (of which a notable example is furnished by Maulvi Mohammad Sajjad of Phulwari) are suggested mostly pertaining to the procedure to be followed, but some are more or less irrelevant to the terms of the reference made for us. But when the Pact enters upon its final stages, some of these suggestions, particularly those just pointed out, will be found to form a good basis for discussion.

In conclusion we are of opinion that:

(1) The necessity for a National Pact as fully borne out by the opinions received is urgent as ever; but
(2) Our draft has not so far received the attention which it deserves and, therefore,
(3) We strongly recommend that a gathering of the representatives of all classes of interests, both secular and communal, be convened at the earliest opportunity to consider and settle the terms of the Pact we now submit for the consideration of the All-India Congress Committee with the analysis of opinions, selected so far.

We are still of the opinion that the final adoption and promulgation of a Pact such as the one we submit for the All-India Congress Committee's approval is one of the immediate needs of our present political life.

ANNEXURE II

Resolutions Passed at the Delhi Unity Conference 26 September to 2 October 1924

RESOLUTION NO. 1

THE CONFERENCE places on record its deep grief and concern at the fast which Mahatma Gandhi has undertaken. This Conference is emphatically of opinion that the utmost freedom of conscience and religion is essential and condemns any desecration of places of worship to whatsoever faith they may belong and any persecution or punishment of any person for adopting or reverting to any faith and further condemns any attempt by compulsion to convert people to one's faith or to enforce one's own religious observances at the cost of the rights of others.

The members of the Conference assure Mahatma Gandhi and pledge themselves to use their utmost endeavours to enforce these principles and to condemn any deviation from them even under provocation. This Conference further authorizes the President to convey personally to Mahatma Gandhi the united wish of this Conference that Mahatma Gandhi should immediately break his fast in order to permit this Conference to have the benefit of his cooperation, advice and guidance in deciding upon the speediest means of effectively checking the evil which is fast spreading over the country.

RESOLUTION NO. 2

This Conference deplores the dissensions and quarrels that are now going on between Hindus and Muslims in several places in India resulting in loss of life, burning and plunder of property and desecration of temples. The Conference regards them as barbarous and contrary to religion. This Conference is of opinion that it is unlawful and irreligious for any person to take the law into his own hands by way of retaliation or punishment. The Conference is of opinion that all differences, no matter of what nature should be referred to arbitration and if that be impossible even to a court of law.

RESOLUTION NO. 3

There shall be a Central National Panchayat of not more than 15 persons, with power to organize and appoint local Panchayats in consultation with the local representatives of the different communities to enquire into and settle all disputes and differences including recent occurrences, where necessary and desirable. The said National Panchayat shall have power to frame rules and regulations for carrying out this resolution.

The Conference appoints the following to act as the Central National Panchayat with power to add to their number up to 15 and co-opt local representatives as additional members:

1. Mahatma Gandhi (Chairman and Convenor)
2. Hakim Ajmal Khan
3. Lala Lajpat Rai
4. Mr K.F. Nariman
5. Dr S.K. Datta
6. Master Sunder Singh of Lyallpur.

RESOLUTION NO. 4

With a view to give effect to the general principles for promoting better relations between the various communities of India laid down in Resolution 1 and to secure full toleration of all faiths, beliefs and religious practices this Conference records its opinion:

(*a*) That every individual or group shall have full liberty to hold and give expression to his or their beliefs and follow any religious practice with due regard to the feelings of others and without interfering with their rights. In no case may such individual or group revile the founders, holy persons or tenets of any other faith.

(*b*) That all places of worship, of whatever faith or religion, shall be considered sacred and inviolable and shall on no account be attacked or desecrated whether as a result of provocation or by way of retaliation for sacrilege of the same nature. It shall be the duty of every citizen, of whatever faith or religion, to prevent such attack or desecration as far as possible and where such attack or desecration has taken place it shall always be promptly condemned.

(*c*) (i) That Hindus must not expect that the exercise of the right of cow-slaughter by Muslims can or will be stopped by the use of force, resolution of a local body, act of legislature or order of court but only by mutual consent and must trust to the good sense of Muslims and the establishment of better relations between the two communities to create deeper respect for their feelings.

(ii) Nothing stated in the above clause shall unsettle or affect any local custom or agreement between the two communities already in existence, nor will it authorize cow-slaughter in a place where it has not taken place before; any dispute on facts should be settled by the National Panchayat formed under Resolution No. 3.

(iii) Cow-slaughter shall not take place in a way offensive to the religious sentiments of the Hindus.

(iv) The Muslim members of the Conference hereby call upon their co-religionists to do everything in their power to reduce cow-slaughter.

(*d*) (i) That Muslims must not expect to stop Hindu music near or in front of mosques by force, resolution of a local body, act of legislature or order of court except by mutual consent but must rely upon the good sense of Hindus to respect their feelings.

(ii) Nothing stated in the above clause shall unsettle or affect any local custom or agreement between the two communities already in existence nor shall it authorize the playing of music in front of mosques where it has not been played before. Any dispute with regard to the latter shall be referred for settlement to the National Panchayat formed under Resolution No. 3.

(iii) The Hindu members of this Conference call upon their co-religionists to avoid playing music before mosques in such a manner as to disturb congregational prayers.

(*e*) (i) That Muslims must not expect to stop by force, resolution of a local body, act of legislature or order of court, except by mutual consent, the performance of *arti* or the playing of music including the blowing of *shankhs* by Hindus during worship and on other occasions in their houses or temples or public places at any time even if the house or temple or place in question is situated in close proximity to a mosque; but they should trust to the good sense of the Hindus to accommodate them.

(ii) Nothing stated in the above clause shall unsettle or affect any local custom or agreement between the two communities already in existence; any dispute on facts should be settled by the National Panchayat formed under Resolution No. 3.

(*f*) That Muslims are at liberty to chant *Azan* or offer prayers in their own houses or in any mosque or public place not set apart for the religious observance of any other community.

(*g*) (i) Where the slaughter of an animal or sale of meat is permissible on other grounds, no objection shall be taken to the method of slaughter, whether by *Jhatka, Bali* or *Zibah*.

(ii) Wherever there is any dispute regarding the sale of any kind of meat in a particular locality or quarter it shall be referred for settlement to the local Panchayat formed under Resolution No. 3.

(*h*) That every individual is at liberty to follow any faith and to change it whenever he so wills and shall not by reason of such change of faith render himself liable to any punishment or persecution at the hands of the followers of the faith renounced by him.

(*i*) That every individual or group is at liberty to convert or reconvert another by argument or persuasion but must not attempt to do so or prevent its being done by force, fraud or other unfair means, such as the offering of material inducement. Persons under 16 years of age should not be converted unless it be along with their parents or guardians. If any person under 16 years of age is found stranded without his parent or guardian by a person of another faith, he should be promptly handed over to persons of his own faith. There must be no secrecy about any conversion or reconversion.

(*j*) That no community should attempt to stop by force the construction of a new place of worship by a member of another community on his own land but such new place of worship should be built at a reasonable distance froman existing place of worship of any other community.

RESOLUTION NO. 5

This Conference is of opinion that a section of the press, specially in the North, is responsible for increasing the tension between different communities by publishing wild exaggerations, reviling each other's religion and by every means fomenting prejudice and condemns such writings and appeals to the public to stop patronage of such newspapers and pamphlets and advises central and local panchayats to supervise such writings and from time to time to publish correct version.

RESOLUTION NO. 6

It having been represented to this Conference that in certain places acts of impropriety have been committed in relation to mosques the Hindu members of this Conference condemn such acts wherever committed.

RESOLUTION NO. 7

The Hindu and Muslim members of this Conference call upon their co-religionists to extend full tolerance to the minor communities of India and to deal with them in all questions of communal intercourse with justice and generosity.

RESOLUTION NO. 8

This Conference is of opinion that attempts on behalf of members of one community to boycott members of any other community and to stop social or commercial relations with them made in certain parts of the country are reprehensible and are an effective bar to the promotion of good relations between the various communities in India. The Conference therefore appeals to all communities to avoid any such boycotts and exhibitions of ill-will.

RESOLUTION NO. 9

This Conference calls upon men and women of all communities throughout the country to offer daily prayers during the last critical week of Mahatmaji's fast and to organize mass meetings on the EIGHTH of OCTOBER in every town and village to express the nation's thankfulness to the Almighty and to pray that the spirit of goodwill and brotherliness may pervade and unite all the communities of India and that the principles of full religious toleration and mutual goodwill declared in this Conference may be adopted and given effect to by members of all communities in India.

Delhi
2 October 1924

SHUAIB QURESHI
JAWAHARLAL NEHRU
Secretaries of the Conference

7

Leading the Congress

> The Council-splendour has dazzled me in vain.
> Oh! take me to the lowly thatched cottage again.
> The village-man will love me and come to my call.
> His service to Swaraj dearer than all.
>
> *Basumati* (Calcutta), 7 September 1927

ON HIS RETURN to India in July 1926 Ansari noticed the changes on the political horizon. He was dismayed to find the Congress riven with dissension and its prestige sunk to a low ebb. He found the Swaraj Party in disarray because the 'Responsivists', supported by Malaviya and Lajpat Rai, had revolted. Having defeated Motilal Nehru's Swarajist alliance in the local elections held in 1925, the Malaviya group organized the Independent Congress Party. In the build up to the provincial and central assembly elections Hindu concerns provided most of the ammunition for the assault on the Swaraj Party. Motilal was accused of being a beef-eater, and the Congress was stigmatized as a prostitute of Muslim India. Such was the communal hatred aroused that he afterwards considered retiring from public life.[1] Gandhi, who had himself withdrawn from the hurly-burly of active politics and had at the beginning of 1926 imposed upon himself a year of silence on political matters, advised the dispirited Motilal to let the evil forces of communalism play themselves out and, in the meantime, to 'wait, watch and pray'.[2]

With the storm of inter-communal antagonism blowing with fury in the summer of 1926, no voices could make themselves heard against the clamour of the rival partisans. Though the Congress attributed the rise in the communal temperature to either the government's divide and rule policy or the militancy of the Khilafat Committees and the Hindu Mahasabha,[3] it did not launch a mass campaign to curb violent eruptions. Ramlila occasioned widespread tension even in areas where Congress exercised much influence; its celebration at Aligarh in September led to one of the worst riots of the year. Delhi was transformed into something like an armed camp during the Id celebrations; yet a minor incident—the scare created by a bolting horse—left three persons killed and sixty injured. Violence erupted in Calcutta from June to October 1926. Inter-communal relations in several other regions were generally strained. There was hardly any development of importance in politics other than the slow and steady resurgence of Hindu-Muslim fracas and its establishment on new, wider and deeper foundations.[4] The vision of swaraj had dimmed in the dust of internal strife.

Ansari pinned his hopes, as always, in the Congress which enjoyed a special national status as the spokesman for India's diverse peoples. Other organizations were, in his judgement, enmeshed in narrow and sectarian politics and had therefore become peripheral to the nationalist mainstream. For this reason, he resigned from them on 16 July 1926, stating explicitly that he owed allegiance to the Congress alone. Jawaharlal approved of his decision. Writing to Syed Mahmud from Geneva, he observed, 'I can see no way out of our difficulties except by prodding on—more or less secular lines in politics'.[5] Addressing a conference in Lucknow a few months later, Ansari exhorted Muslims not to have any truck with communalism and join the others in liberating the country from the clutches of foreign rule.[6]

On 20 March 1927, Ansari attended a conference at Delhi where a group of Muslim politicians, led by Jinnah, agreed to forego separate electorates if their four demands were met by the Congress *in toto*. The first of these was that the Bengali and Punjabi Muslims should be represented in the legislative council in proportion to their population; the second was that one-third of the seats in the central legislature be reserved for the Muslims. Also that Sind be separated from the Bombay Presidency and constituted as an independent province and, finally, reforms be extended to the North-West Frontier Province.[7] 'We have after all succeeded,' Mohammad Yaqub wrote triumphantly, 'in finding out a formula on which there was a unanimity of Muslim opinion and which has shifted the burden of proof on the other party; it is for them [Hindus] to clasp the hand of friendship which the Muslims have extended.'[8]

When these proposals were placed before the AICC, Ansari, Motilal and Srinivasa Iyengar (1874-1941), the Congress president, pressed for their acceptance as a basis for a political accord with the League. Their view prevailed. The only concessions they offered to dissenters like Malaviya, Lajpat Rai and Moonje was to make reforms for the North-West Frontier Province conditional on the provisions of a suitable judiciary and the separation of Sind conditional on the separation of Andhra.[9] Neither of these conditions militated against the spirit of the four proposals and both Ansari and Mohamed Ali were happy to swallow them. Meanwhile, the spate of communal riots continued unabated. Between April and September 1927, twenty-five riots were reported: ten in UP, six in Bombay Presidency, two each in the Punjab, the CP, Bengal, Bihar and Orissa and one in Delhi (Table 7.1). During the seventeen months that the viceroy, Irwin (1881-1959), had been in India, the entire landscape was overshadowed by the lowering clouds of communal tension, which repeatedly discharged their thunderbolts, spreading their devastating havoc throughout the country.[10]

Irwin proposed a conference to address the problem of growing Hindu-Muslim strife. But such summits offered no magic or quick solutions. The ensuing discussions were essentially a dialogue of the deaf, with Muslim delegates—Mohamed Ali, Zafar Ali Khan, Shaukat Ali and Mohammad Yaqub—insisting on tackling the political disputes first, while Malaviya, Lajpat Rai,

TABLE 7.1: COMMUNAL RIOTS IN INDIA: APRIL 1926 TO AUGUST 1927

Province	*No. of communal riots*	*Dead*	*Injured*
Punjab	3	61	380
UP	8	3	131
Delhi	3	4	116
Bengal	12	181	1,512
Bihar	7	14	114
CP	1	Nil	7
Bombay	9	4	253
Madras	1	1	7

SOURCE: Home Poll. F. No. 10/16, 1931 & K.W., NAI.

Moonje and Raja Narendranath (1864-1945) were only prepared to discuss social and religious discord.[11] The recalcitrance on both sides led to a stalemate. The conference floundered without progressing towards its avowed goal. In the end, violent and scurrilous charges were bandied about, with the spokesman of each community blaming the other for its break up. The tendency to bargain for political concessions 'under cover of a settlement of what has been admitted to be religious differences was hardly calculated to create an atmosphere favourable to harmony and settlement', pontificated the *Amrita Bazar Patrika*.[12] The *Mohammadi*, on the other hand, reproached the 'Hindu members' for their uncompromising attitude. They 'have indirectly said that no true unity should be established unless and until the Mussalmans agree to live in this country as a race of slaves like the *Sudras* and other untouchables'.[13]

On 27 October 1927, the AICC, inspired partly by the necessity of maintaining some semblance of solidarity in the Congress and partly by the genuine alarm at the growing Hindu-Muslim clashes, discussed afresh the all-absorbing theme of communal relations.[14] Ansari set the tone early on with an eloquent appeal for unity, spent hours in delicate negotiations, and pleaded with Hindus and Muslims to remain non-violent. But such implorings did not carry matters very much further and the fundamentally irreconcilable aims of certain groups ended in open rupture. The problem at hand was left precisely where it had been before the conference. Though consensus was reached on conversion, cow-slaughter and music near mosques—issues on which Ansari made a detailed statement—its effect was blunted by the boycott of the Mahasabha and League delegates from the conference.[15] Besides, the consensus was more in the nature of an appeal to each side to avoid offending the other. 'Who is going to restrain the enthusiasts and fanatics if they deviate from civilized methods of conversion by persuasion and argument and to take them to task for doing so?', enquired the *Leader* of Allahabad. At the same time, a dispute over, say, music before mosques, could not be solved by means of a formula which assumed tolerance and reasonableness on either side.[16]

The failure of the unity conferences was a foregone conclusion: there was not much chance of reconciling the claims of certain groups in the Congress, the League and the Mahasabha. They were afraid of giving away anything and felt it incumbent on them to stick to their demands. They were like parties in a lawsuit who thought the more extravagant their claims the more likely were they to secure a judgement in their favour.[17] More importantly, an understanding on the immediate causes of conflict, such as the one attempted at Simla and Calcutta, could potentially undercut their support base and render them politically ineffectual. They made good in politics by exploiting religious sentiments. Their favourite rhetorical device was to accuse the British of instigating Hindu-Muslim discord.[18]

There seemed to be some malign fate attending unity conferences, for every one held since September 1924 drove the two communities still farther apart. But Ansari's own doggedness in negotiating a viable settlement did not go unnoticed;[19] it was a commitment that never wavered. Contemporaries were impressed by his loyalty to the Congress, especially when many of his comrades were, in the words of Motilal, 'tumbling over each other to shake hands with officials' and were afflicted by fear, prejudice and lust for power and wealth. It was easy for him to amass a fortune by concentrating on his flourishing practice, but he spent much of his time in politics and whatever he earned—his earnings were substantial because among his clients were some wealthy rajas and nawabs of northern and central India—was placed at the disposal of the Delhi Congress Committee. His house in Daryaganj was virtually a Congress headquarter and the venue of the AICC and CWC meetings. Congress workers frequented his clinic in Fatehpuri to be treated free of charge. To his clinic in Daryaganj came the sick and the needy; they lined up every morning to receive the attention of one of India's most reputed physician-surgeons.

With his record of service, Ansari's choice as Congress president in 1927 was widely acclaimed. Even though Sarojini Naidu, egged on by Jinnah and the Maharaja of Mahmudabad, pressed Motilal's candidature,[20] Gandhi ultimately called the shots from the sidelines. 'There are many forces just now working against Motilalji', he wrote to Sarojini Naidu. He did not either favour the younger Nehru, who, in any case, took himself out of the running. Gandhi wanted Ansari to wear the Congress crown.

His reasons were quite simple: the doctor would be able to pilot a Hindu-Muslim pact through the Congress, his choice would command general acceptance, and his selection by a 'national association containing a preponderating majority of Hindus' would foster Hindu-Muslim friendship.[21] He lauded Ansari's efforts to promote 'union' and pointed out how if he, Sarojini Naidu and Iyengar had not been pitchforked into the presidency of the Congress at the last three sessions, Ansari would have been elected on any of those occasions. His claim was postponed for 'special reasons', though his name was on everybody's lips when elections took place.[22] Gandhi wrote:

> Things, as they are shaping in the Congress, confirm the opinion that it is not yet time for Jawaharlal to shoulder the burden. He is too high-souled to stand the anarchy and hooliganism that seems to be growing in the Congress and it would be cruel to expect him to evolve order all of a sudden out of, chaos. . . . For the present, we should press Dr Ansari to take the reins. He won't control the hooligans. He will let them have their way; but he may specialise in the Hindu-Muslim question and do something in the matter.[23]

Ansari preferred Jawaharlal who, he believed, would match the 'clever' and 'astute' leadership of the League and the Mahasabha. Motilal, according to his reckoning, was unlikely to be backed by most PCC's, especially those which were 'over-run by Mahasabhites'.[24] With Gandhi's backing assured, Ansari's election was a foregone conclusion. Yet, he set forth his views on Indian politics so that those who disagreed with him would have the opportunity of opposing his candidature.[25]

In his statement of 17 August 1927, Ansari admitted that non-cooperation was dead, even though he still believed firmly in non-cooperation, and that the policy of blind obstruction within the councils had failed. He assailed Swarajist policies and advocated direct action as was done in the non-cooperation days. While appealing to those who agreed with his assessment to keep away from the central and provincial legislatures, he urged others who still desired to go to the councils to confess that they were cooperators, to sink their differences and compose their quarrels, and form a people's party constituting the opposition.

The country, was a vast camp of warring factions bent on

destroying each other, and he appealed to the authorities to protect them from the murderous onslaught of one another. It was therefore necessary to accord the highest priority to the communal malaise in its future programme. His own mission was to weld the various communities into a 'single solid nation'. For this, he enumerated three lines of activity to minimize friction: extensive propaganda for communal amity and the establishment of safety bureaus and conciliatory boards in every city and town. The safety bureaus were expected to scrutinize and, if necessary, contradict writings and news items which were calculated to incite communal passions. At the same time, Congress leaders were expected to tour riot prone areas and settle, if possible, contentions issues on the spot.

Ansari's panacea was a tried one. Public safety boards were started as a sequel to the decision arrived at the Unity Conference held in Delhi on 26 September 1924, but they were ineffectual. Also, it was not for want of propaganda that the communal chasm persisted, for Congress resolutions and speeches extolled the virtues of Hindu-Muslim unity and comradeship with unfailing regularity. The slaughter of a cow, the beating of a drum, the reception of a convert into onefold or the other, or the publication of something like *Rangila Rasul* acted as sparks which fired the powder and produced an explosion. They were more often symptoms of a deep rooted socio-economic malady.

Ansari's views did not go uncontested. His criticism of the Swaraj Party was attacked. Some thought that his fine words and phrases were borrowed from the vocabulary of 'defeated' and 'downtrodden' people; others that his sentiments and ideas were 'inopportune' and 'impracticable'.[26] Criticism came from another unexpected quarter. The Communists concluded that Ansari—'the die-hard gandhist'—would lead the peace-making process with British imperialism. In a pointedly ideological attack, the *Masses of India* stated:

> The Swaraj Party whole-heartedly stuck to the bankrupt tactics of parliamentary obstruction in order to satisfy the restlessness of the petty-bourgeois intelligentsia. Now one of the stalwarts [Ansari] of gandhism comes forward to declare that the petty-bourgeois intelligentsia no longer insist upon these tactics for they have become detrimental to capitalist interests. Ansari has proved that petty-bourgeois reaction

(gandhism), just as the petty-bourgeois radicalism of the Swaraj Party, only serves the interests of capitalism.[27]

Motilal ridiculed the suggestion to 'obliterate the last vestiges of the tattered aims of non-cooperation' and pointedly belittled Ansari by saying that he did not have any political programme of his own.[28] Gandhi, too, bombarded Ansari with long letters full of admonition and advice, to which Ansari replied either not at all or briefly and dryly. In trying to persuade him to keep his views to himself and not to publish them, Gandhi wrote:

I [therefore] ask you to tear your statement to pieces. Keep that opinion to yourself, accept the election with grace, dignity and thankfulness, and announce that you have no political policy of your own to place before the country, that so far as that is concerned, you will take up a strictly judicial and impartial attitude and act merely as chairman of meetings guiding deliberations, keeping order and enforcing decision of majorities, that you have accepted the election with the sole intention of guiding the country during your year of office, by all the power at your command, to domestic peace. For, you owe it to the country as a Mussalman and a staunch nationalist to vindicate the religion of the Prophet and the honour of the country by giving all the talents you have for securing a domestic peace honourable to all parties. *Nobody expects more of you. And, if you meddle in anything else, you will be travelling outside your province . . . you dare not refuse the crown of thorns that is offered to you by a grateful country and you dare not publish your statement, however precious your views are* [emphasis added]. If you wish to place them before a few friends gathered together in a drawing-room enjoying hookah, you may certainly enliven the company with your views. But beyond the four walls of such a drawing-room, your views may not travel.[29]

Ansari's response to this patronizing—some said offensive—tone is not known. What is known is his stout refusal to comply with his command. He was not cowed into silence and the statement was promptly released to the press on 15 August. Indignant at this act of defiance, Gandhi suggested 'spontaneous retirement' on the part of Ansari. Although changed his mind soon thereafter, he insisted that Ansari should clarify that he would not impose his views upon the Congress.[30] Ansari agreed to stay in the running for the presidency but did not respond to Gandhi's one-sided harangues. He probably felt that as a leader of long-standing he had the freedom to hold and the right to express his views.

Given a choice, Gandhi may have promoted somebody else for the presidential *gaddi*. But he was not prepared to risk embarrassing the High Command which had, in principle, endorsed Ansari's candidature. He therefore assured the Provincial Congress Committees [PCC] that Ansari would not use the presidential office to enforce his political views through the Congress. 'His integrity is the surest guarantee of his guiding the deliberations of the Congress as an absolutely impartial chairman and of his giving full effect to any agreement that may be arrived at by the various parties in the Congress.'[31]

The Congress reception committee elected Ansari as its forty-second president on 4 September. Fourteen out of the seventeen PCC's voted for him; the only other nominee—Kelkar—had been nominated by three PCC's, including his home constituency. Wrote the *Hindustan Times:*

> The nation is to be congratulated on the singular sobriety of judgement displayed at a crucial period of its history. A fitter recipient than Dr Ansari for the highest honour in its power could not have been found at the present juncture. His election at the crucial period of our history when the country is groaning under communal antagonism appears . . . to constitute a valuable national asset.[32]

Elevated to the presidency, Ansari invited prominent leaders, Hindu and Muslim, cooperator and non-cooperator, to attend the Congress at Madras. Referring to the disastrous results of divided counsel and disunion, he called for reuniting nationalist forces. Divisions in the body politic were merely over details: on matters of principle there was virtual unanimity. The reception accorded to Birkenhead's (1872-1930) 'lily white list', the all-British Statutory Commission, provided an occasion to reunite the drifters and fence-sitters 'If we can take advantage of the opportunity thus presented to us to organize public opinion and focus it on the speedy attainment of our goal, we shall have created a force in our political life which shall be irresistible.'[33]

Ansari received a number of encouraging replies, some from unexpected quarters. Annie Besant, T.B. Sapru (1875-1949) and B.C. Pal (1858-1932) found the atmosphere favourable for teamwork and suggested the getting together of various parties to draw up a constitution on the lines of the 1916 Congress-Muslim League scheme. Hasan Imam (1871-1933) and the Raja of Mahmudabad were for boycotting the Simon Commission; Mohammad Yaqub agreed that a large number of Muslims should attend the Congress; Abdur Rahim (1867-1952), though unprepared to meet other leaders on its platform, endorsed plans for concerted action; Ibrahim Rahimtoola (1862-1942) affirmed that political progress could only be advanced by pulling together.[34]

The Home Rule Leaguer, Joseph Baptista (1864-1931), argued that the boycott would offer a pretext to the government to 'restore autocracy on the ruins of dyarchy'. G.S. Khaparde (1854-1938), once a close lieutenant ofTilak, doubted the effectiveness of the boycott plan. The two Arya Samaj leaders—Bhai Parmanand (1874-1947) and Lala Hansraj (1860-1938)—on the other hand, expressed disdain for manifestos containing either platitudes on unity or schemes of compromises which found little favour with most groups. According to Parmanand, the two communities were so far wide apart that cooperation on a common platform was neither desirable nor possible.[35] In a similar strain Haji Hidayet Hosain (1881-1935) of Kanpur expressed his misgivings.

> It is admitted on all hands that no political advancement is possible till the Hindus and the Muslims unite; what have even the Congressmen done to secure this unity. Indeed some of the Congress workers have been the worst offenders in this respect. Has the Congress even as a body attempted to go to the root cause of the Hindu-Muslim riots? Have you realized that it is only since 1923, when the *shuddhi* and *sangathan* were started, that these riots began to repeat themselves with such frequent obstinacy? Nobody has got a right to take exception to these movements but if the object of the *shuddhi* were merely political and pursued by physical force, threat, violence and fraud in order to reduce the numerical strength of the Muslims, then I think these movements can secure no other purpose except the creation of an unbridgeable gulf between the two communities. . . .
>
> Mere honeyed phrases and appeals couched in eloquent and winsome phraseology to the communities to live in amity and grace has never proved to be of any avail. You cry in the wilderness every year and this year you repeat the same process over again. It may do your

soul some good, but it does nothing to us. The Congress does not represent the Hindus now, it has never represented the Muslims. You are then a group of men, well meaning, well intentioned, honest and sincere, but all the same afraid to look at things at their face, incapable of tapping the root cause of differences and therefore impotent to devise effective means of cure.[36]

This was strong language. The Haji knew this. He confessed that he was being impertinent. But he was stating, as well as it was possible for a contemporary, unendowed with the advantage of hindsight, the tangled state of communal prejudices that inspired people either with cynicism or with woolly idealism.

Ansari's entourage for the Madras Congress included politicians of the old Delhi-Aligarh axis: Khaliquzzaman, Shuaib Qureshi, Abdur Rahman Siddiqi, Aziz Ansari, the Ali Brothers, Faridul Haq Ansari and Zakir Husain. For the time being they buried party rancour, eschewed differences, and set aside political rivalries. All Madras, in feet, seemed awash in enthusiasm for Ansari, who won nearly unanimous applause for being in the national spotlight.[37] His appeal seemed to work and party unity—on the surface, at least—was achieved against heavy odds. Flanked on either side by Congress stalwarts and amidst cries of *Bande Mataram*, *Mahatma Gandhi ki jai ho* and *Hindu-Muslim bhai bhai,* the forty-second president of the Congress strode to the podium to deliver his address: that may have been Ansari's best political moment ever.

In his hour and a half long presidential pronouncement, Ansari stressed unity—unity among communities, among political parties, among Congressmen and among legislators. Minor political irritants, he advised, need not stand in the way of purposeful cooperation to thwart the sinister designs of the common adversary. He devoted a substantial part of his speech to the Statutory Commission. The high-handed manner in which government disregarded the wishes of the people must serve as an eye-opener even to the most confirmed optimist. The enemy was thus met head on by Ansari, at least rhetorically, and the thematics of the campaign against the Commission were set forth with precision and daring. 'No sane or self-respecting Indian,' he continued, 'can ever admit the claim of Great Britain to be the sole judge of the measure and time of India's political advance. We alone know our needs and requirements best and ours must be the decisive voice in the determination of our future. It is our inherent and inalienable right.' He therefore announced: 'We can have no part or lot in a Commission which has been appointed in direct defiance of the declared will of the people of India'—a line that brought an approving roar from the audience.

Quite understandably, Ansari's major concern was 'the ubiquitous microbe' which had infected every sphere of national activity. A nation trying to shake off foreign domination could not afford to carry on an internecine struggle, that freedom and communalism were incompatible and both self-respect and self-interest required looking beyond momentary and sectional advantage to the lasting national gain. He detailed the history of Congress efforts to resolve the political and religious differences, urged Congressmen to explain and popularize them, and called upon Hindus and Muslims to exercise the demon of communal and political discord. And crucially, given his image, Ansari insisted that Hindus and Muslims sink their differences and abide by the agreement reached at the Calcutta Unity Conference.

Ansari was not expected to suggest a radical or even a substantial change in the Congress programme; he was only expected, in view of the need for both political and communal unity, to make a forceful plea to all sections and communities to join the Congress and make it a strong national organization. The speech was logical, moralistic, intense and humourless. It was clear and forceful and as good-natured as the man himself. The *Tribune* complimented Ansari on his speech, adding: 'It was exactly the kind of lead to the Congress and the country that one had a right to expect from a man called upon to take up the national leadership at this supreme crisis.'[38] He did not play to the gallery, avoided the use of catchwords calculated to confuse and mislead, and refrained from suggesting heroic and spectacular methods for attaining swaraj.[39] His message was not 'one of retrogression or stagnation, of depression or despair, but one of unflinching determination and unswerving faith in India's great destiny'.[40] The speech as a whole was admired and praised across party lines.

The Madras Congress adopted three vital decisions which had formed the main burden of Ansari's address. In the first place, it reached a consensus on the communal question; the 'Unity Resolution' adopted was on the lines suggested by Ansari. The second resolution called for an effective boycott of the Statutory Commission 'at every stage and in every form'; Ansari had given the lead first in his letter of 1 December 1927 and later in his presidential speech. Finally, the Congress committed itself to complete national independence at the insistence of Jawaharlal. On 27 December, he had moved a resolution declaring the goal of the Indian people to have complete National Independence. Gandhi and the Right-wing Congressmen thought that it was 'hastily conceived and thoughtlessly passed'. Privately, Gandhi rebuked Jawaharlal for encouraging 'mischief mongers and hooligans' and for not thinking out the whole situation and the resolutions which might be appropriate.[41] The *Leader* summed up significance of the Madras Congress:

> The Madras Congress session has been the most remarkable and successful one since the waning of the non-cooperation movement. The Presidential address was also unique of its kind, breathed a spirit of unity and harmony, and was characteristically outspoken. The complete independence resolution betokens the high moral courage of the Congress and is a necessary corollary of the dictum that Swaraj is the birth-right of the people. The boycott resolution has placed a practical programme before the country and the unity resolution marks the culminating point of the success of the last session of the Congress.[42]

THE NEHRU REPORT AND ITS AFTERMATH

From the early days of their entry into the legislative councils, the Swarajists had pressed for revising the Montagu-Chelmsford reforms. Motilal, leader of the Swaraj Party in the legislative assembly, called for dismantling the half-way houses of dyarchy and the setting up of full provincial autonomy. When the assembly considered the Muddiman Committee report in September 1925, he proposed fundamental changes in the constitutional machinery. His motion was adopted. In November the government announced the appointment of a Statutory Commission, and from April 1926 to November 1927, the viceroy and the secretary of state worked out the form, the terms of reference, and the composition of the Commission. On 8 November, the British Government appointed a Statutory or Parliamentary Commission, known from its chairman's name as the Simon Commission, two years before the time laid down by the Act of 1919.

As we have discussed, the exclusion of Indians from the commission caused quite a consternation. When that 'all-white' commitee reached Bombay's port, its years of projected labour were already doomed, torpedoed before it got underway, by the pig-headedness of a narrow-minded coterie of imperial managers who put their selfish interests above the needs, aspirations and just demands of most Indians. The Muslim League, led by Jinnah and the Jamiyat al-ulama declared that the commission and the procedure, as announced, were unacceptable. Jinnah declared on 30 December 1927: 'Jallianwala Bagh was a physical butchery, the Simon Commission is a butchery of our souls.'[43]

When the Congress met at Madras at the end of the year, it voted to boycott the commission, proclaimed independence as its goal and resolved to draft a constitution of its own. Earlier, party representatives of the Liberal Federation, the Muslim League, and the Hindu Mahasabha held their first meeting on 12 February 1928 in order to respond to the British challenge that Indians could not produce a constitution of their own. Motilal and Jawaharlal were there, as were Jinnah, Lajpat Rai, Malaviya, Jayakar and most of the other leaders of political India.

From February to July 1928, Ansari was engrossed in advising members of the All-Parties Conference on matters small and large and providing a welcome leavening influence within the buttoned-up Motilal entourage. As president, he was more stretched, with more work and more responsibility, than ever before. It was the kind of situation in which he throve and which brought out the best in him. He spent long hours in negotiations and manoeuvres that were as obscure and confused at the time as they remain in retrospect. On 18 May he chaired a crucial meeting which decided to draft a nationalist constitution under Motilal's chairmanship.

When the Nehru Committee Report was published on 15 August 1928, Ansari emerged as its foremost campaigner. In so doing, he made many enemies as Muslim activists, mainly from UP, hammered away at the recommendations: the abolition of separate electorates, abandonment of reservation of seats for Muslim majorities in Bengal and the Punjab and of weightage in those provinces where Muslims were in a minority. During the All-Parties Conference and the All-Parties National Convention, he found himself in a series of prickly exchanges, one involving Shaukat Ali who reproached Ansari for treating the so-called Muslim viewpoint with contempt and betraying the community's interest.[44] However, Ansari, expecting the same precision in the cut-and-thrust of a political battle as in a medical paper, pointed out that he had been unjustifiably smeared and he drew up a statement that the *Bombay Chronicle* published.

Without displaying flashes of toughness, Ansari maintained a statesmanlike reserve. He tried hard to set the fears at rest, pursuing his task against a running barrage of ridicule, but without success. In the end he concluded pityingly that the opposition was based on ignorance and confusion of the rights of minorities with the principle of representation. 'I have been writing and sending telegrams to Muslim friends all over India,' he informed Motilal, 'to start an organized campaign in support of the constitution and against the senseless and unreasoned opposition started by Shaukat Ali and his party along with his henchmen, the Muslim reactionaries.'[45] The report, according to him, provided more 'real' and 'solid' safeguards than the League of Nations to racial minorities of the newly-constituted states of Europe. The value of constitutional safeguards, in any case, was questionable, for they were 'bounties on inefficiency'. 'The more a minority has of them,' he said, 'the more it will need protection from the bracing spirit of free competition by charitable provisions of constitution, it will sink deeper and deeper into ignorance, fanaticism and sloth to be stifled ultimately by the very cords which had appeared to offer it a partial support.'

The Nehru Report, according to Ansari, 'heralded the dawn of a brighter day'. At the Calcutta Convention he warned the delegates of an alien government attempting to widen the religious divide and the communalists, 'inspired by the gospel of more bread and butter', fanning the fires of unrest. At the same time, he saw no reason to fear them. 'Already a new generation is coming to the front,' announced Ansari, 'to which differences between Hindus and Mussalmans are unknown and which will not and cannot think in communal terms'. This was an unprophetic view. Over the years, political demands stiffened and it was no longer possible to either ignore them or to dismiss them lightly. It served no purpose to deny the deep divide and to smother opposition with ridicule or vituperation. If anything, it led certain circles to believe that the Congress was unwilling to come to terms with the Delhi proposals. This was the burden of Jinnah's speech at the Calcutta Convention. But his arguments carried no conviction with his audience which, according to one of his biographers, marked an even sharper veering off from the road of the Congress than Nagpur had been in December 1920. Nagpur had ended Act One. Calcutta finished Act Two. 'This time there would be a larger intermission.'[46]

Shaukat Ali, delighted at Ansari's discomfiture, burst forth in his best denunciatory vein, chiding Ansari for playing the 'generous liberal minded patriot at the expense of one's people' and for supporting a report which 'intentionally treated the Muslim point of view with undeserved contempt'.[47] 'I know the present Hindu mentality well,' he told him, adding that 'they do not want our friendship; they want our allegiance and God-willing, they will never get that.' He charged that

> in your blind adherence to Motilal Nehru and other Hindus, you betrayed Muslims and your co-workers and we both are free now to take our lines of action. Non-cooperation was ruined by these people, chances for Hindu-Muslim friendship have been throttled, an understanding between princes and people thwarted, Swaraj Party dismembered and now you yourself see what is being done to kill Congress, which has ceased to be National now. It has become an adjunct of the Hindu Mahasabha and will soon be a seeker of favours at the door of the English.[48]

Mohamed Ali, fresh from his trip to Europe, pilloried Ansari in his public speeches; indeed the Nehru Report ushered in a new phase of personal bitterness between the two men. The report, he stated, would establish 'a legalized tyranny of numbers', jeopardize Muslim interests everywhere, and lead to the ascendancy of the Hindu Mahasabha.[49] Ansari had actually warned Motilal in mid-September that 'it would be a hard fight as it is, but if Jinnah and Mohamed Ali both go against us the tussle will be harder still'. Mohamed Ali's outburst confirmed his worst fears. At the same time it did not come as a surprise. Over the years, the Maulana had developed a point of view from which everything said or done by any Hindu or Congress Muslim was attributed to the Mahasabha influence.

Mohamed Ali, the man with a caustic tongue, seized the opportunity at the Khilafat Committee meeting—convened on 21 December 1928 to elect delegates for the forthcoming All-India Khilafat Conference—to snuff out opposition. With the connivance of Shafee Daoodi, Shaukat Ali and Haji Abdullah Haroon of Sind, he upbraided those who stood by the Nehru Report. He caused a similar uproar at the Central Khilafat Committee meeting by rousing the partisans behind him. In consequence, about forty-five prominent members of the Central Khilafat Committee, including Ansari, T.A.K. Sherwani and Mujibur Rahman, staged a walk out.[50] A few days later, Mohamed Ali attended Delhi's All-Parties Muslim Conference, which was convened by the pro-government lobby and their allies in the assembly and the legislative councils.

The rough and overbearing attitude of the Ali Brothers disgusted Ansari. He found Shaukat Ali, in particular, opinionated and conceited, a dictator who shouted down his opponents and treated those who disagreed as if they were trying to start a breakaway body. Having idolized him for the last eighteen years, worshipped the very ground on which he tread, he was no longer willing to follow him. 'When I saw the clay feet of my idol,' he wrote some months after the incident, 'I felt as if the world had turned topsy-turvy and that I could never, in future, trust anyone whoever it might be.' He painfully added that friendship with the robust Maulana would never be the same. 'At an age,' he wrote,

> new friendship and new attachments are difficult, if not impossible to make. Therefore, life in future would be the less fuller, the less richer for want of such friends as you and I have been. I, however, bow to the inexorable march of events and have fortified myself against whatever the future may have in store, and have prepared myself to go

on working in the service of my faith and my country, in the best manner that I can do.[51]

Ansari referred to their association with the 'Aga Khan & Co' whose only 'distinction is that they have always been reactionary both to Indian and Muslim affairs'. He added that their differences which initially concerned a few provisions of the Nehru Report 'have now grown into a conflict of the very outlook'.[52] He could hardly be expected to allow his political views to be permanently governed by the friendships of his youth. At some stage—probably after the Khilafat movement had petered out—he weighed the wisdom of following Mohamed Ali and found it wanting; references to him in Ansari's private letters were at best equivocal and sometimes derogatory. He realized that he could not take the views of anyone, however, distinguished, on trust; he had to work out his own views for himself.

Ansari refused to become the drift-wood of the communal tide. During the worst period of communal animus, he did not allow his broad national outlook to be perverted. Indeed, he adhered to the Congress which, according to his firm belief, served the larger 'national' interests and derived legitimacy from its impressive record of launching countrywide crusades against the raj. The Ali Brothers had held the same view until the mid-1920s. The Congress, wrote Mohamed Ali in 1925, 'is and must remain the only national political organization. . . . Let the Muslim League and the Hindu Mahasabha both perish, let the Congress and the nation survive.'[53] In 1928-30, however, he revised his opinion. The hero of the Khilafat days came to believe that the Congress had ceased to be a national organization. As a Hindu body it was unprepared to work towards the creation of an India in which all communities could live in harmony. The Nehru constitution threatened to subject the minority province Muslims to a communal Hindu majority. Those Muslims who supported such a constitution, chief among whom was Ansari, were Congress stooges.

Mohamed Ali's relationship with Gandhi also reached a breaking point. There was no sign of this happening until the mid-1920s when the Maulana venerated the Mahatma and held him in great esteem.[54] 'There is none more free from selfish motives, from jealousy and personal ambitions,' observed Mohamed Ali.[55] He reaffirmed that he held certain views 'with regard to the way in which India can win her freedom, which for the most part I share with Gandhi, whom I am proud to regard as my chief.'[56] But during the Nehru Report controversy Mohamed Ali quoted from Gandhi's writings of 1924 and 1925 to show that his erstwhile chief was now converted to a different creed, sought different goals, defeated all Muslim attempts for a compromise, and gave 'free reins to the communalism of the majority'.[57]

The gulf separating Gandhi and Mohamed Ali seemed unbridgeable; in fact, Gandhi conceded that the Ali Brothers 'had a fairly heavy list of complaints' against him and that he could not make an impression on them as they distrusted the role of his associates. Mohamed Ali's outburst in April 1930 confirmed this impression. 'We refuse to join Mr. Gandhi,' he stated, 'because his movement [civil disobedience] is not a movement for complete independence of India but of making the seventy millions of Indian Muslims dependent on the Hindu Mahasabha.' Symbolic of the collapse of the old alliance on which Gandhi had built non-cooperation was Mohamed Ali's appeal to Muslims not to join civil disobedience because Hindu raj was its goal.[58]

The vehemence of Mohamed Ali's attack, while certain to alienate many of his apolitical friends as Ansari, was not certain to attract new support; in fact, its immediate effect seems to have been even to increase his unpopularity. And it could not have helped his uneasy frame of mind to know—as he must have done—that his reputation, both personal and political, had not been improved by his outburst. Cooperation requires give-and-take, but there was no give in Mohamed Ali's politics. He became a political isolationist and preferred ploughing a lone furrow. Many of his erstwhile comrades who had been the butt of his ridicule, his satirical verses and cutting epigrams were glad to find an opportunity or an excuse to turn against him and to think and speak ill of him.

It has been necessary to dwell at some length on Mohamed Ali's role because, in the years to come, Ansari had to counteract his influence through the All-India Nationalist Muslim Party. Mohamed Ali represented a stream in politics which threatened to destroy Ansari's vision of a secular polity. Though he died in 1931 and was buried in the Al-Aqsa mosque in Jerusalem, he bequeathed a divisive legacy. Ansari's task was to stem this process and to weld the two communities into a coherent whole.

NOTES

1. D. Page, *Prelude to Partition*, pp. 134-5; Gyanendra Pandey, *The Ascendancy of the Congress in Uttar Pradesh 1926-34* (Delhi, 1978), pp. 121-4; C.A. Bayly, *The Local Roots of Indian Politics—Allahabad 1880-1920* (Oxford, 1975).
2. B.N. Pandey, *Nehru* (Delhi, 1976), p. 119.
3. Mushirul Hasan, *Nationalism and Communal Politics*, chs. 5 and 6.
4. J. Coatman, *India in 1926-1927*, p. 3; Page, op. cit., ch. 2. The only detailed study of communal and revivalist movements in the 1920s and of communal riots is by G.R. Thursby, *Hindu-Muslim Relations in British India* (Leiden, 1975); J. Coatman, *Years of Destiny-India, 1926-1932* (London, 1932), p. 117.
5. 11 August 1926, S. Gopal (ed.), *Selected Works of Jawaharlal Nehru [SWJN]*, vol. 2, p. 241.
6. *IAR*, January-June 1927, p. 424.
7. Mushirul Hasan, 'The Delhi Proposals: A Study in Communal Polities', *The Indian Economic and Social History Review*, vol. 17, no. 4.
8. *Leader*, 27 March 1927.
9. Hasan, 'The Delhi Proposals', pp. 389-91.
10. Speech on 29 August 1927, *India in 1927-28*, p. 17.
11. See press clippings in Ansari Papers, JMI.
12. 25 September 1927; *Ananda Bazar Patrika*, 26 September 1927, Native Newspaper Reports (NNR), Bengal, 1927; *Abhyudaya,* Note on the Press, United Provinces of Agra and Oudh, for the week ending 1 October 1927, microfilm, NMML.
13. 7 October 1927, NNR, Bengal, 1927.
14. *Leader,* Note on the Press, UP, 22 October 1927.
15. Ibid., 22 October 1927.
16. Ibid., 5 November 1927; *Ananda Bazar Patrika,* 29 October, NNR, Bengal, 1927.
17. The Earl of Lytton, *Pundits and Elephants: Being the Experiences of Five Years as Governor of an Indian Province* (London, 1942), p. 172.
18. *Madras Mail*, 23 May 1926.
19. *Swarajya* (Urdu), 10 September 1927; *Hamdard* (Urdu), 9 September 1927; *Khilafat* (Urdu), 9 September 1927, Ansari Papers, JMI; also see Home Poll. 32, 1927, NAI.
20. Gandhi to Motilal Nehru, 2 June 1927; to Jawaharlal Nehru, 20 June 1927. *CWMG*, vol. 34, p. 87 and fn. 2, p. 207.

21. *Young India*, 21 July 1927, *CWMG*, vol. 34, p. 214.
22. Ibid., 21 July 1927, *CWMG*, vol. 34, p. 214.
23. To Sarojini Naidu, 25 June 1927, ibid., p. 57; to Motilal Nehru, 19 June 1927, ibid., p. 31.
24. Ansari to Sarojini Naidu, 26 June 1927, Hasan (ed.), *Muslims and the Congress*, p. 20.
25. For Ansari's statement, see *Times of India*, 19 August 1927.
26. Note on the Press, UP, for the week ending 3 September 1927. The statement was, however, welcomed by a section of the Muslim press in UP. See *Oudh Akhbar, Aligarh Mail, Sadaqat* and *Medina*. Note on the Press, UP, 27 August 1927; also, Home Poll. 32, 1927, NAI.
27. G. Adhikari (ed.), *Documents of the History of the Communist Party of India* (Delhi, 1979), vol. III-B, pp. 283-4.
28. *Tribune*, 24 August 1927; *Times of India*, 23 August 1927.
29. Gandhi to Ansari, 10 August 1927, *CWMG*, vol. 34, p. 305.
30. Gandhi to Ansari, 26 August 1927, Hasan (ed.), *Muslims and the Congress*, p. 22.
31. Statement, n.d., ibid., p. 23. Also, speech at Madras, see *Hamdard*, 9 September 1927.
32. *Hindustan Times*, 7 September 1927; *Basumati*, 13 September, Ansari Papers, JMI.
33. Hasan (ed.), *Muslims and the Congress*, p. 24. M.N. Roy wrongly believed that Ansari desired peace with British imperialism. In a statement published in the *Times of India* on 10 November 1927, Ansari had already stated that the difference between the government and the people of India was so great and fundamental that 'they would be considered self-sufficient for the people to stand aside and abstain from any participation in the work of the commission'. See Adhikari (ed.), *Documents*, op. cit., p. 103.
34. Ibid., pp. 25-42.
35. *Hindustan Times*, 15 December 1927.
36. 12 December 1927, Hasan (ed.), *Muslims and the Congress*, pp. 41-2.
37. *Hindu*, 23 December 1927, *Daily Express*, 24 December 1927; *Justice*, 24 December 1927, Ansari Papers, JMI.
38. *Tribune*, 26 December 1927. For comments on Ansari's presidential address, see Ansari Papers, JMI.
39. *Leader*, Note on the Press, UP, for the week ending 7 January 1928, ibid.
40. Ibid.; *Bombay Chronicle*, 27 December 1928.
41. Pandey, *Nehru*, p. 129; Judith M. Brown, *Gandhi and Civil Disobedience: The Mahatma in Indian Politics 1928-1934* (Cambridge, 1977), p. 22.
42. Note on the Press, UP, for the week ending 14 January 1928; Adhikari (ed.), *Documents*, op. cit., p. 313.
43. Stanley Wolpert, *Jinnah of Pakistan* (Oxford University Press, New York, 1984), p. 90.

44. The recommendations of the Nehru Report have been discussed and analysed at length by me in *Nationalism and Communal Politics*, ch. 8. For Shaukat Ali's criticism, see *Hamdard*, 3 September 1928. Ansari, however, issued a general statement answering criticisms levelled against him by Shaukat Ali and a section of the Urdu press. He denied the charge that Muslim speakers were not allowed to express their views. Ansari to Motilal, 9 September 1928, F. No. 105, 1928, AICC Papers (Suppl.); also, *Hamdard*, 5 September 1928.
45. Ansari to Motilal, 19 September 1928, ibid. For Ansari's speech at the All-Parties National Convention, Hasan (ed.), *Muslims and the Congress*, pp. 306-10.
46. Wolpert, op. cit., pp. 101-2.
47. To Ansari, 6 September 1929, F. No. 105, AICC Papers.
48. To Ansari, 19 May 1929, Hasan (ed.), *Muslims and the Congress*, p. 70.
49. For details see Hasan, *Mohamed Ali Ideology and Politics*, pp. 94-7.
50. An interesting analysis of the Muslim Conference has been attempted by David Page. I am not aware of any other study on the subject.
51. 14 June 1929, Hasan (ed.), *Muslims and the Congress*, pp. 65-6.
52. To Mazharul Haq, 7 September 1929, ibid., pp. 86-7.
53. *Comrade*, 9 January 1925.
54. 'I regard and call my "Bapu" more than a political chief and more than a brother', *Comrade*, 9 January 1925.
55. Ibid., 1 May 1925; *Hamdard*, 24 August 1926.
56. Ibid., 16 October 1925. Afzal Iqbal (ed.), *Select Speeches and Writings of Maulana Mohamed Ali* (Lahore, 1944), pp. 331-2, 337.
57. Hasan, *Mohamed Ali: Ideology and Politics*, p. 191.
58. Ibid., pp. 101-2.

8

Leading the Congress Muslims

> Communalism is too harmful to be left to itself in the hope that it will die a natural death some day in the definite future. . . . Your first duty, therefore, is to carry on a relentless crusade against communalism as an active guiding principle of Indian political life.
>
> [M.A. Ansari in 1928]
> *Modern Review*, July 1929, p. 104

IN THE AFTERMATH of the Nehru Report controversy, the Congress had to reckon with Jinnah's 'Fourteen Points' and the demands echoed at the Khilafat and Muslim League meetings in the Christmas week of 1928. Gandhi tried to soothe suspicions with assurances that swaraj did not mean Hindu raj and met Jinnah in February and August 1929 to explore possible avenues to peace. But Lajpat Rai, Malaviya, Jayakar, Moonje, working president of the Hindu Mahasabha (1927-35), thwarted his initiative. Kelkar urged the Mahatma not to reach a solution outside the terms of the Nehru Report.[1] Lajpat Rai would have no modification,[2] while Jayakar warned Gandhi not to yield to the Muslim demands on the ground that the government, as in 1919, would deliberately make any concessions part of a constitution.[3] Caught up in this cross fire, Gandhi wrote to Motilal in anguish: 'How that can be done [resolving the communal deadlock] or whether it should be done, you know best. My mind is in a whirl in this matter. The atmosphere is too foggy for me to see clearly.'[4]

With the crusade against the Nehru Report gathering momentum, the Lahore Congress prudently decided to let it lapse. To woo the Sikhs and Muslims it resolved not to accept any solution of the communal problem without the concurrence of the minorities concerned.[5] Gandhi hoped that the two momentous decisions—declaration of complete independence and civil disobedience—would enable leaders of various shades of opinion to draw their followers into the anti-colonial struggle. He wrote in *Navajivan*: 'If we have true freedom we will shed communal fear. Hindus and Muslims will cease to fear one another.'[6]

It was not enough to soothe Muslim feelings; it was important to arrest their growing alienation from the Congress. Their estrangement was attributed to a wide range of factors, including the supposed hegemony of the Hindu Mahasabha, Congress' inability to curb assertive and militant expressions of Hindu revivalism, and its reluctance to recognize Muslim political aspirations. Such had been the burden of Abdur Rahim's highly inflammatory presidential address at the Muslim League session in December 1925.[7] The charges he levelled against the Congress were exaggerated. But publicists and propagandists like him, aided and abetted by the government, were able to convince their followers that their 'salvation' lay in either forging an alliance with the government or in pursuing independent political action. Their success in reaching out to them led to the steady communalization of politics as well as the gradual decline in Muslim participation at annual Congress sessions.

Table 8.1 indicates the attendance of Muslim delegates at Congress sessions from 1918 to 1923. Without access to complete figures for later years, we can say that the number of Muslims gradually dwindled from a few hundred to less than a score. Likewise, their representation in the AICC showed an increase from 11.1 per cent in 1919 to 24.5 per cent in 1923 (Table 8.2).

TABLE 8.1: ATTENDANCE OF MUSLIM DELEGATES AT THE SESSIONS OF THE INDIAN NATIONAL CONGRESS, 1918-23

Year	*Total no. of delegates*	*No. of Muslim delegates*
1918	3,975	205
1919	6,717	314
1920	13,532	1,050
1921	4,201	521
1922	NA	NA
1923	1,550	111

SOURCE: Compiled from Reports of the Annual Sessions of the Indian National Congress.

TABLE 8.2: COMPOSITION OF THE AICC, 1919-23

Religion	1919 (*161 members*)	1920	1921	1922	1923
		(*163 members*)		(*338 members*)	
Hindus	139	133	124	242	248
Muslims	18	21	33	84	83
Sikhs	–	2	2	9	8
Parsees	3	4	2	–	–
Christians	1	2	2	3	2

SOURCE: Gopal Krishna, 'The Indian National Congress, 1918-1923' (D.Phil. thesis, Oxford, 1960), p. 747.

In 1922-3, 84 of the 338 AICC members were Muslims. By 1928, their number was reduced to 54 out of 332.[8] Provincial and district Congress committees, too, had very few Muslims. In UP, only seven Muslims served on various district committees: one each in Gonda, Allahabad, Jhansi, Moradabad, Fyzabad, Azamgarh, and two in Barabanki.[9]

Muslims had also begun to desert the Swaraj Party. In 1922-3 Motilal had built his support among an influential group of Lucknow and Allahabad-based professional men in UP: Sherwani, Rafi Ahmed Kidwai, Khaliquzzaman, and M.H. Kidwai.[10] In Bengal, Das allied with several leading Khilafatists by offering a set of extravagant concessions to the Bengali Muslims. In consequence, he swept the November 1923 polls, capturing an overall majority of seats, including half the Muslim seats. Muslim support was strongest in the eastern division of Chittagong and the northern division of Rajshahi, the storm centres of the Khilafat movement in Bengal. Likewise, the Swarajists won 10 of the 15 Muslim seats in the Calcutta Corporation elections in April 1928. Here the Muslim vote was strongest in the city's central mercantile wards among the Urdu-speaking merchants, property owners and artisans, who had formed the backbone of the Khilafat movement and who now chose pro-nationalist, and anti-British candidates in 10 of the 11 wards in which they voted.[11]

The repudiation of the Das pact eroded this impressive support. There were 15 Muslim Swarajists in 1923: there were none in 1926. The *Mussalman* found the Swaraj Party to be inimically disposed towards its erstwhile allies, while the *Satyagrahi* (16 February), *Taraqqee* (4 May) and the *Soltan*

(29 June) lambasted the Bengal Congress for preaching *shuddhi* and *sangathan*.[12] Husayn Suhrawardy (1893-1963) and Abdul Karim (1863-1943), leading negotiators of the Das pact, led their followers in Calcutta deeper into the labyrinth of distinctly communitarian politics.[13] The picture was the same in UP.[14] As against 11 Muslims nominated and 4 elected in 1923, 6 were renominated in 1926 and only 1 returned. Some Muslims who had, in the recent past, contributed to Congress' popularity were now arrayed among its enemies.[15]

Of the eight Swarajist Muslims returned in 1923 to the Central Assembly, only 3 were elected in 1926. Many of them were irked by Motilal's attitude towards reforms in the North-West Frontier Province. Syed Murtaza, a Swarajist from Madras, was one of them. He accused Motilal of sacrificing the Frontier Muslims in order to woo Lajpat Rai on the eve of the 1926 elections.[16] Equally harsh was Shafee Daoodi's indictment. 'Temporary success in your political endeavours has got greater value for you than the more enduring rapprochement of the two great communities of India.' He charged that the Congress had been gradually drifting towards the Mahasabha and that it had now reduced itself to being its tool.[17] Both Murtaza and Daoodi quit the Swaraj Party in 1926.

However, the silver lining from the Congress point of view was the sporadic and fragmented political activity among Muslims. In fact, the polarization of communities along religious lines had yet to occur. Conflicting regional, local and class interests—a consequence of the uneven development of the Muslims in different parts of the country—exposed the hollowness of the League's claim to represent all Muslims. The formal split between the Jinnah and the Shafi factions in 1927 revealed, in fact, the deep-rooted divisions in the so-called monolithic Muslim polity. Any new party, whether cobbled together by the Khilafatists or the Leaguers, promised to be a splintered structure that could collapse at any moment. Such was the fate of the Muslim Conference after 1932. The organizers, like the Dutch army, were all generals but no soldiers. Most belonged to the landowning class and none of them was prepared to spearhead the movement or to follow the other.[18]

Equally noteworthy is that, while Muslims were moving away from the Congress, they were not necessarily swelling the ranks of the League, a highly unrepresentative body. Jinnah's attempts to infuse some life into it were poorly rewarded; the Leagues' total membership rose from a mere 1,093 in 1922 to a mere 1,330 in 1927.[19] Provincial Leagues did not fare better; the branch in the Bombay presidency had 71 members in 1928.[20] The organizers had to adjourn the 1929 session for lack of a quorum. When they met four months later in Delhi, the meeting ended in a fiasco.[21] When Iqbal presented his historic address in 1930 demanding a Muslim state in north-western India, the meeting at Allahabad did not even have its quorum of 75 members.[22] The *Mussalman* bemoaned that the only connection, an ordinary member had with the League was to be visited with a V.P.P. for his membership fee. 'It appears that nowadays there are very few who honour those V.P.Ps as the members have been disgusted with the Muslim League on account of its culpable inactivity. The provincial Leagues have imbibed the inactivity and the character of the parent body.'[23]

While the local and regional expressions of 'Muslim communalism', 'Muslim separatism' and 'Muslim nationalism' could not go unnoticed, the Congress, with its claim of being the sole spokesmen of all Indians, drew comfort from the 'most distinguished and trusted leaders and counsellors'.[24] They were designated as 'Nationalist Muslims'. 'They are men,' said Ansari, 'to whom the freedom of the country from alien rule comes merely as a bad second to communal privileges.'[25]

The exclusive application of the label 'Nationalist Muslim' conjures a false image of a largely communally-oriented community, with only a handful integrated with the dominant nationalist trend. (Notice that the expression 'Nationalist Hindu' is not used to distinguish the activities of Gandhi, Nehru, Das and Bose from those of Lajpat Rai, Malaviya, Jayakar and Kelkar.) It also needs to be emphasized that the dividing line between a professed nationalist and a so-called communalist was often blurred. It is thus not easy to place Mohamed Ali in this supposed dichotomous framework. Though a relentless critic of the Congress, he did not waver in his commitment to swaraj. This was amply borne out by his famous speech at the Round Table Conference and his 'Last Letter' to the British prime minister. Ansari conceded that, despite being led into the 'camp of national reaction', the Ali Brothers had not 'surrendered their loyalty to the fundamental principle of Indian politics, freedom from foreign domination'.[26]

There were two main sources of inspiration for the Congress Muslims. Some like Azad and Husain Ahmad Madani (1879-1957), head of the Dar al-ulum at Deoband, derived their nationalist ardour from their interpretation of Islam as a religion of freedom and equality, of justice, of cooperation with, and respect for, all mankind.[27] In May 1930, the Jamiyat al-ulama came around to accepting Gandhi's leadership in the civil disobedience movement; their conference at Amroha called upon Muslims to join Congress and appointed a committee to prepare a programme of action for attaining freedom; the rival conference—Anjuman-i Tausi-i Islam—set up by government and encouraged by the Nawab of Chhatari (1889-1982) and the Ali Brothers was a fiasco. By mid-June, the Jamiyat enrolled 15,000 volunteers and over 100 of its leading members languished in jail; in Delhi, Jamiyat volunteers secured pledges from Muslims that they would discard the use of foreign cloth. Kifayatullah, president, and Ahmad Said, secretary and director of the 'War Council', were arrested on 11 October 1930 and sentenced to six months' imprisonment. In the mid-1930s, Madani defended full and individual Muslim participation in the freedom struggle by advancing a theory of territorial nationhood rather than by appealing to concepts of safeguards and community confederation. He expressed his ideas in a public controversy with Iqbal shortly before the latter's death in 1938.[28]

The Western-educated Muslims had one basic thing in common: a shared perception of nationalism as a legitimate expression to achieving swaraj. Without a firm nationalist tradition, stated Ali Imam, the Bihar lawyer-politician, it was impossible to visualize a free India.[29] Likewise, they regarded the Congress as a symbol of popular aspirations, and therefore the largest, the most important and the most representative organization. It alone could act as a vehicle for bringing about the much-awaited political, social and economic transformation. By joining the

Congress in large numbers, stated Mujibur Rahman (d. 1940) at the Bakarganj District Muslim Conference in May 1931, Muslims of Bengal would take a greater share in suffering and sacrifice and a greater part in the freedom struggle.[30] The Frontier leader, Khan Abdul Ghaffar Khan (b. 1890), said at a public meeting in December 1931 that the Congress alone would free the country, feed the hungry and clothe the naked.[31] The *Jirgah* of India, he reaffirmed elsewhere, was called Congress—a common *Jirgah* of all the communities. Justifying his alliance with the Congress, he said: 'In order to save himself from the enemies did not the Holy Prophet make alliance with the Jews and the politheists [*sic*]?'[32] His audience beamed approvingly.

The Congress Muslim groups spanned several provinces of British India. In the Frontier province, the Khudai Khidmatgars (Servants of God), led by the charismatic figure of Ghaffar Khan, were at the head of a nationalist and socially progressive movement. Their presence was first noticed at the Lahore Congress in 1929 and within two years of its creation the Khudai Khidmatgar Party claimed a membership of 200,000.[33] Quotations from the Quran against slavery served as rallying points for nationalist enthusiasm and the struggle to liberate the country from foreign rule became the Holy War of the Khudai Khidmatgars. 'No section of India,' observed W.C. Smith in 1943, 'has been more thoroughly nationalist'.[34]

During civil disobedience in 1930-1, Khudai Khidmatgar activists were linked with the general Congress movement—the connection being strengthened in August 1931 when the Afghan *Jirga* merged with the PCC. The local *Jirgas* became local Congress committees, while 'Red Shirt' volunteers became part of the Congress at various levels. The whole movement was conducted in accordance with the Congress constitution and the flag used was the Congress flag. Ghaffar Khan explained in November 1931:

> People complain against me for having joined the Congress by selling my nation. The Congress is a national and not a Hindu body. It is a jirga composed of Hindus, Jews, Sikhs, Parsis and Muslims. The Congress as a body is working against the British. The British nation is the enemy of the Congress and of the Pathans. I have therefore joined it and made common cause with the Congress to get rid of the British.[35]

The intensity of civil disobedience was reflected in the number of prosecutions and convictions. Until September 1932, the figure was 5,557 in a total population of 25 lakh. In neighbouring Punjab, on the other hand, the number was 1,620, though the population was more than eight times that of the NWFP.[36] Convictions were also higher than the Bombay Presidency [see Table 8.3]. Towards the end of 1932, out of 1,500 civil disobedience prisoners in Peshawar, 5 were Hindus, 2 Sikhs, the rest being Muslims. The Haripur central jail housed 1,938 Muslims and 24 Hindus. In the province as a whole over 90 per cent of the civil disobedience prisoners were Muslims.[37] Clearly, Ghaffar Khan's message struck a favourable chord in an area which had remained relatively tranquil during non-cooperation and was not fully exposed to either the institutional or agitational politics of most other parts of British India. Ghaffar Khan's motto 'We are Pakhtuns but until we attain freedom we do not deserve to be called Pakhtuns'[38] remained the rallying slogan during the decades before the Partition of India.

The Majlis-i-Ahrar-i Islam, organized in 1929 by a group of Punjabi Muslims who had seceded from the Khilafat committees, was based on the well-to-do peasantry and the lower-middle classes. Its followers combined economic grievances and religious passions to formulate their militant policies.[39] They expressed something of the old Khilafat movement tradition: an ardent and explicit enthusiasm for freedom. Like the Khudai Khidmatgars, they steadily, fervently and inspiredly plunged into the civil disobedience movement and went to jail in large numbers.[40] In Delhi, they combined with the Jamiyat al-ulama in organizing processions and picketing liquor shops, leading to the arrest of Azad, Kifayatullah and twenty-five Ahrars in early March 1932.

TABLE 8.3: CONVICTIONS IN BOMBAY AND NORTH-WESTERN PROVINCE DURING CIVIL DISOBEDIENCE MOVEMENT

	Convictions in Jan.-Feb. 1932	*Convictions in Mar-Sept. 1932*	*Total*
Bombay	5,165	6,311	11,476
NWFP	4,318	1,239	5,557

SOURCE: Home Poll. F. No. S/72, 1932, NAI.

Reminiscent of scenes during the Rowlatt satyagraha was a mammoth meeting at Fatehpuri mosque where 4,500-5,000 Muslims pledged their cooperation with Gandhi's civil disobedience movement.[41]

The Ahrars were active in Kashmir against the Dogra ruler, Maharaja Hari Singh, to redress the grievances of the Muslim subjects.[42] These were set out in the memorial submitted to the Maharaja on 19 October 1931,[43] and taken note of by B.J. Glancy who headed a commission to enquire into the demands of the memorialists.[44] Led by Mazhar Ali, Habibur Rahman of Ludhiana (1892-1956), Abdur Rahman Ghazi and Ataullah Shah Bukhari (1891-1967), the Ahrars sent *jathas* of red-uniformed *razakars* (volunteers) to Kashmir in order to bear pressure on the Maharaja to meet the demands of his Muslim 'subjects'.[45] The outcome was large-scale rioting in Jammu on 2 November 1931 and violent clashes at Mirpur between the *jathas* and the state forces. British troops were pressed into service to quell the disturbances.

The spur in political activity strengthened nationalist and progressive forces among the Kashmiri masses, more than three quarters of whom were Muslims. The Jammu and Kashmir Muslim Conference, founded in 1932, symbolized their aspirations. The Conference, stated its founder Shaikh Mohammad Abdullah (1905-82), though Muslim in name was 'in spirit national and was concerned with the welfare of all communities'.[46] He declared in 1931 and, again in 1935 that the country's progress depended on harmonious communal relations[47] and his fight was for the country's emancipation. 'Let us all rise above petty communal bickerings and work jointly for the welfare of the masses,' he said.[48] In the years to come, the economic programme of the Muslim Conference, embodied in the 'New Kashmir' Plan, and its political orientation was akin to that of the Congress. Abdullah repudiated the two-nation theory and hitched the fortunes of his people with Indian nationalism.

In Bombay, Syed Abdullah Brelvi (1891-1949), editor of the *Bombay Chronicle*, launched the Congress Muslim Party on 8 July 1929 to induce Muslims to join the Congress.[49] His chief support lay among urban-based politicians, such as Yusuf Meharally (1903-50), editor of the English weekly *Vanguard*, Abbas Tyabji (1854-1936), a lawyer with long-standing associations with the Congress movement, and M.C. Chagla (1900-82), also a lawyer who came to the forefront as a vociferous champion of the Nehru Report. Gandhi blessed them with the message: 'If it is fully supported and does not go to sleep, it may prove a tower of strength to the Congress and an instrument of real service to India generally and to Mussalmans in particular.'[50] The fact is that the Congress Muslim Party, in spite of stiff opposition from Shaukat Ali and his followers among the Urdu-speaking Muslims, established its hold in Bombay city. Brelvi, backed by several Muslim mercantile associations in Bombay, led a mile-long procession on 2 June 1930 and presided over a meeting of about 10,000, which called on Muslims to join the civil disobedience movement.[51] 'Conspicuous amongst organizers of procession and speakers at meeting,' noted a government report, 'were certain Maulanas and Muslim propagandists from other provinces. To this extent, [the] procession must be regarded as success of Congress propaganda and it must be admitted that during the last fortnight many Muhammadans have been gathered into the Congress fold.'[52]

Such examples provide a corrective to the impression that the Muslim community stood aloof from the civil disobedience.[53] This is not to deny that, compared to 1920-1, their enthusiasm was much less. But to compare their response in these years to the civil disobedience days, and, then to draw evidence of their indifference or hostility is misleading. The religious passions evoked by the Khilafat question were both unique and unprecedented: there was no such issue in the early 1930s to evince the same degree of interest.

THE ALL-INDIA NATIONALIST MUSLIM PARTY

Among the Congress Muslim groups in the late 1920s, the All-India Nationalist Muslim Party (NMP) acquired greater significance because it mirrored local and regional manifestations of Muslim nationalist aspirations. It occupied a vital position both in terms of its influence in urban areas as well as in articulating the views of Congress Muslims. For the first time, they addressed themselves exclusively to communitarian issues either in relation to or independently of the party to which they owed allegiance. The

NMP offered a platform which ideally suited their political objectives.

Formed on 27-28 July 1929, the NMP resolution stated:

> The political struggle started in 1919 is being gradually weakened by inter-communal conflicts and repeated attempts are being made in different quarters to wean Muslims away from political activities. The present disruption among political-minded Muslims and the consequent apathy of the mass of the Muslim community towards the problem of Indian freedom are due to a confused appreciation of the political obligations implicit in the fact of the community being a part of the Indian nation. Muslim political activity is now confined under the auspices of the existing Muslim institutions, to winning political responsibility as the main objective and with freedom for the country as merely incidental thereto. Hence the need for the new party. The formal objects of it are to promote among Muslims a spirit of nationalism, to develop a mentality above communalism and to inspire into them greater confidence in Indian national ideas, to induce Muslims to take their proper share in the national struggle and to create such relations between the majority and minority communities as would lead the former to consider the rights of the latter in a spirit of broad-minded patriotism.[54]

Khaliquzzaman claimed to have founded the NMP. 'As there was nobody of opinion inside or outside the Congress for ventilating organized nationalist view frankly and honestly,' he wrote in his autobiography, 'I hoped that the establishment of this organization might serve to arrest such an undisciplined exhibition of loyalty to Congress, misleading its leaders and dragging it into dark alleys. I talked to Ansari about my views.'[55] This claim is not sustained by existing historical evidence, which points to Ansari as the architect of the NMP and the man who also held it together. Others closely associated with him were Rafi Ahmad Kidwai, Sherwani, Azad, Ghaffar Khan, Khaliquzzaman, Brelvi, Khwaja, Mujibur Rahman, Kitchlew and Abdul Bari (d. 1947) of Bihar. The *ulama* support came from Kifayatullah Mohammad Sajjad and Ahmad Said—all of the Jamiyat al-ulama and from Qutubuddin Wali of Firangi Mahal in Lucknow.[56]

At its first meeting held at Sherwani's house in Allahabad on 27 July 1929, a central body was constituted of 28 members elected from Bengal, 27 from the Punjab, 3 from the Frontier,

24 from UP, 14 from Delhi, 17 from Bihar and 10 from Bombay and Sind. Seven provincial and seventy-one district branches were established. District branches in UP were set up in Lucknow, Rae Bareli, Allahabad, Banaras, Fyzabad, Hardoi, Bijnor, Saharanpur, Bareilly, Meerut, Aligarh and Shahjahanpur.[57] In Punjab, NMP committees operated in eight districts. Ten of them functioned in Bihar and at least four in Calcutta, Dacca, Bogra and Faridpur. The Dacca committee was headed by Shamsul Huda and Ghulam Qadri, the Calcutta committee by Mujibur Rahman, Akram Khan, K. Nooruddin and Abdur Razzack (both Calcutta Corporation councillors), while the Bogra and Faridpur branches were controlled by a scattering of others who had participated in the Khilafat and non-cooperation movements.[58] On the strength of this wide network built in a relatively short time, the NMP claimed to represent the 'entire Muslim intelligentsia'.[59] Ansari scoffed at the League, pointing out that it had long ceased to be a reality, while the Khilafat committees, once so powerful in the country, 'were now but a shadow of its former self'. He asserted that the NMP was the 'real representative group of the Mussalmans of India today'.[60]

These were exaggerated claims. Yet, the NMP, in spite of its limited political base, had the *potential* of becoming a powerful force.[61] The first warning signal came when Ansari and his comrades staked their claim to attend the Round Table Conference in London. Gandhi insisted on taking Ansari with him,[62] and told the viceroy that without him he would be 'perfectly helpless' in Hindu-Muslim negotiations.[63] But the viceroy did not acquiesce. The Mahatma announced in London that whoever prevented Ansari from being selected as a delegate committed a 'fatal blunder'.[64] Fazl-i Husain who, as member of the Viceroy's Council, influenced official policy on Hindu-Muslim relations, did so. Backed by his allies in the Muslim Conference and a section of the Urdu press, the Punjab leader first opposed the inclusion of Ali Imam and the Raja of Mahmudabad[65] and then sought to prove the hollowness of Ansari's claim to represent the Muslims. He admired his character and his motives, adding, however, how 'during the last few weeks he [Ansari] seems to have done his best to convince all his friends and admirers that [his] partisanship of the Congress had deprived him of any sense of fair-play and propriety'.[66] Fazl-i-Husain reserved his harsh comments for Gandhi. 'To confuse the issues, to indulge in irrelevance and to begin to talk of Muslim demands, and then talk of Congress Muslims, of Dr Ansari and so on', he told friends in October 1931:

> are all devices with which Hindus as well as Muslims are quite familiar. Gandhi's insistence upon Dr Ansari's inclusion and his parading readiness for complete surrender in case complete unity is forthcoming have nothing new about them. They are the very old devices which the Congress, Gandhi and the Indian Hindus have been condemning in the British Government and the British statesmen. They are doing now exactly what they alleged Lord Birkenhead was doing—asking for complete unanimity and resorting to the well-known principle of Divide and Rule; but Gandhi should know that the people are not so unsophisticated today as they used to be and that the game he is now indulging in is one which has been played out for some time.[67]

Ansari did not enjoy being drawn into the controversy. The Mahatma, he reported on 28 September, 'is harking back on me and wanting me even at this eleventh hour to be invited. . . . It is like a baby crying for his wet-nurse.'[68] Convinced that government would not give in, he stated:

> I am positive that the government has deliberately left the Nationalist Muslim Party unrepresented . . . because they do not want the Hindu-Muslim question to be settled without their intervention. And they know that if there is any party in India which can bring about Hindu-Muslim unity it is the Nationalist Muslim Party. It is, therefore, against their interest to have the representatives of that party at the Round Table Conference, for they would be able to cement the unity of the various parties in India and thus deprive the government from playing their trump card against the representatives of India who are pressing hard for complete freedom from the British tutelage.[69]

He also felt that Gandhi should not insist on his inclusion but Jawaharlal dissuaded him not to be 'so rash as to cable him to do what he chooses'.[70] In early October, Gandhi, in fact, concurred that Ansari 'will be of no use unless the Muslim delegation desires or approves of his selection as a delegate'.[71]

Meanwhile, the NMP meetings at Lucknow (18-19 April 1931), Faridpur (27-28 June 1931) and Lahore (24 October 1931) were well-attended, and its pronouncements left a favourable impression in the NWFP, Punjab, UP and Bombay.[72] 'One of the most gratifying signs of the times,' commented the *Leader*, 'is the rapid growth of nationalism among Indian Muslims. The opponents of Indian progress and their allies, the Muslim communalists, will not be willing to admit this fact. But the impressive gathering of the nationalist Muslims at Lucknow from all parts of the country tells its own tale.'[73] The editor of the *Indian Annual Register* hoped that an influential party of nationalist Muslims would 'in the fullness of time, dominate the vast bulk of Indian Mohammedan opinion'.[74]

Ansari worked feverishly to weld together the Muslim factions and persuade them to accept his party's proposals on joint electorates and adult suffrage;[75] on other issues, there was no fundamental difference between Jinnah's 'fourteen points' and the main NMP resolution adopted on 18-19 April 1931.[76] On the question of electorates the NMP reiterated that separate electorates negated nationalism. Political problems, argued Ali Imam, president of the Lucknow conference, were a reflex of social forces. 'If you erect an iron wall between community and community in their politics, you destroy the social fabric. . . . Nationalism can never evolve from division and dissension.'[77] Ansari, too, stated that the measure and method of representation in the federal and provincial legislatures should be settled on the basis of joint electorates and adult suffrage, and that the Muslims would not accept a constitution which did not contain these provisions. He proposed a round table conference to iron out their differences.[79]

This statement set the stage for the real business at hand: ongoing talks between representatives of the NMP and the Muslim Conference. On 10-12 May they met at Bhopal. Ansari insisted on joint electorates for the first ten years with a provision for a referendum thereafter. Alternatively, 50 per cent of the seats were to be contested on the basis of joint and the other half on the basis of separate electorates in the first general election. The arrangement were to change in the second election when two-thirds of the seats were to be contested by joint electorates. Thereafter, joint electorates with adult suffrage, had to come into effect. Iqbal, Shafi, Shaukat Ali and Nawab Ismail Khan (1884-

1958) pressed for joint electorates and adult suffrage after ten years, provided they could be introduced earlier if a majority of legislators so desired. Their other proposal provided for five years of separate electorates with a referendum on joint electorates at the beginning of the fifth year.[80]

Ansari announced with characteristic optimism that the discussions at Bhopal raised the prospect of a settlement.[81] But his hopes were soon belied by the intransigence of delegates from both sides,[82] combined with Fazl-i Husain's stout refusal to endorse a compromise.[83] When talks resumed in Simla on 21 June 1931, the Punjab leader re-ignited the controversy by insisting on separate electorates and wanting Congress to state its position on weightage and reservation of seats for the Muslim majorities in Bengal and the Punjab.[84] Ansari found the atmosphere 'very inauspicious' for any compromise.[85] Ultimately, the conference accomplished little more than to restate a daunting agenda of continuing problems and differences.

Much of the blame for the failure of the Bhopal and Simla meetings was put on Ansari and his colleagues; a well-orchestrated campaign was also launched to deride the NMP.[86] Its policies, stated Shafaat Ahmad Khan (1893-1947), were 'like the bloom on the peach; you touch it and it is gone. Where is the party now? Nowhere! The exact, minute and detailed account of its branches and activities may be found in the secretariat of the Indian National Congress, but so far as Muslims of India are concerned they exist only on paper.'[87] Shafee Daoodi repeated the charge. Rafi Ahmad Kidwai replied that the number of Muslims in Congress exceeded the combined strength of all provincial Muslim Leagues and Khilafat committees.[88] Others excoriated the NMP for selling out the community's interest and the interest of Islam.[89] Ansari stoutly refuted the allegation: 'We are surely not worse Mussalmans because we refuse to turn our faith into a greedy superstition or an ignoble exercise in political hide and seek. . . . Our nationalism is part of our loyalty to our faith and not a betrayal or an infidelity.'[90] Shaukat Ali, who had no pretensions to detachment and only the flimsiest to moderation, made no effort to disguise his hostility. 'I consider you all to be weak men,' he told Syed Mahmud, 'and renegades, and, yielding to the open threats of the Hindus, [to] have chosen to live at their mercy.'[91] This was an ill-chosen way to dramatize his contention that the Congress Muslims had 'sold out' to the Hindus. Ansari tried to convince him that religion and faith were private matters, not symbols to be exploited by partisan politicians. But Shaukat Ali persisted with his barrage of ridicule, causing much distress to Ansari, a man with strong feelings and a deep instinct of loyalty. He attached importance to keeping his word and observing obligations. The unforgivable crime, in his eyes, was treachery: once he suspected anyone of not playing straight, he could be implacable, and once his confidence was lost, as in the case of Shaukat Ali, it was almost impossible to recover.

The Hindu Mahasabha did not spare Ansari. Moonje was convinced that some Muslims, masquerading as nationalists, were trying to infiltrate the Congress in large numbers in order to exert pressure from within.[92] In substance, he thought, there was no difference between the demands of the communalist and the nationalist Muslims.[93] C. Vijaraghavachariar (1852-1944), president of the Hindu Mahasabha in 1931, believed that the NMP resolutions adopted at Faridpur were 'subject to all the infirmities of the proposals of the other section of Muslims to which Mr Jinnah's fourteen points give expression'.[94]

The Hindu Mahasabha adopted a two-pronged strategy: it compared the NMP favourably with the Muslim League and the Muslim Conference, on the one hand, and prevented the party from extracting any concessions from the Congress, on the other. This was demonstrated during the Gandhi-Jinnah talks in 1929 and later when Sapru tried reaching an agreement with the non-Congress groups. Moonje was morbidly apprehensive of any move that might conciliate the Muslims, while Jayakar and Kelkar insisted that the Liberals declare themselves on the communal question and state the limits beyond which they would not go in negotiating with the Muslims.[95] Disheartened by their outburst, Sapru considered calling off the conference. But some of his Liberal friends urged him not to do so. 'If you abandon the calling of the conference,' wrote C.H. Setalvad (1901-71), 'you at once make them dictators and give them a new importance'.[96] Ramaswamy Aiyar (1890-1950) felt equally disgusted. 'Under the guise of communalism,' he pointed out, 'the Sabha is perhaps the most aggressive communal body in India and any day one would choose to work with the Raja of Mahmudabad, Jinnah and Ali Imam rather than with Moonje, Kelkar and Co.'[97] The conference was eventually held in March and the Hindu Mahasabha participated uneasily. The preliminary meeting decided to meet in May before the delegates to the Round Table Conference proceeded to London. While the Liberals and the Muslims held to this agreement, the Mahasabhites backed out.[98]

In July 1931, Ansari, Malaviya and Sardar Sardul Singh (b. 1886) recommended, and the Congress Working Committee adopted, a scheme based on 'undiluted communalism and undiluted nationalism'. Its main features were: joint electorates and adult suffrage, with reservation for minorities of less than 25 per cent. The NWFP and Baluchistan would have the same form of government and administration as other provinces, Sind would form a separate province provided its people were prepared to bear the financial burden of the separated province, and in the future federal constitution residuary powers would rest with the provinces unless found prejudicial to the country's interests. Gandhi commended these proposals and made special mention of Ansari's incessant labours. 'I have never known Dr Ansari so identified and absorbed in anything,' he wrote in *Young India*, 'as he has been about the communal question.'[99] But the Muslim Conference was unimpressed. Its organ, the *Star*, remarked that, despite the 'hotchpotching' by the Ansari-Azad group, the substance of the Muslim demands were not met.[100] The Mahasabha's rejection was equally unequivocal. The Congress formula, stated the *Abhyudaya*, 'had laid itself open to the charge of having deviated from the path of nationalism, and that it sought to benefit the minority at the expense of the majority community'.[101] Even with the issue squarely placed in the context of the country's interest—which is where he thought it ought to be—the Mahasabha was anything but enthusiastic. Ansari poured out his anger and frustration in a stream of letters to his friends.

Ansari watched helplessly as his overtures fell on stony ground. Meanwhile, he had been carrying a tremendous load of work and responsibility and pushed himself very hard. He therefore toyed with plans for going to Bad Neuheim (Germany) for treatment and a prolonged period of rest in Europe. He planned to travel some time in January 1930, but was caught up by the turn of political events and in domestic chores. In May, he arranged the wedding of his friend and political comrade, Shuaib Qureshi; in August, he lost his brother Abdur Razzaq; and in the same month (28 August), the government sentenced him to six months' imprisonment in Central Jail, Delhi, for organizing civil disobedience in Delhi. He was transferred the following day to the Gujarat Special Jail where, according to Ghaffar Khan, 'under the guidance of Dr Ansari we had formed a parliament of our own to train us to run our government which, we thought, was in the offing'.[102]

Out of jail at the end of January 1931, Ansari was constantly kept in a 'whirlpool of excitement'. He finally sailed on board the *S.S. Victoria* at 11 a.m. on 11 August 1932 in the company of T.A.K. Sherwani. There were others as well, but few of them possessed Ansari's practical experience of men and politics and it was this, unfolded in a series of rich anecdotes and drawn upon at every turn in support of his arguments, which fascinated his fellow travellers.

Ansari was treated for his heart trouble at Bad Neuheim. He, then, spent an educative week in Vienna where a select Viennese society of professors, literary, scientific and artistic people welcomed him. His next halt was in Ouchy-Lausanne. Here he felt lonely as he did not have a friend or acquaintance, but enjoyed the peace and quiet of his surroundings and kept himself busy writing to Aziz Ansari and Shaukatullah, reading books, sightseeing and making arrangements for sending his son, Ahmad Harold, born from his second marriage, to an English public school.[103] From Lausanne he travelled to Paris in November and then to London where he stayed till 13 December. This was one of his many visits to Europe; it reawakened his old joy in scenery and open air.

Ansari returned to Delhi on 14 January and went up to see Jawaharlal at the Naini Central Prison in Dehradun. Jawaharlal noted in his prison diary on 17 February:

> Ansari suddenly turned up without any previous warning. . . . Freshly returned from Europe full of stories of common friends and memories

of old haunts in Switzerland and elsewhere. He looked much better than when he came in July. But his heart still gives trouble. He has wandered all over Europe while I sat and fed and slept in this same old little cell.[104]

Ansari reached India in a thoroughly gloomy frame of mind. The old communal spectre, far from withering away, assumed a new and more malignant guise. Moreover, the NMP, of which he was the chief architect, had disintegrated. Khaliquzzaman, no longer inhibited by fear of Ansari's disapproval, signed its death warrant in UP by founding the Muslim Unity Board. In Punjab, the NMP was unable to make much headway because of Fazl-i-Husain and the Unionists, and it disappeared in Bengal owing to Fazlul Haq and the United Muslim Party. The new Muslim Majlis, formed in UP and Bengal to join hands with progressive and nationalist elements, could not make a dent on the communal forces. Abdur Rahman Siddiqi, another of Ansari's favourites and founder of the Bengal New Muslim Majlis, joined Husayn Suhrawardy, while Mujibur Rahman found it difficult to cope with the confusing plethora of groups among Muslims.[105] By 1934, the Congress Muslims stood 'divested of every shred of principle or practice on the basis of which they formed their group and which they had proudly nailed to their masthead—of everything, all, except their name!'[106] By its very nature, observed Khaliquzzaman many years later, the NMP could not progress. Under its name, several conferences were held, but it had no rules or regulations, no separate membership and no office. Being backed by the Hindu Sabha Press it lived in the newspapers all right but beyond that it had no positive existence. Jawaharlal's idea that it might serve to bring about discipline in Nationalist Muslim ranks did not materialize because the remedy was not potent enough to eradicate the evil.[107]

Jawaharlal attributed the NMP's decline to the upper middle class background of its members, and their method of drawing-room meetings and mutual arrangements and pacts. At this game, he argued, the communal leaders were greater adepts and they

drove the Nationalist Muslims from one position to another, made them give up, one by one, the principles for which they stood. Always the Nationalist Muslims tried to ward off further retreat and to consolidate their position by adopting the policy of the 'lesser evil', but always this led to another retreat and another choice of the 'lesser evil'. There came a time when they had nothing left to call their own, no fundamental principle on which they stood except one, and that had been the very sheet-anchor of their group: joint electorates. But again the policy of the lesser evil presented the fatal choice to them and they emerged from the ordeal minus that sheet-anchor.[108]

To Jawaharlal's explanation, one must add the voices of protest from two Hindu Mahasabha, the Muslim Conference, and their diametrically opposite directions—local and regional allies. Working under severe constraints, the NMP could not, for instance, replace the Unionists in Punjab and the Proja Krishak Party in Bengal. It was therefore reduced to arbitrating between the Congress and communally-inclined parties—a role Ansari played in the early 1930s. At the same time, there were serious difficulties in being effective in this role. That is why while such constituents of the NMP as the Khudai Khidmatgars, the Jamiyat al-ulama and the Ahrars retained their individuality, Ansari and his compatriots went their separate ways. Consequently, the NMP lost its *raison d'être* as an independent political entity.

With their image linked with the Hindus, the Congress Muslims were pictured as renegades and accused of a sell-out. The *Himmat*, the *Al-Khalil*, *Mansur* and the *Aligarh Mail*—newspapers published in UP—denounced them for sacrificing the community's interests at the altar of the Nehru Report. The *Al-Khalil* dubbed them as 'traitors' and 'mercenary agents' of Motilal and other Hindus.[109] Even though such charges were bandied about, the NMP leaders did not do much to dispel such impressions. Ansari was, of course, a notable exception. He persevered doggedly, because of his awareness of the need to respond to the pressures for change. He also possessed the courage and the conviction to assert his political will and face the daunting challenge posed by both the Hindu and Muslim communalists with tenacity. He often met criticism and at times bitter attacks, but he did not hesitate carrying the issue to the floor and fighting it out with his critics. But his lieutenants in the NMP were weak, disorganized and unwilling to solve their problems of tactics, coordination or leadership; in fact, Ansari soon became aware of how wayward were the elements he was seeking to fuse into one. Used to playing second fiddle—first to Mohamed Ali and later to Ansari—some NMP members gradually succumbed to communal pressures; others sulked when faced with the combined assault of the Muslim Conference, the Muslim League and a section of the *ulama*. Jawaharlal observed in April 1937:

> Our experience of the Nationalist Muslim Party in the past was not a happy one. Such half-way groupings confuse the issue and the masses are perplexed. . . . Those who agree (with the Congress) should not stand on the doorstep; they should enter the nation's chamber and take full share in shaping the nation's policy.[110]

The failure of Congress Muslims to confront the ideologues of the Muslim Conference and the League can be attributed to their inability to formulate a coherent ideological programme within a framework acceptable to their own constituency. A section in the Jamiyat al-ulama worked out a theory of Islamic nationalism *versus* imperialism—one which was grounded in the basic tenets of Islam. They came round to the view that the future of Islam in India lay in combining with the forces of nationalism in opposition to the raj. Thus the All-India Momin Conference and the Khudai Khidmatgars reconciled their *nationalism* with the specific demands and distinct interests of their constituents. The Congress Muslims made no such endeavour.

The NMP was composed of a small number of professional men—lawyers, doctors and journalists—who did not operate in politics from a position they could claim their own. They depended on the goodwill of leading Congressmen who, in turn, patronized them in order to lend credence to their own claim of representing all Indians. There was nothing wrong in relying on Congress; in fact, it was consistent with NMP's political objectives. What proved detrimental to its credibility and eventual collapse was the absence of any endeavour to extend the political base outside the Congress circles. It was, moreover, caught up in constitutional issues, somewhat obsessively. Ansari was associated with the All-Parties Conference, Shuaib Qureshi served as a member of the Nehru Committee and Khaliquzzaman, Syed Mahmud, Sherwani and Khwaja were enmeshed in constitutional controversies which raged from the time of the first Round Table Conference and culminated in the squabbles over the Communal

Award. Given the alignment of forces, the capacity of such men to negotiate a compromise was limited. They could neither bargain for nor on behalf of their co-religionists. In consequence, they operated on the fringes and were made, in the words of Shaukat Ali, a cat's paw by their Congress co-workers.

Admittedly, some Congress Muslims identified themselves with the Kisan movements in UP during the Khilafat and non-cooperation movements, but beyond the expressions of sympathy and concern, the Congress Muslims had no role in the working class movement in Bombay or the Kisan agitation in UP, Bihar and Bengal. Their speeches and manifestos were devoid of any socio-economic content because they only dimly understood the economic and social changes that were taking place around them. This would probably explain why political depth, comprehension and wisdom were missing in their comprehension and analysis of communalism. Viewing it largely in the context of the struggle for power, influence and authority, they demonstrated no awareness of the socio-economic structures which engendered tensions and animosities.

The position of Congress Muslims was weakened by the apathy of their comrades in Congress. It is true that the Congress assiduously courted them in the 1920s. It is also true that Gandhi flattered and cajoled them during the Khilafat campaign and used Ansari and Ajmal Khan, for instance, to follow a middle-of-the-road policy. Later, he used them to secure the electoral support of the Muslims.[111] Motilal wooed Ansari, Shuaib Qureshi and Khaliquzzaman from the time of the All-Parties Conference in early 1928 till the National Convention in December of that year. Gandhi made laudatory references to their fervent commitment to Hindu-Muslim unity and insisted on Ansari's participation in the Round Table Conference.

Such symbolic gestures did not help the Congress Muslims, who faced the combined opposition of the Mahasabha and the Muslim Conference. Moreover, they did not receive the strong ideological and political backing from the Congress. They were merely used on occasions, given decorative positions in the Congress hierarchy and loudly proclaimed as selfless and devoted leaders. At the same time, their point of view was often disregarded with undeserved contempt.[112] This was so at the Lahore Congress in 1929. It was a situation which left people like Ansari restless and frustrated, conscious of his abilities as an organizer and seeing the job that needed to be done, without the chance to take a hand in it. 'We found the atmosphere in Lahore,' wrote Khaliquzzaman,

> very secretive and when in private talks the leading Congressmen decided to throw the Nehru Report into the Ravi, even Dr Ansari was not consulted. . . . Dr Ansari, Tasadduq and myself were leaving Lahore in the evening for our destinations, humbled, disappointed and angry. . . . At the station we had enough time to decide between ourselves that the Nehru Report having been drowned in the Ravi, we could not take the responsibility of shouldering the burden of fighting for the independence of India, for the Muslims were bound to consider it to be a purely Hindu fight.[113]

Assuming that the Congress Muslims had no large following, they were treated at best as bargaining counters; when not so, they could easily be stored in the deep freeze.[114] This placed Ansari and his friends in a quandary. Thus, when Gandhi agreed to compromise on separate electorates, Khwaja reacted in the following way: 'It means,' he wrote indignantly,

> that you are prepared to surrender the Congress Muslims who have fought the battles of the country side by side with you to those Mussalmans who have done nothing except for themselves, their seats, their posts, their salaries and their lunches and dinners at the Government Houses. . . . So far they [Congress Muslims] have fought against the Government and against the self-seekers of their own community. . . . If now they are thrown overboard by the Congress or by you, they must either clear out of the field altogether or must henceforth fight against the Congress. Khwaja opposed both separate electorates and communal representation as he felt that the 'salvation of the Muslims lies in the salvation of the motherland and the salvation of the motherland in its turn lies in the mutual trust and goodwill of the two great communities.'[115]

Ansari summed up his own predicament in early January 1930—soon after the Congress ignored his criticism of the Lahore Congress:

> We must not leave the Congress, nor must we do anything to weaken the Congress. After all the will of the majority must prevail, that is the only guide for any democratic institution. . . . To leave the Congress

would be to commit political suicide, to oppose the Congress would be a crime. Therefore we must remain in the Congress and let those who believe in the present policy and programme carry on.

Again,

as. . . . for joining the Liberals or the communalists it is unthinkable for you and me. The Liberals will never do anything, even though they are kicked out of the Round Table Conference. . . . As regards the Muslim communalists, we have . . . extricated ourselves from them. We have formed the 'Nationalist Muslim Party' and it would be the height of unwisdom to leave that party or to cease working for its objects. *To my mind, that is the only avenue left for our political activities* [emphasis added]. We must put all our mind to it and carry on a vigorous campaign to wean the Muslims away from the influence of communalists and reactionary leaders and think and act in terms of "nationalism". *That is the only channel left for our political activities* [emphasis added].[116]

It is surprising to find such a sober, commonsense approach in a man who combined strict standards of political honesty and political obligation with a passionate emotional involvement in what he was doing. This is not to argue that Ansari was right—that is a question of opinion which every historian will answer for himself: only that in opposing Gandhi, Ansari acted from conviction and in his own opinion would have been false to the principles which brought him into the Congress movement if he had acted otherwise.

NOTES

1. Jayakar to Gandhi, 23 August 1929, Jayakar Papers (437), NAI. In his reply, Gandhi assured Jayakar that he had not 'found anybody' because he had no representative capacity. 'I simply listened to Mr. Jinnah's exposition of his position. Similarly with the Ali Brothers too, I heard what they had to say. With the latter the talk turned upon their grievance against me for my reticence.' Gandhi to Jayakar, 24 August 1929, *CWMG*, vol. XLI, pp. 289-319.
2. Lajpat Rai to Motilal Nehru, n.d., F. No. 108 (Suppl.), AICC Papers; Moonje to Malaviya, 31 July 1928, Moonje to Gandhi, 5 August 1929, Jayakar Papers (437).
3. Uma Kaura, *Muslims and Indian Nationalism: The Emergence of the Demand for India's Partition* (Delhi, 1977), p. 50; R.J. Moore, *The Crisis of Indian Unity 1917-1940* (Delhi, 1974), p. 101.
4. Kaura, op. cit., p. 51.

5. Resolution on the communal problem passed by the CWC, July 1931, F. No. G-37/1931, AICC Papers; *IQR*, July-December 1929, pp. 310-11; Motilal to secretary, reception committee, Jamiyat al-ulama, 29 April 1930, Motilal Nehru Papers.
6. 9 January 1930, *CWMG*, vol. XLVII, p. 381.
7. Pirzada (ed.), *Foundations of Pakistan*, vol. 2, pp. 42-4.
8. F. No. G/59, 1928, AICC Papers.
9. F. No. 11, 1926, ibid.
10. Motilal was a patron of such men, as indeed of other Muslims, whom he helped to find jobs. See, for instance, the case of Hakim Wali who was recommended for the post of executive officer in Banaras municipality. Motilal to T.A.K. Sherwani, 29 July 1928, F. No. 60 (Suppl.), 1925-6, ibid. Motilal also ensured that the PCC's found Muslims of Congress and Swarajist views to elect candidates for elections. In a directive to the Sind PCC he insisted that 'the PCC even though constituted wholly by Hindus must rise above communalism and show that it makes no distinction between Nationalists whether they are Hindus or Muslims'. F. No. 76 (Suppl.), 1928, ibid.
11. Mcpherson, *The Muslim Microcosm*, p. 80.
12. *Mussalman*, 27 April 1926. Report on Native Newspapers, Bengal, January-December 1927, pp. 127, 204, 271.
13. Mcpherson, op. cit., sections 5 and 6 in chapter 5.
14. Pandey, *Ascendancy of the Congress*, section 5 in chapter 5.
15. Quoted in ibid., p. 145.
16. Page, *Prelude to Partition*, pp. 132-3.
17. Shafee Daoodi to Motilal Nehru, 26 March 1929, F. No. 96, Motilal Nehru Papers. Also, see *The Frontier Question in the Assembly, being the Statements of Pandit Motilal Nehru, MLA, Maulvi Shaft Daudi, MLA, and Syed Murtaza, MLA* (Delhi, 1926).
18. Khaliquzzaman, *Pathway to Pakistan*, p. 117.
19. The membership of the All-India Muslim League was 1,093 in 1922, 1,097 in 1923 and 1,184 in 1924. *Annual Report of the All-India Muslim League* (Lucknow, n.d.), Chagla Papers, NMML.
20. Sayeed, *Pakistan*, p. 176.
21. *Mussalman*, 3 July 1930.
22. Sayeed, *Pakistan*, pp. 176-7. 'It is a wonder that when this clarion call was made from the Muslim League platform (Iqbal's demand) no one took any notice of it and no one moved any resolution in the session approving the scheme enunciated at Allahabad.' Khaliquzzaman, op. cit., pp. 108-9. The total attendance, according to Fakhrul Islam, was between 400 and 500, including a large number of students. It is noteworthy that Iqbal's address was not even taken note of by the *Leader* of Allahabad. Mukhtar Zaman, 'Duaazda Manzil se Manzil-i Pakistan tak', *Nuqush* (Iqbal Number), September 1977, vol. 121, p. 501.
23. *Mussalman*, 3 July 1930. The League, observed its honorary secretary

in his 1931 annual report, was unable to perform its functions effectively because of the Muslim Conference 'which has divided our energies and caused a great deal of harm to the All-India Muslim League'. The situation remained unchanged in 1932-3 when the joint secretary warned that 'a little oversight or a little expression of inactivity on the part of Muslims today means lifelong suffering and bondage'. In order to gain members, the annual subscription was reduced from Rs 6 to Re 1 and the admission fee was abolished. *Annual Report of the All-India Muslim League for the year 1931* (Delhi, n.d.), pp. 1, 4; *Annual Report of the All-India Muslim League for the years 1932 and 1933 (upto November)* (Delhi, n.d.), pp. 2-3.

24. Jawaharlal to S. Mohamed Husain, 1 July 1931, F. No. G-37/1931, AICC Papers.
25. Ibid.
26. *Modern Review*, July 1929, p. 104.
27. Smith, *Modern Islam in India*, p. 251.
28. Peter Hardy, *Partners in Freedom and True Muslim: The Political Thought of Some Muslim Scholars in British India 1912-1947* (Lund, 1971), p. 37. For the support of the *ulama* attached to the *Jamiyat*, see *Bombay Chronicle*, 2, 5, 8, 10, 13, 15 May 1930; F. No. G-94/II, 1930, AICC Papers.
29. *Mussalman*, 16 April 1931. Mahmudullah, secretary of the UP Nationalist Muslim Party, explained that the Congress Muslims did not seek communal safeguards which would be a negation of a free constitution. 'We do not stand for the division of India into "Hindu India" and "Muslim India". We do not stand for an isolated political existence in the Federated India.' *Bombay Chronicle*, 9 November 1931.
30. *Liberty*, 1 June 1931, quoted in Bhola Chatterji, *Aspects of Bengal Politics in the Early Nineteen Thirties* (Calcutta, 1969), pp. 14-15.
31. Home Poll. F. No. 5/72, 1932, NAI.
32. Ibid., F. No. 5/54, 1932, NAI.
33. D.G. Tendulkar, *Abdul Ghaffar Khan* (Varanasi, 1969), p. 116.
34. Smith, op. cit., pp. 266-7.
35. Home Poll. F. No. 5/54, 1932, NAI.
36. Ibid. F. No. 5/72, 1932, NAI.
37. Ibid. F. No. 3/7, 1934, NAI.
38. Ibid. F. No. 5/54, 1932, NAI.
39. Humayun Kabir, *Muslim Politics 1906-47 and Other Essays* (Calcutta, 1969), p. 22.
40. Smith, op. cit., pp. 270-1.
41. Home Poll. F. No. 4/46, 1932, NAI.
42. Afzal Husain Malik, *Kashmir awr Dogra Raj, 1848-1931* (Delhi, 1970 edn.).
43. Among the demands listed were representation in ministries and in all

grades of services in proportion to the Muslim population, religious freedom, the right to hold public meetings and the freedom of speech and press. In other areas, such as Mirpur *tahsil,* Major-General R.G. Finlayson took note of the common grievance relating to high grazing tax and high rent assessments which were double of what they were in neighbouring Punjab, inadequate representation in civil administration, insufficient resources being spent on the development of the *tahsil* and rampant corruption, inefficiency and maladministration. Home Poll. F. No. 10/28, 1932; Home Poll. F. No. 5/2, 1933, NAI.

44. P.N.K. Bamzai, *A History of Kashmir* (Delhi, 1962), pp. 660-1.
45. Home Poll. F. No. 13/23, 1931, NAI.
46. Foreword by S.M. Abdullah in *New Kashmir* (New Delhi, n.d.), p. 6.
47. Cited in Bamzai, *History of Kashmir*, p. 661; M. Ishaq Khan, *Perspectives on Kashmir: Historical Dimensions* (Srinagar, 1983), pp. 146-7.
48. *New Kashmir*, op. cit., p. 6.
49. *IQR*, July-December 1928, pp. 405-7.
50. Ibid., p. 351.
51. Brown, *Gandhi's Rise to Power*, p. 137.
52. Viceroy to secretary of state, 18 January 1930, Home Poll. F. No. 257/V, 1930, NAI. The *Bombay Chronicle* commented optimistically: 'Mussalmans have returned to the old fold to take their place side by side with their Hindu, Sikh and Parsi brethren . . . and all talk of minority suspicions is merely a clumsy justification of *Divide and Rule*', *Bombay Chronicle*, 5 June 1930.
53. 882 persons were convicted in Delhi from 1 April to 15 November 1930. Of these, 88 were Muslims. This is by no means an inconsiderable figure and should at least help historians to qualify their judgement on Muslim aloofness or hostility to civil disobedience in all parts of the country. Home Poll. F. No. 23/26, 1931, NAI. In the Punjab, reported the Provincial Congress Committee, 'among the leaders (Muslim) there are a good number in Jail. Among the volunteers there is a fairly decent number, probably about 600 or 700 out of the total. The Muslim public is apathetic, but not exactly hostile.' F. No. 40, 1931 AICC Papers. Also, see S.L. Malhotra, *From Civil Disobedience to Quit India* (Chandigarh, 1979), pp. 6, 9, 10; Jagdish Chandra, *Gandhiji and Haryana* (Delhi, 1977), p. 86.
54. Khaliquzzaman, *Pathways to Pakistan*, pp. 101-2: *IQR*, July-December 1929, p. 350.
55. Khaliquzzaman, *Pathways to Pakistan*, p. 102.
56. For list of those present at the Allahabad Conference, see *IQR*, July-December 1929, p. 350; for Jamiyat al-ulama, see *Leader*, 19 April 1931.
57. Funds for their support came from several sources, including the Raja of Mahmudabad. He was much active in nationalist campaigns, leading

the boycott of the Statutory Commission in Lucknow, presiding over the All-Parties Conference in Lucknow in September 1928, and lending his name to the list of those who endorsed the Nehru Report. He also proposed launching a newspaper and invited Syed Abdullah Brelvi to join as editor. 'In view of the importance of the political situation and also in view of the Nehru Committee Report it is most necessary to start propaganda in right earnest to educate the people and get the report ratified by all recognized institutions.' To Brelvi, 8 September 1928, Brelvi Papers. Earlier, the Raja had supported similar journalistic ventures in support of nationalist causes. The *Comrade*, the *New Era* (Lucknow) and the *Hamdam* (Lucknow) were among them. Both James Meston and Harcourt Butler tried unsuccessfully to persuade the Raja to withdraw his patronage from such 'extremist' papers. See, for instance, Butler to the Raja of Mahmudabad, 4 September 1920, Mahmudabad Papers, NMML.

58. *Mussalman*, 21 March 1931; for Punjab, see *Bombay Chronicle*, 4 July 1931; also, statement of secretary, UPNMP, *Bombay Chronicle*, 9 November 1931.
59. Ibid., 27 June 1931; for Syed Mahmud's claims, see *Bombay Chronicle*, 20 April 1931.
60. *Modern Review*, May 1931, p. 611; A.Z. Zaidi (ed.), *The Evolution of Muslim Political Thought in India* (Delhi, 1980), vol. 4, p. 476. Also, Gandhi's interview to *New Leader*, 25 November 1931, *CWMG*, vol. XLVIII, p. 333 and Ansari's statement in Bombay on the NMP's support in Bengal, *Bombay Chronicle*, 8 July 1931.
61. 'The Muslim members have chosen,' observed Shaikh Mohammad Abdullah (1878-1965) of Aligarh, 'a most psychological moment for launching their campaign and if they succeed in controlling the situation, there is a chance for them to rally the Mussalmans in large numbers.' Letter to the Editor, 15 April 1931, *Leader*, 19 April 1931.
62. The Raja of Mahmudabad stated that the list of delegates forthe first Round Table Conference was not 'balanced' because the 'Muslim separatists and communalists' predominated. He believed that the 'Muslim Nationalists have larger followings than the authors of the Muslim All-Parties Conference and if Muslim Nationalists are to be invited . . . their numbers shouldbe in accordance with the volume of nationalistic views to be found among Muslims'. The Raja of Mahmudabad to T.B. Sapru, 8 July 1931, Sapru Papers, National Library, Calcutta. According to M.C. Chagla, the only reason why the government was trying to keep the Congress Muslim out of the Round Table Conference was to 'impress upon British public opinion that Mussalmans are determined and united upon the retention of separate electorates.' He said that if the government wished 'to escape the accusation of having always followed the policy of "Divide et Impera" and of always profiting

by communal dissensions and differences there is still time to do what is only fair and just.' *Bombay Chronicle*, 8 July 1931.

63. Gandhi to Irwin (telegram), 20 July 1931, Gandhi to viceroy, 29 August 1931, *CWMG*, vol. XLVII, p. 156.
64. Interview to *Bombay Chronicle*, 14 September 1931, p. 12, Gandhi to Ansari, cable, 14 October 1931, *CWMG*, vol. XLVIII, p. 148.
65. To E.C. Mievell, 27 July 1931, Fazl-i Husain Papers (10); and earlier, M.H. Kidwai to Fazl-i Husain, 18 May 1930, Fazl-i-Husain Papers (12).
66. Indian Muslims do not believe that Gandhi is serious in the matter of Muslim rights. His desire to have Ansari in London is only a continuation of his tactics at Delhi to demonstrate the existence of cleavage in Muslim opinion, while, as a matter of fact, it does not exist.' To Shafaat Ahmad Khan, 28 July 1931, Fazl-i-Husain Papers (12). Shafee Daoodi also protested to the viceroy, arguing that the inclusion of Ansari and Ali Imam would be regarded as an attempt to create division in the Muslim delegation and an endorsement of the Congress formula on the communal question. He warned that Muslims would start an agitation and reconsider their attitude towards further participation in the Round Table Conference. *Bombay Chronicle*, 25 July 1931. Also, Home Poll. F. No. 18/7, 1931, NAI.
67. Waheed Ahmad (ed.), *Diary and Notes of Mian Fazl-i Husain*, p. 228. In February 1932 he told Sarojini Naidu of the 'big mistakes' committed by Gandhi—'mistakes of a nature which are associated with shady politics'. In consequence, Gandhi stood lower in public estimation—'at war with all minorities and in his cabinet a strong body of Hindu Mahasabha and strong body of extremists, the former supporting the latter and the latter supporting the former in their anti-Muslim policy'. 22 February 1932, Diary, Fazl-i Husain Papers (6).
68. To Shaukatullah Ansari, 28 September 1931, Hasan (ed.), *Muslims and the Congress*, p. 129.
69. To Shaukatullah Ansari, 29 September 1931, ibid. An emergency meeting of the NMP was convened on 6 October by Ansari to consider the questions arising from the Round Table Conference and to discuss the future of the party. Ansari, according to the government report, was made a virtual 'dictator' of the party 'to deal with the rapidly changing situation. He is believed to be unwilling to proceed to England even if he were summoned'. Home Poll. F. No. 18/10, 1931, NAI.
70. To Ansari, 4 October 1931, *SWJN*, vol. 5, p. 98. Devdas Gandhi (1900-57) reported from London how difficult it had been for Bapu to discuss the possibility of Ansari coming to London and that he could 'no longer press with dignity for Dr Ansari'. The first argument was that the proceedings of the Minorities Committee could not be held up merely for Ansari's sake and the second objection was that he would make a settlement impossible by prevailing upon Gandhi not to accede to the

Muslim demands. 'Mr Shafee Daoodi quite openly admitted that he had been instrumental in keeping Dr Ansari out and others were eager to share the responsibility with Shafee Daoodi. The whole discussion was sordid.' B.N. Pandey (ed.), *The Indian Nationalist Movement 1885-1947: Select Documents* (London, 1979), p. 71.

71. Statement to press, 14 October 1931, *CWMG*, vol. XLVIII, p. 150; Devdas Gandhi to Jawaharlal, 2 October 1931, *SWJN*, vol. 5, p. 48, fn. 3.
72. See draft note on the success of Punjab Nationalist Muslims, n.d., Brelvi Papers. 'Lucknow seldom had a bigger gathering of Mussalmans than one seen yesterday in connection with Muslim Nationalists' Conference,' reported the *Tribune* of 23 July 1930, and *Indian Daily Mail*, 24 July 1930, Ansari Collection, NMML.
73. Note on the Press, UP, for the week ending 23 April 1931.
74. *IAR*, January-June 1931, p. 80.
75. For resolutions adopted on these issues at the meetings on 15-17 April, see *Leader*, 19 April 1931, *Mussalman*, 16 April 1931.
76. *Mussalman*, 23 April 1931.
77. Ibid., 16 April 1931.
78. *Bombay Chronicle*, 27 April 1931.
79. *Leader*, 19, 20, 22, 23 April 1931, Page, op. cit., p. 238.
80. Brelvi Papers; Iqbal to Fazl-i Husain, 14 May 1931, *Letters of Mian Fazl-i Husain*, p. 143.
81. *IAR*, January-June 1931, p. 304.
82. Syed Mahmud to Jawaharlal Nehru, 27 June 1931, V.N. Datta and B. Cleghorn (eds.), *A Nationalist Muslim and Indian Politics* (Delhi, 1974), pp. 115-16.
83. *IAR*, January-June 1931, pp. 303-6; K.K. Aziz (ed.), *The All-India Muslim Conference 1928-1935* (Karachi, 1972), pp. 75-8.
84. *Mussalman*, 25 June 1931; Page, *Prelude to Partition*, pp. 238-40; Moore, *The Crisis of Indian Unity*, p. 190, Fazl-i Husain to Shafee Daoodi, 16 May 1931, Fazl-i Husain to Iqbal, 30 May 1931, *Letters of Mian Fazl-i-Husain*, pp. 144-8; *Bombay Chronicle*, 23 June 1931.
85. *Mussalman*, 25 June 1931; *Bombay Chronicle*, 24 June 1931.
86. Home Poll. F. No. 18/6, 1931, NAI; The Nawab of Chhatari to Fazl-i Husain, 3 July 1931, *Letters of Mian Fazl-i Husain*, p. 158. Fazl-i Husain, who did much to undermine the possibility of a settlement, wrote that there were no Muslims in the Congress strong enough to persuade that body to act in a 'just' and 'righteous' manner. To Umar Hayat Khan Tiwana, 20 June 1931, ibid., p. 152.
87. *IAR*, July-December 1931, p. 225.
88. *Leader*, 19 April 1931. For Ansari's response, *Bombay Chronicle*, 6 July 1931.
89. Speech of Shaukat Ali at the UP Muslim Conference, 8 August 1931, *IAR*, July-December 1931, p. 228.

90. *Bombay Chronicle*, 21 April 1931.
91. 26 April 1929, Datta and Cleghorn (eds.), *A Nationalist Muslim*, p. 94.
92. 22 August 1929, Moonje Diaries, National Library, Calcutta; Moonje to Jayakar, 31 July 1926, Jayakar Papers (437).
93. Speech at the Bengal Provincial Hindu Conference, *IAR*, July-December 1931, pp. 260-1.
94. Speech at Akola, 8 August 1931, ibid., pp. 252-3.
95. Jayakar to Sapru, 26 January 1930; Kelkar to Sapru, 27 January 1930; Sapru to Aiyar, 21/23 January 1930. Referring to his meeting with Malaviya, Sapru wrote: 'When I raised the Hindu-Muslim question with him frankly I did not find his attitude to be very satisfactory. It was theatrical and academic and did not seem to take note of the reality of the situation.' To Aiyar, 8 January 1930, Sapru Papers.
96. Setalvad to Sapru, 22 January, 6 February 1930, ibid.
97. Aiyar to Sapru, 18 January 1930, Sapru Papers.
98. Moore, *The Crisis of Indian Unity*, p. 106.
99. *Young India*, 16 July 1931, *CWMG*, vol. XLVII, p. 141; *Bombay Chronicle*, 13 July 1931.
100. Note on the Press, UP, for the week ending 25 July 1931. Also, see Page, op. cit., pp. 241-2.
101. Note on the Press, for the week ending 25 July 1931. For the position of the Hindu Mahasabha, see *IAR*, July-December 1931, p. 254, and for the Bengal Provincial Hindu Sabha Conference, see p. 261.
102. Tendulkar, *Ghaffar Khan*, p. 211.
103. To Shaukatullah Ansari (Shaukoo), 28 September 1931; to Sherwani, 30 October 1931; to Aziz Ansari (Ajjoo), 10 November 1931, Hasan (ed.), *Muslims and the Congress*, pp. 129-30. Ansari married for the second time to a Christian lady whose name and background is obscure. A son was born soon after the marriage, but 'the family never accepted him' or his mother who lived mostly in Dehradun or Mussoorie. The son—Ahmad Harold—studied medicine in England, settled in that country and is now a consultant. Based on Zohra Ansari, Oral History transcript.
104. *SWJN*, vol. 5, p. 458; Ansari to Latif, 26 January 1933, Abdul Latif Bijnori, *Latif ki Kahani* (Bijnor, 1967), p. 278.
105. Mcpherson, op. cit., pp. 111, 121-2.
106. Nehru, *An Autobiography*, p. 139.
107. Khaliquzzaman, op. cit., p. 102.
108. Nehru, *An Autobiography*, p. 139. K.M. Munshi, *Pilgrimage to Freedom*, vol. 1 (Bombay, 1967), p. 29.
109. Note on the Press, UP, for the week ending 29 June, 6, 20, 27 July, 17 August 1929.
110. Statement to the Press, 25 April 1937, *SWJN*, vol. 8, p. 128.

111. Thus in 1926 Ansari, Ajmal Khan, Azad, Mazharul Haq and Shafee Daoodi issued an appeal to the Muslim electorate of the Madras presidency 'to stand by the Congress and to vote solidly for the Muslim candidates who stand under the banner of the Congress which is the sole common national organization of India'. F. No. G-66, 1926, AICC Papers.
112. Notice Shaukat Ali's comment at the UP Muslim Conference, Allahabad, *IAR*, July-December 1931, p. 228, and the complaint of the Ahrar leader, Habibur Rahman that those Muslims, especially over 1,000 workers in the Punjab, who made sacrifices during the civil disobedience movement, were ignored by the Congress. To Abul Kalam Azad, 31 August 1946, in Urdu, Habibur Rahman Ludhianvi Papers.
113. Khaliquzzaman, *Pathway to Pakistan*, p. 104.
114. Chatterji, *Aspects of Bengal Politics*, p. 73.
115. Khwaja to Gandhi, 12 March 1931, A.M. Khwaja Papers; *Bombay Chronicle*, 21 April 1931.
116. Ansari to Sherwani, 6 January 1930, Hasan (ed.), *Muslims and the Congress*, pp. 90-1.

Member of the Congress Working Committee at Dar-us-Salam during the Gandhi-Irwin negotiations.

At the inauguration of the Congress Hospital at Allahabad. In the front row (from left except the third) Mahadev Desai, Rajendra Prasad, Vallabhbhai Patel, M.A. Ansari, Jawaharlal Nehru, M.M. Malaviya, J.M. Sengupta, Perinben Captain and Maniben Patel. *Behind* Malaviya and Abdul Kalam Azad are Purshottamdas Tandon and C. Rajagopalachari. In back row fifth from left, is Rafi Ahmad Kidwai and third from right is Asaf Ali.

With Sarojini Naidu and their Congress comrades.

With the Liberal leader Tej Bahadur Sapru.

9

Civil Disobedience and After

> I want to declare that we, the Nationalist Muslims, have never been before, nor are we at present, nor shall we be any time hereafter, communalists. We are Congressmen and we never intend leaving the Congress at any time. Our aim is to convert the communalist Muslim to the nationalist viewpoint and make them think on national lines [M.A. Ansari].
>
> *Bombay Chronicle*, 8 October 1935

THE DECISION OF the Congress to launch civil disobedience created a breach between Ansari and his mentors and led to his isolation, at least for the time being, from the humdrum of political life. Ansari promptly relinquished the positions he held in Congress and became 'only an ordinary member'.[1] This was a painful decision for one who had occupied so central a position in its hierarchy for nearly two decades. But given Ansari's sense of propriety it was not a surprising course of action. He had done the same in 1926 following his differences with the Central Khilafat Committee.

Ansari's estrangement with the Congress was over the efficacy of starting civil disobedience, an issue on which he had a greater degree of agreement with the Liberals than with his partymen. He could not attend the Congress Working Committee meeting on 14-16 February where plans for defying British authority were laid out, but had warned Gandhi not to be carried away by the popular response to Independence Day, which was observed on 26 January 1930. It was easy to join processions, he had written, but quite difficult to face hardships and withstand repression.[2] This was followed by an impassioned appeal from Jaora, a princely state. Ansari argued that political conditions were quite the reverse of what they were in 1920; Hindu-Muslim-Sikh unity was wanting and there was impending danger of the non-violent campaign being submerged by the breaking out of violence.[3] Civil disobedience would therefore cause 'incalculable damage'. The Congress should thus retrace its steps and, among things, concentrate on restoring communal amity, one of the basic items in its programme, and, according to Ansari's conviction, '*the one and only* basic thing'.[4] 'Your movement,' he wrote to Gandhi:

> would thus fail to fructify and all the sacrifices made by you and those who would follow you would be wasted. This is how I have visualized the whole movement. Believe me, if I saw it as you do, I would have taken the marching orders and had been with you in the thick of the fight and not merely giving my blessing to the movement by mere words. You have that without asking for it.[5]

Some suspected that Ansari had gone over to the side of the Ali Brothers and betrayed Gandhi. The fact is that he rebutted Shaukat Ali's outburst against civil disobedience as 'a piece of monstrous falsehood and unworthy of any Mussalman'.[6] With these honest statements, the decks were cleared for an equally honest admission of his feelings for Gandhi. Far from hostility, Ansari confide in Gandhi his troubles in general and his emotional ones in particular.

Gandhi agreed that the Hindu-Muslim tangle was the 'problem of problems', but felt that it had to be approached differently. He told Ansari that political adjustment between the two communities was possible only after the removal of the 'evil' British power and not before; 'there will be no charter of independence before the Hindus and the Muslims have met but there can be virtual independence before the charter is received'.[7] According to him, a meeting of minds could only be accomplished through fighting for common causes, and he wanted Ansari to recognize the new orientation to the civil disobedience campaign.[8] Having failed to heal the communal wound through his own methods, he concluded that independence would precede and not succeed the resolution of the communal question.[9] Ansari, on the other hand, felt that Gandhi's way of bringing about unity had already proved ineffective when conditions for joint action were ideal and reiterated his faith in mutual adjustments through dialogue and discussion. In a candid elaboration of this argument—one which illustrates Ansari's differences with Gandhi as well as offers clues to his way of dealing with the communal tangle—Ansari observed:

Immediately after the setback of the NCO movement, there was a reaction which, instead of keeping the Hindus and Muslims together, made them fight each other as they had never done before. Unity patched up to fight a common foe always breaks down as soon as the fight ceases. Unity during a deluge or in the face of any elemental force is brought about by common danger and lasts till the danger lasts. Unity to be lasting should be achieved during normal and peace time after careful thought and based on collective judgement. The parties should have occasion to fully weigh the gains and losses and should accept them with open eyes and full knowledge. *This is possible only through conferences, as in the present pressing circumstances led by a great urge* [emphasis added]. This is how other countries have achieved it. I believe that urge is felt today by the contending parties. Along with the Liberals, the imprimatur of the Congress would have aided much to help them onwards.

I have all along pinned my faith in mutual adjustments through formal and informal conversations [emphasis added].[10]

Lastly, Motilal concurred with Gandhi and disagreed with Ansari's proposition.

You say the country is not ready for civil disobedience. If so, when and how are you going to make it ready? Do you believe that in the present temper of the so-called leaders of the two communities it is possible to arrive at any formula? Even if it were possible which I seriously doubt how will the existence of that formula on paper carry us in our conflict with the foreign Government? . . . . I have definitely come to hold the opinion that *no amount of formulae based upon mutual concessions which those making them have no right to make will bring us nearer Hindu-Muslim unity than we are at present* [emphasis added].

Motilal concluded by claiming credit for realizing what it means to me and mine

to throw in my lot with Gandhiji in the coming struggle. Nothing but a deep conviction that the time for the greatest effort and the greatest sacrifice has come would have induced me to expose myself at my age and with my family obligations to the tremendous risks I am incurring. I hear the clarion call of the country and I obey.[11]

Some contemporary observers noticed a shift in Congress priorities.[12] Ansari, in particular, felt that his party had not done enough to achieve Hindu-Muslim unity and regretted that Gandhi and Motilal were not so 'persuasive, so active, or so masterful as the great importance of this question required'. 'Perhaps you were not very confident of yourselves,' he told Gandhi, 'or perhaps you felt you could not succeed in bringing about a communal settlement by means of conferences. Whatever the causes that is how it struck me and many others.'[13] Some of the others disapproved of some of Gandhi's pronouncements during this period, such as his speech in Delhi on 7 March and at the Jamiyat al-ulama on 1 April 1931.[14] The *Mussalman*, a Calcutta newspaper took exception to his remark that Hindus should not 'return blow for blow but treat the Muslims as brethren, even if the Muslims are wrong'. The paper contested the implicit notion of an 'aggressive' Muslim *versus* a 'defensive' Hindu. Communalists were among both the communities. The only difference was that the Hindus, being in a majority, could palm off their communalism as nationalism or altruism.[15]

Gandhi created doubts in Syed Mahmud's mind as well. He sought advice, torn between loyalty to Jawaharlal and dislike of the Lahore resolution, reinforced by his need to earn a living at the Bar.[16] Sherwani felt that his reply showed utter indifference to the feelings of those who stood by him in his movement just like soldiers.[17] Khaliquzzaman wondered about the future of the Congress Muslims. If they were to accept Gandhi's order of priorities and time scale, they would, in effect, proclaim to find their leaders in people who played the communal game unabashedly. That said, Khaliquzzaman wanted to form a group committed to independence and, at the same time, insistent on Hindu-Muslim unity. He discerned support for this view and hoped that many Muslims who left the NMP on the issue of the Nehru Report would return to its fold in sheer disgust with the aggressive attitude of Jinnah and Shafi.[18]

It was all very well to feel aggrieved and nurse grandiose plans. But the Congress Muslims realized could ill-afford to stay aloof from civil disobedience. Ansari stated the obvious: 'to leave the Congress would be to commit political suicide'.[19] His heart was not in civil disobedience,[20] but he ultimately joined it partly because of his loyalty to Gandhi and partly because of his desire to remain in the political mainstream. Thus when Vallabhbhai Patel (1875-1950) appealed for his return to the Working Committee in July 1930 after the arrest of the two Nehrus,[21] he agreed owing to the government's stern counter measures, the 'unparalleled fidelity of a people to the principles of non-violence', and the shockingly retrograde recommendations of the Statutory Commission report.[22] He rejoined the Working Committee in August, as he could neither 'view with equanimity the policy of ruthless suppression' nor allow government to 'kill the paramount national organization of India, loyalty to which has been my lifelong creed'.[23]

Ansari succeeded Azad as Congress 'dictator'; he was arrested on 27 August 1930 during the Working Committee meeting at Dar-us-Salam.[24] He served another term in prison. Succeeding Rajendra Prasad (1884-1963) as Congress president, he was arrested in Delhi on 8 January 1932 and was sentenced to six months' imprisonment. Ansari's comrades followed their leader after Gandhi's arrest on 5 May. Syed Mahmud was arrested on 30 June for being secretary of the 'unlawful' Working Committee; Sherwani was convicted in Bombay in connection with the 'Tilak Day' procession on 2 August; Azad, acting president, was sent to gaol on 21 August; Khaliquzzaman served for a while as Congress 'dictator'; and Hasrat Mohani, Saifuddin Kitchlew, Rafi Ahmad Kidwai, Khwaja and Brelvi were incarcerated for defying government ordinances. The Congress Muslims were now visible in a movement they had joined with extreme reluctance. Their conference in July, chaired by Ansari, supported mass action, such as general strike and movement of non-cooperation, especially because all resources to protest by means of representation had been exhausted.[25] Ansari repudiated the charge that Muslims, particularly those connected with the NMP, were wary of joining civil disobedience.

> We had to stop this misrepresentation of the community by parties and persons who would exploit the Muslim community to serve ends that are neither Indian nor Indian Muslim. We had to give the direct lie to libellers so that future generations might not point their finger of scorn at the supposed indifference of Mussalmans in their country's hour of trial.[26]

Much of the drive behind this enthusiasm followed the crucial decision of the Jamiyat al-ulama to participate in civil disobedience.[27] If the *ulama* could do so, so ran the argument, the Congress Muslims had no reason to distance themselves. Furthermore, they could not risk being found in the company of the Ali Brothers and their credibility, as indeed their political survival, depended on their ability to retrace their steps and choose the one course which made them part of the national mainstream. With the *ulama* and the NMP behind the Congress, Ansari could rightfully claim that large segments of the Muslim community backed civil disobedience.

The rigours of a hectic political life damaged Ansari's health. He went to Europe for treatment—in October 1932, August 1933 and May 1934—but his heart condition deteriorated. He complained of hard work and heavy responsibilities. 'I don't think I would last long at this rate,' he wrote in December 1933.[28] He informed Jawaharlal around the same time that he could not stand the rigours of political life and apologized in advance for not attending meetings and conferences.[29] But he was pressed into service just when he contemplated resigning from the Congress. He returned to active politics and in the form which most suited him. He became the go-between, the man who tried to arrange compromise between the contending political parties.

THE MAKING OF THE SWARAJ PARTY

The opportunity of playing a major political role was provided by the slackening of civil disobedience and the feeling among Congress leaders outside jail that its momentum could not be maintained any longer.[30] By mid-1933, there were open demands for revising the Congress strategy as civil disobedience had outlived its usefulness as a method and devising a practical plan to turn the energies of the nation into 'channels of fruitful activity'.[31] Such views were voiced at the Poona Conference on 12-14 July 1933, but they were opposed by Gandhi. Ultimately, the Mahatma agreed to a compromise on his own terms: without an unconditional withdrawal, disobedience would take the form of individual civil disobedience. As Congress had been unable

Nationalist Leaders are taking counsel together in Delhi on future policy as to the direction in which they should next proceed.

'Wither India?'

to communicate the essence of satyagraha to the masses it was now to be conveyed by the example of individuals acting in a true spirit of resistance.[32]

Ansari had sensed the political mood on his return to India in early November. S. Satyamurti (1887-1943) founded a provincial Swarajya Party a month earlier to contest elections to the local boards and legislatures and planned holding a conference to launch a party at the all-India level.[33] K.F. Nariman (1883-1948), a Working Committee member, declared his intentions of restoring the Congress 'from the wrong track to which . . . it was drifting'. But Satyamurti and Nariman did not tread warily; Gandhi and the Congress thwarted their initiative. Nariman tried in vain to seek a referendum on revoking, modifying, or retaining the civil disobedience movement started in 1932.[34]

Soon thereafter, Ansari and B.C. Roy (1882-1962) carried on Nariman's unfinished work. They met in Bombay in late December, conferred with Azad, Sarojini Naidu and K.M. Munshi (1887-1971),[35] and then drafted a letter, preceded by consultations with Gandhi, inviting forty prominent Congressmen to implement the constructive programme outlined in the Poona Conference and later amplified in Gandhi's statement.[36] Plans were then set afoot to meet in March. Ansari hoped this would revive the Swaraj Party and its political programme.[37] Having opposed civil disobedience, he wanted a change realizing that Muslim seats in the legislatures would all go to the communalists unless Congress rehabilitated itself in his co-religionists' eyes.[38] Besides, with the communal situation deteriorating steadily and individual civil disobedience proceeding haltingly, he searched for a way out of the growing impasse. Jawaharlal learnt of the 'demoralization' outside afflicting Ansari, Sherwani and Khaliquzzaman, though he expressed surprise that Rafi Ahmad Kidwai was also part of the same flock.[39]

The initial move to hold a conference ran into trouble, but Roy's meeting with Gandhi on 17 March straightened matters. The latter informed Ansari the next day that he would not stand in the way of a Council entry party because the paralysis of the intelligentsia had to be removed. He would therefore welcome Congressmen prosecuting the programme rather than remaining sullen, discontented and inactive.[40]

The conference that followed Gandhi's signal was held at Dar-us-Salam, with Ansari as the star performer. Many of those present already belonged to provincial parties which had formed themselves on the ruin of the Congress party machine and had taken Council entry as their avowed or tacit objective. 'For God sake,' Ansari implored, 'end this deadly political paralysis that is slowly creeping on the nation and has resulted in a political lethargy and blankness that may ultimately lead to disaster.' 'Believe me,' he assured his detractors, 'that I am still as staunch a Non-changer as before and I have been compelled to adopt this course as the only possible alternative to end the present deadlock.'[41] He spoke effectively and convincingly; in fact, an hour's forceful oration gave the final touch to the proceedings and decided on the revival of the Swaraj Party.[42] Two days earlier, Ansari had gathered that government intended to hold assembly elections in the autumn. He seized on this 'God-sent opportunity' as a handle for a new programme to side-step the thorny question of withdrawing civil disobedience and making an immediate decision on the new legislatures.[43] He put his argument to Brelvi, who, having condemned the council entry policy as divisive in November 1933,[44] now backed Ansari:

I know that you would stand by me realizing fully well that what I have done is entirely conceived in the interest of the country and solely with a view to remove the paralysis and death-like inertia . . . as a result of complete inactivity on the part of Congress workers. . . . I admit that the scheme has many drawbacks and is far from perfect, but I want you to see what other schemes would have been devised which would be dynamic, would catch the imagination of the people, would offer a challenge to the Government and would at the same time be fighting the government on constitutional lines. . . . You would also see that, as it confines itself to the election of the Assembly, it would be possible for the Swarajya Party to send the most outstanding men to contest the elections and thus ensure not only their return but the raising of the opposition in the Assembly and all Congressmen in the country. . . . The Swarajya Party after its campaign for the assembly elections would have reached the electorate and familiarized the people to its aims and ideals and therefore it would be in a position to stand up in opposition to the forces of bureaucracy, of reaction, of capital and of communal organizations, which you may rest assured would all combine against the Congressmen.

Ansari concluded on a cautious note, making it clear that he had no delusions regarding the limited scope of the assembly work. But, in the existing state of 'deadlock and paralysis', there was no alternative to the plans chalked out at the Delhi gathering.[45] Ansari's optimism, was not misplaced. When he and Roy met Gandhi at Patna in early April, they convinced him that the Swaraj Party's revival was a political necessity and that many Congressmen were reticent to go to jail in pursuance of individual civil disobedience.[46] Gandhi pledged his support to the idea.[47] He, then, suspended civil disobedience, a decision which agonized, among others, Jawaharlal. His statement of 7 April seemed to Jawaharlal an insult to the nation and to the Congress. He felt with a stab of pain that the chords of allegiance that had bound him to the Mahatma for many years had snapped.[48] The Congress Socialist Party, inaugurated at Patna on 17 May 1934, also felt that the decision to enter the Delhi assembly violated the 1929 Lahore resolution which had called for boycotting legislatures and had demanded nothing less than complete independence. The new policy illustrated that the national movement was drifting inevitably towards constitutionalism and accommodation with the British.[49]

Jayaprakash Narayan (1902-79), writing in 1936 in *Why Socialism,* characterized Gandhism as a mixture of 'timid economic analysis, good intentions and ineffective moralizing'. To socialists like him Gandhi, was a reformist, who offered only palliatives for chronic and grievous social ills, when a purgative was required.[50] Yet, as Acharya Narendra Deva (1889-1956), a Congress socialist, stated: 'Howsoever one may criticize and denounce the Congress, it is the only broad platform of anti-imperialist struggle in India and it is the only centre today from which such a struggle can be conducted.'[51]

Amidst scenes of enthusiasm, nearly a hundred Swarajists met in Ranchi on 2 May to implement the Delhi decisions. Being unanimously voted to the chair, Ansari again occupied the centre stage. He detailed the history of the efforts which went into the making of the Swaraj Party and urged all concerned to accept Gandhi's definition of satyagraha and civil resistance and to abide by his advice.[52] At the AICC meeting on 18-19 May, he placed the Swarajist view, moved the resolution for suspending civil disobedience and shrugged socialist opposition by pointing out that most of their demands were contained in the Karachi Congress National Demand.[53] 'We have achieved in six weeks,' he proudly announced,

> what the most sanguine amongst us could not have expected in six months or a year and we have achieved what to us is the most priceless of all the assets: the recognition, the moral and political support of the greatest Indian National organization, the Indian National Congress.[54]

The wheel had taken full circle. Although the 'no changers' of 1922-3 were ridiculed for executing a *volte face*, Ansari brushed aside their criticism with disdain. He enjoyed being at the centre of a controversy and heard with pleasure the words of praise showered on his leadership. He had not received such compliments before and relished them in his final hour of glory. Friends and detractors alike commended his role and he received credit for that 'great and wonderful miracle'—the conversion of the author of non-cooperation 'into a silent blesser of parliamentary methods'.[55] Nariman commented that the Mahatma's assent was entirely due to Ansari's 'advocacy of such transparent sincerity and honesty'.[56] The praise did not end here. As president of the Congress Parliamentary Board, there were more kudos for the man who emerged as the chief election campaigner—issuing policy statements, settling factional feuds, raising funds and laying down guidelines for candidates. It was a position of prominence Ansari greatly welcomed. Such was the goodwill he earned that, on the eve of his departure for Europe on 24 May, he was specially feted in Bombay.[57] Both Gandhi and Jawaharlal kept him posted with political developments and solicited his advice. On his return to Bombay on 5 October, Patel eulogized his contribution at a massive public meeting held at the Chowpatty sands.[58] This was Ansari's hour of triumph as he gazed at the massive gathering which applauded at the mention of his name.

Ansari was drawn into the fray immediately after returning from Europe. He opened the assembly election campaign on 6 October in Bombay.[59] This was followed by an assurance to the electorate that the Swaraj Party would press for self-determination and pursue national reconstruction. 'Every voter,' stated the appeal, 'must look upon himself as the custodian of the country's honour and of both collective and personal interests and therefore he should not waste his vote on small or subsidiary issues or allow it to be exploited by candidates who are not supported by the most powerful party of the country'.[60]

The Congress did well in the assembly elections, winning 44 of the 88 elected seats. Brelvi, for one, felt no surprise; 'there is not the least doubt that during the last few years the Congress had a tremendous hold over the people'.[61] Rajendra Prasad attributed the party's success to its record of sacrifice and service.[62] Later, he talked of the hold on the masses and their respect 'not for the individual but for the institutions'. Indeed, the large gatherings at public meetings were due to Gandhi's charismatic personality as well as the support for the Congress policies.[63] What Rajendra Prasad ignored was Ansari's contribution in organizing the election campaign with imagination, purposefulness and efficiency. He minimized friction within the Congress, sorted out the all important problem of raising funds and ensured, much to everybody's satisfaction, its proper distribution. His personal contribution to the election expenses, raised through a private loan, was substantial and entailed quite a burden to pay it off; 'the result has been that I have had to go on grinding day after day and month by month without, taking any rest or holiday,' he wrote to B.C. Roy in October 1935.[64] But this was scarcely recognized, a fact which seemingly distressed Ansari. This would probably explain why some of his statements, issued soon after the assembly elections, reflected his disappointment.[65] What added to his irritation was the irresponsible criticism of his statement of 16 October: his critics charged that his views were 'calculated to bring down the dignity of the Congress'.[66] B.C. Roy came to his defence,[67] but Ansari's feelings were not assuaged. In disgust, he contemplated resigning from the Congress Parliamentary Board.[68]

THE COMMUNAL DIVIDE

Ansari had little cause to complain, for his political trajectory had worked out quite well from 1930 to 1935. There were of course some setbacks but they were a necessary part of a politician's life. He was disappointed with the performance of the NMP, which had long ceased to be an effective force. The failure of the Round Table Conferences, followed by the Communal Award on 16 August 1932, created intense communal friction.[69] Those present in London noticed the self-proclaimed a Muslim spokesmen, standing on the platform of the Delhi resolutions of January 1929, seeking assurance of statutory majorities in Bengal and the Punjab, veto to such legislation which appeared inimical to Muslim religious interests, an elected 33 per cent representation in the central legislature and a loose centre with full administrative and financial autonomy resting in the provinces. On the other side was the group under the Mahasabha's influence. Representatives of other religious minorities were anxious to defend themselves against majority

A certain section of No-changers in the United Provinces is reported to be firmly against the Council-entry Programme.

'Wanted Careful Driving'.
Hindustan Times, 31 March 1934.

In the Arabian Nights, there is a queer story of the "Fisherman and the Genie."

'Danger of Releasing the Geni'.
Hindustan Times, 22 April 1934.

domination. The Sikhs were, in particular, vigilant with regard to their interests in Punjab.

The Congress was conducting the civil disobedience campaign against the government's refusal to accept dominion status as the presupposition of all discussions. After his talks with Irwin in February and March 1931, Gandhi attended the second session of the conference, held between 14 September and 1 December 1931, as Congress' sole representative. 'I happened to be in Delhi,' recalled Khaliquzzaman, 'when Gandhiji was staying at Dr Ansari's house [during his talks with the viceroy] and to my great surprise I used to see many inveterate enemies of Congress and well-known supporters of the British raj, both Hindus and Muslims, hovering round Dr Ansari's residence.'[70]

Gandhi brought with him the Congress plan which proposed, among other things, separate representation on the basis of joint electorates for both Hindus and Muslims in provinces where they were less than 25 per cent of the population, with the provision to contest additional seats. He made it clear that adult suffrage would enable him to satisfy the reasonable aspirations of the Muslims, the so-called Untouchables, the Christians and all kinds of 'classes'. As negotiations went on, the Mahatma, with his customary flair, agreed to modify some of his proposals.[71] But most Muslim delegates, following the directives of Fazl-i Husain, stuck to their demands.[72] Shafi and Shafaat Ahmad Khan insisted on a statutory majority in Bengal and the Punjab and 33 per cent representation in the central legislature.[73] Neither the Sikhs nor the Hindus, led by Raja Narendranath, Malaviya, Moonje and Jayakar, agreed to the Muslim claims. As time went on, a series of contradictory and irreconcilable claims and counter-claims emerged, the hair-splitting became finer and finer and the arguments more and more abstract. 'The sum total of all our work,' wrote the Aga Khan, 'was a vast array of statistics and data, a great many speeches and little or no positive understanding.'[74]

By 25 October, negotiations between various parties came to a standstill. Gandhi tried to break the impasse, but 'with deep sorrow and deeper humiliation' he announced his failure to secure an agreed solution of the communal question. Even after their return to India, delegates to the Round Table Conference tried in vain to reach a consensus. Not long after the conference, the Congress resumed civil disobedience. 'The first Round Table Conference was as round as a circle, the second one was rounder still and when the third round table conference ended it became a well round zero.'[75] With no constitutional progress on the horizon, Ramsay MacDonald (1866-1937), the British prime minister, announced the Communal Award.

The Award prolonged the system of separate electorates for Hindus, Muslims and Sikhs and extended it to those described as the Depressed Classes. The Act of 1909 was the beginning and the Communal Award the culmination of the government's strategy of leaning heavily on the Muslims and giving them a distinct political identity. Said Jayakar: 'The Lucknow Pact divided India into Hindus and Muslims. This Award will divide it further into Hindu *versus* Muslim women, Europeans *versus* Anglo-Indians, white Christians *versus* coloured Christians, high castes *versus* Depressed classes and, eventually, north India *versus* south India.'[76]

The Hindu Mahasabha denounced the Award on the grounds that it gave the Muslims control of Bengal and Punjab, denied to the Hindus in those provinces representation in proportion to their population, granted too much weightage to Muslims in the Hindu-majority provinces, and that it implied the formation of Sind as a separate province.[77] The Sikhs were embittered because the Award did not give them and the Hindus together a majority of the seats in Punjab. Muslims alone felt satisfied. Even though their main demand—statutory majorities in the Punjab and Bengal legislatures—was not conceded, but in both the provinces they retained not only their separate electorates but also more seats than any other community in the provincial assemblies (Table 9.1). Provincial autonomy was now a pleasing prospect for Muslims in Bengal and Punjab and also for Muslims in the newly-created province of Sind as well as the NWFP, which was to be elevated to the status of a Governor's province.[78] For these reasons, except for Bengal, where Fazlul Haq and his followers made some noises and proposed modifications,[79] Muslim organizations, including the Muslim League, welcomed the Award. 'In the provinces,' wrote Azim Husain, the biographer of his father Fazl-i Husain, 'the Muslims now woke up from somnolence and for every meeting held by the Hindu Mahasabha asking for joint electorates a meeting was held by the local branch of the Muslim Conference to approve of the Award'.[80] Thus the government's design of setting one group against the other worked. It created new areas of conflict which, as intended, kept on enlarging in the years to come.

The Congress could neither acquiesce in nor reject the Award without causing a rift within its own ranks and driving the Muslims further into the Muslim League camp.[81] At first, civil disobedience postponed the dilemma. Many of its leaders were in gaol and the Mahatma, who was not released until August 1933, advised his followers to keep mum.[82] But the issue could not be deferred for long, specially after the Swaraj Party's decision to fight the assembly elections. At this stage, the Congress Working Committee on 17-18 June 1934 adopted the course of neither accepting nor rejecting the Award.[83] It was an extraordinary decision, yet this was consistent with its policy of the past. If the Congress had adopted a strong line previously and followed it regardless of short-term consequences, it would have been able to resist all forms of strident communitarian demands. But, as it had been unwilling to do so, there was no other course open to the Congress Working Committee except the one it took.[84]

Congress' neutral—some said ambivalent—position raised a storm of protest in different circles. Its own structure, built on the principle of 'consensus', came under severe strain, particularly after Malaviya, Aney and their followers formed the Congress Nationalist Party on a programme of total opposition to the Communal Award. When they began marshalling their forces at the Anti-Communal Award Conferences on 23-24 February and 25 October 1934, most of the old faces from the Mahasabha breakaway of 1926 were visible. Predictably, they castigated the Congress attitude towards the Award as 'a virtual acquiescence in the decision'.[85]

There were loud protests from other quarters as well. Shadi Ram Sharma, member of the Hoshiarpur Congress Committee, spoke of his party's anomalous position.

Blowing hot and cold in the same breath the Congress says: *"We are Nationalists, we oppose communalism, we reject it."* But after a pause

TABLE 9.1: COMMUNAL AWARD: ALLOCATION OF SEATS IN LOWER HOUSES OF PROVINCIAL LEGISLATURES

Province	*General*	*Depressed Class*	*Representatives from Backward Areas*	*Sikh*	*Muhammadan*	*Indian Christian*	*Anglo Indian*	*European*	*Commerce and Industry, Mining and Planting Special*	*Landholders Special*	*University Special*	*Labour Spec2al*	*Total*
Madras	134 (including 6 women)	18	1	0	29 (including 1 woman)	9 (including 1 woman)	2	3	6	6	1	6	215
Bombay (including Sind)	97 (including 5 women)	10	1	0	63 (including 1 women)	3	2	4	8	3	1	8	200
Bengal	80 (including 2 women)		0	0	119 (including 2 women)	2	4 (including 1 women)	11	19	5	2	8	250
United Provinces	132 (including 4 women)	12	0	0	66 (including 2 women)	2	1	2	3	6	1	3	228
Punjab	43 (including 1 women)	0	0	32 (including 1 women)	86 (including 2 women)	2	1	1	1	5	1	3	175
Bihar and Orissa	99 (including 3 women)	7	8	0	42 (including 1 women)	2	1	2	4	5	1	4	175
Central Provinces (including Berar)	77 (including 3 women)	10	1	0	14	0	1	1	2	3	1	2	112
Assam	44 (including 1 women)	4	9	0	34	1	0	1	11	0	0	4	108
NWFP	9	0	0	3	36	0	0	0	0	2	0	0	50
Bombay (without Sind)	109 including 5 women)	10	1	0	30 (including 1 women)	3	2	3	7	2	1	7	175
Sind	19 (including 1 woman)	0	0	0	34 (including (1 woman)	0	0	2	2	2	0	1	60

NOTE: As explained in paragraph 9 of the statement, the number of special Depressed Class seats in Bengal—which will not exceed 10—has yet been fixed. The number of General seats will be 80, less the number of special Depressed Class seats.

SOURCE: *East India (Constitutional Reforms), Communal Decision*, pp. 1931-2. XVIII, Cmd. 4147.

when called upon to declare their policy on the Communal Award they say, "*We neither reject it nor accept it.*" Congressmen, he wrote, are expectant that these clouds of uncertainty and dubiousness will be blown off and blown away by a clear-cut declaration by the President of the Indian National Congress and the AICC against the Communal Award in the near future.[86]

This demand was most vigorously made in Bengal where educated Hindus, aggrieved by the denial of their claims to weightage, were up in arms. Besides organizing public meetings, they drew up a memorial, signed by all the Hindu members of the legislative council, by twenty-three chairmen of municipalities, by eight chairmen of district boards and by thirty-six 'representative Hindu leaders' urging London to amend the Communal Award. The signatories included Ramanand Chatterji (1865-1943), editor of the *Modern Review*, and the Nobel laureate Rabindranath Tagore (1861-1941).[87]

The Bengal Congress, beleaguered by numerous factions, was one in opposing the Communal Award.[88] Sarat Chandra Bose (1889-1950) drew attention to the popular opinion against it, attributed Congress' defeat in the assembly elections to its ambivalence on such a vital issue, and warned Jawaharlal that Bengal's Hindu electorate was impatient with the party's uncertain and equivocal stance. 'To ignore that fact would be to court defeat at the coming elections and we shudder to think what the effect of such a defeat would be on the Congress organization as a whole.'[89] However, the thrust of the Mahatma's argument was that the Congress, claiming to stand for all the communities, should do nothing which would make Muslims feel that it had departed from that position. He said that it would be a betrayal of the Muslims to oppose their view of the Communal Award.[90] 'The more I think about it,' he wrote to Aney, 'the clearer it becomes that the Working Committee resolution is faultless. Non-committal is the only position the Congress can take up. We must not tease the communal boil. The more we tease it, the worse it becomes.'[91] He made it clear to the Calcutta Congressmen that everybody condemned the Award, 'but a Congressman, because he is a Congressman, can neither accept it nor reject it because if he did one or the other he would be taking sides and therefore not represent the whole nation'.[92]

Jawaharlal agreed that the Award was dangerous, but took pains to explain that an agitation against it did not figure in Congress' order of priorities. With independence being the main issue, the real question was not one of principle but of methods to give effect to that principle. He hoped that those who thought in terms of political freedom and economic issues would some day see the Communal Award in perspective and join hands in fighting it.[93] This view glossed over the context in which opinions on the Award were shaped and crystallized. It was futile to expect any of the parties to dilute their demands or soften their attitudes in the years 1932-5; the historical currents were inescapably moving towards a hardening of attitudes. Jawaharlal was aware of this, but he did not adequately comprehend the intensity of the communal differences. Addressing the All-India Trade Union Congress on 18 May 1936, he said:

> I consider the Communal Award to be a dangerous thing. . . . But everyone should seriously engage himself in the major problem of achieving freedom for the country and then the *communal question will automatically be solved* [emphasis added].[94]

Again, speaking at Amritsar on 31 May 1936, Jawaharlal stated:

> The issue of the Communal Award, important as it is, is not the main issue before the country. *The day on which India achieves her freedom, communal differences and jealousies will get solved of themselves* [emphasis added].[95]

Ansari learnt his lesson the hard way. His experience of conducting parleys with the Muslim Conference and later with Shaukat Ali and Jinnah demonstrated that make-show attempts at achieving reconciliation widened existing rifts. Such was the fate of his initiatives as leader of the NMP and of the Unity Conference at Allahabad, held towards the end of 1932. Memories of the Lucknow Pact (1916) were no doubt fresh in his mind, but it was equally clear to him that the Congress-League concordat happened in somewhat exceptional circumstances, created by an unusual configuration of forces. It was therefore not easy, though he did not say so, to achieve the same agreement in the mid-1930s for reasons which were linked with either British policies or connected with the experiences and perceptions of large segments of the Hindu and Muslim communities in the aftermath of the Khilafat and non-cooperation movements. It is worth summarizing a dialogue between Ansari and Halide Edip, as recorded in *Inside India* (pp. 217-18):

'We Muslems are being generous and more consistent when we uphold Communal Award both in Muslem majorities and minorities. It is the only safeguard against communal friction. The Hindu, when in a minority, can no longer have a grievance if he has definite representation and proportional posts.'
Ansari: 'But it will be accepting the fact that Hindus and Muslims will neither trust each other, nor are able to co-operate without interference of a third power.'
'What if they came to a mutual understanding on the subject?'
Ansari: 'I would oppose it still. It would perpetuate two things which prevent us becoming a nation in a modern sense: the fight for jobs by this on that community; the continuation of nations within a nation.'
'But what do you say to the way the Muslem minority is treated?'
Ansari: 'Let the Muslems then vote for the best Hindu, and let the Hindu minority vote for the best Muslem, one who will work for the good of all.'
Edip: 'May not the Communal Award be temporary expediency to prevent Hindu-Muslem friction, until there is a civic education which will change this communal mentality.'
Ansari: 'No . . . civic education begins with experience. Let us face the disaster of even friction, rather than retard our civic education. If the Muslems as a body throughout India would back the Hindus who are against Communal Award in principle we could do away with the canker of Communal Award. This bone of contention over which we are fighting so shamelessly constitutes both the strength and the perpetuation of foreign domination.'

Ansari characterized the Award as a vicious document based on the principle of divide and rule.[96] Reaffirming the NMP's position that joint electorates with adult suffrage constituted the only acceptable basis for India's constitution, he asserted that the Award would impede future prospects of Hindu-Muslim cooperation. In a statement issued from Freiburg in Germany, he said: 'Rescue our common motherland out of chaos and extricate ourselves from the most humiliating position and fervently hope that the Award will open the eyes of both the communities and an era of sense of goodwill will be ushered.'[97] Given the choice, Ansari would have campaigned against the Award and rallied his band of followers in the NMP, who seemed uncertain and confused, on to his side. But Congress' strategy to play it safe clipped his wings and offered him little scope for manoeuvre. In the end, he performed the role expected of him: to explain and defend Congress' policy. He did so in a press statement on 21 May 1934:

> The Congress knows that while a large number of Hindus and Sikhs have taken strong exception to the Communal Award, a considerable section of Mussalmans, Harijans and Christians have accepted it for so long as an agreed substitute is found. The Congress will always strive to find a national solution of the question, but in my opinion such a solution of the question cannot be found except by a Constituent Assembly convened to frame a national constitution. Until then, the question of acceptance or rejection of the mode or proportion of representation as contained in the Award does not arise. It would not be dignified for any self-respecting people to ask any outsider to decide what is purely a domestic matter, nor would any such decision succeed in satisfying all.[98]

Soon thereafter, Ansari turned to Jinnah, who had been re-elected that October to represent the Muslims of Bombay city in the central assembly. He wanted to know the basis on which the elected members could cooperate.[99] They had met earlier—in April 1934—when Jinnah offered a formula: acceptance of the Communal Award for the time being on the understanding that joint electorates would be substituted for separate electorates after a specified period. Though Ansari, Bhulabhai Desai and B.C. Roy, who were confronted with what seemed a reasonable offer, remained non-committal because of the Congress Working Committee mandate,[100] Jinnah's proposal opened up the prospect for yet another round of negotiations.

Jinnah endorsed Ansari's suggestion;[101] he was prepared to turn back towards the Congress to see if its leadership was prepared to concede all that the Communal Award had promised to the Muslims, thus clearing the way for the Hindus and Muslims to join forces against the White Paper, presented by Samuel Hoare (1880-1950) to parliament in March 1933.[102] He hoped the time was ripe for launching a new series of talks aimed at weaning Congress from its dependence upon the Hindu Mahasabha position. He made his offer thus:

> I have nothing in common with the Aga Khan. He is a British agent. I am devoted to my old policy and programme. . . . If the Congress can support the Muslims on the question of the Communal Award, I would be able to get all the Muslim members except 7 or 8. . . . As things stand, the practical way would be for just a few leaders of political thought to combine for the purpose of preparing a formula which both the communities might accept. The Congress I admit would have to change its attitude in some respects, but looking to the great interests at stake Congress leaders should not flinch. I think the future is with the Congress party and not with me or the Aga Khan.[103]

These were not empty words. In the assembly, Jinnah and the Muslim Independents cooperated with the Congress members on several issues. The 'Ambassador of Hindu-Muslim Unity' secured their backing for three resolutions of his own, the first acquiescing in the Communal Award pending an alternative settlement by the communities themselves, the second criticizing the provincial part of the Act of 1935 but not condemning it outright, the third denouncing the federal part as 'fundamentally bad and totally unacceptable' and demanding the prompt establishment of full responsible government in a federated British India. This alliance was more or less consistently maintained. In 1935, and again in 1936, it brought about the rejection of the budget and forced the governor-general to 'certify' it. 'Never before,' wrote the official British historian, 'had the nationalist opposition pressed the Government so hard as it did in this period of Hindu-Muslim cooperation.'[104] This augured well for the talks between Jinnah and the Congress president, Rajendra Prasad, in January 1935.

Discussions between Prasad and Jinnah started at the Dar-us-Salam on 23 January and continued until the end of February at 13 Ashok Road. After protracted deliberations they agreed on the following as a basis for further discussion:

1. Franchise to be framed and adjusted to reflect the proportion of population of the various communities in the electoral rolls for the province as well as the centre. For that purpose

differential franchise would be adopted wherever necessary.

2. There would be no overlapping of electorates or constituencies.
3. The Sikhs in Punjab would choose the number of constituencies for the seats allotted to them in the Communal Award. Thereafter, the Hindus would have the choice to fix on such constituencies as they might desire for the number allotted to them. The remaining constituencies would go to the Muslims in accordance with the provision in the Award, excluding the seats given to Europeans, Anglo-Indians, Indian Christians and special constituencies.
4. In Bengal if any seats were obtained from Europeans they would be divided between Hindus and Muslims in proportion to their population. However, seats reserved for the Muslims under the Award would stay, excluding the seats given to Europeans, Anglo-Indians, Indian Christians and special constituencies.
5. In other provinces and in the central legislature, the number of seats reserved for the Muslims would be the same as in the Award.
6. On this basis it was agreed that joint electorates would replace separate electorates in all the provinces and in the centre.[105]

Bhulabhai Desai (1877-1946), Patel and the Congress president accepted this formula.[106] Gandhi, too, nodded in approval.[107] Serious opposition was, however, mounted by the Sikhs in Punjab and a section of urban Hindus in Bengal. Whereas the Sikhs rejected the Punjab formula,[108] the Hindu Mahasabha denounced the Bengal formula. Their spokesmen were C.Y. Chintamani (1880-1941), president of the Anti-Communal Award Conference,[109] and Malaviya, the voice of Hindu orthodoxy in north India.[110] Yet, Prasad and Patel, impressed by Jinnah's accomodating spirit and the Muslim Leagues' acceptance of joint electorates, ignored the dissenters.[111] When Prasad met Jinnah on 27 February he suggested confining the agreement to the Congress and the League, leaving aside the more intransigent bodies. Jinnah refused. The Congress president's own notes described Jinnah's position:

As regards future procedure he [Jinnah] said that Mussalmans had told him that on several previous occasions the question had been discussed and ended in no agreement. They wanted to know whether the Hindu Sabha leaders and Sikh leaders were agreeable and particularly what was Pandit Malaviya's attitude. If I could get the signatures of these people he hoped to carry it through so far as the Mussalmans were concerned. I asked him if resolutions of Provincial Legislators and the Assembly would do. He said they might as mere expressions of opinion but the Government might insist on resolutions of communal organizations and signatures of individual leaders. I told him that organizations might be easier to tackle than some individuals and perhaps legislature could be managed best. He said an individual like Malaviyaji could in no case be ignored. He pointed out that with propaganda being carried on his position was becoming very difficult and even negotiations were made very difficult.[112]

With the Congress president refusing to accept Jinnah's conditions, the talks came to an 'infructuous end'. Prasad's own version reflects his disappointment.

In the conversations which I had with Mr Jinnah in 1935 we were able to evolve a formula. I accepted it not only in my personal capacity but as President of the Congress and offered to have it ratified by the Congress. I was keeping in touch with prominent Congressmen while the conversations were going on and had received universal support for it from them. There were several members of the Congress Working Committee at Delhi at the time and were in full agreement with me. There was absolutely no difference among Congressmen and I was successful in obtaining the support of the leaders of the Hindu Mahasabha of the Punjab also. But Mr Jinnah insisted on having the signature of Pandit Madan Mohan Malaviya and other leaders of the Hindu Mahasabha. This I was unable to secure and the matter had to be dropped. It was not dropped because Congressmen were not agreeable but because those leaders of the Hindu Mahasabha on whose signature Mr Jinnah insisted were not agreeable. . . . I had gone further and had told Mr Jinnah that the Congress and the League should accept the formula and the Congress would fight those Hindus who were opposed to it, as it had fought them during the recent Assembly elections quite successfully in most Provinces. But this was not considered enough by Mr Jinnah and as it was impossible to fulfil his demand that Hindu Mahasabha should also join, the matter had to be dropped.[113]

It would thus appear that as far as Prasad and Jinnah were concerned, the negotiations brought about a substantial degree of consensus and left to themselves, they would have reached a settlement.[114] But the president's attempt to make others outside the Congress agree to the terms yielded nothing. To expect Moonje, Parmanand and H.N. Dutt, president of the Bengal Provincial Hindu Conference, had thwarted all the previous Congress-League pacts and there was no reason for them to act differently in January-February 1935. 'How is it that Moonje, Jagatnarainlal can be better Hindus than Vallabhbhai, Rajendra Babu and others?' enquired Birla who was much concerned with the failure of the talks. He continued:

> Have not we ourselves given them undue importance and so by unanimous votes, they are the real leaders so far as communal matters go? I fear that in any constructive work that you may do in future, these false prophets would put obstructions in your way.[115]

Thus, once again, a few stubborn leaders refused to stretch that extra inch of representational concession to close the gap dividing India's pluralistic society and keeping it constitutionally fragmented. They alienated Jinnah, the only Muslim leader capable of reining his community into harness with Congress' bullock team. He was driven to the position of obduracy and belligerence towards the Congress.[116]

Ansari remained in 'constant attendance'. After all, he had prepared the ground for the Jinnah-Prasad talks and had coaxed the latter into inviting Jinnah for discussions. But he could not sustain his active interest. Strained by his involvement in the Parliamentary Board and the subsequent election campaign, his health was in a 'chronic state of deterioration'. For two months he travelled extensively, hosted meetings of the Working Committee and the Board at his residence, and kept a vigil on the Jinnah-Prasad parleys. 'Are you surprised that with all this care and responsibility, my damaged health has completely broken down and I find myself totally unable to go any further?' he wrote to Brelvi in April 1935.[117]

In early March 1935, Ansari dropped a bombshell by quitting public life 'under great compulsion of pressing personal and private necessity'.[118] His anguished outpourings were followed by his resignation from the Working Committee and the Parliamentary Board, a move which caught many by surprise.[119] Some thought that it was due to his feuds with Bhulabhai Desai and Malaviya in the Parliamentary Board, who made his effective functioning difficult.[120] Both Ansari and Desai contradicted such reports.[121] The *Bombay Chronicle* found it necessary to print in bold letters that Ansari's retirement was due solely to reasons of health and speculation as to other possible reasons were without any foundation.[122] Gandhi, who cared for Ansari more than anybody outside his close and inner circle of friends and followers, insisted that he should not desert the Board or the Committee.[123] Nariman pointed out that 'a general has no right to retire till the fight is over and the rank and file can demand at least his association, if not active service, so long as the objective is not reached'.[124] He wanted Ansari in the Parliamentary Board because he occupied

> a peculiar and unique position, both in Congress and the country. His unassailable nationalism and his uncompromising anti-communalism give a peculiar value to his association to all political organizations in general and to the Congress Parliamentary Board in particular. With him at the helm, none dare charge the Board with communalist tendencies. . . . He is a strong link between the two great communities and his nationalism and cosmopolitanism serve as an inspiring example to young political India . . . and also as an effective check to the canker of communalism. To remove both this inspiration and check at a time when both are most needed would be a suicidal and retrograde step.

Unmoved by such earnest pleas, Ansari quickly withdrew into Dar-us-Salam's quiet surroundings. However, his retreat into the background did not mean that he was now free of political entanglements: from this time onwards. He was consulted on the election of the Congress president for the 1935 session,[125] though he in public affairs.[126] 'Now that I am free from all responsibilities for the future,' he wrote to B.C. Roy, for long a political companion, 'I shall breathe freely and feel my own master, a luxury which I have not enjoyed all these years owing to my intimate connection with the Congress.'[127] He had been engaged in writing his book on *Regeneration in Man* and was happy to see it through the press. Published in early 1935, this extremely readable work gave a historical retrospect and a review of the advances in the knowledge of the endocrinal activity of the sex glands.[128] Gandhi was among those who read it with interest, though he refrained from offering any comments.

Ansari's main interest lay in nursing the Jamia Millia which had suffered years of neglect. His appeal for funds in mid-February[129] met with a favourable response; grants came pouring in from different quarters.[130] This enabled him to organize the foundation ceremony of a new building at a site in Okhla, now in South Delhi, where 100 acres of land was acquired for Rs 10,000. Performed by the youngest child in Jamia,[131] Rajendra Prasad, Patel, Sarojini Naidu, Bhulabhai Desai and the Turkish guest, Halide Edip, witnessed the ceremony. The *Amir-i Jamia* said on the occasion: 'We desire to build an institution which, while being Islamic in its traditions, will be national in its outlook.'[132] Although his dreams were partially fulfilled, he was not destined to be associated with Jamia's progress for long. By the time Halide Edip returned to Turkey, Jamia had expanded its horizon in several different spheres. This was her final impression:

> The last I saw of the Jamia was when its members assembled outside Delhi to lay the foundation-stone of their new building. . . . The youngest child was to lay the foundation-stone. He stood on the platform and seemed rather restless among the grown-ups. Opposite the platform were all my young friends. They behaved very well, listening patiently to the inaugural speeches made from the platform. But after a while they became fidgety and began to talk. . . . A little girl of seven restored order. She was a puny creature with sharp black eyes. Her eyes glared, and certain ribs felt her sharp elbows stuck into them. There was no more fidgeting. She seemed to me a symbol of the modern Indian woman, asserting her rights by proving her ability to make her men behave.

This was on 1 March 1935, and the youngest child was Abdul

Aziz. 'To perform this sacred formality', Zakir Husain observed:

A person is chosen who is neither from the rulers nor from the dignitaries of the Government; he is neither from the leaders of the land, nor from the lords of the community; he is nothing at all, but he could be everything. He is the youngest child in Jamia. Those with vision would appreciate the selection and would accept the fact that this master of the future is far suitable to perform this ceremony than most of us who are the slaves of the present.

Next day the celebrations continued. Halide Edip distributed prizes, and Urdu poets recited *ghazals* (lyric love poetry in the form of rhyming couplets) at a *mushaira* (poetry session) held in Sarojini Naidu's presence. In April, Ansari had entrusted the work for raising contributions for the Jamia building fund to Shafiqur Rahman Kidwai and Zakir Husain;[133] thereafter, he did little beyond performing his minimal duties as *Amir-i Jamia.*

So ended a distinguished public life which spanned over two decades and encompassed some of the most tumultuous years in India's fight for freedom. Some still hoped that he would be restored to his normal health and take his place 'in the political life of the country to which few living men have made a more disinterested, glorious and invaluable contribution'.[134] But, while returning from Mussoorie where he had gone to attend on the Nawab of Rampur, Ansari suffered a heart attack near Jainpur Saun station and died a little after 12.30 a.m. on 10 May 1936. 'Few deaths leave me disconsolate as this has done,' wrote Gandhi in his tribute to the man he admired and respected. 'Quite wrongly, I know, but I had pictured Dr Ansari as one destined to finish his century. . . . He had become part of the lives of many.'[135]

NOTES

1. To Brelvi, 2 April 1930, Brelvi Papers. Ansari refused election to the Congress Working Committee and as a general secretary. He resigned from the presidentship of the PCC of Delhi, as well as membership of the Working Committee of the Delhi province and district.
2. To Gandhi, 10 February 1930, Hasan (ed.), *Muslims and the Congress,* p. 93. Also, Khaliquzzaman to Jawaharlal, 1 February 1930, Ansari Papers, JMI.
3. Statement, 6 July 1930, ibid., p. 115.

4. He compared the situation in the following manner:

(1920)	(1930)
1. Great dissatisfaction against the Govt. owing to wartime promises not having been kept. Dissatisfaction against Rowlatt Act, Martial Law and Khailafat wrongs.	1. Large number of people believe in the goodwill of the Labour Govt. and sincerity of the Viceroy, rightly or wrongly.
2. Highest watermark reached in Hindu-Muslim unity.	2. Lowest watermark reached in Hindu-Muslim unity.
3. Sikhs entirely with the Congress.	3. Sikhs almost entirely against the Congress.
4. Complete unity inside the Congress. Great enthusiasm among the workers and the rank and file.	4. Disunity in the Congress, diversity of purpose, complete lack of enthusiasm amongst the workers. Lukewarmness amongst the rank and file.
5. Complete non-violent atmosphere and yet breaking of violence in Chauri Chaura.	5. Obvious existence of violence, even large number of leading Congressmen believing in it and the certainty of violence breaking out.

Ansari to Gandhi, 13 February 1930, ibid., pp. 99-100. This letter is also published in *CWMG*, vol. XLII, pp. 518-22.

5. The first page of this letter is missing, but it was obviously written by Ansari to Gandhi soon after 3 March 1930. See Ansari Collection, NMML.
6. To Brelvi, 2 April 1930, Brelvi Papers.
7. Gandhi to Ansari, 16 February 1930, Hasan (ed.), *Muslims and the Congress*, pp. 101-2; also, *CWMG*, vol. XLII, pp. 510-11.
8. Gandhi to Ansari, 3 March 1930, Hasan (ed.), *Muslims and the Congress*, p. 118.
9. This was the essence of Gandhi's letter of 16 February to Ansari.
10. Ansari to Gandhi, n.d., Ansari Collection, NMML.
11. Motilal Nehru to Ansari, 17 February 1930, ibid., pp. 103-4.
12. It seems to us that Gandhi has not so far tried so much as he ought to have done to bring about a Hindu-Muslim settlement . . . [and] has not yet made any sustained efforts to make the Hindus as a community to take up an attitude that may make for a settlement.' *Mussalman*, 20 June 1931. This assertion was true to a certain extent but was not supported by the impression of other contemporaries. Sapru, for instance, found him anxious for a Hindu-Muslim settlement and felt, quite rightly, that it was unfair to judge Gandhi's intentions by his public statements or by what some of his followers said. Earlier, Gandhi had written to Sapru that he was 'trying in my own way to reach a solution of the communal tangle. If there is no success I would not

have the heart to go to London. I said as much to Irwin.' Sapru to Sankey, 24 May 1931, Gandhi to Sapru, 22 April 1931, Sapru Papers (23).

13. Ansari to Gandhi, n.d., Ansari Collection, NMML. It is noteworthy that Ansari did not change his view until 1934 when he again complained of Gandhi not doing enough to restore communal amity. Gandhi wrote in reply: 'If you entertain this fear I would like to disabuse you of the fear. My views are just as strong as they were on the necessity of this unity. But I have come to the conclusion that this is the time for real lovers of unity to sit still and simply pray showing in their individual action what a living unity of hearts can mean. Do you not meet in your practice with boils which grow worse with teasing? I find communal discord such a boil. The more you tease it the worse it becomes. It needs a rest cure.' Gandhi to Ansari, 18 March 1934, Hasan (ed.), *Muslims and the Congress*, p. 145.
14. *Mussalman*, 10 March, 4 July 1931.
15. Ibid., 4 April 1931.
16. Syed Mahmud to Ansari, n.d., Hasan (ed.), *Muslims and the Congress*, pp. 106-7.
17. Sherwani to Ansari, 3 March 1930, ibid., p. 113.
18. Khaliquzzaman to Ansari, 1 March 1930, ibid., pp. 110-11.
19. Ansari to Sherwani, 6 January 1930, ibid., pp. 90-1.
20. He put it somewhat differently in his letter to Gandhi. 'My heart,' he wrote, 'is with you but ray brain is not, in spite of all the bias in your favour.' To Gandhi, n.d., Ansari Collection, NMML. Also, Ansari to V.J. Patel, 29 May 1930, Hasan (ed.), *Muslims and the Congress*, p. 123.
21. Vallabhbhai Patel to Ansari, 13 July 1930, ibid., p. 126.
22. Ansari to Brelvi, 2 April 1930, Brelvi Papers; press statement by Ansari, 7 July 1930, Hasan (ed.), *Muslims and the Congress*, pp. 123-4. *Bombay Chronicle*, 7 July 1930, and *IQR*, July-December 1930, p. 331.
23. Ibid., 13 August 1930; Home Poll. F. No. 5/46, 1932, NAI. Writing to the *Manchester Guardian* after Ansari's death, Horace Alexander recalled his meeting with the departed leader during civil disobedience. 'He had disapproved Mr Gandhi's starting of civil disobedience and was eager for peace. On my visiting him, he admitted that he had been opposed to civil disobedience, but as the weeks had passed by, with daily lathi beatings of unarmed peaceful men and women and other brutalities, he had felt unable to stand aside any longer. On that very day, as a result of the arrest of another Congress leader, he had become acting president of the Congress.' *Manchester Guardian*, 13 May 1936, Nehru Papers, vol. 45.
24. Wrote Azad: 'Before I was arrested, I nominated Dr Ansari as my successor. At first he was not willing to join the movement but I was able to persuade him.' *India Wins Freedom* (Delhi, 1959), rpt., p. 11.

Horace Alexander and his companion were in *Dar-us-Salam* when 'it was surrounded by the police, who had come to arrest the whole committee. In the midst of all this anxiety Dr Ansari came out on the balcony and smilingly said: "Well, you see how it is. I apologize for receiving you in this manner. I hope to be able to offer you better hospitality at some future time when we are free." . . . Then the members of the Congress Committee were carried off in police cars; last of all, the police superintendent himself drove his own car, containing Dr Ansari, the Muslim president, and the veteran Hindu leader Pandit Malaviya. As they passed us in the Drive Dr Ansari and Malaviya waved to us as if they were schoolboys off for a holiday.' Ibid.

25. *IQR*, July-December 1930, p. 331.
26. *Bombay Chronicle*, 24 July 1930.
27. After three days of strenuous discussion on the question whether Muslims should participate in the struggle for independence, the Jamiyat at its session at Amroha resolved: '(a) Whereas the Indian National Congress has adopted complete independence as its political goal which has so long been the creed of the Jamiyat, and whereas it has nullified the Nehru Report and has resolved that no constitution will be acceptable to the Congress unless it gives full satisfaction to the minorities concerned, this session of the Jamiyat considers that under the present circumstances there is no reason why Muslims should keep themselves aloof from the Congress. (b) In view of the religious and national interest of Muslims, this session of the Jamiyat wants to make it clear that any future programme of the Congress will not be regarded as the final word for Muslims, unless the Jamiyat accepts it. (c) Whereas the Sarda Act is an open interference with Islam and is an outrage upon the Islamic personal law and whereas the Government, in spite of widespread agitation and protest, has not exempted Muslims from it. (d) Whereas complete freedom of the country and the nation from British domination is the only means to put a stop to all this mischief and to safeguard the honour of Islam, this session of the Jamiyat appeals to Muslims that for the sake of the freedom of the country and to protect from the outrage the Islamic personal law, they should, in cooperation with the Congress, carry on the non-violent struggle for freedom with courage, zeal and determination. (e) This session of Jamiyat appoints a Committee, consisting of Maulana Kifayatullah, Maulana Ataullah Shah Bukhari and Maulana Muhammad Naeem to prepare a programme of action on the following lines for the attainment of freedom and the protection of personal law and invites Muslims to execute it:—(i) Publication of proscribed *fatwa* and other literatures, (ii) Picketing of liquor shops, (iii) Boycott of British cloth and to carry on a propaganda in favour of British goods and specially British goods

and cloth made in India, (iv) The Jamiyat expects that, if the Congress makes an attempt to remove the doubts and suspicions of some of the Muslims who are not yet satisfied with its attitude, prompt success is bound to come through the united actions of the Muslims.' *IQR*, January-June, p. 43.

28. To Shaukatullah Ansari, 9 December 1933, Hasan (ed.), *Muslims and the Congress*, p. 141. He had earlier written to Jawaharlal to say that there was an acceptable improvement in his heart condition. A week before sailing for India he wrote from France: 'A week in London was enough to make me run away from there. I am here for this week before taking my boat on 26th. One at least sees the sun here.' To Jawaharlal, 19 October 1933, Nehru Papers (3).
29. To Jawaharlal, 20 December 1933, Nehru Papers (3); Ansari to A.I. Bijnori, 19 October 1934, Bijnori, *Latif Ki Kahani*, pp. 280-1. Horace Alexander met Ansari at London in 1933 and remembered how his health had been broken by his imprisonment, and 'he had become an old man'. Nehru Papers (3).
30. There is much useful secondary literature on the subject. I have mainly relied on: Brown, *Gandhi and Civil Disobedience*, chapter 7, section 2; B.R. Tomlinson, *The Indian National Congress and the Raj 1929-1942: The Penultimate Phase* (London, 1976), pp. 37-9; B.B. Misra, *The Indian Political Parties* (Delhi, 1976), pp. 299-307. Some of the essays in D.A. Low (ed.), *Congress and the Raj: Facets of the Indian Struggle 1917-47* (London, 1977) revise some of the existing notions on civil disobedience.
31. *Hindu*, 19 August 1933, *A Hundred Years of the Hindu: The Epic Story of Indian Nationalism* (Madras, n.d.), pp. 438-9.
32. Tendulkar, Nanda and Brown have described the process. I have tried to keep the details to the minimum. Also, the chronological order of events has not been followed in the subsequent narrative.
33. Satyamurti to Ansari, 11 November 1933, Home Poll. F. No. 4/19, 1933, NAI.
34. Nariman to Ansari, 11 December 1933, Hasan (ed.), *Muslims and the Congress*, pp. 142-4.
35. Roy to Ansari, 8 January 1934, B.C. Roy Papers, NMML; Ansari to Brelvi, 1 February 1934, Brelvi Papers.
36. Ansari and Roy to Munshi, 10 January 1934, *Pilgrimage to Freedom*, vol. 1, pp. 358-9, and enclosure in Roy to Ansari, 8 January 1934, Roy Papers.
37. Ansari to Brelvi, 1 February 1934, Brelvi Papers.
38. Brown, *Gandhi and Civil Disobedience*, p. 368.
39. Prison Diary, 23 June 1933, *SWJN*, vol. 5, p. 485.
40. Gandhi to Ansari, 18 March 1934, Home Poll. F. No. 3/6, 1934, NAI.

41. *IAR*, January-June 1934, pp. 261-3, for the proceedings.
42. *Bombay Chronicle*, 3 April 1934.
43. Ansari to Brelvi, 10 April 1934, Brelvi Papers; Brown, *Gandhi and Civil Disobedience*, p. 364.
44. Brelvi to Satyamurti, 12 November 1933, quoted in Brown, *Gandhi and Civil Disobedience*, p. 364.
45. Ansari to Brelvi, 10 April 1934, Brelvi Papers.
46. *IAR*, January-June 1934, vol. 1, pp. 262-3.
47. Gandhi to Ansari, 5 April 1934, Hasan (ed.), *Muslims and the Congress*, p. 147. The journalist Durga Das concluded after his discussions with Gandhi that he had realized that 'whereas the Swarajists counted on his movement as a sanction for their fight within the legislatures, hereafter the constructive programme for which he stood could receive an impetus through the power that the coming Reforms Act would place in the hands of popularly chosen Ministers in the province'. Durga Das, *India From Curzon to Nehru and After* (London, 1969), p. 164.
48. *SWJN*, vol. 6, p. 272; Gopal, *Jawaharlal Nehru*, vol. 1, pp. 186-7; Pandey, *Nehru*, pp. 178-9.
49. *IQR*, January-June 1930, pp. 340-4. J.P. Haithcox, 'Left Wing Unity and the Indian Nationalist Movement: M.N. Roy and the CSP', *Modern Asian Studies*, vol. 3, i, 1969, pp. 19, 21; Minoo Masani, *Bliss was it in that Dawn: A Political Memoir Upto Independence* (Bombay, 1977), pp. 46-50. For reactions to socialist pronouncements, see Tomlinson, op. cit., pp. 52-5.
50. For a recent study, see Bimal Prasad, *Gandhi, Nehru and J.P.: Studies in Leadership* (Delhi, 1985).
51. *Bombay Chronicle*, 24 May 1934.
52. *IAR*, January-June 1934, pp. 271-2.
53. Ibid.
54. *Bombay Chronicle*, 25 May 1935 (editorial comment).
55. Ibid., 11 April 1935, and editorial comment, 6 April 1935.
56. Ibid., 7 October 1934.
57. Ibid., 25 May 1934.
58. Ibid., 6 October 1934.
59. Ibid., 7 October 1934.
60. Hasan (ed.), *Muslims and the Congress*, pp. 165-7.
61. Brelvi to Ansari, 24 November 1934, Hasan (ed.), *Muslims and the Congress*, p. 192.
62. Rajendra Prasad to Ansari, 26 December 1934, Hasan (ed.), *Muslims and the Congress*, p. 227.
63. Rajendra Prasad to Sri Prakasa, 11 December 1935, Sri Prakasa Papers, NMML.
64. Ansari to B.C. Roy, 10 October 1935, Roy Papers.

65. Statement of 26 November 1934 and letter to Congress members of the Legislative Assembly, 11 December 1934, Hasan (ed.), *Muslims and the Congress*, pp. 196-7, 213-14.
66. *Bombay Chronicle*, 7 January 1935.
67. Ibid.
68. Ansari to G.B. Pant, October 1934 (telegram), Hasan (ed.), *Muslims and the Congress*, p. 167.
69. For official and semi-official accounts of the Round Table Conference, see Reginald Coupland, *India: A Re-statement* (Oxford, 1945), pp. 137-41; William Roy Smith, *Nationalism and Reform in India* (Yale University Press, 1938) follows the official version closely. The communal question is discussed by Brown, Moore and Uma Kaura. The role of Sapru is examined by D.A. Low in *Soundings in Modern South Asian History* (University of California Press, 1968), though his account does not shed much light on the communal issue at the Round Table Conference. Moore, *The Crisis of Indian Unity*, pp. 218-23; also, Aga Khan, *The Memoirs of Aga Khan: World Enough and Time*, pp. 214-22, 228-31, is an account of one who was closely involved in the negotiations. His suite in Hotel Ritz was the venue of several informal discussions.
70. Khaliquzzaman, *Pathway to Pakistan*, p. 111.
71. For a detailed discussion, see Note by P. Stewart, 4 November 1931, appendix I, Templewood collection, MSS. EUR. E. 240 (65). IOL. Appendix II is Moonje's memorandum on the Congress formula, while the demands of the Sikhs are set out in the memorandum submitted by Ujjal Singh and Sampuran Singh. This is included as appendix IV. For secondary accounts of Gandhi's role, see B.R. Nanda, *Mahatma Gandhi: A Biography* (London, 1958), pp. 313-15; Tendulkar, *Mahatma*, vol. 3.
72. Fazl-i Husain to Shafaat Ahmad Khan, 6 November 1930, Fazl-i Husain to Mohammad Shafi, 6 November, 1 December 1930, Fazl-i Husain to Shafaat Ahmad Khan, 7 September 1931, Waheed Ahmad (ed.), *Letters of Mian Fazl-i Husain*, pp. 106-9, 190.
73. *Indian Round Table Conference 12th November 1930-19th January 1931. Proceedings of Sub-Committees (Part II) (Sub-Committees II-IX)* (London, 1931), pp. 98-9; and, *Proceedings of Sub-Committees (7 September-1 December 1931)*, (London, 1932), p. 4.
74. Aga Khan, *The Memoirs of Aga Khan*, p. 232. For the Aga Khan's role, see Mihir Bose, *The Aga Khans* (London, 1984), pp. 241-3.
75. Speech by Jamnadas Mehta, *Free Press Journal*, 10 February 1933, Sapru Papers (30). There was much bitter controversy at the outcome of the conference. The *Pratap* and the *Abhyudaya* blamed the Muslim delegates—'hirelings of the British Government'—for the deadlock over the communal question. The *Himmat, Hamdam* and the *Naiyar-i Azam*, on the other hand, attributed the failure of the talks to the

obstinacy of the Hindu and Sikh delegates. They even disputed Gandhi's claim that the Congress represented all communities, classes and creeds and asserted that it was a purely Hindu organization which the Muslims had abandoned long ago. This was a typical example of the scurrilous and irresponsible writings in a section of the vernacular press. Charges were bandied about without any realization of its implications on communal relations.

76. Statement on the Communal Award, Sapru Papers (29). Sapru agreed that the Award had 'ugly features', though he added that 'we never seized the opportunity of settling it [Hindu-Muslim problem] ourselves'. To Jayakar, 23 August 1932, Sapru Papers.
77. *IAR*, January-June 1933, p. 420; and presidential address of Bhai Parmanand at the Ajmer session of the Hindu Mahasabha on 14 October 1935. *IAR*, July-December 1933, p. 204.
78. Fazlul Haq moved a resolution at the 1933 Muslim League session which, while welcoming the Award, recorded dissatisfaction that one-third of the seats were not guaranteed to the Muslims in the central legislature and Bengali Muslims were not given the number of seats to which they were entitled by virtue of their strength in population. Pirzada (ed.), *Foundations of Pakistan*, vol. 2, p. 203. For details of reactions in Bengal, *IAR*, July-December 1933, pp. 212-13, 217-18; Mcpherson, *The Muslim Microcosm*, pp. 117-18, 120, John Gallagher, 'Congress in Decline: Bengal 1930 to 1939', *Modern Asian Studies*, vol. 7, 3, July 1973, pp. 615-25.
79. On this point, see Kaura, op. cit., pp. 86-7. For its implications in the Punjab, see Page, op. cit., pp. 253-8 and Ayesha Jalal and Anil Seal, 'Alternative to Partition: Muslim Politics Between the Wars', *Modern Asian Studies*, vol. 15, 3, 1981, p. 443. It was noted that the Award gave Muslims of Bengal and the Punjab 'considerable opportunities to win a clear majority for themselves'. If they were able to capture 2 out of the 10 special seats in the Punjab and 7 out of 10 special seats in Bengal, they were to obtain a majority over all other communities combined. 'And this should not be an impossible or even a difficult task if they are able properly to organize themselves.' Reforms Dept., F. No. 86, Box No. 3, UPSA. Also, see Ayesha Jalal, *The Sole Spokesman: Jinnah, the Muslim League and the Demand for Pakistan* (Cambridge, 1985), p. 13.
80. Husain, *Fazl-i-Husain*, p. 263; *IAR*, July-December 1933, pp. 9, 11, 15, 20.
81. Notice the comment of Rajendra Prasad, Congress president elect. *Bombay Chronicle*, 3 August 1934.
82. Gandhi to Birla, 21 January 1933, quoted in Gallagher, op. cit., p. 621.
83. The Working Committee resolution laid down that the 'Congress claims to represent equally all communities composing the Indian Nation and

therefore, in view of the division of opinion, can neither accept nor reject the award so long as the division of opinion lasts'.

84. Nehru, *An Autobiography*, pp. 575-6.
85. *The Communal Award? Examined and Criticised* [with a foreword by C.Y. Chintamani] (Allahabad, 1934). 'The entire outlook from which the problem of communal award is approached,' wrote Aney in his letter of resignation from the Congress Working Committee, 'is in my opinion opposed to the very fundamental principles of nationalism and at variance with the policy of the Indian National Congress pursued during the last fifty years.' 18 June, 29 July 1934; and Malaviya and Aney to Gandhi and the members of the Congress Working Committee, F. No. G-24, 1934-36, AICC Papers.
86. Sharma to Jawaharlal, n.d., F. No. G-24, 1934-36, ibid. Jawaharlal expressed surprise at the association of some Congressmen and 'even persons calling themselves socialists' with the Anti-Communal Award Conference at Lahore. 'The socialism that prevails amongst some quarters in the Punjab is of a peculiar variety'. Jawaharlal to Satyapal, 10 July 1936, *SWJN*, vol. 7, pp. 366-7.
87. See *Bengal Anti-Communal Award Movement: A Report* (Calcutta, 1939). For a fairly perceptive account of the anti-Communal Award movement in Bengal, see Gallagher, op. cit., pp. 615-25.
88. Gallagher, ibid., pp. 618-19.
89. Bose to Jawaharlal, 19 September 1936, F No. G-24, part I, AICC Papers.
90. Speech at the Congress Parliamentary Board on 16 June 1934 Gandhi reiterated this view in his interviews to provincial Congress leaders (13 July 1934), Akali and Khalsa Durbar deputation (15 July) and the deputation of Punjabi Hindus and Sikhs (15 July). *CWMG*, vol. LVIII, pp. 83, 181, 191-2.
91. 27 July 1934, ibid., p. 253. Yet the Mahatma took the extraordinary stand that in the elections to the central assembly, the Congress should 'unreservedly' vote for Aney as opposed to the non-Congress candidate. To V.G. Joshi, 20 October 1934, ibid., vol. LIX, p. 204.
92. 19 August 1934, ibid., p. 234. The lack of any consistency in the Gandhi-Jawaharlal advice to Congressmen in the assembly was indicative of the general confusion in Congress circles. Gandhi directed that Congressmen must vote against a resolution or amendment accepting the Award. 'And since they cannot vote for rejection, naturally they must abstain from voting in regard to a resolution or amendment rejecting the Award'. Gandhi to B.C. Roy, 25 August 1934, ibid., p. 365. Jawaharlal, on the other hand, believed that the Congress members must 'inevitably' give their opinion against the Award 'but they will add that it must be changed by agreement'. Jawaharlal to Habibur Rahman, 13 December 1936, *SWJN*, vol. 7, p. 403; also, *Bombay Chronicle*, 15 February 1935.

93. *SWJN*, vol. 7, p. 37; Jawaharlal to Jagatnarainlal, 30 September 1936, F. No. G-24, part I, AICC Papers; Jawaharlal to S.C. Majumdar, 6 August 1936, *SWJN*, vol. 7, p. 273.
94. *SWJN*, vol. 7, p. 268, also, speech at Lahore, 29 May 1936, p. 268.
95. Speech at Amritsar, 31 May 1936, ibid., p. 270.
96. Interview to the *Bombay Chronicle, The Communal 'Award'*, op. cit., pp. 16-17.
97. Ibid., p. 73.
98. *IAR*, January-June 1934, p. 296.
99. Ansari to Jinnah, 30 December 1934, Hasan (ed.), *Muslims and the Congress*, p. 235.
100. *IAR*, July-December 1934.
101. To Ansari, 3 January 1935, Hasan (ed.), *Muslims and the Congress*, p. 235.
102. Wolpert, *Jinnah of Pakistan*, pp. 135-6.
103. 'Summary of conversation between Mr Jinnah and myself', Vallabhbhai Patel Papers, quoted in Gallagher, op. cit., p. 628.
104. Coupland, *India: A Re-Statement*, p. 151.
105. Notes of Conversation held between Jinnah and Prasad on 13-14 February 1935, AICC Papers.
106. Prasad to Patel, 14 February 1935, Rajendra Prasad Papers, NAI; also, Gallagher, op. cit., pp. 630-1.
107. 'If the kind of compromise you have outlined in your letter can be brought about, I would love it.' Gandhi to Prasad, 7 February 1935, Valmiki Choudhary (ed.), *Dr Rajendra Prasad Correspondence and Select Documents*, vol. 1 (Delhi, 1984), p. 6. Again, he informed Rajendra Prasad: 'As I am willing to do everything, why would I be averse to the joint electorate? If Muslims can accept even this and if Sikhs and Hindus agree, I have no doubt it will be extremely good. To bring around Malaviyaji appears to be a difficult proposition, but he would put up no opposition if Sikhs could be persuaded.' Gandhi to Rajendra Prasad, 28 February 1935, *CWMG*, vol. LX, p. 266.
108. See Birla to Gandhi, 25/26 February 1935, *Bapu*, vol. 1, p. 35.
109. The Anti-Communal Award Conference, held on 23-24 February 1935 and presided over by Chintamani, coincided with the Jinnah-Prasad talks in the same city. Rajendra Prasad noted on 23 February that Chintamani had expressed scepticism over the outcome of the negotiations, for 'his experience had been that on every occasion when settlement had been talked about, the demand of Mussalmans had increased and on Hindus failing to agree, the Mussalmans and some Hindus also had blamed the Hindu leaders'.
110. 'Panditji (Malaviyaji) is here and he has turned down Jinnah and Rajendra Babu's formula.' Birla to Mahadev Desai, 21 February 1935, *Bapu*, vol. 2, p. 33.

111. Gallagher, op. cit., pp. 630-1. The Muslim League Council had declared JPC Report as reactionary and agreed to cooperate with any community or party to secure a constitution satisfactory to the people. *Bombay Chronicle*, 28 January 1935.
112. Daily Notes taken by Rajendra Prasad, 20 February 1935, Rajendra Prasad Papers.
113. Statement of 6 July 1937, F. No. G-65, A1CC Papers.
114. Birla to Mahadev Desai, 28 February 1935, *Bapu*, vol. 2, p. 38.
115. Birla had advised Rajendra Prasad to accept the formula and was hopeful of persuading the 'Hindu masses' to do the same 'I am quite optimistic about the results,' he wrote, '*if only the Congress will take up a definite attitude* [emphasis added]. Even the Hindu Sabha could ratify the formula in its session provided the Congress would work for it. I hope Bapu would approve of such a move.' Birla to Mahadev Desai, 21 February 1935, ibid., p. 33.
116. Wolpert, op. cit., p. 137; Rajendra Prasad, *India Divided* (Bombay, 1946), p. 134; Khaliquzzaman, op. cit., p. 139.
117. Ansari to Brelvi, 15 April 1935, Brelvi Papers; Ansari to Jawaharlal, 11 October 1935, Nehru Papers (35).
118. Ansari to Rajendra Prasad, 23 March 1935, Hasan (ed.), *Muslims and the Congress*, pp. 253-4.
119. Ibid., p. 255.
120. *Bombay Chronicle*, 5 April 1935; on differences between Ansari and Malaviya, see Tomlinson, op. cit., pp. 39-40; *IAR*, January-June 1934, pp. 281-4.
121. *Bombay Chronicle*, 18 April 1935.
122. Ibid.
123. 'I hope you will not desert the Board or the Committee. You need not take any great active part requiring much strain. But your counsel cannot be dispensed with.' Gandhi to Ansari, 16 February 1935, *CWMG*, vol. LX, p. 237. Later, of course, Gandhi acceded to Ansari's request. 'I shall not strive with you but plead with Rajenbabu to release you,' he wrote. To Ansari, 8 March 1935, Hasan (ed.), *Muslims and the Congress*, p. 253, and *CWMG*, vol. LX, p. 285.
124. *Bombay Chronicle*, 12 April 1935. Also, editorial comment of 6 April 1935.
125. Ansari expressed his preference for Rajagopalachari, 'the best suited man to occupy the responsible post'. As regards Jawaharlal, Ansari wrote: 'He is undoubtedly the idol of the people and specially of Congressmen. Whether he is elected to the Congress Presidentship or not, his place in the hearts of the people and of Congress is ensured forever. . . . I feel that owing to Jawahar's domestic condition and his prolonged incarceration, it would be cruelty on our part to put him at once to the yoke without giving any respite. . . .' Ansari to Rajendra

Prasad, 6 October 1935, Rajendra Prasad Papers. He reiterated the same to Jawaharlal. 'I have felt all along that all of those who are responsible for your election this year are very very thoughtless and unkind to you both from the point of view of your domestic difficulties and from the public point of view. I do not think that in the present condition of things even your dynamic personality would be able to do much during your year of Presidentship. And if nothing is achieved at the end, the fact that one of our very best men have failed to achieve something would produce a great set-back'. Ansari to Jawaharlal, 11 February 1936, Nehru Papers (3). Ansari to Satyamurti, 27 November 1935, K.V. Ramanathan (ed.), *The Satyamurti Letters* (Delhi, 2008), p. 226.

126. 'And having retired from active politics, I consider it presumptuous and uncalled for to be always writing about current events to those who are responsible for guiding the policy of the Congress. If they seek my private advice, it would be gladly given. But, without any desire on their part, I feel I should abstain from doing so.' Ansari to Brelvi, 25 July 1935, Brelvi Papers.
127. Ansari to B.C. Roy, 6 October 1935, Roy Papers.
128. Mohammad Amin, *'Ada-i Shabab' (Regeneration in Man)* in Malik Ram (ed.), *Nazr-i Hameed* (Delhi, 1981), pp. 525-32; Shahabuddin Ansari, 'Dr Ansari ki Kitab: Regeneration in Man', *Jamia* (special number), July 1981, pp. 65-8.
129. He said: 'I believe what counts as the most remarkable contribution of the Jamia to our national life is that it has carried on a constructive educational and cultural enterprise . . . without seeking any aid from the government. And the fifteen years of its life are a proof that cannot be challenged that there is no lack of idealism, patience and organizing capacity.' *Bombay Chronicle*, 19 February 1935.
130. Jinnah, Shaukat Ali, Fazlul Haq and Asaf Ali were among those who associated themselves with Ansari's appeal. Ibid., 26 February 1935.
131. Gandhi welcomed the idea and congratulated Zakir Husain on the 'originality of the conception'. He thought that Jamia had a 'great future' and through it he expected the 'seed of Hindu-Muslim union to grow into a majestic tree'. Gandhi to Zakir Husain, 20 February 1935, *CWMG*, vol. LX, p. 244.
132. *Bombay Chronicle*, 2 March 1935.
133. Ibid., 23 April 1935.
134. Ibid., 6 April 1935, for editorial comment.
135. To Zakir Husain, 12 May 1936, Ansari Papers (Miscellaneous files), JMI.

10

The Legacy

> Dr Ansari has passed away and the nation of which he was a shining ornament and of our national movement of which he was so long a pillar and guide, feels desolate and shaken. We remember afresh his brilliant gifts and his services to the nation and his sacrifices for the cause of freedom [Jawaharlal].
>
> *Bombay Chronicle*, 11 May 1936

ANSARI WAS BURIED in Jamia. The funeral was intended to be private, but the immense popular interest turned it into a public, even a national event. In areas where Ansari's name was so firmly associated with the freedom struggle, people spontaneously expressed their grief at his premature death. Dar-us-Salam, a familiar landmark in Delhi's political history, was thronged with mourners. Public meetings were held in the capital where, for nearly a quarter of a century, Ansari survived the kicks and buffetings of political life and symbolized the composite cultural ethos of the Indo-Gangetic region. His face showed character and his movements, thought and talk all suggested a sincere and passionate temperament. He gave a tone to public life that promoted goodwill and had smoothed away the harsher discords of politics. Elsewhere, people remembered him as a Congress stalwart, a freedom fighter and an apostle of Hindu-Muslim unity. Wrote the *Bombay Chronicle:* 'While the spectre of communalism stalked the land and many a nationalist even among the Congressmen fell victim to it, Dr Ansari remained unshaken in his faith in democratic nationalism. . . . His nationalism was pure, unadulterated and undefiled.'[1]

Ansari was with his gentle manner a most attractive person, with an endearing streak of sometimes childlike simplicity. Kindness came naturally to him; he was thoughtful and considerate even to strangers. Those to whom he was personally attached always found him ready to involve himself sympathetically in their affairs. His Congress comrades held him in esteem for his devotion to nationalist causes, his humanity, generosity and kindness.[2] Gandhi and the Nehrus treated him with respect and deference. He was their friend and confidant and, after Mohamed Ali's estrangement from the Congress, the most important front rank leader they could rely on for rallying the Muslims around the Congress banner. From 1924-5 to 1935, he occupied the same position in Congress that Azad enjoyed in the 1940s. During this period, he was a man of action in the best sense: what he had learnt from practical experience he used to exhort, advise and implore. Having led a life of almost ceaseless endeavour and commitment, he proved himself in the most searching of political tests.

He got on well with the Liberals. He worked closely with Sapru whom he had known since 1915. He invited him to preside over the lecture of Husain Rauf Bey, first president of the Angora National Assembly, at the Jamia Millia Islamia,[3] backed his move to resolve the communal deadlock,[4] and appreciated his firm advocacy of constitutional rights. 'Although it has not been possible for Congressmen during the last 14 or 15 years to see eye to eye,' Ansari told Sapru, 'there have been more occasions than one when your cooperation on critical junctures such as, for instance, the Gandhi-Irwin negotiations, has proved of considerable value.'[5] Sapru, in turn, admired his 'genuine type of nationalism'.[6] In his final tribute to Ansari, he wrote:

> There was scarcely any man in the public life of the country for whom I had greater respect and for whom personally, if I may say so, greater affection. In these days, when it is a fashion for so many to claim to be nationalists, there was no man among the Hindus or the Muslims to whose real feelings of nationalism I felt more drawn than those of Ansari. Whatever else he may or may not have been, he was, in my humble opinion, *a very true, a very selfless and a very earnest nationalist* [italics added]. We have lost in him not only a great patriot, a great nationalist, a great doctor, but what is more, a great gentleman.[7]

Of all his friendships, perhaps that with Hakim Ajmal Khan had been the closest; in fact, rarely in political affairs had such a partnership persisted, so intimate and so loyal. But the hakim died in 1927 and Ansari became increasingly dependent on Sherwani,[8] Khaliquzzaman, Abdul Majid Khwaja, Abdur Rahman Siddiqi and Shuaib Qureshi. Azad, Syed Mahmud, Rafi Ahmad Kidwai, Ghaffar Khan, Mujibur Rahman, Brelvi, Kitchlew and Hasrat Mohani sympathized with him on certain issues; but none could be described as belonging to his personal following. His protégé, Khaliquzzaman, also did not act closely with him. For much of the period after 1929-30, he was on the other side searching for a role outside the Congress. Exuding insincerity to some, he seemed at times to embody the popular image of a cynical politician. In fact, Ansari painfully discovered that Khaliquzzaman had stood for the Assembly elections without informing him about it. 'But I must not forget my place. Who am I to grumble, what am I to take offence to such things?'[9] Leadership demanded that the emotions be kept directly from the public gaze.

Ansari inspired an entire generation of young Muslims by his consistent defiance of colonial rule,[10] his unassailable loyalty to the Congress, his contribution to fostering communal amity, and his attractive personality which was free from rancour and bitterness and untouched by any personal or political scandal. He lived long enough to see his ideas accepted, then become part of history and, as such, vulnerable to dissection and revision. Many who gathered around Jawaharlal in the 1930s were Ansari's friends and followers. Many leading lights in the Muslim Mass Contact Campaign, launched in August 1937,[11] had learnt their political lessons at his feet. And many at the Azad Muslim Conference in April 1940 were members of the NMP. Equally, Ansari's example inspired various isolated, though ineffectual, endeavours in the 1940s to stem the Muslim League tide. His followers knew that he did his best, usually with success, to cope with the task in hand.

Ansari's message was straightforward. The destiny of the Indian Muslims was inextricably linked with their fellow countrymen with whom they had everything in common except religion. Second, the Congress was engaged in a historic struggle against a colonial power and it was therefore incumbent upon all sections of the society to rally round it. Third, the debate whether a Muslim was loyal to the country first or to his faith bore no relevance, for Islam and nationalism were compatible in the Indian, as indeed in any other situation. Lastly, nationalism represented the true and genuine aspirations of the people generally; so the Hindus and the Muslims, with their shared common historical experiences and a common destiny, had to forge a united front to create a secular and democratic polity. Existing differences between them were to be amicably settled through pacts, agreements and unity conferences. The Congress offered, Ansari argued, an adequate and appropriate framework for resolving communal disputes.

Perhaps, Ansari assumed that unity conferences would put an end to communal discord. When these failed, he complained that Gandhi and Motilal had not shown sufficient interest in the matter. The fact is that he wrongly assessed that their influence was so pervasive that any agreement could be pushed through without taking care of the interests, fears and aspirations of their other constituent groups. What is more, Ansari did not notice that the resolution of communal differences was conveniently deferred until the attainment of swaraj. He was unable to come to terms with this reality; hence his outburst in February-March 1930. His resignation from the Congress was a step reluctantly taken. It was feared that he might lead a revolt, but he made no such attempt and resisted the considerable pressure placed upon him to align himself with the Muslim League. In the months that followed his resignation, he spoke rarely in public or Congress meetings. When he did speak, he underlined the theme of national unity. Men with lesser convictions succumbed to communal pressures, but he refused to change course. Although his own efforts to bring about an agreement had come to nothing, he persisted in his search for a consensus, continued to champion Hindu-Muslim unity and, in the end, represented the best traditions of Indian nationalism. 'We are not likely to see the like of Dr Ansari again,' concluded Mahadev Desai in his tribute.[12]

In the midst of his crowded time in March 1946, Gandhi had a quiet, family gathering with the students and staff members of Jamia. Pyarelal describes the visit in *Mahatma Gandhi: The Last Phase*:

> One of the students asked what they could do to bring about Hindu-Muslim unity. The way was, Gandhiji replied, that even if all the Hindus

turned rowdies and abused them, they should not cease to regard them as their blood-brothers and vice versa. 'If one returns decency for decency, it is a bargain. Even thieves and dacoits do that. . . . Humanity disdains the calculation of profit and loss. . . . If all the Hindus listened to my advice, or in the alternative the Muslims listened to me, there would be peace in India which nothing would be able to shatter. The mischief-maker will weary of the sorry business of stabbing, when there is no retaliation or counter provocation. An Unseen Power will arrest his uplifted arm and it will refuse to obey his wicked will. . . . God is good and does not allow wickedness to proceed beyond a certain length.[13]

Before returning from the campus, the Mahatma visited Ansari's tomb. This is how Pyarelal describes the pilgrimage:

The doctor had been like a brother to Gandhiji. During his twenty-one days' self-purification fast at Poona in 1933 when Gandhiji's condition suddenly became critical, Gandhiji sent him a message at Delhi that he would love nothing better than to die in his lap. Back came the good doctor's reply; he would not let him die either in his or anyone else's lap! And interrupting his visit to Europe, he hastened to the bedside of his friend to see him safely through the fast. A platform thrown up into a series of terraces marked the burial place. A plain marble tablet at the foot bore the doctor's name and the dates of his birth and death. The austere simplicity of the monument added to the poignancy of the visit. The visit symbolized Gandhiji's undying faith in the ultimate inevitability of Hindu-Muslim unity.[14]

The warmth of sentiment is not surprising. Gandhi had reposed his confidence in Zakir Husain immediately after Ansari's death, his 'infallible guide', in May 1936. He wrote to him on 24 May:

The question I wanted to ask was and I still want to ask is, will you be to me what the doctor was on the Hindu-Muslim question? What distracts me is not the absence of the warmth of a gentleman-friend, of a God-believing and God-fearing doctor. It is the absence of an unfailing guide in the matter of Hindu-Muslim unity. My silence at the present time of this question is not a sign of my apathy, it is a sign of an ever-deepening conviction that the unity has got to come. Then I ask, will you take Dr. A[nsari]'s place? In answer, do not think of your status in society. If you have self-confidence, you must say 'Yes.' If you have not, you must say 'No.' I shall not misunderstand you. I know and love you too well to misunderstand you.

. . . You have now become that for me. I did not need to utilize that special function of this very often. I may not have to trouble you so frequently as to take a lot of your time. But the fact that you are always available for reference at critical moments is a great consolation.

Gandhi continued to approach Zakir Husain as 'the spiritual successor to Dr. Ansari', and, in 1938, sought his views and advice on the Hindu-Muslim riots in Bombay and the Hindi-Urdu controversy in Bihar and Madras. Zakir Husain replied by referring to 'a floating mass of inter-communal distrust and suspicion' that was ready to be exploited by the practioners of hate.

NOTES

1. *Bombay Chronicle*, 11 May 1936.
2. Gandhi wrote that Ansari can't refuse anybody, rich or poor. 'He was once visited by a woman out to rob him, and he emptied his purse into the fold of her sari.' Gandhi to V.J. Patel, 8 April 1935, *CWMG*, vol. LX, p. 400.
3. To Sapru, 26 February 1933, Hasan (ed.), *Muslims and the Congress*, p. 135.
4. To Sapru, 25 March 1933, ibid., p. 137.
5. To Sapru, 28 April 1934, ibid., p. 152.
6. Sapru to Ansari, 23 April 1934, ibid., pp. 147-50.
7. Sapru to Asaf Ali, 12 May 1936, Sapru Papers.
8. He died on 22 March 1932. Wrote Jawaharlal in his prison diary: 'We had been arrested together on Dec. 26, 1931, and had spent a month together in barrack No. 6. That month and the preceding months during the strenuous true period we had a great deal to do with each other and my liking for him had progressively grown. When he went to Europe with Ansari in the summer of 1934 for treatment he wrote to me to prison almost an apologetic letter for leaving the country at that juncture. A brave man, true man, rather limited in outlook as all of us are, but not to be frightened or bullied.' 24 March 1935, *SWJN*, vol. 6, p. 337.
9. Ansari to Khaliquzzaman, 24 February 1923, Hasan (ed.), *Muslims and the Congress*, p. 107.
10. It is interesting to note that Ansari used professional bodies, such as the All-India Medical Conference, to voice his anti-colonial views. See *IQR*, 1933, vol. 2, pp. 23-4. I was told by the Maharajkumar of Mahmudabad that Ansari insisted on prescribing medicines produced in India to his patients.

11. Mushirul Hasan, 'The Muslim Mass Contact Campaign: An Attempt at Political Mobilization', *South Asia*, New Series, vol. VII, no. 1, June 1984.
12. Mahadev Desai to Birla, 12 May 1936, *Bapu*, vol. 2, p. 235.
13. Pyarelal, *Mahatma Gandhi: The Last Phase*, vol. 1, Bookone (Ahmedabad, 1956), pp. 176-7.
14. Ibid., p. 176.

APPENDICES

APPENDIX I

*Names of Muslims Elected from Muslim Constituencies to the Assembly with the Name of the Party to which they Belonged**

Congress

T.A.K. Sherwani.

Mohd. Ahmad Kazmi (also nominated by Unity Board).

Unity Board

Maulana Shaukat Ali (also Khilafat and Jamiyat al-ulama).

Azhar Ali (also nominated by Oudh National Agriculturists) (also Congress).

Red Shirt

Dr. Khan Sahib.

Ahrar

K.L. Gauba.

League Conference

Bombay

M.A. Jinnah.

Ibrahim Jaffer.

Sind

Seth Haji Abdulla Haroon.

Bhutto.

Punjab

Syed Ghulam Bhik Nairang.

Makhdum Syed Rajan Buksh.

Nawab Sir Mehr Shah.

Hafiz Mohammad Abdullah.

Sheikh Fazli Haq Piracha.

*Home Poll. F. No. 150/1934, NAI.

United Provinces
Maulvi Sir Mohammad Yaqub.
Dr. Ziauddin Ahmad.

Bengal
A.H. Ghaznavi.
A.K. Fazlul Haq.
Anwar-ul-Azim.
Sir Abdulla Suhrawardy.
Abdulyahel Baqi (also nominated by the Congress).

Bihar and Orissa
Maulvi Shafee Daoodi.
Maulvi Badiuzzaman.
Maulvi Mohammad Noman.

Madras
Umar Ali Shah.

Central Provinces
Khan Sahib Siddique Ali Khan.

Assam
Abdul Matin Chaudhri.

Independents

Madras
Maulvi Murtaza Sahib (also supported by League Conference).
Haji Abdul Sattar (also supported by League Conference).
Umar Ali Shah (also supported by League Conference).

Assam
Abdul Matin Chaudhri (also supported by League Conference).

C.P.
Khan Sahib Siddique Ali Khan. Independent.

Muslims elected from other Constituencies

From General Constituency
Asaf Ali (Congress).

From Landholders' Constituency
1. *Sind.*—Sir Ghulam Husain Hidayatullah (League Conference).
2. *Punjab.*—Ghiasuddin.

APPENDIX II

*Muslim Organizations in India, 1906–1947**

Serial No.	Name of Organization	When established	Constitution	Aims and Objects	Remarks
1	All-India Muslim League, Delhi	1906	*President*—M.A. Jinnah *Secretary*—Hafiz Hidayat Hosain. *Joint Secretaries*— 1. K.B.S.M. Abdulla 2. Mr. Anwar-ul-Azim M.L.A. 3. Shah Masood Ahmad, M.L.A.	To protect the religious and political rights of the Muslims in India.	This is the oldest of all the prominent Muslim organizations in India. The scope of the activities of the League is limited and unlike the C. Khilafat Committee it seldom dabbles in affairs relating to foreign countries. About 1928-29 the League was split into two rival sections, one led by M.A Jinnah and the other by the late Sir Mohd. Shafi. Both of these groups continued to work separately till the beginning of this year when they were amalgamated under the presidentship of M.A. Jinnah through the efforts of H.H. the Agha Khan. The League is now working hand-in-hand with the A.I.M.C.
2	Jamiyat al-ulama-i Hind, Delhi	1919	*President*—M. Kifayatullah. *Secretary*—Ahmad Said.	*Original* 1. To safeguard the Khilafat.	This organization is mainly composed of *Ulama*. It was established in 1919 through the efforts of Kifayatullah

(Contd.)

*Home Poll., F. No. 150/1934, NAI.

Appendix II (Contd.)

Serial No.	Name of Organization	When established	Constitution	Aims and Objects	Remarks
			Treasurer—Haji Abdul Ghaffar.	2. To preach Islam. *Subsequent to the abolition of the Khilafat.* 1. To work for the restoration of the Khilafat. 2. To preach Islam *Present Aims and Objects.* 1. To preach Islam. 2. To prepare the Muslims for the Congress creed.	and Ahmad Said of Delhi. Took an active part in Khilafat agitation and after the abolition of the Khilafat turned its attention towards the Hejaz and Arabia—stressing upon the freedom of these countries from non-Muslim influence. Thereafter the Jamiyat took some interest in the Riffian struggle and when the latter was over it devoted itself entirely to preaching unity among Muslims and protecting Islam. In 1929 the Jamiyat was split into two sections—viz., Delhi and Kanpur—the former led by Kifayatullah and the latter by the Ali Brothers. The Delhi section took an active part in the Civil Disobedience Movement in 1930 in support of the Congress by which it was well supplied with funds.

3	Jamiyat al-ulama-i Hind, Kanpur.	1929	*President*—Shah Mohd. Sulaiman of Phulwari. *Vice-President*—Abdul Qadir of Budaun. *Working Secretary*—M. Mazharuddin of Delhi. *Financial Secretary*.—Kh. Ghulam-us-Sibtain, B.A.	Aims and objects as regards the propagation of Islam are identical with those of the Delhi Jamiyat but it is opposed to Congress creed	Was founded in 1929 by the Ali Brothers with the main object of widening the narrow circle of the *ulama* by including those who thought ignorant of Arabic were well informed of the Muslim religion and further to include in the definition of religious *ulama*, all *ulama* and *Mujtahids* of all sects. This *jamiyat* was backed by the *ulama* of Firangi Mahal, Badaun and M. Mazharuddin of Delhi. When M. Shaukat Ali and his party consisting of M. Inayatullah of Firangi Mahal went over to the Delhi Jamiyat the Kanpur Jamiyat issued a disclaimer severing its connection with them. The latter body is in full agreement with the A.I.M.C. and the A.I.M. league.
4	All-India Central Khilafat Committee, Bombay.	1919	*President*—Abdul Majid Sindhi M.L.A *Vice-Presidents* 1. Haji Abdulla Haroon. 2. Maulvi Shafee Daoodi. *Secretaries* 1. Shaukat Ali. 2. Allah Bukhsh Usafi.	1. To secure the solution of the Khilafat question strictly in accordance with the *Sharia*. 2. To launch a comprehensive programme for the moral, political and	Was founded during the Great War by the Ali Brothers and Maulana Abdul Bari to safeguard the Khilafat and to watch over the safety and integrity of the Holy Places of Islam but since the disclaimer of Mustafa Kemal

(Contd.)

Appendix II (Contd.)

Serial No.	Name of Organization	When established	Constitution	Aims and Objects	Remarks
			3. H.S. Suhrawardy. 4. Mohiuddin of Ajmer. 5. Mohd. Irfan. 6. Ghulam Rasul 'Mehr'. *Honorary Treasurer* Umarbhai Chaudibhai	educational uplift of the Muslim of India. 3. To establish brotherly relations with Muslims of other countries.	Pasha and the termination of the Khilafat the aims and objects of the organization are now confined to (2) and (3) mentioned in previous column only. Is a political body with anti-British aims and propaganda. It is now anti-Congress and wields influence over those Muslims who have communal tendencies. The Central Khilafat Committee has its headquarters at Bombay and affiliated to it are the Provincial and District committee's in all parts of India.
5	All India Majlis-i Ahrar-i Islam, Punjab. Amritsar.	May 1931	*President*—M. Habibur Rahman *Vice-President*—Chaudhri Afzal Haq. M.L.C. *Secretaries* M. Daud Ghaznave. Mazhar Ali Azhar. *Treasure*—Dr. Abdul Qadir.	1. To work for the economic, educational and social uplift of the Muslims. 2. To awaken political consciousness and infuse the spirit of Islam among Muslims.	Was started by the pro-Congress Muslims with the main object of maintaining the position of the Muslims in the Congress itself and to secure seats in the Working Committee. The Congress formula regarding the settlement of communal question

3. To strive for the freedom of the country by peaceful methods.	was found to be unacceptable and was consequently rejected by the Majlis which thereafter turned its attention towards the Kashmir agitation. The Majlis carried on an intense propaganda in the form of a press campaign, meetings, processions of Kashmiri labourers and the celebration of a 'Kashmir Day', against the State. It also sent *jathas* of volunteers to Kashmir in defiance of the orders passed by the Static authorities forbidding their entry in Kashmir. The arrest of prominent leaders and lack of funds and volunteers owing to great distrust of the leaders served to decrease the enthusiasm for the Kashmir agitation and as a result the Majlis was forced to change their programme and turn their attention towards the alleged Government excesses in the N.W.F.P. but the agitation was shortlived. The agitation in Kapurthala and Jind States evoked

(Contd.)

Appendix II (Contd.)

Serial No.	Name of Organization	When established	Constitution	Aims and Objects	Remarks
					considerable interest among the Ahrars who contemplated to stir the Muslim masses in the same way as was done in the case of Kashmir but fortunately the movement died a natural death. Of late the Ahrar Party in order to enlist fresh support has been carrying on a tirade against the Ahmadiya community. The Majlis still wields a considerable influence in the Punjab and has branches in almost all the big cities in that Province.
6	Anjuman-i Khaksaran. Lahor.	1931	*Executive Committee* 1. Inayatullah Khan Mashriqi. 2. Mufti Sahib, Mozang Lahore. 3. Masud Ahmad Khan, B.Sc., of Lahore. 4. M.A. Majid of Lahore. 5. Hakim Mohd. Din of Lahore.	Social service and political advancement. To unite all Islamic power and to achieve independence for India.	The founder of Anjuman is Inayatullah Khan Mashriqi, of the "Tazkira" fame who was employed in the N.W.F.P. Educational service. He is reported to be eccentric and an ardent pan-Islamist. The Anjuman has branches in various cities in the Punjab and one in Peshawar. In July 1933 the Lahore Anjuman despatched, by

					way of advertisement, a *jatha* of 9 volunteers for pilgrimage to Mecca. The movement has made no further progress as Inayatullah has incurred the hostility of the Ahrars.
	Red Shirts (Khudai Khidmatagars or Afghan Jirga) Utmanzai-Charsada.	1929		To propagate the congress creed and to carry on the Civil Disobedience Movement.	It commanded great influence over the rural populace in the district through the medium of Khan Abdul Ghaffar Khan. Has been declared unlawful since 1931. Some unimportant persons are now carrying on the organization secretly.
8	All-India Muslim Conference.	1929	*President*—Nawab Ahmad Said Khan of Chhatari. *Vice-Presidents* Sir. Mohd. Iqbal. Dr. Shafaat Ahmad Khan. Shafee Daoodi. *Secretary*—Seth Abdullah Haroon. *Working Secretary*—Khan Bahadur Haji Rahim Baksh.	(1) To safeguard and promote the rights and interests of the Indian Muslims at all stages of constitutional advance towards full responsible Government in India. (2) To organize the Indian Muslims and to co-ordinate the existing Muslim organizations having an All-India character for the purpose	Was founded early in 1929 on the occasion of H.H. the Agha Khan's visit to Delhi. It passed unanimously the famous 14 points of Mr. Jinnah which represented the Muslim demands in the new Constitution. The conference firmly stood by these demands (including separate electorates) during the Civil Disobedience Movement from which it remained quite aloof. After the C.D. Movement discussions

(Contd.)

Appendix II (Contd.)

Serial No.	Name of Organization	When established	Constitution	Aims and Objects	Remarks
			Joint Secretaries K.B. Syed Abdul Hafiz, Husain Imam, A.H. Ghaznavi. Mohd. Moazzam and Zahur Ahmad.	of giving expression to Muslim opinion on questions affecting the Indian Muslims without interfering with the special features which distinguish such organizations.	crept in with the result that the constitution of the conference was re-shaped early in 1934 through the efforts of its promoter, viz., H.H. the Agha Khan. In conjunction with the A.I.M.L. the conference decided in August 1934 to from a Parliamentary Majlis with a view to contest seats in the Assembly in direct opposition to the efforts made by the Unity Board formed by the rival organization, viz., the A.P.M.C. to send their own candidates to the Assembly.
9	All Parties Muslim Unity Conference, Lucknow.	1930	Constitution of the Unity Board— *President* Nawab Mohd. Ismail Khan. *Working Committee.* Consisting of 21 members.	1. To create a sense of duty and love for Islam. 2. To organize all Muslims in order to enable them to take their proper share in struggle for freedom. 3. To unite the various sects of Muslims and	This conference was organized at Lucknow at the close of 1933 by Muslims of a nationalist turn of mind who were anxious to save their reputation by bringing about unity among the Muslim ranks. It is composed of members belonging to the nationalist school of thought,

Secretaries 1. Shaukat Ali. 2. Shah Masood Ahmad. 3. Syed Zakir Ali.	to strive for unity with other communities. 4. To improve the condition of peasants and zamindars and to fight against unemployment.	of the Delhi group of the Jamiyat al-ulama, a section of the Jamiyat al-ulama-i Hind, Kanpur; some members of the old C.K.C. and the A.I.M.L., the Shia community and more particularly by Shaukat Ali and his coterie, formerly enthusiastic workers of the A.I.M.C. The conference formed a Unity Board consisting of 21 members with the object of contesting seats in the Assembly elections in opposition to the efforts of the Parliamentary Majlis formed by the rival organization, viz., the A.I.M.C. At its meeting held at Lucknow in May 1934 the Muslim Unity Majlis endorsed the Congress programme regarding the revival of the Swaraj Party and deprecated all agitation to get the Communai Award modified by the British government in the absence of an agreed settlement among the various communities.

(Contd.)

Appendix II (Contd.)

Serial No.	Name of Organization	When established	Constitution	Aims and Objects	Remarks
					The results of the election clearly show that the Unity Board has attained a position of influence and importance slightly better than that held by its rival organization, viz., the A.I.M.C. Judging by the results of the elections the influence of the A.I.M.C. appears to be declining.
10	All-India Shia Conference, Lucknow.	1910	*President.*—Prince Mirza Mohd. Akram of Calcutta. *General Secretary.*—Mojez Husain (of Amroha).	To safeguard the religious and political rights of the Shia community.	The Conference was affiliated to the All-India Muslim Unity Majlis about the middle of 1934. The latter is in favour of the institution of separate electorates.
11	Jamiyat Shabbanul Muslimin, Delhi.	1929	*President.*—Mohd. Usman Azad. *Vice-President.*—Shah Abdul Jabbar. *Secretary.*—Dr. Noor Ahmad. *Joint Secretary.*—Mohd. Ibrahim. *Treasurer.*—Sufi Noor Elahi.	Aims and objects are similar to those of Jamiyat al-ulama-i Hind, Delhi, of which it is a branch.	Was founded with the object of enlisting support of the Muslim youths for the Jamiyat al-ulama of Delhi and to induce them to take part in the Civil Disobendience Movement. There are branches (or similar organizations) of the Jamiyat al-ulama-i Hindi in Lahore and Bombay but they are practically inactive.

APPENDIX III

Statement of Hakim Abdur Razzaq Ansari

My Family Comes from Ghazipur in the division of Benares. My grandfather Shaikh Muhammad Bakhsh had three sons, Shaikh Muhammad Sadiq, Jan Muhammad *alias* Abdur Rahman, and Maulvi Abdul Ghaffur. Shaikh Muhammad Sadiq, the eldest, was an Inspector of Police in the Punjab. He took his pension and died 7 or 8 years ago. He has two daughters but no sons. I married one of the daughters and the other married one Maulvi Muhammad Latib of Ghazipur. He died without issue.

Abdur Rahman was my father. He was a judicial *Amin* at Rasara in the Ballia district. He took his pension and died 12 or 14 years ago. He had four sons, Hakim Abdul Wahab, Hakim Abdur Razzaq, Muhammad Raza, Dr. Ansari. Hakim Abdul Wahab learnt medicine in the Tibbia School in Delhi, run by Hakim Ajmal Khan's father and Hakim Abdul Majid. He also studied at the Deoband *madrasa*. I was taught medicine by my brother at Ballia. Muhammad Raza and Dr. Ansari read in the Mayo College, Allahabad. When I was 26 or 28 years old I went to Hyderabad (Deccan) with Hakim Abdul Wahab. My mother's maternal uncle, Maulvi Shujaat Husain Maulai, was a *Sarishtadar* in the High Court there before his death and his son Maulvi Abdul Hamid was a High Court Vakil at the time. Six or seven years ago he was made a *Nazim Adalat* (District Judge). He is still there.

We went and stopped with him and started a practice there. We soon began to practice apart and lived in separate houses. We both had considerable success there and got large fees. My eldest brother is still practising there.

Muhammad Raza became a *Naib Tahsildar* in Jaunpur and afterwards went to Hyderabad and is now a Collector there.

Dr. Ansari passed the F.A. at Allahabad and then came to Hyderabad where he passed the B.A. from the Nizam's College. He then got a State scholarship and went to England to study medicine.

I stayed in Hyderabad all my life until a year and five months ago. My mother used to live with me formerly but came to Dr. Ansari. She insisted that she was very old and wanted at least two of her sons with her, so I also came to Delhi and lived with Dr. Ansari. I began to practise here but found it no good as no one pays fees in Delhi so I began to look for work elsewhere. Nawab Zulqadar Jang called me to Lucknow where he said I could make a good practice. I went there for about a fortnight in January and February and a lot of people came to be treated by me.

They asked me to settle down in Lucknow but I had to come back to Delhi as my mother was ill and I got a wire from Dr. Ansari. I had to stop with her till April as she was very ill. I then went to Yusufpur in Ghazipur to attend the marriage of Maulvi Abdul Kadir's daughter, a connection of mine. Maulvi Abdul Kadir was a *Sarishtadar* of the Collector of Benares. I went from there to Lucknow where I treated a number of people and from there went to Lahore to Mr. Raja Ram, a landowner, whose wife I had to treat and whose brother's marriage I was to attend, I stopped there ten days or so and then came back to Delhi. All this time I was trying to get a good house in Lucknow but failed to get one to my liking and I stayed in Delhi for the *Ramzan*. In August I went to Indore to treat the Maharajah Holkar, and came back after 10 or 12 days. I returned again in September and went with His Highness to Bombay. At Bombay all the doctors except myself said that the Maharajah had a stone, and said my treatment was wrong. The Maharajah believed them and dispensed with my services at the end of October, so I returned to Delhi. My pay with him was fixed at Rs. 5,000 per mensem but he only paid me Rs. 6,000 altogether though he broke the contract. I hope to get a house shortly in Lucknow.

A few people come and are treated by me in Delhi, but I have made no effort to get a practice here as people don't give fees. I simply stay as a guest in Dr. Ansari's house while in Delhi and if any one comes to the house for treatment; I give it to him. I have no dispensary in Delhi and no share in any house in Delhi.

I forgot to say that I also went to Benares on my way from Ghazipur. The *Kotwal*, K.S. Qazi Muhammad Faruq, is Abdul Kadir's son-in-law and my sister's son-in-law is *Munsiff* there. His name is Shah Munir Alam.

My family was very loyal during the mutiny and my father was granted exemption from the Arms Act. My family's history is written in a history of Ghazipur by, I think, Mr. Oldham. I have no connection with Ansaris other than those of Ghazipur.

I know Maulvi Abdalla Ghazipuri. He was in a school at Arrah and afterwards came here when Maulvi Nazir Husain died. I never met him here. I haven't seen him for years.

My father and uncles were *murids* of Hafiz Muhammad Ali of Gorakhpur. I was not anyone's *murid* till I became the *murid* of Hazrat Maulana Mahmud Hasan about 3 or 4 years ago. I have known Maulana Hafiz Ahmad Shamsul Ulama for 12 or 14 years. He used to come to Hyderabad a lot. I had heard of Hazrat Maulana for years as a very pious man and the *Khalifa* of Maulana Rashid Ahmad Gangohi. It happened about four or five years ago that Dr. Ansari's wife had to go to Amritsar to undergo an eye operation under Colonel Smith. Dr. Ansari asked me to come up from Hyderabad and we all went to Amritsar together. The Shamsul Ulama asked us to stop at

Deoband on the way back, so we stopped for a few hours and I then met Hazrat Maulana for the first time. The next time I saw the Maulana was 2½ or 3 years ago. I came to Delhi on a visit to Dr. Ansari. I had a great respect for the Maulana and had determined to become his *murid* so I went to Deoband and told him that both I and my mother wished to become his *murids*, but my mother was too old to travel to Deoband. After some persuasion the Maulana agreed to break his usual rule and came to Delhi where my mother and I both became his *murids*. Dr. Ansari became his *murid* at the same time. The Maulana went back alone.

Of the other Deoband maulvis I knew Maulvi Habib-ur-Rahman well. He used to come to Hyderabad with the Shamsul Ulama.

I went back to Hyderabad, and 3 or 4 months later my brother Muhammad Raza's wife was called to her father's as she was ill with leprosy and they wanted to have her at home. Her home is in Azamgarh. I took her there and then came on to Delhi. I went from Delhi to Deoband to see Hazrat Maulana and stayed a day and a night. I met the maulvis at the *madrasa* there but only for a moment. The Maulana asked me to treat his wife, the Pirani, who had been ill for years with liver trouble, and her feet are useless. She can't walk or even stand up. I went back to Delhi and sent some medicine for her.

I then went back to Hyderabad and stayed there till 1 year and 5 months ago, when, as I have said, I brought my mother here. She was very fond of Dr. Ansari, who is her youngest son and insisted on living with him. She begged me to stop here too, and though I did not want to I consented to spend most of my time in Delhi.

While in Hyderabad I never heard any suggestion that as Turkey had joined in the war against England we should take her part in any way. As far as I could see everyone was perfectly loyal.

I came to Delhi in the month of *Shaban* (July 1916). I did not meet the Maulana till after *Ramzan*. Shortly after the *Id* I went to Deoband to see the Maulana. It was then for the first time that I heard that Maulana was going to Hedjaz. I asked Maulana if this was so and he told me it was. He never told me at all that he was going on *Hijrat* and I never knew that he had this intention.

Continued on 8th November 1916. I saw the Pirani and treated her again for her illness. I saw the Shamsul Ulama, Maulvi Habib-ur-Rahman, Maulvi Muhammad Hanif who took me in to the Pirani, and several students who used to live with Hazrat Maulana. Auzer Gul was one of these: another was addressed as Mahmud. I treated him as he was not well. I do not know what his full name is. I do not know the names of the others.

We had no further conversation about the Maulana's departure on this occasion. So far as I know no one suggested to the Maulana that he should wait until the war was over on account of the difficulties caused by the war.

Nor did anyone ask him why he particularly wished to go that year, nor did anyone say how long the Maulana had had this idea. It was not for me to question my Pir's intention. I did not even consider in my own mind whether it was a bad year to choose.

I think I left Delhi by the 6 p.m. train and arrived at Deoband about 10 p.m. When I arrived everyone was asleep except the Maulana who was praying inside. Muhammad Hanif asked me if I had dined and on hearing that I had not insisted on getting me some food. He went inside and soon brought me some bread and eggs. The Maulana came in while I was eating. I said my prayers and was given a bed upstairs where I slept. In the morning I came down and heard that the Maulana was in the Masjid. I went there and prayed and then came back with the Maulana. We talked about the Pirani's health and he told Hanif to take me in. The Pirani only talked about her health and did not mention the Maulana's impending departure. I went out and talked to the Maulana about her, recommending the same treatment. The Maulana then told me he was going to the Haj. I said that it was *bahut munasib.* (*Note.*—I reminded him that yesterday he said he first heard the news from one of the others and then asked the Maulana if it was true. He denied this and said the Maulana told him the news.—P.L. ORDE.)

This was how I heard the news. I first had some tea and biscuits and then hurried off to catch the 9 a.m. train.

I got back to Delhi about 2 p.m. and told Dr. Ansari and my mother that the Maulana was going to Hedjaz. They made no comment.

About 10 or 12 days later I again went to Deoband in the 6 p.m. train to see the Pirani principally. The Maulana was sitting outside when I arrived. I sat on a stool by his bed. He said he had seen in the papers that several ships were soon leaving for Hedjaz, and asked me if I had any friend who could arrange for the berths of his party, etc. I said I would certainly go myself and see about it. He begged me not to take the trouble, but I insisted that it was no trouble to make arrangements for my Pir.

I forgot to say that when the train stopped at Muzaffarnagar I saw Shah Zabir Alam, Deputy Collector, who had come to see off some other Deputy Collector. He is a resident of Ghazipur and I have known him a long time. He said he had gout in his foot and had meant to come to Delhi and get treated by me or Dr. Ansari but had not had time. He begged me to stop and see him but I refused. He then said he would come to Delhi and meanwhile insisted that I should have some tea or cake. I accepted this after some demur. He came in to Delhi and stopped with me 8 or 10 days later for a few days, and I treated him. The other Deputy Collector and a Hindu companion sat in my carriage but I did not talk to them. I do not know their names. (*Note.*—He first said he was introduced to the other Deputy and when I asked what his name was, said he had not been introduced.—P.L. ORDE.)

I told the Maulana that I had had some food and did not want any more.

The Maulana then went in to pray and told someone to give me a bed on the roof. I said my prayers and went upstairs. The Maulana's brother Maulvi Muhammad Mohsin, *Peshkar,* Muzaffarnagar, was with him when I arrived. He was there as it was a Sunday and he had leave. I had known him some time. I met him previously at Deoband.

I went upstairs and slept and in the morning came down. I overslept myself and did not like to go to the Masjid to pray. I found the Maulana downstairs and soon was taken inside to see the Pirani by Muhammad Hanif. She again said nothing about the Maulana's departure for Hedjaz. She was very ill. I promised to send her some other medicine. We had no more conversation about the Haj and I left by the 9 a.m. train.

Three or four days later I got the Pirani's medicine ready and was going to send it by post, but I noticed in the papers that the ships were soon leaving for Hedjaz, so I changed my mind and took the medicine myself intending to find out the Maulana's requirements in Bombay. I arrived at night. I saw several students reading there and asked them where the Maulana was. One of them said he was inside with his wife, so I sat down and waited. About 10 minutes later the Maulana's grandson came out, saw me and went in again and the Maulana came out at once. He told me the Pirani was very ill. We talked about the treatment for some time and then went in to see her. We talked about her health. I thought she was in great pain but there was no danger of dying. She then said she was going to die and the Maulana was going to Hedjaz and no one would look after her. I said I would always be in attendance and she should have no fear. The Maulana also consoled her and we went out. I gave the Maulana the new medicine I had brought and he put it in his room. I went out and said my prayers and the Maulana's grandson brought me food. I ate the food and the Maulana came out and suggested that we should go to bed. We went upstairs and went to sleep. I got up early and went to the Masjid to pray. The Maulana and others were there and we came back to the house after prayers. The Maulana's brother, Muhammad Hanif, and I sat down apart from the Maulana who was reading. We sat silent in order not to disturb him. Then he stopped reading and offered me some tea. He persuaded me to stop till the 2 p.m. train as I could not get a good meal if I went by the 9 a.m. We had some tea and biscuits. Then I told the Maulana that the ships would soon leave, so I intended to go to Bombay and make arrangements for him. I asked him how many men would go with him. He said about 7 or 8 men would go. I asked him to let me know if possible the exact number as I had to buy food and stores for the journey and must know how much to get. He again said that 7 or 8 men would go and he only wanted a little flour, rice, tea, etc., and did not expect any arrangements on a grand scale. That was the end of our conversation on the subject. The Maulana then went to the *madrasa* saying he would be back in an hour or two and I should have my meal with him. The Maulana's brother and Muhammad

Hanif were present when we were talking about the Haj but left before the Maulana went away. They took no part in the conversation.

I went upstairs and lay down on my bed. About a couple of hours later a student told me that the Maulana had come back. I came down and as it was after 11 a.m. the Maulana sent for food. The Maulana's brother, Muhammad Hanif and two or three students ate with us. After the meal the Maulana went inside and brought out some *pan*, for me. We sat down and he asked me to stop and say my prayers as the train would not leave for two hours. He went in to lie down, I asked Muhammad Hanif for some cold water as I was accustomed to ice and the water was very warm. He said he would get some from a well. He came back half an hour later with some water. I drank the water and told him it was not very cold. We then started talking. He told me the Maulana had told him to take 6 or 7 months' leave from the school at Muttra or it may be Mainpuri and live at his house. He asked me to come and treat the Pirani when Hazrat was away. I agreed. The Maulana then came out and went to the Masjid: I followed him and Muhammad Hanif remained to get me a tonga. After prayers I had some *pan* and then went off after telling the Maulana I would send him news of the arrangements from Bombay.

Four or five days later I went to Bombay alone. I had been several times before. I went to the Railway Hotel in Grant Road. I went in the Great Indian Peninsula mail 2nd class, with a return ticket. I went in a victoria the same afternoon to Mehmal Muhalla to a friend of mine called Haji Ahmad. He was not in but there were several men there. I asked them if they could tell me the exact dates of the departure of the ships for the Haj. One of them told me that a ship left the next day and that a Maulana from Saharanpur was going in it. He did not know who he was but said he was a famous Maulvi and many people had gone to see him. He said he was stopping at Sapa Sadiq's *musafirkhana*. I went back to the hotel. I met no one that day. In the morning I went to the *musafirkhana* to see who the maulvi was who was going and to make arrangements for berths on some other ship. All the pilgrims were leaving for the harbour so I went there too and there I saw Maulana Khalil Ahmed with a lot of followers. I met him at Saharanpur first once when I went to Gangoh seven or eight years ago to Maulana Kashid Ahmad's tomb. On my way back I went to see him at his *madrasa*. That was the only time I had seen him before. He recognised me and told me that he was to have gone with Maulana Mahmud Hasan and had waited for him and sent letters to him but he had not arrived, so Khalil Ahmad was going off alone. I told him I had come to make arrangements for the Maulana and wanted to find out about the next ship but did not know who to ask about it. He pointed out Maulvi Abdullah* a Superintendent of Police, in charge of the Hajis and said he was the man to tell me. I went up to him

*?Maulvi Abdulla Ahmad, Pilgrim Protector.

and told him my name and what I wanted. He asked me to come to his office the next day and he would let me have all the information I wanted. He told me his office was close to the *Anjuman Islamia* school near the Victoria Terminus. I then went back to Maulvi Khalil Ahmad. He had a few women among his followers. Everyone had a mark stamped on his hand except the Maulvi who was allowed to pass through without it. There were lots of people there to see him off. I did not know any of them. I had no idea before I got to Bombay that Maulvi Khalil Ahmad was going. After he had gone I went back to the hotel. I got there about 3 p.m., and had lunch and went to sleep. I did not go out again nor did I meet anyone that day.

Next morning at 10 a.m., I went to Maulvi Abdullah's office. The *gariwala* did not know the way to the office and we did rot find it till about 11-30. I saw Maulvi Abdullah and he got me the information. He told me a ship of Turner Morrison was leaving on some date I forget, probably about the 15th September. It was about four or five days thence. He also said one of Kanwani's ships was going soon but he did not know the date. The ship was coming from Calcutta and tickets were being sold very cheap, including single tickets. I then went back to the hotel and wrote to the Maulana all the details.

After writing the letter I went off again to see my friend Haji Ahmad and took him to the hotel. I explained to him that I had to buy stores, etc., for the Maulana's party and did not know the best places to get them. He promised to get all the things for me at the best shops. I then told him I would like to take a house in Bombay in which I could put the stores and where we could all live when the Maulana arrived. He said it was very difficult to get a house and I should go to the *Anjuman Khuddam-i-Ka'aba* and live there. I said I had nothing to do with the *Anjuman* and did not like to live there, and asked him again to get a house. He went off apparently to search for me, but really went to the *Anjuman*, and told the people there what had happened. Next day they all came back with him and insisted not only on my stopping there but on the Maulana stopping there also when he came. There was a room in the same building as the *Anjuman* which I got for Rs. 18. The members of the *Anjuman* told me that it would cost a lot to furnish the room and I should use it simply as a store room for the food, etc., and sleep and live in the *Anjuman's* rooms. I agreed to this, went back to the hotel, had a meal and took my luggage to the *Anjuman*.

There were two men* living in the *Anjuman*. One was called Taj Muhammad Sindhi and the other Maulvi Ghulam Ahmad or Ghulam Muhammad.† They were servants of the *Anjuman*. I did not join the *Anjuman*. I discovered that the object of the *Anjuman* was to make

*Taj Muhammad, Mir Muhammad *Shaidai.*

†Of Simla, *Shaidai.*

arrangements for Hajis. I did not know this before. I had heard of the *Anjuman*, read about it in the papers, etc., but had taken no interest in it.

Continued on 9th November.—The two men used to go round collecting money to pay for the poor Hajis' tickets, buying tickets for others, and generally making themselves useful. Meanwhile Haji Ahmad got in supplies of flour, rice, biscuits, tea, etc., for 8 or 10 men and I stored them in the room under the *Khuddam-i-Ka'aba* premises. Some friends of Haji Ahmad came to see me and get treated by me. One of them was Haji Yusuf Haji Sharif. He is a Seth and deals in timbers. I don't remember any other names.

After I had been in the *Anjumam* 2 or 3 days I got a wire from the Maulana that he was coming in the Nagda Mail. Taj Muhammad and I went in the morning to meet him. I had met Sultan Chinoy the day the wire came. I had met him 2 or 3 years ago in Bombay, and he came to see me. I asked him to arrange about the tickets, as he knew Turner Morrison's manager. I told him Hazrat was coming and I would let him know the details as soon as he arrived. He told me he lived in Colaba but his flour mill was near the *Anjuman* and I should let him know there.

A lot of Hazrat's followers arrived by the train but not Hazrat. They said he had got down at Surat and was coming by the next train. We got carriages and I with 6 or 7 men left for the *Anjuman* while Taj Muhammad and 2 or 3 men stayed with the luggage. Maulvi Muhammad Hanif, Nurul Hasan, Maulvi Murtaza Hasan, a man called Haji Khan Muhammad whom I had seen in Deoband, one Khuda Bakhsh whom I had not met before, Abdul Wahid, a boy whose father or uncle lives in Medina and who was going there with Hazrat Maulana (I had seen him in Deoband) and Maulvi Muhammad Mian went with me. I forget who were with the luggage. They had brought food with them. I asked how many tickets were required and they said I should wait till Hazrat Maulana came and ask him. They did not know in what train Hazrat Maulana would come. Muhammad Hanif, Taj Muhammad and I went to the station to meet the next train in the evening but he was not in it, so we went hack. I got food from the bazaar for every one and we had dinner, after which we all went to a neighbouring Masjid to pray. The luggage filled up all the room I had taken and there was very little space for all the men to sleep, so I sent to Haji Ahmad for some *durries* to spread on the floor of the *Anjuman* rooms.

He sent them and some pillows and by moving the table we got plenty of room. Next morning Taj Muhammad and 2 or 3 men went to the station to meet the mail. I followed them alone in a victoria. I found Hazrat had arrived and a son of Hakim Muhammad Ismail Ajmeri, a resident of Gangoh, who practises in Bombay, had also gone to meet him. Hazrat was in his carriage. In my carriage someone else sat, I forget who. Hazrat went up to Hakim Ismail Muhammad's house and Maulvi Murtaza Hasan also went there. I do not know exactly who came with Hazrat as I was late at the station. I got food ready for everyone at the *Anjuman*, but then heard that they were all having a meal at Hakim Muhammad Ismail's. There were a few men still with me at the *Anjuman*. They wanted to go to the Hakim's dinner, but I persuaded them to eat mine instead as I did not want to waste it. Hazrat Maulana then arrived with Murtaza and Qazi Mohiuddin of Bhopal. I had not met him at all before. Qazi Mohiuddin was stopping with the Hakim and I remember now that Murtaza also lived there though he used to come a lot to the *Anjuman*. The Qazi said the *Anjuman* room was very cool and airy and the Hakim's house was shut in, and asked if he might get his luggage from the Hakim's and live there till Hazrat Maulana left. Murtaza said the same and they both got their luggage. I asked Hazrat to let me know how many tickets were wanted. He told me Maulvi Sahul was coming from Calcutta and he did not know what tickets he wanted, but I could take them for those who were already present. There were ten tickets to be taken for those with the Maulana. So I went to Sultan Chinoy and asked him. He said he wanted the names so I went back to Hazrat who told Nurul Hasan to write the names, and give the money for the tickets. Nurul Hasan wrote out the names but suggested that he should not pay the money until the remainder arrived and he could then pay up a lump sum for the lot. I said it was sufficient at present to give the names and we could pay for the tickets when they arrived. I took the list to Sultan Chinoy and he asked me to read it as it was written in Urdu which he does not know well. I read it out and he wrote it again in English. The names were Hazrat Maulana Mahmudul Hasan, Maulvi Murtaza Hasan, Khan Muhammad, Abdul Wahid, Auzer Gul, Hadi Hasan, Khuda Bakhsh, a man called probably Mahbub Khan, Maulvi Muhammad Mian, Maulvi Matlub-ur-Rahman. I think these were all the names. Sultan Chinoy said he would either bring the tickets or send them to me.

I then went hack to the *Anjuman* and found a large crowd to see off the Maulana. There was a man from Khurja who lives in Delhi too. I don't know his name but he is often in the Billimaran, and probably has a shop there. There was also a maulvi called Mubin whom I had not met before but have since seen in Deoband. I do not remember any others. Anyhow, I saw that there were far too many people to sleep at the *Anjuman*. There is a Muslim Club opposite the *Anjuman* and one or two of the members used to *salaam* me, so I went across to see if they could help. I found them playing cards and asked them if they would mind some of the Maulana's party sleeping in their club. They at once said they had no objection and offered to get beds. I said the Maulana certainly ought to have a bed and perhaps the Qazi Sahib too and they went off and got two beds which were placed in the room. I then got dinner and we all had food some in the *Anjuman* and some in the room below, which I had hired. Some of the party were not there and so I kept food for them. When they came they had food in the

Muslim Club. I remember Maulvi Sahul had arrived and he was one of these. Hazrat Sahib said that we could now send for the other tickets as Maulvi Sahul had arrived. I said that it was too late and the best plan would be to send the men themselves with Sultan Chinoy's clerk when he brought the tickets I had already ordered. He agreed and we all went to sleep. Hazrat Sahib and Qazi Mohiuddin slept on the beds in the Muslim Club and others on the floor. The rest including myself slept in the *Anjuman*. About 2 a.m. Maulvi Sahul called me and said Hazrat Sahib had hurt himself. I ran across and found that he had been sitting under the tap getting water and had suddenly got up and hit his head against the tap. Blood was flowing from the wound. I bandaged the wound with my *kurta* soaked in cold water and we went to bed again.

We got up very early as all the Hajis and their luggage had to be ready for inspection at 8 a.m. We had tea and then put the luggage in some carriages which Haji Ahmed had got for us at my request. I took Hazrat Maulana and Qazi Mohiuddin downstairs and we met Sultan Chinoy's clerk. Hazrat sent for Nurul Hasan and told him to send those who had not tickets with the clerk to get them.

I forgot to say that Sultan Chinoy's clerk had brought the tickets a few hours after I left their office. I was not in the room at the time but upstairs in the *Anjuman*. Nurul Hasan told me he had paid for all the tickets which he handed over to me. I sent Taj Muhammad with them to Maulvi Abdullah to get the passports. Maulvi Abdullah sent him back with the passports and a message to say I should send the remaining tickets and he would issue passports.

We three went off to the harbour and Muhammad Hanif also came in my carriage. I had sent off' Haji Ahmad's *durrie* to the harbour and it was spread beneath a tree there. I left the rest there and went off to look for the luggage. It came soon and we put it down on one side of the *durrie*. This was about 8 a.m. Then a meal which I had ordered arrived and we all had a meal as the inspection would soon begin and there would be no time later. Nurul Hasan and his party had not arrived at first but he came while the meal was going on and said they had got the tickets and had gone for passports. The remainder arrived after the meal with their passports and they had a hurried meal. I then saw Maulvi Abdullah and he told me to make every man hold his ticket in his hand in order to pass through the gate. Soon after there was a great rush of Hajis which showed that the inspection had begun. I told Hazrat and Qazi to wait on the *durrie* and sent the rest off. I took Abdul Wahid by the hand and brought him along and passed him through. When all the rest were inside I saw Maulvi Abdullah and said Hazrat Maulana was outside and suggested that he should be excused having a mark stamped on his hand. He said it was the rule to stamp everybody but the Maulana should wait till the crowd had subsided as the ship would not start at 11 a.m. as advertised but at 1 or 2 p.m. I then went back and met Sultan Chinoy on the way to Maulana. He asked for the Maulana and I took him along. I found that Hazrat Sahib and Qazi were not on the *durrie* but were sitting in Hakim Ismail Ajmeri's carriage. There was a large crowd round him. I introduced Sultan Chinoy and asked him if he had arranged with the captain of the ship for a good place for the Maulana, etc. He said he had asked the Manager but had not seen the captain. I asked him to do so now and he went. He came back after 15 minutes or so and said the captain had promised to let them say their prayers on an empty part of the deck where others were not allowed. He then went off to his house. I asked Maulvi Abdullah if I should bring the Maulana and he told me to wait a little longer. Then I saw some constables signalling for the remaining Hajis to come along so I brought the Maulana to the gate. The policeman would not let me in but I asked Maulvi Abdullah and he asked a Sahib and I was then allowed to go in. We went in and found all the Hajis sitting down, having their hands stamped. They all stood up on seeing the Maulana. The officials told them to sit down again and the Maulana also signed to them to do so. Qazi Sahib was left outside. When the inspection was over I sent all the Maulana's party to take their luggage on board. When they had gone I went with Maulana to the other gate. Murtaza arranged about where the luggage was to be put. The Maulana asked me if I could manage to get Qazi Sahib in to say goodbye. I persuaded an old *jamedar* at the gate to let Qazi Sahib in and we went back to Maulana. We both took leave of Hazrat and we both wept. In parting he asked me to look after his family and the Pirani. I promised to do this. Then Hazrat went to the ship. I think he had not had his hand stamped though he had probably been examined. Then suddenly Muhammad Hanif appeared and talked to Hazrat from where he stood. Hazrat charged him to look after the family well, Hazrat was standing in the sun talking to us so I said that he should sit down in the shade and we would go. We all *salaamed* all the party and they went over to the shady side of the ship. We three went and sat in some shade by the gate. Soon the ship left. We watched it out of the harbour and then went back to the *Anjuman*. I had some food as I had not eaten at the harbour and Qazi went to sleep in the Muslim Club. He is an old man and was very tired.

I forgot to say that when the Maulana arrived in Bombay and I was asking him about the tickets he said that if we could get single tickets by the Kalwar's ship it would he better as the tickets were cheap. But as there was no news of when the ship would leave he said we had better get return tickets by Turner Morrison's ship. He never said to me that he had an idea of remaining in Hedjaz. We never discussed his return and I never made any plans to meet him when he came back, though I took it for granted that he would return after the Haj. I am perfectly certain that we never had any discussion at all about the question of Maulana remaining in Hedjaz. Obviously the reason why the Maulana in his letter to me asked my opinion *re* the necessity of a speedy return from Hedjaz, was that the Pirani was very ill and I was attending her and would be able to let him know whether he ought to come back in case her condition became critical.

Well, I asked the Maulana at this time whether he would allow me to pay for his ticket. After some demur he agreed and I paid Sultan Chinoy about Rs. 200 or Rs. 300. I cannot remember the exact sum. I got a second class ticket for him and not a 3rd class. Hadi Hasan was the only other who had a second class ticket. I did not pay for any one except the Maulana. The Maulana remonstrated with me about taking a second class ticket as they were all one party, but I insisted as with a second class ticket he would get a bed. I paid the money for the stores to Haji Ahmed. It was about Rs. 150 I think. I told him if he spent more than this that Nurul Hasan would pay for it. He said he would manage all right and would not take anything, but I asked him later and he said he had fixed up everything with Nurul Hasan. I never asked him how much more or less than the Rs. 150 from me he had spent. I made no arrangements for them in Arabia. My arrangements were to last them on the voyage. I never got any *hundi* on an Arabian firm from any one for them.

The Maulana did not dine with any Seth in Bombay. He only had a midday meal with Hakim Ajmeri. I provided the rest of his meals.

I took all the money I spent from Delhi with me. I had I suppose Rs. 500 or Rs. 600.

I have never saved any money in my life. No doubt in Hyderabad I had a good income and got large fees. My mother gets all the money from our family property. I used to spend all my income in this way. First of all Dr. Ansari went to England. He had a first class State scholarship for four years of £300 or £350 a year. I used to send him some money then but not very much. However he stayed in England for 11 years and after the first four years I sent him about Rs. 500 a month. He came back in 1911. Then I have a cousin, my mother's sister's son, Muhammad Asghar, Bar-at-law. He went to England some three years after Ansari and stayed for five years. I used to send him about Rs. 300 a month. Then I also spent money on my family and myself and thus saved nothing. Muhammad Asghar came back and has now a very good practice in Hyderabad. I had to help him for a few months and then he managed for himself.

Dr. Ansari went to Hyderabad on his return and had to wait 6 months under the rules of his scholarship in case the State demanded his services. After 6 months he had not been given any post so he went to Calcutta to start a private practice. Sir Ali Imam and the Raja of Mahmudabad advised him to go to Delhi instead as it had just been made the capital. So he did so. I had to set him up in Delhi and sent him several thousand rupees for this but he soon started well and I had no more need to send him money.

Still I went on spending all my income on my friends and in charity, etc., and never kept any accounts or put any money in the bank, etc.

(*Note.*—The Hakim is lying about his income. The first day I saw him he said he only paid for the Maulana's share of the food, about Rs. 23 in all. Now he appears to have given Rs. 150 and in a lordly way asked for no account of the money. During the search we saw an old letter from some Jang of Hyderabad offering him Rs. 100 as subsistence out of the money which the Nawab allowed him for the upkeep of his stable. Now he talks of sending Rs. 800 a month home to Ansari and Muhammad Asghar. It seems fairly obvious that the Hakim posed as the rich patron whereas the money came from elsewhere. It is perhaps significant that Dr. Ansari arrived from Jaora last night, went to his house, saw the Hakim, and hurried off to Rampur early this morning.—P.L. ORDE.)

Continued on 10th November 1916. I happened to have this Rs. 600 and more by me. I had probably saved it from Hyderabad and I think I had a little more too. I thought Rs. 500 or 600 would be necessary so I took that. I took no money from any one else. Dr. Ansari did not offer me anything.

The reason why I had a letter offering me any money from a follower of the Nawab is this. When I first went to Hyderabad I had a private practice and continued thus for 12 or 13 years, then the Nizam sent for me and appointed me his doctor, so I had to live in the Palace and had no private practice. The custom then was not to pay state servants for some time and then to pay them a large sum. Meanwhile they were naturally short of money. My friends knowing this offered to provide for me until I was paid but I managed to get on without it. About 8 or 10 months after my appointment the Nawab began to give me large sums for medicines, etc., but I never got any fixed pay. The Nawab later said he would give me fixed pay of Rs. 3,000 a month as well as money for medicines, but he died without settling anything, and the present Nawab gave no satisfactory answer to my petitions, so I started my private practice again. This was in 1911. The money I sent to Dr. Ansari, etc., was out of the sums the Nawab gave me for medicines and the rewards, he gave me several times a year.

To go back to the Maulana's departure—I remained in Bombay for 10 or 12 days and went twice to the Poona races. I stayed the whole time in the *Anjuman Khuddam-i-Ka'aba*. Several big merchants, etc., came to me for treatment. I made about Rs. 20 or 40 a day and my patients begged me to start a practice in Bombay. I do not remember the names of any of my patients. One of them came again to me when I was in Watson's Hotel with the Maharajah Holkar of Indore last month. He was always addressed as Haji Sahib. I don't know his full name. Qazi Mohiuddin left the day after the Maulana and Muhammad Hanif too. I left about the 1st October and came to Delhi. I stopped here a few days only and then went to Deoband to see the Pirani. She was very miserable. I consoled her and treated her and came back to Delhi after a day I saw Muhammad Hanif there. So far as I remember I did not mention the question of expenses to him but I certainly told the Pirani that I would be responsible for all expenses.

Seven or eight days after my return to Delhi I got a letter from Muhammad Hanif saying that the Pirani had had severe fever for two days so I went back there next day and changed her medicine. I stopped a day and two nights at Deoband and on that occasion gave her Rs. 50 for expenses. I then came back to Delhi and talked over with my mother the idea of going to Bombay. I gave it up principally because I had promised to look after the Pirani and this would not be easy from Bombay.

My letter from the Maulana arrived before I went to Deoband the first time and a letter had also arrived there probably to Hakim Muhammad Hasan or Muhammad Hanif. I was told what was in the letter. It was much the same as mine. I think he said much the same about coming back. I did not question them about the matter. I know this letter had been censored because they asked me to explain the meaning of the censor's stamp. I did not send any answer to the Maulana and have not written to him at all. I thought the post was closed for Arabia.

Since then I always went once or twice a month to Deoband and used to give Rs. 40 or 50 a month for expenses. I also sent money once by money order as I had not had a chance of going myself for over a month. On that occasion I sent Rs. 100 to Muhammad Hanif. This was in April last. Once also Muhammad Hanif came to Delhi. I do not know why he came but he came to Dr. Ansari's house and had dinner and stopped with us and went back in the morning. I gave him Rs. 50. This was last cold weather I think but I cannot say what month it was.

During November and December I only went to Deoband, not elsewhere. In January I went to Lucknow and got a concession ticket as the races were on. I stopped there for 8 or 10 days. I went for the wedding of Nawab Sarbaland Jang's son. He married Nawab Zulqadar Jung's daughter. I know Maulana Abdul Bari but did not meet him there. I came back to Delhi and treated a few people who came to me, but I made no attempt to start a practice as none paid me. Saiyid Bahauddin, Deputy Collector, Gorakhpur used to send his family to me to be treated and pressed me to go there but I did not.

In February, I think, when at Deoband I heard from Muhammad Hanif that Murtaza and others had returned and had been to Delhi and found that I was away.

In March, as I have already said, I went down to my house in Yusufpur and sent the money which I have mentioned from there in April. Thence I went to Benares for this reason. There is one Shankar Raj, son of Maharaja Shivraj Dharmawand Bahadur of Hyderabad, who came to Delhi to enter for the Matriculation examination of the Panjab University. He took a house on the Egerton Road. He did his examination in St. Stephen's High School and used to come from there to see me at Dr. Ansari's which is close by. He waited to see the Barwa Bangal at Benares and asked me to arrange for him in Benares as I came from that part of the country. I wrote to the *Kotwal* of Benares to arrange for a house and carriage or motor, etc., for him. I got a satisfactory reply from him and told Shankar Raj to wire him when he was coming. I went to Benares to see if everything was arranged for him. The *Kotwal* said he had heard nothing from him but he had come and put up at the house of Gopal Lal Chobu Pinda near Dewal Nilkanth, Mahadeo, Benares City. The note bearing this address was written by Shankar Raj and sent to the *Kotwal* who gave it to me. The *Kotwal* had arranged another house for him but he had taken this one, as his father had arranged it. I went and saw him.

The same day I went to see Kailash Chandra Bhattacharji whom I knew in Hyderabad. He lives in Oudh Mohalla, P.S. Bhelupara. He told me his son was under police surveillance and asked me to do some thing with the police about it. I made a note about it which was found in my room. I spoke to the *Naib Kotwal* Naqi Muhammad Khan about him and he promised to make enquiries. On the same bit of paper I made a note about a glass which I wanted, and which is made in Benares. I then went back home and stopped there till May, when I went to Lucknow, as I thought of practising there, and stopped with Nawab Zulqadar Jang. I stopped there a fortnight or so. I asked the Nawab who said it would be an excellent thing if I settled in Lucknow. I asked him to find me a good house. He told his Munshi Abul Hasan to find one I treated some patients there and made Rs. 250 or 300 and then came back to Delhi. I stayed in Delhi a few days and then went to Deoband and saw the Pirani. She was much better as the result of my treatment. I don't think I saw Muhammad Hanif then, I think I only had the one letter from him which you have got. I came back the same day and a few days later went to Lahore, as I have already said, to see Mr. Raja Ram. While there Dr. Iqbal who had heard of me asked me to treat his wife. I prescribed for her. He was the only Muhammadan I met in Lahore, where I stayed 5 or 6 days.

From Lahore I went to Lucknow as Iftikhar Husain, Deputy Collector, had sent me a wire to treat his daughter. He lives in Kaiser Bagh and I stopped with him for a week or so. His daughter died then and I came back. Before doing so I spent a few days with Nawab Zulqadar Jang who pressed me to remain, but as the *Ramzan* was approaching and I did not want to work during it I went back to Delhi. I remained here during the *Ramzan* and never went out at all. After the *Id* I went to Deoband again. I saw the Pirani but Muhammad Hanif was not there. I saw the Pirani and treated her, and came back. She was much depressed because there was no news of the Maulana. I consoled her and said he was sure to come back some time, though we had had no news of him. I only stayed the day there and then came back to Delhi.

When the Viceroy came to Delhi in August the Nawab of Rampur came to visit him and dined afterwards with Dr. Ansari. On that occasion he asked me to come to Rampur for his birthday festivities, so I went there in August and stopped for 3 days. A man from Qazi Mohiuddin came to Rampur to tell me that the Qazi was in Moradabad and I should see him before going back to Delhi. So I went to Moradabad with this man. He is a young man and I don't know his name. I went to Qazi's house and saw him and Maulvi Murtaza Hasan also came. I only stopped there a few hours. He wanted me to treat him as he was ill and then asked me for news of the Pirani, etc. He was ashamed of not having been there and said he would go at once and begged me to go with him. We arranged to go in a few days' time. So I went back to Delhi and met him at Deoband on the appointed day. Hakim Muhammad Hasan was there and Maulvi Habib-ur-Rahman. His brother Maulvi Aziz-ur-Rahman was there too to see the Qazi Sahib. The Pirani again complained that there was no news of Maulana's return. The Qazi said Khalil Ahmad had returned and the Maulana would doubtless soon come though he had not sent any news. The Qazi went off to Moradabad and I went to Delhi. I have not seen him since.

The letter of Khalil Ahmad which was found in my house arrived some time before this happened. I had not met Khalil Ahmad but had heard he had arrived.

I forgot to say that before this happened I had been to Indore. I went to Indore on the 10th August and came back on the 24th. The visit to Rampur took place after I had returned from Indore. So this must have been in September.

When I was at Moradabad Murtaza told me he and Muhammad Mian had been in Delhi after returning from Hedjaz but had found me away so had not seen me.

Continued on 11th November 1916.—About 5 or 6 days later I got a postcard from the Pirani telling me to come at once. I went to Deoband and met Hakim Muhammad Hasan and asked him what had happened that I had been so hastily summoned. He said all was well. He went in at my request to warn the Pirani of my arrival, and soon afterwards I was called inside. I asked what the matter was and she replied that she was going to tell me something which she had never told to any one before. This was that for 20 or 25 years she had been laying by small sums of money, whenever she could save anything. She intended that this money should be used for her funeral expenses and had never told her daughters even lest they should try to persuade her to give it up to them. She said that now that I was looking after her she had no fear about her burial expenses, and so she wished to send her money to the Maulana, who she feared must be without money to pay for his return to India. I asked her how much money she had. She said she could not say yet as she had not counted it, she would let me know later. She then sent me out, saying she would soon call me in again. I went outside and saw Masud who told me he was going on Haj. Four or five hours later I was called inside again. The Pirani told me that there were Rs. 1,400 in a box which she said I should take away with me and arrange for Masud to go and take it to the Maulana. I knew by this that she knew Masud was going already and wished me to make arrangements for him and see that he got the money for the Maulana. I agreed and offered her Rs. 100 for Masud for the Haj, which she took. She impressed on me that I should not mention this matter to any one as she had kept it secret all these years and did not wish any one to know. I took an oath not to reveal it to any one. I said I could not take the box away in the day time as the people outside would see it. I said I would wait till nightfall and then go by the night train, thus I would be able to smuggle it away in the dark. It was an old wooden box. (*Note.*—He showed me the box; it is about 1½ ft. by 8″ by 8″. An old box with a lock and key.)

I remember now that the Pirani had previously told me that one Muhammad Kasim was going to the Haj. I had never met him but heard he was in the Canal Department. I saw him once in Madrasa Abdur Rab at the annual prize-giving. When she gave me the box the Pirani told me that Muhammad Kasim could not go and Masud would go instead. I went outside and waited for dark and about 10-30 p.m. I went inside again, took the box up and carried it out. No one was there and I put it in the Maulana's room where I waited for an hour or so and then sent a boy for a tonga. The tonga came about 11 p.m. and I got the box to it without difficulty and took it away. I got rid of the boy by telling him to go and tell the Hakim that I was leaving. As soon as he had gone I put the box underneath the seat of the tonga. The boy came back and said the Hakim's door was shut and all were asleep. So I went off. I got to the station and took the box in my own hands and put it on the station steps. After paying the tonga driver I took the box in and put it under a bench in the station and sat on the bench myself. The train came very late, but I got to Delhi without incident, and put the box in my room. In the evening I opened the box and counted the money. There were altogether Rs. 1,400 in cash, some in two bags and some loose underneath the bags.

Three or four days later Masud arrived and said he was off to Hedjaz. He said the Pirani had given him Rs. 100. I said I would make all arrangements for him. That same evening a boy called Bholu came up from Deoband and said the Pirani had called back Masud with his luggage. We did not understand this and Masud wanted me to send back word that the tickets, etc., were taken and he could not go back. I said no, it was the Pirani's order and he must go and see her. So he went off at 6 p.m. I had told him nothing about the Pirani's money. Next day Masud came back from Deoband. I asked him what the matter was. He said they had heard at Deoband that Maulvi Khalil Ahmad had come back and had been arrested in Bombay. So the Pirani got afraid that if Masud went to Hedjaz he might be arrested on his return, and told him not to go. Masud said he did not know the reason for Khalil Ahmad's arrest but it could not be for going on Haj and he persuaded her to let him go. I arranged then that he should leave by the mail train next day. I also said that I would write a letter to Sultan Chinoy whom he should go and see and who would see that everything necessary was done. I went inside then and asked Dr. Ansari's wife if she had any notes as I wanted some in exchange for Rs. 1,400. She gave me 14 notes of Rs. 100 each and I gave her the rupees and took the box back. I then wrote to Sultan Chinoy to ask him to get Masud's ticket and food, etc., and make all arrangements. I had no idea when the ship left or what ship it was, etc. I asked him to take the Rs. 1,400 which I was giving to Masud, to pay for his expenses out of it and to send what was left with him to Arabia.

Next morning I took Masud to the station and got him a 3rd class ticket by the Nagda Mail. I told him to take my respectful *salaams* to Hazrat, etc., and to say we would all be glad if he would come back as he had been away so long. The train then left and I saw nothing more of Masud.

(*Note.*—I have looked up the dates of Masud's departure and Khalil Ahmad's return from Hedjaz. I find that Khalil Ahmad arrived on the S.S. *Akbar* at Bombay on the 8th September 1916, while Masud left Deoband on the same day at 2-25 p.m., arrived in Delhi at 7-34 p.m., and left for Bombay at 6-30 on the morning of the 9th September. According to the Hakim, Masud first came here on the 7th and received a message from the Pirani that he should return at once, the reason, as subsequently transpired, being that Khalil Ahmad had been arrested. But as Khalil Ahmad did not arrive till the 8th and the Pirani sent the message on the 7th the Hakim is evidently lying.—P.L. ORDE)

Seven or eight days later I went again to Indore. This was the 25th September. I stopped there with the Maharaja and then plague broke out and we went to Bombay. The Maharaja stayed in Malabar Hill and arranged for me in Watson's Hotel. I was in room 85 and my medicines, etc., and servants in room 106. Here I met Sultan Chinoy. He told me this.

Masud arrived and met him. The last ship was leaving Bombay that very day at 12 noon. He went at once and found there were no 3rd class tickets left but there was one first class ticket which he took for him and gave him. He took him to the ship and sent him on board. (He said nothing about getting passports.) He also said that he got the ticket for Rs. 300 or 350 and hastily got some food for the voyage, and got a friend named Muhammad Ali Raza, I think, to give a *hundi* on some firm* in Jeddah for the remainder, which was Rs. 1,000 or 1,100.

I stayed in Bombay, dined with Sultan Chinoy once in Malabar Hill. Nothing of interest happened and, as I have already said, I got back to Delhi on, I think, the 30th October. I had meant to go to Deoband but was stopped by this enquiry.

*Zain-ul-Ali Raza.

The poem which was found in my house was written by someone in Lucknow, I think. When I was there last someone came to the house reading this poem and gave it to me to read and I happened to put it in some book. I do not know who read it or who wrote it there. I had not seen it again till you searched the place.

I have never to my knowledge abused Obeidullah, Muhammad Mian or Hamdulla. I am certain I did not do so. I always abused any one who was against the Government, but I never even heard Obeidullah's name before, I heard I think that a Fatehpuri *madrasa* Maulvi had gone from Delhi to the Frontier. His name may have been Saif-ur-Rahman, but I never heard of Obeidullah. I never heard anything against Muhammad Mian and Hamdulla nor against the Maulana. I shall tell the Pirani that you pressed me and I had to tell about the money she gave me for Masud and the Maulana. It was because I had given my oath to the Pirani that at first I did not tell about the money for Masud. It was only after thinking it over that I considered it my duty to tell you. I do not now believe that the Maulana is engaged in any work against the Government. It would be quite impossible for him to do so.

(*Note.*—With regard to this matter, the Hakim, when I was talking to him, before taking his statement, flatly denied that he had ever given Rs. 1,000 to Masud and paid his expenses and arranged for a *hundi.* Yesterday when he was leaving me he first mentioned it, and I told him I would record his statement about it in full to-day. I did this as I wished to see if there was any discrepancy between what he said then and his story to-day. There is a discrepancy. Yesterday he said he did not take the money when the Pirani first told him of it. He went away back to Delhi and three days later returned and took it then and when he went to her he found two *Sahibzadis* with her, and the Pirani had to get rid of them before they could talk of the money. His story of the Pirani's giving the money has been well thought out, and is, I think, the result of much consideration and possibly consultation with Ansari. In the first place, he knew that the *hundi* might be traced and Sultan Chinoy approached. Secondly he knew it would be very difficult for us to question the Pirani, and thirdly his oath to the Pirani would explain his previous reluctance to tell the truth.—P.L. ORDE.)

I remember some time perhaps in June or July 1916, Maulvi Murtaza Hasan came from Bhopal and came to Dr. Ansari's house to see me. He was on his way to Moradabad and came to ask me for a prescription for his daughter. I gave him some medicine. Hamdulla had gone to Dr. Ansari's office and telephoned to ask if Murtaza was at the house as he wanted to meet him. Murtaza said his train was just leaving for Moradabad and if he waited for Hamdulla he would miss it, so I telephoned to tell Hamdulla to wait and then took Murtaza to Dr. Ansai's dispensary in the motor. We picked up Hamdulla and went to the station. We got platform tickets for myself and Hamdulla, and one inter class ticket for Moradabad for Murtaza.

He offered me the money for the ticket but I refused to take it. We had no conversation about the Maulana. I left Hamdulla and Murtaza on the station and came back as I thought Dr. Ansari might need the motor. I do not know what happened to Hamdulla after that. I have not seen him since.

APPENDIX TO STATEMENT OF HAKIM ABDUR RAZZAQ ANSARI

Translation of documents seized in Abdur Razzaq's room in Dr. Ansari's house.

1. *Address on the envelope.*—Hakim Abdur Razzaq Sahib at the house of Dr. Ansari, Mori Gate, Delhi, India.

From—Mahmud, Aden, Saturday.

Respected Hakim Sahib, the mine of benevolence and generosity, namely Hakim Abdur Razzaq Sahib, may your virtues last for ever!

Humble Mahmud, with due *salaams*, begs to say that the ship reached Aden safely on Saturday early in the morning to-day. God be praised; all are doing well. Everyone has more or less been affected by headache which is an inevitable result of the travel by sea. But all are well. All the members convey their *salaams* to you. The ship will set sail by this evening D.V.

If you happen to go to Deoband, please console every one there. If you can somehow manage to send letters to me on board the ship, please try to despatch letters from Hakim Maulvi Mahmud Hasan Sahib and Maulvi Muhammad Hanif and Maulvi Hamdulla Sahib, so that on getting letters from these gentlemen, we may get information as well as consolation. But if that is impossible, let it alone.

Please convey my *salaams* to mother and the doctor. May God keep you all sound !

Through your kindness the journey by ship is accomplished with nice equipment, the "Arabia" is next to it. If God wills, no more provisions will be required for some days to come. Adieu.

Aden, I remain,
Saturday Yours obediently,

MAHMUD.

P.S.—Please inform the Abdur Rab's school and the Aminia School of my safe arrival.

Another point worth consideration is whether a speedy return from Arabia is required or not. If you can send your opinion to me please do so without fail.

2. *Name of payee* . . Muhammad Hanif
Amount of Order . . Rs. 100.
Name and address of remitter Hakim Abdur Razzaq, Yusufpur, Muhammadabad, Care of Muhammad Abdul Kadir.

Received the sum specified above on
Received Rs. 100 on 22nd April 1916.

MUHAMMAD HANIF.

3. To—Hakim Muhammad Abdur Razzaq Sahib, Mauza Yusufpur, District Ghazipur.

Dated 25th April 1916

MY RESPECTED GRAND HAKIM SAHIB,

Salaams to you. Received a money order worth Rs. 100 from you : after I received the money from you the doctor had despatched Rs. 100 in two instalments. Afterwards I received Rs. 100 from you. You need not take any trouble for some time. I have got enough for my expenses. I do not know when you will be coming. My leave expires on the 30th April. I shall be going to Muttra on 1st May and shall be back on the 15th, because summer vacations for 2 months will commence from the 15th May. I shall see you then. As soon as you reach Delhi, I hope you will let me know by the address of Government School, Muttra. Mumani Sahiba conveys *salaam* to you and wishes to thank you. And the medicines are almost consumed. The remaining ones have become dry. Adieu.

Yours sincerely,
MUHAMMAD HANIF DEOBAND.

4. Kashi Chandra Bhattacharji, son of Kailash Chandra Bhattacharji, Muhalla Oudh Bhelupura, Police surveillance be removed. Jagar Nath Parshad *alias* Malla Maharaj, first contractor for buildings.

Oudh Muhalla Bhelupura.

A glass with silver cover lid.

Nearly 3 inches high, 2 inches in circumference, 2 inches thick, *Nilam* stone over it, with silver core, ornamental plain work.

5. At the house of Gopal Lal Choba Pinda,

Near Dewal Nilkanth Mahadev,
Benares City.

6. My dear Hakim Sahib,

Salaams to you ! Received from Maulvi Khalil Ahmad at Mecca a letter of Maulana Sahib's welfare. I send it to you. I shall feel obliged if you return it after perusal. As far as possible you should exert yourself in recalling him. Please convey my *salaam* to the Doctor.

Yours.
Sick Younger Mother.

Translation of the copy of a letter from Hazrat Maulana Maulvi Khalil Ahmad Sahib at Mecca.

My dear elders and youngers, Maulvi Hafiz Abdul Latif Sahib, Maulvi Abdulla Jan Sahib and Hafiz Ahmad Jan Sahib, *salaams* to you. May God pour blessings and mercy on you !

It is long since you heard from us of our welfare or we heard from you of the relatives and your own welfare. How could we learn that? The postal communication was cut-off. Only yesterday we learnt at the Post Office that postal communication with India had been restored and we could send letters to whomsoever we pleased. God be praised that state of affairs allow to send information. We with Maulana Mahmud Hasan's party are all well.

We stayed at Medina till the middle of the *Jamadi-us-Sani* (6th month of the Arabian year) and we hoped to reach Mecca at a season when time of Haj drew nigh. But as soon as the summer set in we thought the summer being very hot, it would be very difficult to travel at that time.

So about the middle of *Jamadi-us-Sani* we left Medina and reached Mecca in a fortnight safely and comfortably. We had seven camels in all of which three were *Shaghdafs* and four of burden. The path was well guarded. On reaching Mecca Haji Makbul Ahmad and I suffered from ill-health slightly. Maulana Mahmud Hasan and most of his friends got fever. God be praised. All have recovered.

The Maulana with Maulvi Auzer Gul and Maulana Husain Ahmad and Abdul Wahid have gone to Taif in company with his *Mutawwif.* Only Syed Hadi Hasan and Munshi Muhammad Husain survive here. I stay at Mecca with all my relatives. It is exceeding hot. The Simoom blows hard even after the evening prayers.

Owing to the disagreeableness of climate I had a mind to return to India with family, if some ship arrived at Jeddah before Haj. Since the time of Haj is drawing near, another idea is that I should return after finishing the Haj, if life permits. Whatever is destined for me will be known to me.

Maulana is not yet back from Taif. I do not expect him in near future owing to sultry heat.

I have an absolute intention to return after finishing Haj, but I am doubtful whether I can return before Haj.

I am very anxious to hear the welfare of relatives and friends of that place. Please inform me of the welfare of my relatives and friends immediately. I am specially anxious to hear about my sister, Maulana Hafiz Qamruddin Sahib, dear Hafiz Muhammad Yaqub, dear Syed Zahur Ahmad Nathori, and Maulana Abdullah Jan, all of whom I left sick behind. Please also inform me of Sufi Muhammad Hasan and dear Masud Ahmad and Mahmud's welfare. Please also let me know whether they are still in school or have left it.

Please circulate the contents of this letter round to all the friends and relatives by copying it down on cards. If anybody wishes to leave for Haj, please let me know about his departure. Please convey my *salaams* to all friends, students and teachers, owners of school, neighbours and persons who say their prayers in the mosque especially to Sheikh Habib Ahmad, Hakim Muhammad Ishaq dear Budhu, Sardar Khan and Mohtamin Sahib. Adieu.

KHALIL AHMAD,
Mecca.

Put up at Qari Abdul Haq' school opposite to the post office and Bab-i-Ibrahim, written on Thursday, the 21st *Shaban.*

Please convey *salaam* to all the above named persons on behalf of humble Makbul Ahmad.

The letter is being despatched in compliance with Maulana's orders.

Mahmud Hasan Mutamid Mazharul Islam School, Saharanpur got it printed at the Rashid-ul-Matabe Press.

7. The Opium eater's Rijz from the pen of a joker.

To express loyalty to the British and enmity to Germany.

(1) We are opium eaters. When we are in the best of spirits we will put an end to Germany's intoxication.

(2) If we happen to give reins to the Mushki of opium, we shall stop only when we have reached Berlin.

(3) Whether you are braver or we are braver than you, we will let you know after we have shaken off the effect of opium.

(4) When we send forth the gurgling noise of our crooked *huqqah*, O Germany thy army would think it to be Maxim.

(5) When we put in Bichhwa in the small *huqqahs* such a gas will ensue that you will run away coughing.

(6) We are accustomed to take pills night and day; if you wish to see the opium box, we will show it to you.

(7) We will eat away our king's enemy by pouring down curses on him. We shall efface his name out of our imagination.

(8) We will get stronger than Rustam, when we mix a little cream with tea.

(9) When we show feats with Gadkas in our hands, we shall cause upheavals in the Berlin fields.

(10) We shall become revolving things on holding *banaitis* and will make such a continuous circle as to overwhelm your head.

(11) Wherever we went with our *lathis,* we immediately cudgelled out the head. O Germany we will cause sticks to strike on your guns.

(12) Whether it be Germany or Austria, we shall scare them away by our moulting; if either of them happens to come on the sea.

(13) We do not mind if Germany blows off the earth. We will throw her to the ground after attaching her to our kite.

(14) We will rain so many lumps of clay on you, Germany, that your grey dress will be altogether spoiled.

(15) Though we are sitting in a *chhonja* like *baya* bird, you will witness the scene, let us fire the gun.

(16) We possess knives which do not require a license. It may seem ill yet we will display something.

(17) We will cause you to run with *parakas* of carrot, though we have not even seen what rifle is.

(18) We are jackals, the crumb eaters of tiger; you shall take to heels as soon as we utter a roar.

(19) For 19 years we have been dying of plague, if death approaches we shall cause an inoculation to be done to it as well.

(20) We are famine striken, we are not afraid of death; if we fight for a single grain, we shall put to flight some ten or twenty at a time.

(21) O Germany if you slay us, we will terrify you during night as ghosts.

(22) Let us see your cruisers what they are like. We shall drive them away by sitting on *dongas* on the river Gomti.

(23) When we reach the sea with our *dongas*, we will cause your submarines to be ensnared in difficulties.

(24) O Germany if you boast of anything, come to the open bazar we will beat you and make you dance in distress.

(25) We are British subject; we cannot fight. We will point out the law relating to the evidence in a suit.

(26) Tell the Belgians that when their country is restored to them we will add something by way of commiseration.

(27) Please keep silence and regard our promises as genuine, we shall add Berlin to our territory.

(28) We were displeased with Russia, we are pleased with her now, if she comes to our opium house, we will administer opium to her also.

(29) Bravo ! O Italy !
Go on fighting with Germany, we will pray for you.

(30) Let someone say to Turkey, "Agha, you that are fighting, if you lose your life, what do you expect from Germany in return?"

(31) "You are losing your lives at the instigation of those who will prove traitors to you one day."

(32) Bravo, O Joker! you have written such *rijz* that we all intend to remunerate you with a subscription.

Bibliography

Private Papers

Aligarh Muslim University Archives, Aligarh (AMUA)
Papers relating to the Non-cooperation movement at MAO College, Aligarh.

India Office Library, London (IOL)
Chelmsford Papers.
Fazl-i Husain Papers.
Harcourt Butler Papers.
James Meston Papers.

National Archives of India, New Delhi (NAI)
M.R. Jayakar Papers.
Rajendra Prasad Papers.

National Library, Calcutta (NLC)
B.S. Moonje Papers.
T.B. Sapru Papers.

Nehru Memorial Museum & Library, New Delhi (NMML)
Abdul Majid Khwaja Papers.
Abdullah Brelvi Papers.
All-India Congress Committee (AICC) Papers.
B.C. Roy Papers.
Habibur Rahman Ludhianvi Papers.
Haroon Khan Sherwani Papers.
Jawaharlal Nehru Papers.
M.A. Ansari Collection.
M.C. Chagla Papers.
Motilal Nehru Papers.
Raja of Mahmudabad Papers.
Sri Prakasa Papers.

Oral History Transcripts (NMML)
K.G. Saiyidain.
Mohammad Mujeeb.
Zohra Ansari.

University Library, Cambridge (CUL)
Hardinge Papers.

Jamia Millia Islamia, New Delhi (JMI)
M.A. Ansari Papers.
K.G. Saiyidain Collection.
Mohamed Ali Papers.
Mohammad Mujeeb Collection.

Centre of South Asian Studies, Cambridge
J.C. Curry Papers.

GOVERNMENT RECORDS

National Archives of India, New Delhi (NAI)
Records of the Home Department of the Government of India. Home Political files are divided into A, B and D (Deposit) categories.

The Uttar Pradesh State Archives, Lucknow (UPSA)
Records of the UP government in the General Administration (GAD), Reform and Police departments.

Delhi State Archives, Delhi
Records relating to the Police Department.

NEWSPAPERS AND JOURNALS

Aaj Kal (Delhi), Ansari number, January 1981.
Bombay Chronicle (Bombay).
Comrade (Calcutta and Delhi).
Hamdard (Delhi).
Indian Annual Register, 1922-36, published as the *Indian Quarterly Register*, 1924-9.
Jamia (Delhi), Ansari number, July 1981.
Leader (Allahabad).
Modern Asian Studies (Cambridge).
Modern Review (Calcutta).
Mussulman (Calcutta).
New Era (Lucknow).
Naqush (Lahore), Iqbal number, September 1977.
Report on the Native Newspapers of Bengal, Punjab and the United Provinces.
Tribune (Lahore).
Young India (Ahmedabad).

OFFICIAL PUBLICATIONS

District Gazetteer of the United Provinces of Agra & Oudh, vol. XXIX, Ghazipur (Allahabad, 1909).

Ghazipur Supplementary notes and Statistics to volume XXXIX of the District Gazetteer of the United Provinces of Agra and Oudh (Allahabad, 1915). Government of India, *India in 1917-18 to India in 1933-36*, reports prepared annually for presentation to Parliament.

Indian Round Table Conference 12th November 1930-19th January 1931. Proceedings of Sub-Committees (Part II).

Proceedings of Sub-Committees (7 September-1 December 1931) (London, 1932).

Report of the Working of the System of Government, United Provinces of Agra and Oudh (3 vols., Allahabad, 1925).

Report on Indian Constitutional Reforms (1918). Cmd. 9109.

Report of the Indian Statutory Commission, vol. 1, *Survey* (1930). Cmd. 3568.

The Disorders Enquiry Committee, vol. I, Delhi (Calcutta, 1920).

MATERIALS PUBLISHED BY INDIAN POLITICAL ORGANIZATIONS

Annual Reports of the All-India Muslim League.

Annual Reports of the Indian National Congress.

Aziz, K.K. (ed.). *All-India Muslim Conference 1928-35: A Documentary Record* (Karachi, 1972).

Pirzada, S.S. (ed.). *Foundations of Pakistan: All-India Muslim League Documents, 1906-47* (2 vols., Karachi, 1970).

Proceedings of the All-Parties National Convention (Allahabad, 1929).

PUBLISHED WORKS, ARTICLES AND UNPUBLISHED THESES

Abbas, K.A. *I am not an Island: An Experiment in Autobiography* (Delhi, 1977).

Abbot, F. *Islam and Pakistan* (New York, 1968).

Abdullah, S.M. *New Kashmir* (New Delhi, n.d.).

Ahmad, A. *Studies in Islamic Culture in the Indian Environment* (Oxford, 1964).

———. *Islamic Modernism in India and Pakistan 1857-1946* (London, 1967).

Ahmad, W. (ed.). *Letters of Mian Fazl-i Husain* (Lahore, 1976).

———. *Diary and Notes of Mian Fazl-i Husain* (Lahore, 1976).

Adhikari, G. *Documents of the History of the Communist Party of India*, vol. III-B (Delhi, 1979).

Amin, M. 'Aadaa-i Shabab', Malik Ram (ed.), *Nazr-i Hameed* (Delhi, 1981).

Andrews, C.F. *Zakaullah of Delhi* (Cambridge, n.d.).

———. 'Hakim Ajmal Khan', in *Eminent Mussalmans* (Madras, 1926).

Ansari, K.H. 'The Emergence of Muslim Socialists and their ideas in India Between 1917 and 1947' (Ph.D. thesis, University of London, 1985).

Ansari, S. 'Dr Ansari ki Kitab: Regeneration of Man', *Jamia,* July 1981.
Ansari, Shaukatullah. *Pakistan: The Problem of India* (Lahore, 1944).
Ansari, Z. 'Shamsunnisa awr Dr Ansari', *Aaj Kal,* January 1981.
Azad, A.K. *India Wins Freedom: An Autobiographical Narrative* (Bombay, 1959).
Baird, R.D. (ed.). *Religion in Modern India* (Delhi, 1981).
Bamford, P.C. *Histories of the Khilafat and Non-cooperation Movements* (Delhi, 1975, rpt.).
Bamzai, P.N.K. *A History of Kashmir* (Delhi, 1962).
Barkatullah, M. *The Khilafat* (London, 1924).
Barni, Z.A. *Azmat-i Rafta* (Karachi, 1961).
Bayly, C.A. *The Local Roots of Indian Politics: Allahabad, 1880-1920* (Oxford, 1975).
Bedar, A.R. *Mata-i Faqir* (Delhi, 1969).
Begum Nazli. *Sair-i Europe* (London, n.d.).
Bengal Anti-Communal Award Movement: A Report (Calcutta, 1939).
Bijnori, A.L. *Latif ki Kahani* (Bijnor, 1967).
Birla, G.D. *In the Shadow of the Mahatma* (Calcutta, 1953).
———. *Bapu: A Unique Association,* vol. 1 (Delhi, 1977).
Blunt, W.S. *India Under Ripon: A Private Diary* (London, 1909).
Bose, M. *The Agha Khans* (London, 1984).
Brass, P. *Language, Religion and Politics in North India* (Cambridge, 1974).
Brown, J.M. *Gandhi's Rise to Power: Indian Politics 1915-1922* (Cambridge, 1972).
———. *Gandhi and Civil Disobedience: The Mahatma in Indian Politics 1928-34* (Cambridge, 1977).
———. *Modern India: The Origins of an Asian Democracy* (Delhi, 1984).
Chandra, J. *Gandhiji and Haryana* (Delhi, 1977).
Chatterjee, B. *Aspects of Bengal Politics in the early Nineteen thirties* (Calcutta, 1969).
Choudhary, V. (ed.). *Rajendra Prasad Correspondence and Select Documents,* vol. 1 (Delhi, 1984).
Coatman, J. *Years of Destiny: India, 1926-1932* (London, 1932).
Cotton, H. 'India Old and New', *Asiatic Review,* July 1914.
Coupland, R. *India: A Re-statement* (Oxford, 1945).
———. *The Indian Problem 1833-1935* (Oxford, 1952).
Das, D. *India from Curzon to Nehru and After* (London, 1969).
Datta, V.N. and B.E. Cleghorn (eds.). *A Nationalist Muslim and Indian Politics* (Delhi, 1974).
Desai, M. *Day-to-Day with Gandhi* (Varanasi, 1968).
Edip, H. *The Turkish Ordeal* (London, 1928).
———. *Conflict of East and West in Turkey* (Delhi, 1935).
———. *Inside India* (London, 1936).
Ellisson, G. *An Englishwoman in Angora* (London, 1923).

———. *Turkey To-day* (London, 1928).
Faruqi, Z. *The Deoband School and the Demand for Pakistan* (London, 1963).
Fill Badiya Khutba-i Sadarat (Lahore, n.d.).
Furbank, P.N. *E.M. Forster: A Life: The Growth of the Novelist 1879-1914* (London 1978).
Fyzee, A. *Iqbal* (Bombay, 1947).
Gallagher, J. 'Congress in Decline: Bengal 1930 to 1939', *Modem Asian Studies,* vol. 7, 3, July 1973.
Gandhi, M.K. *The Collected Works of Mahatma Gandhi* (Delhi, in process of publication).
Ghaffar, A. *Jamaluddin Afghani* (Delhi, 1941).
———. *Hayat-i Ajmal* (Delhi, 1950).
Gilbert, I.A. 'Autonomy and Consensus under the Raj: Presidency (Calcutta); Muir (Allahabad); MAO (Aligarh)', S.H. Rudolph and L.I. Rudolph (eds.), *Education and Politics in India: Studies in Organization, Society and Policy* (Delhi, 1972).
Gopal, S. *Jawaharlal Nehru: A Biography,* vol. 1: *1889-1947* (Delhi, 1975).
Gopal, S. (ed.). *Selected Works of Jawaharlal Nehru* (Delhi, in process of publication).
Gupta, N. *Delhi Between Two Empires 1803-1931: Society, Government and Urban Growth* (Delhi, 1981).
Halil Halid. *The Diary of a Turk* (London, 1903).
Hamied, K.A. *An Autobiography: A Life to Remember* (Bombay, 1972).
Hardy, P. *Partners in Freedom and True Muslims: The Political Thought of Some Muslim Scholars in British India, 1912-1947* (Scandinavian Institute of Asian Studies, 1971).
———. *The Muslims of British India* (Cambridge, 1972).
Hasan, Mohibbul. 'Mahatma Gandhi and the Indian Muslims', S.C. Biswas (ed.), *Gandhi Theory and Practice: Social Impact and Contemporary Relevance* (Simla, 1969).
Hasan, Mushirul. *Nationalism and Communal Politics in India 1916-1928* (Delhi, 1979).
———. (ed.), *Muslims and the Congress: Select Correspondence of Dr M.A. Ansari 1912-1935* (Delhi, 1979).
———. *Mohamed Ali Ideology and Politics* (Delhi, 1981).
———. (ed.), *Mohamed Ali in Indian Politics: Select Writings,* vol. 1 (Delhi, 1982).
———. (ed.), *Mohamed Ali in Indian Politics: Select Writings,* vol. 2 (Delhi, 1983).
———. (ed.), *Communal and Pan-Islamic Trends in Colonial India* (Delhi, 1985).
Hasan, Mushirul and Rakhshanda Jalil, *Partners in Freedom: Jamia Millia Islamia* (Delhi, 2007).

Haq, M. *Muslim Politics in Modern India 1857-1947* (Meerut, 1970).
Hayat, Abul. *Mussulmans of Bengal* (Calcutta, 1966).
Holt, P.M. et al. *The Cambridge History of Islam: The Central Islamic Lands*, vol. 1 (Cambridge, 1970).
Hourani, A. *Arabic Thought in the Liberal Age, 1798-1939* (Oxford, 1970).
Husain, A. *Fazl-i Husain: A Political Biography* (Bombay, 1916).
Husain, M.A. *Kashmir awr Dogra Raj, 1848-1931* (Delhi, 1970 edn.).
Husain, Swaliha A. *Jaane Walon ki Yadd Aati Rahi* (Delhi, 1974).
Iqbal, A. (ed.). *Selected Speeches and Writings of Maulana Mohamed Ali* (Lahore 1944).
———. (ed.). *My Life a Fragment: An Autobiographical Sketch of Maulana Mohamed Ali*, reprint of 1942 edn. (Lahore, 1966).
———. *Life and Times of Mohamed Ali* (Delhi, 1978 reprint).
Jafri, R.A. *Karawan-i Gumgushta* (Karachi, 1971).
Jamia Millia Islamia: Some Appreciations (Aligarh, 1923).
Jalal, A. and A. Seal. 'Alternative to Partition: Muslim Politics Between the Wars', *Modern Asian Studies*, vol. 15, 3, 1981.
Jalal, A. *The Sole Spokesman: Jinnah, the Muslim League and the Demand for Pakistan* (Cambridge, 1985).
Jamiyat-i Markaziya Tanzim Ka Mujawaza Dasturul Amal (Amritsar, 1925).
Kabir, H. *Muslim Politics 1906–47 and Other Essays* (Calcutta, 1969).
Kaura, U. *Muslims and Indian Nationalism: The Emergence of the Demand for India's Partition 1928–1940* (Delhi, 1977).
Keddie, N.R. *Islamic Response to Imperialism: Political and Religious Writings of Sayyid Jamal ad-Din "al-Afghani"* (California, 1968).
———. *Sayyid Jamal-ad-Din "al-Afghani": A Political Biography* (Los Angeles, 1972).
Kedourie, E. *Afghani and Abduh: An Essay on Religious Unbelief and Political Activism in Modern Islam* (London, 1966).
Khaliquzzaman, C. *Pathway to Pakistan* (Lahore, 1961).
Khan, A.A. 'Tehrik-i Aazadi ka ek Khamosh Kaarkun', *Jung* (Rawalpindi, 9 June 1944).
Khan, Agha. *The Memoirs of Agha Khan: World Enough and Time* (London, 1956).
Khan, M.I. *Perspectives on Kashmir: Historical Dimensions* (Srinagar, 1983).
Khan, R.A. *Hayat-i Ajmal* (Delhi, 1931).
Kozlowski, G.C. 'The Power of Language and the Language of Power: A Study of Mawlana Muhammad Ali's Political Rhetoric', *South Asia*, vol. 5, 1, June 1982.
Kidwai, A. *Azadi Ki Chaon me* (Delhi, 1980).
Kumar, K. *Peasants in Revolt: Tenants, Landlords, Congress and the Raj in Oudh* (Delhi, 1984).
Kumar, R. (ed.), *Essays on Gandhian Politics: The Rowlatt Satyagraha of 1919* (London, 1971).
———. *Essays in the Social History of Modern India* (Delhi, 1983).

Kumar, R. and D.N. Panigrahi (eds.). *Selected Works of Motilal Nehru*, vol. 3 (Delhi, 1984).

Lewis, B. *The Emergence of Modern Turkey* (London, 1961).

Lewis, G.L. *Turkey* (London, 1955).

Laird, M.A. (ed.), *Bishop Heber in Northern India: Selection from Heber's Journal* (Cambridge, 1971), p. 126.

Lago, M. and P.N. Furbank, *Selected Letters of E.M. Forster; 1879-1920*, vol. 1 (London, 1983).

Low, D.A. (ed.). *Soundings in Modern South Asian History* (University of California Press, 1968).

———. *Congress and the Raj: Facets of the Indian Struggle 1917-1947* (London, 1977).

Lytton, Earl of, *Pundits and Elephants: Being the Experience of Five Years as Governor of an Indian Province* (London, 1942).

Malik, H. (ed.), *Iqbal: Poet, Philosopher of Pakistan* (New York, 1971).

Madani, H.A. *Naqsh-i Hayat: Khudnawisht Sawaanah* (Karachi, 1979 edn.).

Malhotra, S.L. *From Civil Disobedience to Quit India* (Chandigarh, 1979).

Masani, M. *Bliss was it in that Dawn: A Political Memoir upto Independence* (Bombay, 1977).

Mathur, V.S. (ed.). *Zakir Husain: Educationist and Teacher* (Delhi, 1969).

Mcpherson, K. *The Muslim Microcosm: Calcutta, 1918 to 1935* (Heidelberg, 1974).

Metcalf, B.D. 'Nationalist Muslims in British India', *Modern Asian Studies*, vol. 19, 1, 1985.

Millat-i Islamia awr Jamia Millia Islamia, Delhi (Calcutta, 1941).

Minault, G. *The Khilafat Movement: Religious Symbolism and Political Mobilization in India* (Delhi, 1982).

Misra, B.B. *The Indian Political Parties* (Delhi, 1976).

Moazzam, A. *Jamal al-Din al-Afghani: A Muslim Intellectual* (Delhi, 1983).

Mudholi, A.G. *Jamia Ki Kahani* (Delhi, 1965) in 2 vols.

Mujeeb, M. *The Indian Muslims* (London, 1967).

———. *Dr Zakir Husain: A Biography* (Delhi, 1970).

———. 'Dr Ansari: Chand Yaaden Baaten', *Aaj Kal*, January 1981.

Munshi, K.M. *Pilgrimage to Freedom*, vol. l (Bombay, 1967).

Moore, R.J. *The Crisis of Indian Unity 1917-1940* (Delhi, 1974), p. 101.

Nairang, S.G.B. *Jamiyat-i Markaziya Tabligh al-Islam Ambala Shehar ki Satarsala Khidmat ka Khulasa* (Ambala, 1940).

Namboodiripad, E.M.S. *How I Became a Communist* (Trivandrum, 1976).

Nanda, B.R. *Mahatma Gandhi: A Biography* (London, 1958).

Nehru, J. *An Autobiography: With Musings on Recent Events in India* (London, 1936).

——— (ed.). *A Bunch of Old Letters*, 2nd edn. (Bombay, 1966).

Nizami, H. *Tark-i Gayekushi* (Delhi, 1920).

———. *Government awr Khilafat* (Gurdaspur, 1922 edn.)

Nomani, S. *Safarnamah-i Misro-o Shaam* (Agra, 1894).

Noorani, A.G. *President Zakir Husain: A Quest for Excellence* (Bombay, 1967).

Page, D. *Prelude to Partition: The Indian Muslims and the Imperial System of Control 1920-1932* (Oxford, 1982).

Pandey, B.N. *Nehru* (London, 1976).

———. (ed.). *The Indian Nationalist Movement 1885-1947: Select Documents* (London, 1979).

Pandey, G. *The Ascendancy of the Congress in Uttar Pradesh 1926-1934* (Delhi, 1978).

Poynter, M.A. *When Turkey was Turkey: In and around Constantinople* (London, 1921).

Prasad, B. *Gandhi, Nehru and J.P: Studies in Leadership* (Delhi, 1985).

Prasad, R. *India Divided* (Bombay, 1946).

Pyarelal, *Mahatma Gandhi: The Last Phase*, vol. 1 (Ahmedabad, 1956).

Qadiri, K.H. *Hasrat Mohani* (Delhi, 1985).

Rahman, F. *Islam* (London, 1966).

Ram, M. (ed.). *Nazr-i Hameed* (Delhi, 1981).

Ramanathan, K.V. (ed.). *The Satyamurti Letters: The Indian Freedom Struggle Through the Eyes of a Parliamentarian* (Delhi, 2008).

Robinson, F. *Separatism Among Indian Muslims: The Politics of United Provinces' Muslims,1860-1923* (Cambridge, 1974).

Sabri, Imdad. *Dehli ki Yadgar Hastiyaan* (Delhi, 1972).

Sadiq, M. *The Turkish Revolution and the Indian Freedom Movement* (Delhi, 1983).

Sayeed, K.B. *Pakistan: The Formative Phase 1857-1948* (Karachi, 1968 edn.).

Schimmel, A. *Gabriel's Wing: A Study into the Religious Ideas of Sir Muhammad Iqbal* (London, 1963).

Shraddhanand, S. *Inside Congress* (Bombay, 1946).

Siddiqi, M.H. *Agrarian Unrest in North India: The United Province 1918-22* (Delhi, 1978).

Smith, W.C. *Modern Islam in India* (Lahore, 1943).

Smith, W.R. *Nationalism and Reforms in India* (Yale University Press, 1938).

Tendulkar, D.G. *Mahatma*, vol. 3 (Delhi, 1951).

———. *Abdul Ghaffar Khan* (Varanasi, 1969).

Thursby, G.R. *Hindu-Muslim Relations in British India* (Leiden, 1975).

Tomlinson, B.R. *The Indian National Congress and the Raj 1929-42: The Penultimate Phase* (London, 1976).

Watson, W.J. 'Muhammad Ali and the Khilafat Movement' (unpublished M.A. thesis, McGill University, 1955).

Wolpert, S. *Jinnah of Pakistan* (New York, 1984).

Zaidi, A.Z. (ed.). *The Evolution of Muslim Political Thought in India*, vol. 4 (Delhi, 1980).

Index